T0330265

The Human Side
of Outsourcing

The Human Side of Outsourcing

Psychological Theory and Management Practice

Edited by Stephanie J. Morgan, PhD
Kingston University Business School

A John Wiley & Sons, Ltd., Publication

This edition first published 2009
© 2009 John Wiley & Sons Ltd.

Wiley-Blackwell is an imprint of John Wiley & Sons, formed by the merger of Wiley's global
Scientific, Technical, and Medical business with Blackwell Publishing.

Registered Office
John Wiley & Sons Ltd, The Atrium, Southern Gate, Chichester, West Sussex, PO19 8SQ, UK

Editorial Offices
The Atrium, Southern Gate, Chichester, West Sussex, PO19 8SQ, UK
9600 Garsington Road, Oxford, OX4 2DQ, UK
350 Main Street, Malden, MA 02148-5020, USA

For details of our global editorial offices, for customer services, and for information about how to
apply for permission to reuse the copyright material in this book please see our website at www.
wiley.com/wiley-blackwell.

Library of Congress Cataloging-in-Publication Data

The human side of outsourcing : psychological theory and management practice / edited by
Stephanie J. Morgan.
      p.   cm.
  Includes bibliographical references and index.
  ISBN 978-0-470-71870-4 (cloth)
  1. Contracting out.   2. Contracting out–Management.   3. Personnel management.
I. Morgan, Stephanie J.
  HD2365.H86 2009
  658.4′058–dc22

                                                                    2009019205

A catalogue record for this book is available from the British Library.

Set in 10.5/13 pt Minion by SNP Best-set Typesetter Ltd., Hong Kong
Printed in Singapore by Markono Print Media Pte Ltd

1   2009

Dedication

To my husband Roy and daughter Elizabeth –
your love and support make all things possible.

Contents

List of Figures and Tables

Figures

Tables

List of Contributors

Jan Aylsworth

Jan has more than 20 years' experience as a corporate communications writer-consultant and freelance journalist. She holds a B.S. in English, resides in Evansville, Indiana in the U.S.A., and is currently pursuing a master's in organizational psychology through the University of London's Birkbeck College. Her long-term goals are to help bridge the academic–practitioner divide by conducting theory- and evidence-informed small-group workshops that address career guidance at the individual and group levels of analysis. Her organizational psychology interests include downsizing, work and personality variables, career theory, social capital and reciprocity, and networking. She welcomes correspondence at JanAylsworth @aol.com.

Richard Blakeley

Richard has a BA (Hons) in Politics and Mdip in Organizational Behaviour. Recently appointed as Learning and Skills Policy Officer at the Trades Union Congress, he has several years of experience as a researcher working for the finance sector trade union, UNIFI (now part of UNITE), taking a particular interest in workforce development policy. Richard has also worked in local government during major restructuring and change programmes and has been actively involved in a number of projects to improve people management practices. Richard can be contacted on richardb@co-op.com.

Irvine Caplan

Irvine has been a Director of the National Outsourcing Association for three years, with special responsibility for end users. Irvine is an economist by training, and professional Treasurer – a Fellow of the Association of Corporate Treasurers. With a professional career spanning over 30 years, he has worked in government (quangos), public and private sector organizations, and engaged in many aspects of commercial sourcing. Most recently with Royal Mail Group, and now working as an independent outsourcing advisor, Irvine has seen outsourcing from at least four sides as an end user: reviewing outsourcing business cases; contract managing, for 3½ years, what in 2003 was then the largest-ever IT outsourcing in Europe; vendor management; and managing a small RM subsidiary business totally dependent on outsourced services. Irvine can be contacted by email on irvine.caplan@googlemail.com.

Brigitte Cobb
Brigitte has many years' experience helping organizations deliver major transformation programmes and has consulted on or managed the delivery of a variety of approaches to business transformation, including multi-tower shared services, outsourcing, process standardization and re-engineering, technology and culture change. Brigitte has a PGDip in Change Management, lectures on the MSc in Change and Consultancy at Birkbeck College and has done research on the successful management of organizational change. She is a practitioner of NLP and also works as an Executive Coach to managers charged with delivering transformation programmes. Brigitte can be contacted on mail@brigittecobb.com.

Simone Hemingway
Simone has a BSc (Hons) First Class in Business Studies and an MSc in Organizational Behaviour from Birkbeck College, University of London. She has significant experience as a senior HR professional in a number of private sector organizations within healthcare, transport, banking, telecommunications, asset management and logistics, both in the UK and internationally. Over the past 10 years she has spent the majority of her career managing large-scale organizational change programmes, in particular involving outsourcing, offshoring and business restructuring. Most recently she has led on a number of major outsourcing contracts both as outsourcing provider for public sector services at Serco and from within the client organization at Barclays Bank. Now working within the private healthcare sector, Simone has more recently been involved in the acquisition and merger of two private equity owned providers of diagnostic imaging services in the UK as well as a number of smaller outsourcing contracts. Simone can be contacted via email at simone.hemingway@virgin.net.

Royston Morgan
Royston has a BSc in Operations Research, MSc in Industrial Engineering, MBA in Technology Management, and an MA in the Management of Change in the Public Sector. He has many years' experience in programme management and consultancy for a range of organizations, both public and private. This includes the Ministry of Defence, the National Health Service, the Royal Navy and many blue-chip companies. He has carried out research in technology change and business modelling and has developed the Crosslight cost-reduction programme, saving companies substantial sums whilst improving operations. Roy has written chapters and e-publications about outsourcing and on cost reduction. Roy can be contacted on rmorgan@crosslight.co.uk for consultancy and advice.

Stephanie J. Morgan

Stephanie has a BSc in Psychology, MSc in Organizational Behaviour and a PhD in Occupational Psychology, from Birkbeck, University of London. She is a Principal Lecturer at Kingston University Business School where she is Course Director for the Leadership & Management in Health programme. She also holds director positions at Crosslight Management Ltd and Decision Dimensions Ltd, and has worked as a non-executive director in both primary and secondary care NHS Trusts. A chartered psychologist, she consults and researches on various aspects of work, including outsourcing, staff motivation, technology-related change, and managing diversity. Stephanie's early career was in the IT industry, and she has many years' experience as a manager and consultant, including a number of international assignments. She has published in both academic and practitioner journals and has presented at a range of conferences. She can be contacted by email on smorgan@ crosslight.co.uk or Stephanie.Morgan@kingston.ac.uk.

Ian Pogson

Ian is married with three children and lives in Bromsgrove, Worcestershire. He is a Chartered Automotive Engineer who began his career in 1980 as a Graduate Trainee for Land Rover. He worked in many different senior roles in Competitor Analysis, Technical Research, Manufacturing Process Engineering, Logistics, Quality Improvement and Programme Management. As part of MG Rover's last-ditch attempt to court an international partner, Ian worked in Shanghai, PRC, from the start of January 2005 to redundancy upon the collapse of MG Rover in April that year. He returned to work and live there over a one-year period from June 2005 to 2006, continuing as he does to work for SAIC in the UK Technical Centre. He liaises and trains Chinese engineers as part of his day-to-day responsibilities and used this to create the material in this book. Ian can be contacted on 07966 430 806 or ian. pogson@saicmotor.co.uk for copies of his own book *Carry On Car-making, Life in China after Longbridge*, published by Brewin, ISBN 978-1-85858-409-6, and for public lectures on living and working in China and the new *TF*.

Alex Watts

Alex has a BSc in Psychology and is working towards an MSc in Occupational Psychology from Birkbeck College, London. He has 25 years' experience as an IT developer, tester and project manager and has worked as a consultant for a wide variety of organizations in both the public and private sectors and both the UK and the USA. Alex has published several technical IT articles in the past but this is his first management publication. His main academic interest is team dynamics, especially the areas of trust, empowerment, employee engagement and informal working practices. Alex can be contacted at alex.watts@kraftware.co.uk.

Yvonne Williams

Yvonne is Managing Director, MDA – Executive Resourcing and Individual Training Director, National Outsourcing Association (NOA). Yvonne has worked in the recruitment industry for over 20 years and specializes in Human Talent Management and Acquisition. She has worked for a number of industry leaders and owned her own executive search firm. Highly experienced in technology, telecoms, outsourcing, professional services and finance, Yvonne has worked across most disciplines and recruited to CEO level and for board appointments. She has extensive experience of helping organizations to plan and manage their human capital resources, a vital component to the success of an outsourcing programme. An accredited fellow of the Independent Institute for Business, Yvonne has also stood for parliament, and served as a County Councillor in Surrey. She can be contacted on yvonne@mallarddrake.co.uk.

Foreword

Martyn Hart,
Chairman, National Outsourcing Association

Outsourcing is often seen as difficult, prone to failure and vilified by the press, yet outsourcing goes from strength to strength; a growing number of people, organizations and countries embrace it; and it seems to bring many benefits wider than the simple one of a project well done.

In my mind there are only three ways of achieving a goal: do it yourself, do it along with someone else or let someone else do it for you. The complexity and difficulty grows as you move from left to right from DIY, through shared services to full outsourcing, and as you go vertically from a simple infrastructure to a complex full-blown business process. I can imagine a consultant's 2 × 2 matrix, showing that the hardest part is the top right-hand corner, complex full-blown business process being fully outsourced!

But the continued growth of outsourcing demonstrates its maturity; now, areas that only a few years ago that were seen as 'risky' or 'novel' such as HR & Financial outsourcing are commonplace. But to reach true maturity outsourcing must now consider the most complex component of all: people!

If, like me, you think of outsourcing as a business practice, maybe the most challenging of all, you will recognize the importance of people in any business and this is where Stephanie Morgan's book scores, as the people side has had the least exposure and research, until now. It is really a pace setter, as she sets out to combine and explain academic theory plus sections from eminent practitioners from the top of the outsourcing community (some are NOA members, of course!).

So you can't really expect to understand how outsourcing will affect you or your customers until you understand its effects on people, from the customer side in terms of loss of control, to the staff transferred, or those expected to work with you in terms of establishing trust. This book doesn't give prescriptions, it gives you the context in which you can choose the way forward, based on excellent academic references and the experience of its contributors. You will know why you are taking a direction and with these guides at your hand you can confidently approach situations and ensure that you will be able to operate at the very top right hand corner of that 2 × 2 matrix or scale business processes' own Mount Everest!

I commend this book. It is easily accessible, each chapter could stand on its own, 300-plus pages might seem a lot, but think of them as 300 gold-plated references and a stepping stone for your future!

Martyn Hart
Chairman, National Outsourcing Association
Wardour Street, London, 2009
www.noa.co.uk

Preface

An outsourcing poem:

> Sea saw Marjorie daw
> Johnnie's to have a new master
> We don't know
> Where he'll go
> But we'll come tumbling after!

In the 10 years that I have been carrying out research on outsourcing, the industry has grown substantially yet still little attention is paid to the people who make outsourcing happen – the men and women who are transferred from their chosen organization to a company chosen by their 'Masters'. My interest in this aspect of outsourcing started whilst carrying out research on subcontracting. I found that a number of the staff interviewed had joined their current organization through an outsourcing transfer, and it was clear that this process had affected them deeply. Since then, I have carried out research on a range of people experiencing outsourcing transfers, and broadened this out to assess other human factors for those involved in most types of outsourcing. Questions around how outsourcing can be most effective, how staff experience transfers, how outsourcing negotiations 'work', whether cultural differences impact on outsourcing, how disparate teams from possibly multiple organizations work together, what type of people one should employ in outsourcing deals, and how one should develop the staff that stay behind, are all of interest to me and at least some of them are addressed in this book.

We also consider the issues that arise from more general forms of outsourcing, including offshoring and nearshoring, when staff transfers are not the issue, but people still make or break the contracts. Although HR is mentioned in a number of places, this book is not just for HR people, but for all those involved with negotiating, managing and developing outsourced processes.

Stephanie J. Morgan

Acknowledgements

The initial research for some of the chapters in this book was carried out under ESRC grant number R42200024292. I will always be grateful to Dr Gillian Symon at Birkbeck College, University of London for her supervision and support during those early years. Some aspects of my early research have been published in books and journals, all of which are acknowledged throughout. However, for this book, everything has been looked at with fresh eyes; this is the first time all of these areas have been brought together, and much of the research discussed has been carried out post these publications. Furthermore, I am extremely lucky to have been joined in this enterprise by the chapter authors, each of whom has brought their own research and/or practice to bear. We all wish to thank the people who took part in our research, giving up time to give interviews or fill in surveys. Finally, I would like to thank Professor Ruth Taplin, director of the Centre for Japanese and East Asian Studies, for asking me to write for her own book *Outsourcing and Human Resource Management: An International Survey* (2008, Routledge), which made me realize how little had been written on the broad subject of the psychological aspects of outsourcing.

Part I
Outsourcing in Practice

Chapter 1

Introduction

Stephanie J. Morgan

Outsourcing, however defined, is big business. Globally the outsourcing market was said to be around 1,500 billion US dollars for 2009. At the time of writing we are unsure of how long or how deep the current recession will be, yet many outsourcing organizations suggest that this 'credit crunch' will lead to a further increase in outsourcing as companies strive to achieve cost reductions. Views on the impact of this recession on outsourcing are mixed, with some suggesting an increase in bringing work back in-house and others arguing for an increase in offshoring. New locations, particularly in IT outsourcing, are likely to become popular,[1] with all the issues that can arise with understanding cultural differences. All seem to agree that costs will drive the business decisions but that efficiency will be crucial. Yet we will argue that it is the human aspects that can make a difference to success or failure in outsourcing. As with all business processes, outsourcing depends on people to make it work, yet it is these people that receive the least attention when outsourcing deals are struck.

In this introduction I will outline the range of outsourcing contracts and some of the issues involved for people management. I will explain the rationale for this book and then introduce the chapters in Part I, emphasizing their contribution to our understanding of management practice. A brief overview of Part II will also be given, although this section also includes a separate introduction where a broad range of theory is outlined. Overall, this book focuses on the importance of human behaviour and relationships in outsourcing contracts, an aspect which in our view is not given sufficient consideration in current publications. Many books and articles have been written about the high-level decision-making processes, selecting

---

[1] See for example www.noa.co.uk/index.php/noa/hartofoutsourcing/

suppliers and contractual aspects, but very few consider the relationships between people that make these happen, or the perspective of those whose jobs and careers are affected. Brown and Wilson (2005) do include a guide to an outsourcing career and tips for outsourcing entrepreneurs; however, these are aimed only at very senior managers – far more people are affected at the lower levels, and all are vital to the success of the contract.

The term outsourcing is used very broadly, often to refer to processes that would previously have been termed subcontracting; for example, Bartel, Lach, and Sicherman (2008) define it as 'the contracting out of activities to subcontractors outside the firm' (2008, p.1). For some researchers, a crucial point is whether the work would have been done internally before outsourcing (Domberger, 1998). Outsourcing is a particular form of externalization of employment, and in many cases involves an outside contractor taking over an in-house function (Purcell & Purcell, 1998). A broad range of activities have been transferred in this way, including catering, cleaning, and security, often termed 'secondary' or 'non-core' functions. However, professional services have also increasingly been outsourced, with IT being a large part of the market, with finance, HR and increasingly complex activities such as business process outsourcing (BPO) and knowledge process outsourcing (KPO) coming to the fore. Outsourcing is also very different from insourcing, when contractors are used to assist with work, for example supplementing internal capacity (although some of the people issues remain, we would argue that they are less problematic). Offshoring is also a major trend, as business processes, especially call-centric services, are handed over to organizations operating from parts of the world that enjoy a labour cost advantage over the local workforce. A range of risks specific to offshoring have been identified (e.g. Kliem, 2004) but although cultural differences are highlighted, they are rarely discussed in detail. Nakatsu and Iacovou (2009) found that language and cultural differences, along with lack of business or technical know-how by the offshoring team, were key risk factors in offshoring versus domestic outsourcing; again, these are all linked to the human aspects. Finally, as the market is maturing, the concept of back-sourcing (or re-sourcing) internal organizations must be considered, as more companies see the need to bring people and processes back under their control. Logan (2008) suggests that 25–30 per cent of outsourcing deals are brought back in-house, indicating a real need to understand the experience of staff in these circumstances. Figure 1.1 gives an overview of the different main forms of outsourcing. With these multiple aspects of outsourcing, most of which require people to be moved back and forth between different companies, no wonder there are some issues to be resolved.

Furthermore, contracts are becoming increasingly complex, with multisourcing, nearshoring, and other new variants arising. Although many of the clients are in the US and UK, the global nature of the outsourcing business is an important feature. India is well known for call centres but as the economy develops they are shifting to the higher end (e.g. BPO) where they can. China is moving out to 'cheaper' parts of China itself. Some suggest that organizations will become completely 'virtual', relying totally on a spread of outsourcing contracts to complete

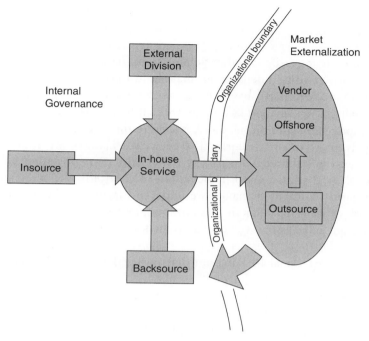

Figure 1.1 Outsourcing types

their business. In the public sector in particular, these changes raise issues around interoperability (sharing and integration of information and business processes), and, again, people are crucial to the sharing of information required (see Gottschalk, 2009).

All of this has implications for the people involved. There are issues of language, culture, legal and ethical differences that will need to be explored. There is increasing evidence that, particularly with transfers and outsourcing-related downsizing, the very health of staff can be affected (Gustafsson & Saksvik, 2005). My own research indicates that there can be a range of concerns for staff involved in transfers that may require understanding during career counselling (Morgan & Symon, 2006) and problems of anxiety linked to feelings of injustice and low engagement (Morgan, 2007). While the world of outsourcing contracts is likely to have changed even by the time this book is published, with new concepts and approaches likely, the basic people management principles will remain as important as ever. I hope that, thanks to this book, they may be better understood.

A wide range of stakeholders are involved, suppliers and clients, senior directors, managers, team leaders and staff. Lacity and Willcocks (2000) discuss the complexities of these relationships and warn against underestimating the importance of the staff aspects. A variety of departments should participate at all stages (including but not restricted to procurement and HR), which is good practice but again increases complexity.

All of these activities demand a new balance of skills. These include contractual and commercial understanding, coordination and control of suppliers, change management and strategic planning. These are all skills that can take a long time to develop, and are not easily found in organizations, particularly amongst staff who were previously running a department that has just been outsourced.

In situations where staff have been transferred to another organization, there is evidence that the anxiety and lack of control felt by the staff can lead to very low levels of morale and commitment and, related to this, reduced performance. This is not purely linked to job insecurity (indeed, for some, the only consolation is that they still have a job, although downsizing is often a factor in outsourcing transfers). The psychological stress caused by being out of control of the situation and the anxiety created by imposed change are important factors in the development of future work relationships. For the organization, research has shown that ignoring the human side of outsourcing can lead to the following issues after a transition:

- lack of organizational learning and 'memory' (the intellectual capital has all gone);
- difficulties with relationships with (ex) colleagues;
- reduction in innovation and creativity;
- reduced long-term responsiveness from staff;
- misunderstanding of roles and resistance to the 'client';
- poor negotiating, linked to above, and cultural differences (both organizational culture and national culture, especially in offshoring);
- uncertainty regarding how to develop the skills of remaining staff (and which skills are really needed).

There is evidence of financial losses due to contract misunderstandings and relationship history. As many outsourcing contracts are based on cost-savings and improved performance, this can be extremely problematic.

Even where the outsourcing deal did not include people transfer, issues have occurred during all stages. Negotiations can be fraught with problems, being reliant on suppliers requires ongoing relationship and contract management, and measuring the quality of governance and deciding when to change suppliers or bring work back in-house requires substantial time and resource to manage. Furthermore, there are still issues around the motivations of staff who are working on the contract, the trust between key negotiators and indeed the staff, and the difficulties in generating knowledge and expertise in-house when contractors are used – particularly if they are remote. Clearly, the people aspects of outsourcing need to be understood to increase the chances of success.

The first section of this book concentrates on the practice of outsourcing, and allows these different stakeholders or 'voices' to demonstrate the importance of people management based on their many years of experience. Irvine Caplan has been involved with the process for many years, working in senior management as a client of outsourcing. Although he explains issues that arise throughout the life cycle, he particularly emphasizes the issues with finding and using the right skills of those retained after an outsourcing contract has been signed, and the problems that this can create throughout the contract. Simone Hemingway has many years of senior HR management experience on the other side – for an outsourcing supplier. She too emphasizes the skills of the people involved, and the different types of 'deals' that take place. Simone also discusses the potential differences between types of contract, public and private being one key area. My own research indicates that although public sector employees do often have very specific values that are sometimes compromised when moving to the private sector, issues of identity are problematic for many staff who have come from large organizations, whether public or private. Simone outlines in particular the differences in contract negotiations between the public and private sectors. Yvonne Williams has worked for many years helping organizations to recruit for outsourcing contracts, from both sides, and gives some excellent tips for the type of people needed at different stages in the process. Finally, Ian Pogson gives first-hand experience of culture shock after being sent to China to assist during an outsourced contract. Again, Ian gives a number of tips for those who may be involved with outsourcing that requires regular visits to another country – particularly if the culture is very different.

What these practitioner voices share is a concern for understanding the other party, for enabling trust, and they also demonstrate a desire to work together to achieve the aims of outsourcing (usually to reduce costs and/or enhance performance). However, they also share similar views on the problems that arise when people have different expectations, are from different cultures (national or organizational), and perhaps lack the skills required to negotiate and manage within outsourcing contracts. While all these chapters provide us with useful tips around the human aspects of outsourcing, we argue that to gain a deeper understanding we need theory and supporting evidence. The second part of the book therefore gives us this grounding, which helps us to explain why these issues arise and how we can address them. Each of the later chapters also brings in examples of evidence, often based on in-depth interviews, of the actual experience of working in outsourcing contracts. It is also hoped that by presenting both practitioner and academic viewpoints, we do something to reduce the practitioner–academic divide – sadly, there is substantial evidence that practitioners tend not to use research, feeling it is not relevant to practice, and academics tend not to work with practitioners to address real-world problems (see Rynes, Bartunek, & Daft, 2001). We hope to increase the possibility that this book is used by practitioners in the field.

In Chapter 6 I outline the range of theory and related evidence that can inform outsourcing processes. An overview of research evidence related to downsizing, mergers and acquisitions is given, followed by a short discussion on theories of commitment, identification, identity, socialization, organizational justice, and the psychological contract. Other theories related to trust, knowledge management and culture are only touched upon as these are covered in much more detail in the following chapters. Important to all understanding is an awareness of the context within which we are working; the chapter by Roy Morgan ensures that this context is explained, along with the positioning achieved by discourses or narratives of outsourcing. Brigitte Cobb outlines how differences in national and organizational culture can impact upon outsourcing, and Alex Watts discusses the role of trust when operating remotely from others – virtual teams are increasingly used in outsourcing. Richard Blakeley and I give an overview of the theory and research behind knowledge management and knowledge transfer, demonstrating the problems that can occur when knowledge is power and knowledge sharing relies upon the goodwill of others, who may be feeling less than generous in some outsourcing contracts. Roy Morgan gives evidence based on experience of the full outsourcing life cycle, demonstrating how important it is to think through the implications of each stage for staff. Jan Aylsworth brings an American perspective to our understanding, as there are indeed differences in process due to each country's employment law. Outsourcing and offshoring in the US have received a great deal of attention lately, and although there have been some attempts to prevent contracts, even through legislation, most argue that this is unlikely to succeed (see Earle, Madek, & Madek, 2007). Downsizing is even more likely to occur in the US, and in the US there are fewer situations where decision-bargaining is required (see Miscimarra & Schwartz, 1997), but many of the theories relevant to outsourcing are also found in downsizing, and Jan gives a good overview of the range of theory and research on the subject. After a discussion of the importance of understanding transitioning and the role of expectations and the psychological contract in moderating employee reactions, I conclude with a final chapter that develops a model of employee responses to outsourcing transitions. Although theoretically driven, all of these chapters in the second half include evidence from academic research and from the author's own studies. Indeed, each of these 'academic' authors is a practitioner at heart, with their own experiences as well as rigorous research to underpin their discussions. It is hoped that by understanding employee reactions organizations can do more to ensure good practice during a transfer, and therefore reduce anxiety and enhance performance.

Much of the practitioner literature tends to cast an overly positive slant on outsourcing and, as highlighted in Chapter 7, few people wish to be associated with failure. Although we take a more critical view, we do not wish to make the mistake of being overly negative. There are outsourcing contracts that succeed, negotiations that result in all sides gaining, staff who improve their careers due to a transfer, and transitions that are carried out with full attention to justice and employee engagement. However, there are problems, as both our practitioner and academic chapters attest. Our intention is to highlight things that can go wrong to encourage more people to do things right.

References

Bartel, A., Lach, S., & Sicherman, N. (2008). *Outsourcing and technological innovations: A firm-level analysis*. London: LSE.
Brown, D., & Wilson, S. (2005). *The black book of outsourcing: How to manage the changes, challenges, and opportunities*. Hoboken, NJ: Wiley.

Domberger, S. (1998). *The contracting organization: A strategic guide to outsourcing*. Oxford: Oxford University Press.

Earle, B., Madek, G. A., & Madek, C. (2007). A finger in the dike? An examination of the efficacy of state and federal attempts to use law to stem outsourcing. *Northwestern Journal of International Law and Business, 28*, 89–123.

Gottschalk, P. (2009). Maturity levels for interoperability in digital government. *Government Information Quarterly, 26*, 75–81.

Gustafsson, O., & Saksvik, P. O. (2005). Outsourcing in the public refuse collection sector: Exploiting old certainties or exploring new possibilities? *Work, 25*, 91–97.

Kliem, R. (2004). Managing the risks of offshore IT development projects. *IS Sourcing*, Summer.

Lacity, M. C., & Willcocks, L. P. (2000). Relationships in IT outsourcing: A stakeholder perspective. In R. W. Zmud (Ed.), *Framing the domains of I.T. management: Projecting the future, through the past* (pp. 355–384). Cincinnati, OH: Pinnaflex Educational Resources.

Logan, M. (2008). Outsourcing working paper. London School of Economics.

Miscimarra, P. A., & Schwartz, K. D. (1997). Frozen in time: The NLRB, outsourcing, and management rights. *Journal of Labor Research, XVIII* (4).

Morgan, S. J. (2007). Employee engagement in outsourcing. In R. Taplin (Ed.), *Outsourcing and HRM: An international survey* (pp. 26–56). London: Routledge.

Morgan, S. J., & Symon, G. (2006). The experience of outsourcing transfers: Implications for guidance and counselling. *British Journal of Guidance and Counselling, 34*, 191–208.

Nakatsu, R. T., & Iacovou, C. L. (2009). A comparative study of important risk factors involved in offshore and domestic outsourcing of software development projects: A two-panel Delphi study. *Information & Management*, doi:10.1016/j.im.2008.11.005.

Purcell, K., & Purcell, J. (1998). In-sourcing, outsourcing, and the growth of contingent labour as evidence of flexible employment strategies. *European Journal of Work and Organizational Psychology, 7*(1), 39–59.

Rynes, S., Bartunek, J. M., & Daft, R. L. (2001). Across the great divide: Knowledge creation and transfer between practitioners and academics. *Academy of Management Journal, 44*, 340–356.

Chapter 2

The Client Side – Retained Organization

Irvine Caplan

Introduction

In looking at the retained organization, the purpose is to explore many of the people issues and interrelationships through the life cycle of an outsourcing. Usually we plan for who does what to whom at the start, but then a host of people issues surface which can change the dynamics of an outsourcing. This chapter aims to give an insight into the sorts of change-management issues that an outsourcing will engender, arising merely as a result of a transfer of people from one organization to another, and highlights the issues and tasks of those retained. These are issues that cannot all be provided for in the contract or schedules, assuming that these issues can even be prescribed! Often commitments in this space will be based on 'best endeavours', 'to be agreed', or an 'agree to agree'. One thing to take heed of here is the lawyer's clinical advice to avoid any of these!

The Issue

Put simply, the 'retained' organization (R) is the original in-house (I) organization less that which is outsourced to the external service provider (O). Interestingly, the ROI of an outsourcing in respect of the people involved is nearly always negative, compared to the positive ROI (return on investment) of the whole outsourcing. Experience and practice suggest that this is never understood until well into the life of the contract, when the negatives of the people issues start to impact on both the anticipated cost savings and the anticipated managed service provision.

The Human Side of Outsourcing: Psychological Theory and Management Practice
Edited by Stephanie J. Morgan

While it can be argued that outsourcing is just another way of sourcing, the fact that outsourcing has almost reached the status of an 'industry' would appear to validate that outsourcings do have something unique compared to other sourcing options, namely the transfer of 'I' to 'O'. This people dynamic creates a new paradigm of issues, the dynamics of which are frequently not understood, and not clear to either party, or neither party is aware of them.

Planning the 'Deal'

This tends to be both combative and constructive … in this phase of activity (which can easily last for up to two years) everyone in both camps, i.e. the supplier's bid and the client's 'procuring' teams, including the external advisers, is trying to solve problems and work together collaboratively, and there should be a respectful consideration for getting agreed compromises.

What is the 'people' strategy? Or, more likely, is there a 'people' strategy? Frequently outsourcing deals are done to reduce costs, with the people impacted being a layer in the sandwich – a useful analogy, as they are often squeezed, with issues spewing out of the side.

The planning stage usually involves a team from the supplier and a team from the client, and while each will have an HR lead, most of the time and effort is initially spent looking at the commercial impacts of the agreement and service provision. The people strand will often run in parallel, but at a tangent, through the issues generated: pensions, redundancy, guarantees and location can individually be deal breakers. In the UK, we enter the world of TUPE (Transfer of Undertakings Protection of Employment) with all the inherent employment protection issues to consider.

The regulations are designed to protect the rights of employees in a transfer situation, enabling them to enjoy the same terms and conditions with continuity of employment. TUPE regulations were introduced to comply with relevant European Commission Directives concerning transfers of undertakings. Other countries will have varying levels of employee protection, which need to be understood from an employee and cost perspective. In many industries and countries, trade union representation in the client needs to be at least addressed and possibly agreed (particularly) in the public sector. In many countries TUPE does not apply, and different countries' employment laws will imply different obligations on both transferor and transferee organizations, with different rights for the individuals being transferred.

Outsourcing and trade unions are not happy bedfellows, as there are usually job losses, or at least job instability, arising in both supplier and client organizations. So having briefly given a flavour of some of the issues, how do the staff actually feel?

Supplier 'deal teams' tend to look at this as a project, most frequently with the rationale being cost reduction, so people issues can be underplayed. The deal teams are doing the outsourcing to their respective organizations, and one of the big issues that emerges is the level of buy-in from the client within its existing business operations. The deal teams also include a high proportion of external advisers and contractors, who do not generate waves of empathy to the in-house teams.

The 'deal' creates a 'Maginot Line', i.e. draws the line between those staff retained and those staff transferred. This review is not a science, so lots of individuals will be caught on the wrong side of the line, or feel they are on the wrong side of the line. The consequent issue is that the right skill sets might be caught in the wrong place. Once the deal is contracted, however, moving people between the respective organizations is, at the very least, complicated, and possibly not even feasible under employment law. Inevitably, therefore, outsourcing will create skills gaps.

If the intended retained organization does not buy into the deal, what comes next will be at best hard work, and at worst destructive. The potential for negativity in this space cannot be underestimated. The constant demand for information can build up resentment within business-as-usual teams.

One impact, in the receiving organization(s), is on incumbent employees. Clearly, while the deal will address physically integrating the transferring employees (place of work, payroll, pensions, etc.), will it address the emotional issues associated with 'mergers'?

The impact on the service provider organization doing the outsourcing is more subtle – both in integrating behaviours and in integrating remuneration. Outsourcing organizations are a conglomerate of previous deals, so integrating new teams into their business is part of business as usual. They have managers experienced in assimilating new teams into their business. However, there will always be levelling issues as staff pay and terms and conditions (T&Cs) will always vary, given that transferring staff come in under TUPE or whatever continuous staff provisioning is contractually provided for.

The impact on the people being outsourced is frequently one of frustration, as they are having the outsourcing done to them. They have no direct say in the decision, but clearly there is an influencing strategy which may impede the deal.

How many parties are party to the deal? In more complex outsourcings, there may be several business units on the client side, and several, even many, suppliers providing the services. Irrespective of whether there is a single prime contractor, the reality is that there are many service providers interfacing with the client, and with the prime contracting party. Multifaceted relationships abound.

Cultural alignment (of the involved parties) plays an important part of making a deal work successfully. Few organizations actually try to do this analysis, but rely on perceptions of the key personnel involved. However, all sorts of factors may inhibit success, e.g. the parent company ethos may be different from the subsidiary, may be different in different geographic regions, may not be uniform globally, private sector does not always align to public sector, etc. Having a cultural fit between service provider and client increases the empathy on the ground.

Planning for the outsourcing is crucial for all parties involved, and making sure that there is full consultation and involvement is paramount to 'success'. So planning the people communications is a number one priority. Outsourcing is creating an uncertain world, so regular briefings are a must to instil confidence.

Transition

At this stage, expectations are high. Making things work seamlessly is of prime importance in order to engender confidence in the end users of the outsourcing organization, to create the feel-good factor that outsourcing does not mean disruption to services, and, politically, to avoid criticism and embarrassment! Everyone from the supplier service and the retained service management teams goes the extra mile to ensure that things go smoothly. The same, however, does not always apply to the transferred (to the service provider) or retained (in unfamiliar roles) staff who have had the outsourcing 'done' to them.

Passing over services … (getting) ready, steady, go: on the face of it it's the same people doing the same things immediately before and immediately after someone signs a piece of paper, 'the contract', so why then is this simple handover so fraught with issues?

1. Business continuity: organizations are obsessed with business continuity, owing to the impacts on their customers. It is now unacceptable to blame your service provider when something goes wrong. BAA's outsourcing of its IT for its new baggage-handling system for Terminal 5 showed that it was its (BAA's) customers who complained.
2. Ways of working: there was a way of working pre-outsourcing. However good or bad it was, people knew who did what to whom. It worked. Outsourcing throws all of this into the bin, and replaces it (or rather tries to) with a complete new set of untried and untested processes. If you are lucky the service provider will claim that these are tried and tested from other accounts. Don't let that fool you … at best they may work with that other client, at worst they have been designed on paper with no real understanding as to what will work with the new client's new organization.
3. Understanding who does what to whom is crucial. With changed roles and responsibilities it is very easy for things to fall down the cracks. However, we would categorize this period as not taking your eye off the ball. The exceptions tend to be 'work in progress', where drawing the line as to progress/work completed has financial implications, so will be bounced backwards and forwards. The risk is that this may delay projects in delivery. New work can be slow to commission as new processes rarely work as detailed in the contract, where insufficient resource is allocated to both determining business requirements and pricing new work.

For the supplier the 'deal' team is often seen as too valued a resource to be managing the contracts post completion and is required to move on to the next deal.

Perhaps there is also a perspective that it is in the supplier's interest to move this team on, so that it avoids becoming embroiled in business as usual, with the consequent issues of extricating themselves, or, more cynically, a perspective that the supplier deliberately wants to create change within business as usual, i.e. to move things hanging over that still need to be sorted out into normal day-to-day discussions, to facilitate new revenue opportunities.

So one simple requirement to make the deal transition to a better business-as-usual is to insist that the supplier deal team is required to take on service delivery for at least the transition period. This will provide for continuity, known faces, but more importantly, even though everything is thought to be catered for 'in the contract', those dotted 'i's' and crossed 't's' have an awful habit of being misinterpreted ... only people can sort out these confusions, and having the same people engaged offers the best chance of not reinventing the wheel of what this was meant to mean.

Frequently, as part of an outsourcing, the supplier is offering a 'transformation', usually incurring an investment, which the client organization wished to avoid making themselves (e.g. wanting to avoid a capital investment, not having the in-house skills, using the outsourcing as the 'excuse' for change), in order to deliver a reduced cost base inherent in the deal, or a major upgrade of infrastructure, or major enhanced service provision.

Transformational change programmes are normally over a pre-agreed time-scale as part of the negotiated deal, and can be rolled out over many months. They are often managed by separate 'project' teams from both the supplier and client organizations, rather than part of business as usual, in parallel, to avoid the change being caught up in business as usual. The relationships on both sides with the business-as-usual teams can get strained, as the retained teams have much to do to bed down service levels, and transformation is used by the supplier as a valid get-out-of-jail card for obviating, or mitigating, contracted service levels. This can create a period of instability, with tensions between the 'project' and 'retained' teams.

The retained teams during transition are very much finding their feet. They have had a major 'life' change imposed upon them. For the client organization, the retained teams also represent an element of instability. Yes, they are there for continuity, but many will be unfamiliar with their new roles, may feel they are under threat from further reorganization/rationalization, may feel isolated by the loss of their former colleagues, may be unused to the commercial intensity of outsourcing, but will definitely feel under pressure, as they are now placed in the middle, between the outsourcer and business end user, and loved by neither, as they will be seen by both parties as the source of failure when problems arise.

For those transferring to the supplier, they are now working in an unfamiliar organization, not of their choice, with the only certainty being uncertainty. Their former comfort zone has disappeared, and they are being viewed from scratch as to their 'value'. Yes, under the transferring arrangements, some security will have been contracted for a period of time, but what comes next?

Managing the Deal

Two factors are at work here, frequently mutually contradictory! The supplying organization needs to get extra new work from its client in a spirit of cooperation and innovation. The client organization wants to receive what it says on the tin. Clients in particular need to be aware of 'promises, promises' ... raised expectations and unfulfilled hype!

Relationships, relationships, relationships (leadership, contract management, service delivery). Each of these different tiers of engagement needs to be managed differently. The accepted principle is that everything is down to having the right 'leadership' who champion the relationship. This is true of all change initiatives. However, while this is necessary, it is never sufficient in an outsourcing, because there are multiple relationships that need to work, both within the respective organizations and between them.

Do the 'leadership' objectives align? Can a cost-saving/cost-effective ethos within the client organization align with the profit requirements of the service provider? Did the deal deliver sufficient returns or, at the outset, are either or both parties trying to redress the balance? Is outsourcing an irreconcilable set of conflicting objectives?

The contract management teams have a joint objective: to administer the commercials, monitor service levels and aim to solve problems/resolve disputes. Are their remits aligned or mutually exclusive? Can they operate in a win–win, working together, collaboration, or are their postulations based on agreeing that any change involves an additional cost? The foundations of contract management are founded in the deal as reflected in the contract. The deal teams have been either disbanded or moved to the next deal.

The service provider has just taken responsibility for a large number of the client's staff to manage the deal on the ground. True, their terms are (at least initially) the same as before, but how do these align to the service provider's own terms? What is the management style of the new employer? What are its plans for staff assimilation, development, restructuring, etc.? It is unlikely that the attitudes and behaviours of this pool of staff will be uniformly positive, and at least some will be resentful and even hostile. The consequences are that relationships both within the service provider and with their former colleagues may be fraught. Fraught relationships are unlikely to be positive for working together.

If technology innovation is an agreed objective, and if the transferring staff did not possess this capability (clearly a likely rationale for the outsourcing), why all of a sudden will the service provider deliver this? Similarly, with respect to transformation, speed of delivery, service levels, etc., if the former employees could not deliver, then at the very least the service provider must bring in new resources, restructure the transferring employees or remove them.

So before anything else is brought into consideration, we have to conclude that without further change, the service provider is not going to deliver a silk purse from a sow's ear. Having the right available resources post outsourcing is improbable, given that the line drawn between transferring resources is always a compromise, and the skills required post outsourcing are different for the client, who needs new commercial skills, service managers, and a lot of skills it has just transferred.

The service provider, too, needs skills to manage the client. Inherently this has not been part of the transferees' former roles. The client's former employees may be introspective, in that they have, until now, accepted their client organization's operational hierarchy and ways of working, and are unlikely be looking at how to manage from a supplier perspective. This group may be too acquiescent of client requests which are likely to represent additional costs to the supplier, and which are not matched by additional revenue. It often takes time for the supplier organization to train their new employees not to give away time and resource, but to look on the client as needing to be exploited as a source of revenue.

Skills (of the respective organizations), knowledge base, organizational restructuring to manage an outsourcing, and coping with change/resourcing are now the consequences of outsourcing, i.e. the outsourcing itself has created this new different set of dynamics which are brought into play:

a)   The consequence of outsourcing in both the supplier and client organizations has been to raise the profile for recruiting outsourcing professionals, even to the extent of creating a new career – 'the outsourcing professional'.

b)   There is a trend to create gaps in retained organizations through reorganizing on the back of outsourcing. These gaps are filled by highly paid contractors and interims, as recruiting permanent staff is much more time consuming.

c)   This gap leads to a gap in the organization's knowledge base, with the potential for loss of knowledge, loss of control, and increased costs through having to address these gaps. It is not unknown for it to pull in consultants to re-create data and analysis.

d)   There is also an incidence of contractors managing interims and managing permanents, with the retained permanents then becoming disenchanted and 'revolting' against this style of management.

e)   However, a legacy issue will always be the proportion of the transferring staff that do not fit; they will need to be retrained, relocated or removed. This element can be a destabilizing element in any outsourcing deal. Transferring employees have divided loyalties.

f)   For the retained people, they will also have to go through traumatic change as to whether their role continues, and if it continues, how it will change. A large proportion of their roles will change – as the retained organization is no longer managing the delivery of services, they may not be managing the assets, support for applications, changes, disaster recovery, etc.

Governance is the thing that everyone says makes for a successful deal. Governance is key – not only do you need to dedicate time to overseeing vendors' performance but also to avoid losing control of the scope of an outsourcing. Effective governance in practice is rarely what is provided for within the contract. Working arrangements are unlikely to align to the 'governance schedule'. Realistically, is it unlikely that you can prescribe in a contract what will work in practice? One of the first post-contract challenges is to make governance fit for purpose.

For the retained staff, they will not necessarily have the skills to manage the governance issues created by an outsourcing, so developing the retained staff in this core competence is necessary. However, governance does not apply only to the outsourcer and outsourcee. The outsource service provider will frequently involve a multiplicity of parties – prime, subcontractors and third-party suppliers – which may well spell an 'outsourcerer's cocktail'! Here, there are contractual arrangements that need to be managed between the respective parties, in order to provide full service provision. Therefore, the internal governance will inevitably need to be augmented to provide a seamless interface with the client organization.

But it can get even more complex ... offshoring service provision is often a integral part of an outsourcer's service offering to reduce costs. In an increasingly global world of service provision, offshoring capability is widening, with many offshoring centres in low-cost countries now becoming established centres of excellence. This overlays a new set of governance and cultural issues. Global service requirements are now being serviced through global service provision, creating even more interfaces to be managed.

Most deals provide for customer satisfaction surveys, and some even have supplier surveys as well, where the respective organizations' employees are surveyed for their opinions. However positioned, they are always a reflection of perceptions and reality, representing a reality check on performance. If used properly they can form a reality health check. They are influenced by pre-deal hype and raised expectations, so not meeting high expectations clearly creates a sense of failure. These surveys therefore often reinforce negative behaviours. On the positive side, they can create a shared understanding of what is not working well, and a positive momentum for change initiatives and improvement opportunities. The opposite, when they are not used properly, which can be the case if relationships are poor, is that they create a gulf rather than shared understanding.

One facet of outsourcing that is often underestimated is the impact of ongoing 'renegotiating'. Most deals, even before the ink is dry, move into renegotiation by stealth. The respective commercial teams' juxtapositioning means that every change control is a managed negotiation. While this is inevitable within these teams, the knock-on effect within the service delivery and service management teams is often one of increasing frustration, making implementation of change problematic. This then knocks on to the users, who very soon start to blame the outsourcing or, more specifically, all the people involved in the outsourcing. The risk is that the substantive benefits of the deal soon get forgotten, and that 'business as usual' becomes grating, with a deterioration in relationships ensuing.

So strategic supplier management comes to the rescue. Current theory says that 'key' vendor relationships need to be strategically managed to ensure long-term business value. This involves creating a much more structured approach to vendor management, involvement of business stakeholders, and introducing a number of relationship management tools to health-check the relationship. Suppliers have also recognized the need for more professional account management, rather than using more traditional salesperson account managers. Growing opinion is that one should appoint a senior specialist person to work directly with (each) vendor – if you don't manage and nurture that relationship as if it is your own team, you could get totally out of sync and watch the level of your services drop considerably. Again, this demonstrates that the client organization must undertake a wide-ranging assessment of their retained organization's competencies, not just limited to those directly affected, and balance the mix of the retained people by supplementing or replacing them with individuals with the right skills.

Usually a structured framework, with facilitated governance, does help bring issues out into the open to ease relationship tensions, but this is labour intensive for both service provider and client, and takes considerable effort to put in place. Even with this people management approach, there potentially remains the underlying issue of 'it's the economy, stupid', i.e. that no amount of relationship management can redress underlying cost issues.

One facet of improving service management has been the creation of outsourcing centres of excellence, more common in suppliers with multiple clients and client organizations with multiple outsourcings. Supplier organizations will try to reduce their costs through both economies of scale and creating centres of technical excellence. That way, they can reduce the cost of service provision across a number of clients, and take on more technical expertise to raise their game. The propensity to take this to offshore destinations (usually to reduce the costs of service provision) can accentuate relationship issues, as each client sees its service provision as becoming less personal. There has been a consequent trend for clients to form user groups to exchange information on service providers (obviously generic, rather than commercial), to help them understand how to manage the service provider.

On the client side, within the contract management, vendor management or group procurement departments, these areas are being set up as outsourcing centres of excellence, where the theory is that different outsourcings have so much in common; they need to be managed in a particular way to ensure compliance and visibility. Ideally, organizations should manage their outsourcing contracts as a portfolio in order to get better value (i.e. manage from a central group). However, the converse may be counteracting, that managing a 'stable' of outsourcing partners can be time consuming, complex and expensive.

So How Key Are the People?

Client organizations that don't put in the people with the right skills to manage the supplier will risk getting out-managed and out-executed by the supplier. Supplier organizations that don't assimilate and integrate their newly acquired and existing service organizations risk becoming dysfunctional, and fragmenting their service provision. These organizations must create development opportunities and career structures for their employees to ensure that they retain their knowledge expertise, or risk degrading their services or re-establishing this competency through hiring in new, potentially more expensive, resources.

So is the converse true … that organizations that put in the right resources, and treat them well, succeed? Well, clearly any organization that does this is much more likely to be well managed, which will apply equally to outsourcing situations as it does to non-outsourcing situations.

Exiting/Renewal

This is fractious! It needs to start a year before notice provision. So the life cycle moves into its final phase, and the need for the right sourcing begins again …

A contract exit/renewal is an inevitable consequence of contracting. For both sides this is going to be a costly exercise, but whereas (normally) the incumbent supplier is trying to retain the business, the client has a range of sourcing options to consider. However, it is worth bearing in mind that there is an innate tendency, as the contract progresses, to bring out the negatives. However, if any outsourcing relationship is to develop, you can't escape the need to recognize the achievements of your vendors and introduce rewards (something along the lines of supplier awards).

I will avoid commenting on when the contract ends as a result of a commercial dispute on the threat of litigation. This can happen in any contract and is usually the consequence of an extreme breakdown in the relationship. For normal contract ends, one just needs to recognize that renegotiating is part of the business-as-usual process of running an outsourcing; then, there is normally a recognition that part of this process must be to plan for renewal. Exit is the extreme option of this renegotiation. Exit does not necessarily mean that things between the supplier and client have broken down (though it usually does), but may be as a result of a change of requirements, and a change of sourcing strategy, of the client.

Exiting an outsourcing is always going to be expensive because, as with the original deal, people are involved in providing and receiving the service, and in some way or another will be involved in what comes next. For the supplier, it is rare that they wish to terminate, as a renewal offers the chance to sweat the 'sunk' investment and avoid stranded costs. The extreme circumstances of when the supplier wants to exit are usually when they are losing money, and exiting will both eradicate this recurring loss and allow them to pass at least some of the stranded costs back to the client. However, usually the supplier is using this threat as part of their negotiating strategy for renewal.

Contract end dates in outsourcing deals present as many issues as doing the deal in the first place. Most contracts provide in detail, prescriptively, for what comes next. Exit planning is now well established as part of outsourcing contracting. However, few will address the 'how's with respect to people issues, which are frequently as complicated as those of the original deal. A renegotiation for renewal is likely to involve changes at the margin. Any other outcome involves a major change to how service provision is delivered. Insourcing creates a whole new problem set needing to be addressed; transfer to a new service provider involves meticulous baton passing. Both involve transferring people, frequently involving TUPE.

One of the least understood issues is the impact of the way that service provision has changed through the previous period. The service provider has the requirement to reduce their cost base to improve their profitability and service performance. This will involve changing the infrastructure platform of service provision, offshoring to lower-cost countries, moving services to shared service environments. So over time the ability to segregate an individual client's services is going to be more complicated. Transferring this to another service provider, or insourcing, is not going to be either clean or simple.

Because of the above, most outsourcing deals renew rather than exit. Renewal is likely to be a major renegotiation. However, to reduce any blame culture, and to save face as a consequence of having to re-present to the respective boards, 'realignment' sits more comfortably with both sides, as this feels less contentious. Do not underestimate the implications of realignment. Renegotiation will be a major project, involving costs and people again, and frequently bypasses the service operators and receivers.

So there are a few questions to answer before going down this path:

- Is the service provider really that bad?
- Is the grass greener?
- Do you have, or can you put together, an exit/renegotiation team?
- What will be the impact on ongoing services over this period of uncertainty?

'Plan A' is always to renegotiate for renewal. So what practical options exist if 'Plan A' does not progress – because it's a bridge too far, because either or both organizations can't step up to the mark, because this fails to be deliverable, and/or because there is no sinecure of a solution? The key risks for the contract and relationship continue to be:

a) Organizational capability: are you convinced that the client organization has the right capabilities and behaviours, or does this organization need to change and do something differently? It is unlikely that you have the right organization, accountabilities and responsibilities either. Does the client organization take on sufficient risk, or simply lay off the risks of its business variability and vagueness on to the supplier?

b) Does the internal (to the client organization) change model work? Or is it that you have too many people in the organization who think that existing approaches are sufficient and do not notice how many times the wheel is reinvented nor how often projects drift because they don't know what they are doing?

c) Business strategy: a lack of clear business strategy will tend to lead to a continued lack of significant investment by the client and will likely lead to a need for continuing cost reductions by the supplier in order to deliver their contractual savings. This reduces the focus on strategic direction and has an adverse impact on the relationship. The need is to align work (and sourcing) to business drivers and invest in those initiatives that align to those drivers. In the absence of clear direction in that space now, we should start with the following 'working assumptions' for business drivers:

- improving workforce productivity;
- lowering the company's overall costs;
- improving the quality of products and/or processes;
- acquiring and retaining customers;
- driving innovative new market offerings or business practices.

d) Demand planning: uncertainty/lack of robust demand planning within the organization's business units is likely to result in poor resourcing and capacity management, cementing a risk-averse approach from the supplier and a knock-on effect of poor understanding and delivery of the client's requirements; this all results in a tactical/transactional approach and if you do not get away from that regime then you are unlikely to move far from the existing template, meaning the supplier operating in a no- or low-risk manner (why would they want to raise their game in such circumstances?)

e) Sourcing: lack of responsiveness and understanding from the supplier in meeting the client business requirements may lead to alternative sourcing options being increasingly exercised, which could result in further relationship tensions and increasing costs of supply. Changing a supplier who has competence adds to risks. Some of the current service provision is still likely to be more than adequate, so the client needs to determine what needs changing, what needs modifying.

f) Dispute resolution: extended time for resolving commercial issues affecting the relationship. This is dependent on the level of contractual compliance.

And on the other side:

a) Do you have the supplier's 'A' team? An apparent shortfall in capabilities from the supplier will militate against top service provision, and will undermine the business opportunities of the client organization placing new, planned or potential work with the supplier. Is there a mechanism to keep the 'A' team on the client account? To manage this, there needs to be a clear set of requirements, i.e. an incentive for the supplier to retain their best resources on the account.

b) Plan B: if you are just unable to reconcile whatever differences persist, then what is the 'Exit Plan B'? Clearly Plan B will involve a change of supplier, either a direct switch or 'insourcing'. A change of supplier may involve a change in the supply arrangements.

A direct switch assumes that there are one or more suppliers who are both willing and able to bid for the work. At the very least, this will require an actively managed tender programme. This is no different in principle from undertaking any tender for the supply of services, but clearly, because of the often complex outsourcing arrangements that have been put in place, tendering with an incumbent supplier can be equally complex.

Two added factors come into play: first, the need to consider that many of the current supplier staff providing the services may, or even will, need to be transferred to any new service provider, either because the contract provides for that, or because employment law necessitates it; and second, separating out the service provision from the existing supply arrangements might not be that simple, due to their being potentially, over time, more integrated into wider service provision of the *in situ* service provider.

The other option is to take service provision (back) in-house. I say back, because it is likely that, in most situations, the services were formerly provided (directed, managed and resourced) by the organization using the services.

So Why Insource?

There is always a sense of 'I told you so' in outsourcing relationships, where the original outsourcing doubting Thomases will mentor an in-house option. However, the principal reason for insourcing is to take strategic control of service provision … to be master of one's own destiny. Undertaking this needs a major resourcing programme. These change programmes need management resources. Management means people. With no resource pool to call upon, these programmes will frequently need to be supported by interim managers and contractors. People require people management.

Well, clearly there are benefits of risk reduction by not being dependent on a single outsourcing vendor, but then any multi-vendor proposition will equally need to be understood and managed.

There are now sufficient examples of insourcing that one can consider what is needed, and what best practice in this space is likely to involve:

- re-creating a group of vendors selected to take advantage of technical specialization (i.e. 'best' suppliers in different areas);
- creating panel suppliers may have the potential for cutting costs and fostering competition;
- more management bandwidth needed to manage multiple suppliers.

It will be important that the multiple vendors 'play well' together – so one should consider putting in place something like an 'Operating Level Agreement' that requires providers to work together for the benefit of the client. One consequence of 'insourcing' will be a requirement for managing multiple outsource vendors, which will require creating (or re-creating) a new set of specialist skills and competencies.

So what skills are required? Getting the most from multiple outsourcers involves:

- formal sourcing strategies, requiring sourcing strategists;
- dedicating people to oversee each vendor relationship;
- establishing regular reviews of vendor performance (dashboards/scorecards);
- spelling out in contract negotiations that vendors should cooperate and refrain from blaming, or else risk losing the job;
- running a project management office or similar body that can track all outsourcing agreements, using a software application to track vendor relationships and performance (and to help create regular reports and dashboards).

So Where Do All the People Come From?

For the renegotiation, there may still be people around from the original deal – the existing service teams, the commercial teams – who can be pulled together into a project 'deal' team. However, the likelihood is that these resources will have dissipated, and there will be a need to take in external advisers, contractors and consultants. The supplier will retain bid teams, and will pull together their internal team to specifically 'manage' this.

Postscript on Early Termination

This is usually very fractious as it creates a group of the 'untrusted' (analogous to the undead in a Dracula script!).

So why am I highlighting this as part of the life cycle of an outsourcing? As with any partnering-type venture – and outsourcing is very analogous to any new joint venture – these ventures have a high failure rate. When service provision (for whatever reasons) and/or relationships break down, there is usually an option to terminate the contract early. Here, I am not going to address the normal contract remedies available, but the circumstances around exercising early termination rights.

Many outsourcing contracts, particularly longer-term arrangements, provide the right to give notice to terminate early. The rationale is that, in any long-term service arrangement, the requirement for those services may radically change, and that ongoing service provision may need to be radically re-planned owing to changed circumstances. That said, inadequate service provision may still be an instigating factor.

Early termination options (or merely the threat to exercise) are no different from those associated with normal termination, and clearly this can be part of a renegotiation strategy. However, two factors may be different. First, in an early termination scenario, there are likely to be stranded costs associated with the supplier's initial investment programme, which are likely to give rise to stranded costs for the client organization. Second, getting to this point is likely to mean that the relationship between both parties is likely to be at least strained, at worst broken down, with a heavy involvement of legal advisers!

So if the relationships at the top level are fraught, then what is the effect on all the people involved? Clearly not good, with the probability of reduced service levels and reduced cooperation, and with all the people feeling uncertain as to what comes next. This is not where anyone really wants to be. The one possible upside is that it is probably better to bite the bullet early where things are not panning out as expected, rather than allow the contract to continue into a further period of dissatisfaction.

Conclusion: 'People, people, people … saying me had sod this has long how … people, people, people'. Read this a few times … and then read it backwards. The only purpose of this is to for you to take a pause … to emphasize the importance of people in an outsourcing relationship. So where does this lead us? From many years of experience in outsourcing, the people side tends to be underestimated, to everyone's cost; many of these facets are extremely important points that often get forgotten … many will be taken up and discussed in more detail in the following chapters.

Chapter 3

Outsourcing – A Provider's Tale

Simone Hemingway

Introduction

This chapter provides some thoughts and experiences from a provider's view on the business of outsourcing and identifies how good people management approaches can improve the benefits to both public services and the financial performance of private businesses. The author of the chapter has many years' experience as a 'provider' of outsourcing services in both the private and public sectors and the chapter focuses on her experience and thoughts in relation to the human side of outsourcing.

Private and Public Sector Outsourcing

The rationale given for most outsourcing arrangements is predominantly efficiency and innovation, effectively providing more for the same money or the same for less money. These elements typically involve significant changes for the people involved in delivering the service, in particular the impact on managerial and organizational structures, working practices and skills required. The ability to manage the people changes effectively is therefore key to successfully delivering the objectives of an outsourcing contract. Below is a brief discussion of the differences, in the author's experience, between public and private sector outsourcing contracts.

The Human Side of Outsourcing: Psychological Theory and Management Practice
Edited by Stephanie J. Morgan
Copyright © 2009 John Wiley & Sons Ltd.

Public sector outsourcing

One of the strategic aims of outsourcing for government is to improve service and reduce cost by making significant changes which are deemed not possible in the current public services environment, as well as to gain management expertise that is not available from within. Another key element includes transferring the risk of service delivery and particularly the implementation of needed structural changes.

As a consequence of the high profile and political nature of public sector outsourcing, reputational risk can often be perceived to be much greater in transferring and managing national or local government services. The political agenda and often strong media attention can impact levels of stakeholder buy-in. Likely resistance from unions or the public may be enough to stifle a commercially sound proposition, in particular where required changes are most controversial. As is covered later on under the umbrella of 'culture change', these early processes will significantly impact the ability to manage change in the new outsourced organization as often the views and opinions of employees will be formed at a very early stage, before the new employer has any opportunities to communicate and engage with its new workforce.

Additionally, the procurement processes for public sector outsourcing will often be more complex and the timescales to achieve a successful outsource greater, in order to ensure that decisions on making changes to public services have sufficient stakeholder scrutiny and the bid processes are deemed to be fair to all interested parties. Although the key drivers may still be cost and public service efficiencies and improvements, there is often a significant social element which will drive a public purse argument. There are obvious tensions between providing needed public services versus the cost efficiencies which provide more public money for investment in other areas. The outsourcing processes can be hampered by the perceptions of key stakeholders that the purpose is for cost saving and reducing public services. These tensions can be seen as beneficial to the provision of a public service but more often may be seen as detrimental; for example, the reduction of specific routes on a train service which are underused or the closure of railway stations or local post offices with very limited patronage. The implications for profit making and taking for the outsource provider in comparison to the private sector are therefore much wider and more complex and fair returns for private businesses can be the subject of much political debate.

The above elements create a very different framework for outsourcing in the public rather than private sector and have significant implications for managing change both within a newly 'privatized' service and in the second, third and fourth generation of privatized contracts where there is often ongoing pressure by politically motivated groups to revisit the rationale for 'privatization'.

Private sector outsourcing

The market and experience for private sector outsourcing is mature in the UK and the US and there is greater acceptance of organizations taking commercial decisions on where to do business as cost effectively as possible. Indeed, often the driver for private sector outsourcing may be innovation or acquiring needed skills, as the provider may be specialists in non-core areas of their business (e.g. IT or business processing) but will usually also incorporate a significant element of cost saving. More recently, over the past decade a considerable number of people-based outsourcing contracts have migrated to locations outside of the UK and US, often called 'nearshore' (within Europe) from the UK or 'offshore' (typically to India or Asia). This has added a substantially different dimension to the private sector outsourcing marketplace and often the people implications of these contracts will remain with the current employer to be managed (as there is unlikely to be any 'transfer' of actual employees, despite UK 'TUPE' legislation). This particular 'human issue' of outsourcing adds a layer of complexity around the social and economic arguments on outsourcing and are picked up for discussion in Chapter 7 which focuses more on the context of outsourcing.

Managing People Changes

It is often said that how a people change is managed has more of a lasting impact on those involved than what the change in fact meant for an individual's day-to-day work; and this is never truer than in an outsourcing environment. From a provider's viewpoint, there are two key areas to managing change from the people side of an outsourcing environment: (1) the management of change in the employment relationship and organization of work; and (2) the management of cultural change. These will often define the success of the outsourcing process in terms of meeting all stakeholders' objectives. It is the people element, therefore, that will often affect the commercial reality of what is to be achieved and, for this reason, the human side of outsourcing should be given the same or higher priority than managing all other stakeholders. The transition management process, as the people transfer is often termed, will start as soon as employees are engaged and may often end up to 12 to 24 months past the transfer of people, depending on the phasing of the transfer and the scope of the change required to arrive at the 'new state'. The key aspect of timescales in outsourcing will be covered in Chapter 11; from a provider's perspective, this is a critical part of the whole aspect of managing people transitions.

The Importance of Transition Management

When transferring employees to a new employer, it is imperative to start the communication and consultation process as early as possible. This may often be quite difficult, particularly in the public sector outsourcing arena, for two reasons:

1. Often there will be significant speculation and public consultation before a decision is reached in a first-generation outsource. As the outsourcing provider

will not have been selected, nor any invitation to tender issued, there will be very little on which one can consult employees and their representatives.

2. Access to employees will only be given once the final bidder has been announced, and this process can take several months, or even years, to complete from the initial consultation on an outsourcing proposal.

Even with second- or third-generation outsourcing within a public sector environment, the bidding process can often be so formal and 'arm's length' to ensure parity of opportunity amongst the bidders that appropriate consultation and communication is difficult to achieve in a timely manner. Alleviating employees' fears of the unknown as soon as possible is crucial to their levels of continuing engagement in the service being provided. This consequently creates real issues in managing change and ultimately impacts on achieving the objectives of the outsourcing. It is fair to say, in a private sector environment, that a competitive bidding environment will often also prevail. In the provider's experience, however, the process for consulting and engaging once the preferred bidder has been announced is generally longer and gives opportunity for greater engagement with the transferring employees, certainly in first-generation private sector contracts.

Culture Change and Employee Engagement

The culture of an organization will be heavily determined by its history, its leaders and the environment within which it operates. (See Chapter 8.) It is therefore no surprise to learn that the transition of a business from a public sector organization to the private sector will bring changes in all three of these dimensions.

There is much research in the area of employee engagement, which clearly demonstrates a link between the performance of an organization and the levels of engaged employees. As with any change in environment, there is always uncertainty and this will affect how employees feel about the organization within which they work and also how they identify with it. During an outsourcing, both of these parameters are put severely to the test and both aspects need to be identified, measured and managed through effective transition management practices.

Often the key challenge is to create loyalty both to the 'client' (who may have been the previous employer) and to the new employer. There are often differences in how outsourced employees are integrated into their new employer's organization. Some outsourcing organizations have clear and prevalent processes to attempt to ensure that incoming employees are inducted into their brand and culture in the first few weeks and months of transfer, hence hopefully becoming part of their organization and living their values as quickly as possible. Other outsourcing organizations take a view on keeping 'contracts' whole and ensuring that the loyalty is to the 'client' organization. There is little empirical evidence and study to suggest which is the most effective in ensuring that the outsourcing is successful. In my experience, often less effort is made to integrate employees into the new organization in public to private sector outsourcing contracts than in private to private sector outsourcing. I have also observed interesting results from employee engagement surveys which show that where contracts are left reasonably 'whole' and within the client organization, employee engagement and loyalty to the client organization can often be significantly higher than to the outsourcing organization, even after multiple years of employment within the outsourcer. Loyalty to the new organization can often be very difficult to establish without full integration and significant leadership engagement, supported by employee marketing and branding exercises. All of these efforts are often time consuming and therefore expensive, and in a low-margin blue-collar public sector outsourcing environment they are often not prioritized. In comparison, where professional services are outsourced (such as technology), much more effort is made to ensure higher levels of engagement owing to the scarcity of labour and the costs of replacing leavers, who will often have valuable proprietary and irreplaceable client knowledge.

When involved in a major outsourcing contract, it is important to ask potential bidders how they plan to manage transition; what case studies they can use to demonstrate their approach to managing organizational, terms and conditions and cultural changes and how they measure their success. You may also wish to visit 'outsourced' sites and meet with managers and employee representatives to ask first hand how the transition to the 'new state' was managed. During a major private sector outsourcing in which I was involved, we used a cultural 'employee engagement' survey to measure operational risk during a phased transition process which took place over 10 months. This was a very useful measure of general feelings of engagement pre and post transfer and the likelihood of risk to delivery where engagement levels were particularly low. It also enabled the outsourcing company to have a good measure of how the culture change programme was being embedded in the newly outsourced part of their business.

The impact of culture change is often much greater for public sector employees becoming part of the private sector. In my experience, public sector employees identify very strongly with their roles as 'public servants' and have a high degree of loyalty to the communities they serve. The importance of the provider recognizing and leveraging this in the transition process is key and often overlooked. The positive impacts can, however, also be significant. There is some limited research available in this area which shows that often the benefits perceived by public sector managers going into the private sector are considerable. The feeling that finally they are able to make decisions and needed changes without the restrictions of a heavily bureaucratic and politically driven process has been found to be enlightening and consequently had a positive impact on their engagement (Serco Case Study: Serco Institute article 'Good People, Good Systems' – reference and links at end of chapter).

The management of employees transitioning out of an organization, in my experience, is as important as transitions in, and I have yet to work within an outsourcing environment where either the client or the outsourcer focuses their attention on this important aspect of people management during the bidding and mobilization process. There is as much a requirement to ensure that employees transferring out of your organization go with feelings of fair treatment and respect for their outgoing employer as there is when they transfer in, for all the obvious reasons of reputation, brand and future resourcing and business development. I would certainly recommend any parties entering into an outsourcing environment to ensure that this is adequately covered in the negotiations before the contract is concluded.

The Management of Change in the Employment Relationship and Organization of Work

The level of change expected will have a key impact on the transition and management of people. People being transferred will always fear potentially significant upcoming changes in terms and conditions of employment, shift patterns, the likelihood of a requirement to reduce staffing numbers, the introduction of new technology, or even the potential of a change in location for the delivery of some services. There may even be anticipation by the employees 'in scope' to transfer that the service provider will 'nearshore' or 'offshore' some of the services provided.

The Hard Facts – Public to Private Terms and Conditions of Employment (UK)

Amongst the differences in terms and conditions between the public and private sectors, pensions is by far the most emotive subject in the UK outsourcing environment, despite it having the least legal coverage under TUPE. In the private sector, final salary pension schemes are virtually non-existent for new employees, and have been for quite some time; therefore often this issue is less prevalent. In the public sector, however, final salary pension schemes are the norm. As public sector services are outsourced to the private sector, so the final salary pension becomes the key financial limiter to ensuring that the outsourced service can be provided in a sustainable way. The political implications of closing final salary schemes do not need further mention for the purposes of this chapter; the media continue to ensure that we are all aware of the issues and arguments – most readers will remember the impact of the Grangemouth dispute in Scotland on the availability of fuel in the UK. The arguments related to their final salary scheme and the attempts by the exiting private sector employer to limit its substantial liabilities under the scheme. Often the first-generation public to private sector outsourcing will be the most political and high profile in tackling the pensions issue, and to this end both the outsourcer and outsourcee will go to great lengths to ensure the protection of the pension rights of the employees in scope to transfer in order for the proposal to meet least resistance from employees and their representatives. Once the contract has transferred a number of times, the issue of pensions may become less emotive and it can be possible to close the scheme to new members depending on the political environment within which the service operates and the strength of union opposition; in the Grangemouth case, the strength of feeling and opposition clearly did not dissipate over time. The whole pensions issue is a considerable barrier for public to private sector outsourcing, and this remains a real issue within sectors which are currently facing the requirement to outsource more of their services, but where there are limited solutions available for bridging the pensions issue. One area where this will become more prevalent in the coming years will be in the UK healthcare sector, where there is also significant resistance to 'independent sector' providers and the issues are heavily politicized.

Impact of Contract Length

Contract length will impact the outsourcing company's ability to create successful organizational culture change and employee engagement with the new employer. There is significant debate within the outsourcing community as to the return on investment for developing employee engagement in shorter-term contracts (up to two years). Arguably, the better the engagement, the better the delivery of service, and the more likely the outsource provider's success in retaining the contract. In certain public sector outsourcing environments, however, service provision alone may not be sufficiently compelling to retain contracts and often there is a suspicion that ensuring the business opportunity is appropriately 'spread' between available private sector service providers may be the driver for contract awards. There is clearly a disincentive in shorter, low-margin contracts to invest in ensuring that the employees are highly engaged during their time with the existing provider. This has often led to a 'new badge, same job' culture, particularly within a blue-collar service environment, and employees may be actively disengaged with their new employers owing to the number of transfers they have experienced. In a unionized environment, this can often become a huge blocker to change, as union representatives (and influencers) remain more of a constant in the employees' work life than the employer themselves. This can create a 'vicious circle' as each new service provider fails to achieve high levels of engagement, thus creating a more disassociated workforce and a less efficient service. This again fuels the arguments for lack of success in public sector outsourcing and the answers probably lie in contractors being able to build longer-term service contracts with incentives to succeed and retain the business rather than the requirement to re-tender so regularly. This line of argument does start to take us rather beyond the scope of this text and into business cases for outsourcing, which, if they were to include human capital opportunity costs as described above, may paint a fuller picture.

Another key area of debate worth discussing is the differences, or indeed similarities, of managing the human aspects of an outsourcing contract versus those of an acquisition.

Outsourcing versus Acquisitions

In discussing potential transition management processes and making outsourcing contracts successful, the question is often asked as to whether broadly the same challenges and opportunities exist with both. In my experience, there are great similarities to the people management practices employed in transitioning a new contract in or transitioning a new organization in (and subsequently transitioning out, as I have argued above). The due diligence processes pre-acquisition and outsourcing and the valuation processes may be very similar, as will the plans to transition in around communication and engagement. There are some areas where different approaches may often be taken in the case of an acquisition over an outsourcing. Often, an acquisition will mean a merger of business functions to create more synergies across the new business. In an outsourcing environment this is often not the case and contracts are often required to be left 'whole' to ensure that they can be appropriately transitioned out in the future (as is more often the case in the public rather than private sector outsourcing arena). In most cases, an acquisition will also be long term and permanent and therefore the processes for cultural change are often approached as a 'merger' and best of both, rather than a 'bolted on' contract. I would say, however, that this often depends on the rationale and the environment around acquisitions. I have worked in portfolio-managed businesses both in an outsourcing environment and for organizations that are formed and managed as 'conglomerates' and in both environments the incentive is to retain businesses or contracts as 'whole' entities. The former GEC business is a good example of an organization that integrated only at a financial and purchasing level for a number of years of its existence, allowing it to purchase and divest within its portfolio with relative ease. Only towards the end of its existence did it start to manage-in synergistic savings across the business as its focus turned to a single market.

Implications in Practice

The above content touches on all the aspects that both 'customers' and 'providers' may need to consider when engaging in the human aspects of the outsourcing environment.

As a provider of outsourcing services, the key practical issues to consider, beyond the commercial aspects of securing new business, are the people aspects. If the people aspects are not managed appropriately, then, in my experience, it is highly unlikely that the contract will be a financial or reputational success. Good people practices in outsourcing should therefore ensure that the following aspects are known and carefully considered:

- The elements that define the outsourcing contract, i.e. public or private sector; first-, second- or multiple-generation transfer; the political environment and public opinion surrounding the service, including the union environment; the location and local environment.

- A robust due diligence process and care not to focus solely on the quantitative rather than the qualitative aspects, such as due consideration of all key stakeholders in the process and their impact on the success of the contract at all stages.
- The transition management process in relation to the above, in particular ensuring that robust plans are in place to transition the employees from one organization into another and that promises and timescales are met and maintained during the process.
- The implications on the terms and conditions and organization of work are considered fully at the commercial or bid stages of the contract, and that these meet with client expectations and the likely employee expectations before finalizing the financial business case. In particular, consideration must be given to the legal requirements of TUPE and likely pension issues outside of this, which will be expensive in financial terms and have key impacts on reputation and ability to deliver the service.
- Employee engagement and cultural implications are clear and there are mechanisms in place to manage these. This often requires real leadership engagement and understanding of the people aspects as well as the importance that is placed on this and time spent on the people aspects. Look at how these aspects can be measured through surveys or feedback sessions.

Further Information

Serco Institute (2004). Study interviews with 13 managers. www.serco.com/Images/good%20people%20good%20systems%202004_tcm3-3788.pdf

Serco Institute (2004). Executive summary. www.serco.com/Images/GoodPeopleExecSum_tcm3-3787.pdf

Serco Institute (2006). Study survey results from 150 managers. www.serco.com/Images/Good%20People%20Survey%20Main%20Report_tcm3-11869.pdf

Serco Institute (2006). Survey results. www.serco.com/Images/Good%20People%20Survey%20Detailed%20Findings_tcm3-11870.pdf

Chapter 4

Sourcing for Outsourcing

Yvonne Williams

Introduction and Background

When I was first asked to write a chapter on recruiting into the outsourcing sector, I was flattered but also admit to being a little disappointed; I had always shared the philosophy of many that there is a novel in everyone and had rather liked the idea that my first stab at writing would be a racy and, of course, highly successful novel entitled 'Sleeping with a Headhunter'. So watch this space!

But seriously, having spent the best part of three decades in the recruitment industry working across sectors including financial services, technology, and professional services in both selection and search, I have seen monumental changes. This period has included several downturns and at least three major recessions, numerous and innovative transformations and the challenges that economic globalization brings to the way that business is conducted.

This has been an incredibly fast-moving time for business and has required a proactive and innovative approach to recruitment to enable businesses to stay one step ahead in an increasingly competitive environment. Perhaps because I have been privileged to have worked throughout this extraordinary business and economic cycle, I remain passionate that sourcing the right people is one of the most important and rewarding careers imaginable.

It is worth drawing attention to the way that recruitment has generally evolved over the years. Sometime in the not too distant past, companies changed the name of the department that looked after their people issues from Staff Welfare to Personnel and then to Human Resources Department and some US corporations

The Human Side of Outsourcing: Psychological Theory and Management Practice
Edited by Stephanie J. Morgan
Copyright © 2009 John Wiley & Sons Ltd.

have now gone the extra mile to name their departments Human Capital. De-personalizing personnel is a modern trait and one that, sadly, often carries a high price tag. De-personalizing your recruitment and resourcing process carries an even higher one.

Whatever the modern terminology, we are all surely agreed that your human capital – your people – are your company's future. We read so much on corporate websites and in brochures about their people being the main asset to growing their business and fundamental to building relationships with their clients. Why then do the actions not necessarily follow the words? So many firms invest so little time and effort in resourcing the right people, and sadly even less in retaining them.

In this chapter, I will first outline the aspects of outsourcing that result in a different approach being needed in the outsourcing sector compared to other sectors. I will then discuss the different stages of the outsourcing process and the steps and specific outsourcing skills required for each.

Outsourcing and Recruitment

So what, you may ask, makes resourcing the right people in the outsourcing sector any different to other sectors? The outsourcing industry has been developing over the past 20 years, led by the US, and has enjoyed a rapid year-on-year growth. This has caused an insatiable demand for top talent with experience and the war scars of having run large, complex outsourcing deals.

I entered the outsourcing market as a recruiter several years ago. I had been working in technology recruitment for some time and could see that outsourcing IT was going to be more than a short-term business trend. I was also fascinated by the complexity of outsourcing – the multi skills and talent requirements – and could see the immediate challenges in finding people with these skill sets.

As with any 'new' industries enjoying growth, there have been many times, particularly in the early years, when we were in a Catch 22 situation. Companies wanted to hire experts, but there were very few experts about and, certainly in the 1990s, it was a case for many of learning and developing skills on the job – and dare I say some of this showed in the quality and success or failure of the outsourced deals.

Outsourcing is an extremely complex business tool and requires a range of skills and knowledge across many disciplines. There are at least seven steps in the life-cycle model required to implement a successful outsourcing deal, and all these steps require a good knowledge of contract negotiations and business law, bid processes, due diligence procedures, procurement, relationship and vendor management, commercial acumen, awareness of risk (security, data-protection, intellectual property, and political and economic) business re-engineering, change management, governance, crisis management and technology savvy.

The People and Skill Requirements

The people recruitment considerations follow a cycle, moving from the initial decision to outsource.

Step one: the decision

Not surprisingly, the decision to outsource is usually taken at, or very close to, board level. Before the decision is taken it is imperative that an organization has a very clear and common understanding of its business objectives and the drivers for change. This is often driven by a need to reduce costs, to improve business processes and service levels, to gain access to bleeding-edge technology or a combination of all of these. Often, at this early stage, organizations will engage consultants or advisers to help them to formulate the strategy and understand the options available to transform the business vision into a transformation programme.

There has been a significant growth in the demand for consultants and advisers as outsourcing has matured as a business tool and I see no signs of this slowing. Indeed, quite the opposite, the professional services sector is enjoying significant growth. The slowing down of the economy and the recent credit crunch have meant that more organizations are looking at ways to work smarter while reducing costs, and there are a record number of major business transformation programmes under way or being considered, with outsourcing playing a significant role.

Skills required: Human resources, transition specialists, culture change, business change/transformation specialists, experts. Consider consultants and/or interim managers, business re-engineering, business transformation, cost–benefit realization specialists.

Step two: how to outsource

The options are varied, from setting up a captive centre, or working through a single service provider or multiple vendors, operating a shared service, to deciding to include multi-shoring, nearshoring or single-destination offshoring as part of the transformation plan.

Again, with the complexities of the choices available, many organizations choose to work with specialist advisers who are not tied to a supplier to give them 'honest broker' advice on what to outsource and how to get the very best from an outsourcing deal. In recent years there has been a particular growth in smaller niche advisory firms who give practical guidance built on experience and knowledge of the global opportunities.

All this needs careful planning and management and many advisers recommend that this is treated internally in a similar way to a merger and acquisition (M&A);

certainly the internal communications should be handled as sensitively as an M&A, as rumours can escalate and have a very negative effect if not handled in a timely and appropriate manner.

Step three: vendor selection

During this period, financial management and analysis of costs will pay a large part in the decision, and procurement departments will have a significant influence on the decision. There must also be considerable risk assessment; for example, when offshoring this would include geo-political risks, including local infrastructure, language, culture, political stability, bureaucracy, terrorism and adverse weather trends. Other risks include performance risk – suppliers' failure to provide services which would impact on reputation, and legal and regulatory risk – tax, employment, data protection, intellectual property, and contract enforcement.

The way in which an organization conducts its selection of a vendor varies from organization to organization. However, it is usual for most organizations to go through a competitive tender, inviting a number of suppliers to bid and once down-selected to go through an RFI (request for information) process, usually with term sheets. The organization would then carry out a full due diligence exercise of the short-listed suppliers, which would usually include benchmarking.

Skills required for stages two and three: Risk analysts, cost analysts, procurement specialists, internal lawyers (end-user). Bid teams and commercial contract teams from the supplier side.

Step four: bid process and contract negotiation

It is imperative at this stage to have absolute clarity as to what is being out-sourced and to understand each of the parties' responsibilities and to agree pricing structures. If this is to be the beginning of a successful partnership, the contract must accurately reflect the will and legal obligations of all the parties involved.

There needs to be appropriate and fair balance of risk as well as effective gover-nance, together with some flexibility to take account of strategic business changes, market changes, technology and regulatory changes. One of the keys to a successful outsourcing deal is ensuring that the reporting mechanisms and exit strategy are robust and workable for all parties – thus avoiding expensive and time-consuming litigation downstream. Multisourcing, a relatively new trend, has brought added complexities and a new dimension to the negotiation of contracts.

Skills required: Internal and external lawyers, human resources (union representatives if appropriate), cost accountants, procurement, specialist con-sultants. Contract advisers can also add value as they bring pragmatism and are less expensive than external lawyers and can often get to an advanced stage of negotiation.

Step five: transition stage

This stage of the outsourcing process is the most emotional, when staff are transferring across to a new organization. Communication and timing are vitally important, in both the announcement and the management of the transition. Human resources from both the supplier and the organization will play a very important role at this time.

Even when an outsourcing arrangement does not involve offshoring, there is still a cultural change to manage. It takes time for the incumbents to adjust and conflict can arise. Often there is resentment if two people are head to head for one management role and their reports are also affected by this. Outsourcing can also lead to redundancy and the retained personnel are naturally upset when colleagues are faced with this.

The requirement of senior management also changes during this time, from a strategic requirement to a more hands-on approach to the management of the supplier or client relationship.

Transition is one of the most vulnerable stages of an outsourcing deal and, as a recruiter, I have often found that many organizations often do not engage the appropriate skill sets before transition or retain the right people during and after the transition.

Skills required: Transitional specialists, change specialists, business transformational specialists, lawyers (internal and external employment lawyers) and human resources. New and additional skill sets are often required and this is the ideal time for organizations to consider specialist interim managers to help them through this stage while deciding who and what skills are required for the future.

Step six: vendor management/relationship management/programme management

An organization that has gone through an outsourcing arrangement will understand the importance of managing the vendor/supplier relationship. This step is paramount to the ongoing success of the programme. Gone are the days when contracts were something to be kept in a drawer until a problem arose. Good governance and continued monitoring of the key performance indicators and service level agreement are now, more often than not, normal best practice. Successful outsourcing goes hand in hand with successful relationship management.

Suppliers equally need to value their customer relationships and ensure that appropriate service levels are delivered. Additionally, they will require extensive project and programme management skills to deliver the services and adjust to changes and new requirements.

Skills required: Programme managers, project managers, vendor managers, service delivery managers and directors, trouble-shooters, business turnaround specialists.

Step seven: exit – litigation

There are many reasons why an organization may wish to exit or consider exiting an outsourcing programme: the programme may have reached or be reaching full term, and they may wish to explore new suppliers; there may be business, political or economic issues which affect the deal; or the supplier may be failing. Whatever the reason, it is easier to negotiate an exit from an outsourcing programme that has included an agreed exit and dispute strategy from the outset.

Skills required: Conflict resolution specialists, lawyers, business transformation specialists, trouble-shooters, business change specialists, business process re-engineering specialists and technology architects.

Resource Management

An overarching and vital requirement throughout a successful outsourcing arrangement is appropriate resource management and planning. There will be 'hot spots' during the negotiation stages, as well as through transition, that will require skill sets that an organization would not naturally have available. The use of interim managers while deciding on a full-time solution is usually the best answer for this. However, I would always recommend preparing a resource management plan to enable appropriate resources to be factored into the programme schedule and costs and to ensure that you have the skill sets when you need them. Table 4.1 outlines the range of skills required at each stage.

Although these skill sets are available within a number of professions, it is a rare character that has worked across all of these steps – the end-to-end process. A major criticism of outsourcing professionals is that they often work in a silo and do not have a complete understanding of all the components and processes. Therefore, the lack of broad knowledge can have an adverse effect on the outsourcing programme. When you then add the additional complexity of working across differing business sectors with inconsistent business and processing requirements – retail, life sciences, fast-moving consumer goods (FMCG), financial services, manufacturing etc. – it is easy to see why outsourcing has become an industry in itself and why it is so challenging to find the skills and talent required.

Education and Training

Interestingly, unlike other professions, until recently outsourcing did not have a qualification or any recognized accredited training to develop personal professional development. Therefore, when sourcing candidates from the outsourcing industry, there has been a lack of any professional qualification or certificate to demonstrate

Table 4.1 Skill requirement by contract stage

Making the decision	Who, how, and where	Vendor selection	Bid process	Transition	Programme delivery	Exit and renegotiation	STAGE
							Resources required
Board	Board	Supply chain management	Internal and external lawyers	Change managers	Programme managers	Conflict resolution	
Strategic business advisers	Specialist outsourcing advisers	Internal lawyers	Human Resources	Transition specialists	Project managers	Lawyers (internal and external)	
Accountants	Benchmark organizations	Business stakeholders	Union representatives	Business transformation specialists	Vendor managers	Business transformation specialists	
Economists	Risk assessment, geo-political, economy regulatory, IP data protection	Contract and negotiation teams	Contract and negotiation teams	Lawyers (internal and external)	Business relationship managers	Business trouble-shooters	
Lawyers	Business transformation specialists	Benchmark specialists	Bid management teams	Employment lawyers	Project/programme trouble-shooters	Business change specialists	
		Due diligence	Sales/client directors	Human Resources	Turnaround specialists	Business process re-engineers	
		Cost/service analysis	Cost accountants	Union representatives	Customer relationship managers	IT solution architects	
		Benchmarking	Procurement	Culture change specialists	Service delivery managers	Bid team	
		Procurement	Supply chain management		Support service management		

that the individual understands or has worked to best practice standards – most people have learnt 'on the job' with varying degrees of success!

With outsourcing being such a growth area over the past few years, there are a vast number of people who have had some involvement in deals in one way or another. Because there is also a skill shortage, these skills are naturally highlighted, and quite often exaggerated. I have had personal experience, even at relatively senior level, of finding that a candidate's CV does not accurately reflect his or her experience. Only during an interview, when delving more closely into his or her involvement in an outsourcing deal, are you truly able to really begin to understand the true capabilities or lack of experience. An inexperienced recruiter, without a thorough knowledge of the complexities of the industry, or insight into the outsourcing deals, might therefore be forgiven for recommending individuals for positions when in reality they do not have the correct level of knowledge.

For a number of years I have believed that offering professional development in the outsourcing industry would drive up standards and improve the success rate of projects. Other professions have this – e.g. legal, accountancy – and yet somehow this has been missing in the outsourcing sector. In 2005 I was offered an opportunity to help to make this happen. It seems that I was not alone in my idea to raise standards as many corporate and individual members of the National Outsourcing Association (www.noa.co.uk) also thought a training initiative would benefit the industry. I was elected to the NOA board to lead this initiative and I am delighted that the NOA has quite recently set up a training arm. This is the first time that the UK has had an accredited qualification for outsourcing. The course design offers a modern, flexible approach to professional development, and individuals, or participants from organizations, can choose (once they have completed the entry level) to enter the programme where they feel appropriate and cover all of, or elements of, the prospectus that suit them at the time. The objective is to complete the entire programme and gain an accredited professional certificate and/or diploma.

Other, US-based organizations are reacting similarly and several universities are including outsourcing as a module in their MBA programmes. I am confident that this will raise standards and give subject-matter experts a goal and credibility amongst other professionals.

Growth Areas and Trends

The UK is at the forefront of many major high-profile outsourcing deals and UK firms are now leading Europe which has been slower to recognize the advantages of outsourcing. This success has given rise to recent major growth in global advisory firms. The top four consultancies have strong outsourcing practices and give end users considering outsourcing as a business tool relevant strategic advice.

There is also a strong growth in the UK for niche outsourcing advisory firms, usually not suppliers of outsourcing services, as they are giving 'honest broker' advice and guidance. They often then follow through with hands-on delivery and management of the entire life-cycle programme. Many outsourcing deals are pan-European and currently there are major opportunities in Spain, Germany and France. Language skills may therefore be extremely useful.

The legal profession is doing well in the global outsourcing sector, particularly as the market matures. This maturity has often increased the complexities of the deals, i.e. multisourcing, multi-shoring, and other consortium-led deals have led to more rigorous and sophisticated legal contract arrangements. At the same time, the trend has moved away from a 6-inch-plus thick contract, that no one ever looked at after the deal signing, to a working document that is more operational and referred to on a regular basis.

Outsourcing lawyers are now more business aware – less likely to be working in a legal silo – and less likely to recommend litigation, preferring a more conciliatory approach to benefit their clients.

Service providers have had to continually change their business models to take account of new trends. As the outsourcing industry has matured, it has become much more competitive and pricing and service delivery are high up the agenda. The offshoring providers also pull on the UK market for mid and senior management to be the conduit between the offshoring destination and wherever the service is being provided. The credit crunch is having an impact on these suppliers, as customers are expecting greater savings and improved service, while in some offshoring destinations they are experiencing challenges of higher wages as the market has matured and also very high attrition rates. Western-style management is often sought to handle the culture differences in large and complex offshoring programmes to add value to the programmes by giving management experience sometimes not found in the offshore destinations.

Additionally, there are firms that specialize in business process outsourcing for specific business services – human resources, accountancy, recruitment, payment processes, call centres and data-centres etc. These firms look for individuals with experience in these business functions as well as experience in service and customer delivery.

Of course, organizations that are considering outsourcing will be growing during a downturn in the economy. Outsourcing is an excellent business tool to reduce cost and improve service, exactly what all organizations will be doing for the foreseeable future.

Considering Outsourcing as a Career?

A career in outsourcing offers diversity and opportunity. Entry level can be through programme or project management, procurement, relationship management, service delivery, a particular business service, a conscious decision or simply because your firm has decided to outsource something and you happen to be around at the time!

My advice to anyone entering outsourcing as a profession would be to read as much information as possible on the subject and to attend as many seminars and conferences as you can in order to gain knowledge from people who have a few war scars. Listen and learn and don't be afraid to ask. I would also strongly advise enrolling for training as this will help you to understand the entire life cycle of a programme and give you a very significant competitive edge. To reach the very top of the career ladder individuals need to have a number of personal traits over and above being entirely focused on the business case. You would need to be flexible regarding working long hours and being away from home for sometimes long periods of time. To reach industry guru status you would also need to be a good negotiator, commercially and technologically savvy, and able to create and build teams. Additionally, the highest achievers need exceptional relationship-building capabilities and to be able to demonstrate leadership qualities, as they will be expected to gain stakeholder buy-in from the board to the engine room. The rewards are good, not only in financial terms but, more importantly for most, in the sense of achievement in getting something (which often seemed impossible) achieved.

Conclusion – Golden Rules of Recruitment

There are a few golden rules that are not industry or sector specific that are useful to remember to ensure a successful recruitment campaign:

1. Engage all decision makers at all stages to obtain their buy-in. Without this vital component, there is a significant danger that a key decision maker may, at an advanced stage in the process, declare a completely different set of objectives and this will obviously retard and sometimes lead to the abortion of the entire programme.

2. Decide on your methodology – explore your options to use an external recruitment service provider or handle this internally. Investigate the appropriate technique for the hire – database search, advertised selection, executive search (head-hunt) if you are seeking a full-time employee – or whether an interim or contract manager is more appropriate if you are resourcing for a short-term project or transition programme.

3. Preparation – know whom you want and what you want this person to do. Agree a job brief and person specification, based on your current requirements. If the post is replacing someone, take this opportunity to analyse and refresh the requirements – do not be tempted to replace like with like without a thorough review. Often firms present a five-year-old job description when someone leaves and they require a replacement, not taking into account how the position and person has moved on.

4. Agree and plan the recruitment process – decide how you will run the recruitment campaign, remembering that this is a window display of your company,

an opportunity to communicate who you are and what you do to a wide audience. Project-plan the process with a timetable, making sure you know who is accountable for collating feedback, communicating good and bad news to candidates and making the decisions.

5. Create a positive experience – ensure that all concerned enjoy the process; they will communicate the negative experiences as well as the positive.

6. Onboarding – create a welcoming experience for new hires. Consider a 'buddy' system to blend them quickly into your culture.

7. Talent management and mapping – recruiting is expensive and time consuming; losing good people can also have a negative impact on remaining staff, so make sure you do everything possible to retain your talent and know where it is. Regular mapping of internal and external talent and helping individuals to plan their career path within your organization will help to reduce attrition and make you an employer of choice.

8. Salary and benefit reviews – ensure that you are paying a fair remuneration for the job. Analyse your competition and stay ahead with financial incentives and bonus schemes.

9. Offer training incentives – this not only creates a highly qualified workforce, but allows your employees to benefit from continuous professional development, contributing to your ability to attract and retain top talent.

10. Exit procedures – learn from experience; give leavers an opportunity to tell you why they are going. This will give you invaluable information to inform your future recruitment process. Remember that we live in progressive times and that some attrition is natural and essential to create new opportunities for growth and development.

Chapter 5

Experiencing Cultures: An Automotive Engineer in the Middle Kingdom – Lessons in Life

Ian Pogson

Introduction

My employer for nearly a quarter of a century, MG Rover, had been divested by BMW in 2000 and had made it a strategic imperative since then to find a suitable partner. It had become obvious to all employees who could face it that the company would fold if we were unsuccessful in this. By the end of 2004, after several disappointments and false dawns, success was looking extremely unlikely. The only option left before the money ran out was a link with Shanghai Automotive Industries Corporation (SAIC) of China.

Having heard a presentation from one of my team who had been working on localizing to Shanghai for three months, I volunteered to work in the country and play my part in a last-ditch attempt to save Rover. Our task was to localize or outsource the engines to Shanghai and re-import them for fitment to our cars as well as to provide SAIC with an engine family themselves.

I moved out to Shanghai for a three-month period, leaving family and friends behind. I am essentially a home-bird and not a city-dweller, living as we do in a leafy Worcestershire village. Shanghai, with a population of twice that of London (depending upon where one draws boundaries), was therefore something of a shock. The city and the people, however, welcomed us *lao weis* (foreigners) with open arms – and a lot of noise. Fireworks and city traffic assaulted my ears, but somehow I settled in and regarded Shanghai as my city, guiding fellow ex-pats around the sights whenever they started 'a tour of duty'. It is a wonderful place and the people of China are most hospitable. I no longer live there, but return as and when my employer requires my help. My normal workplace is now (strangely) back

The Human Side of Outsourcing: Psychological Theory and Management Practice
Edited by Stephanie J. Morgan
Copyright © 2009 John Wiley & Sons Ltd.

at Longbridge, where the SAIC Technical Centre is located, and we are making cars – MGTFs – again.

What I knew about China before going there I reckoned could be recorded on a postage stamp. Now I might need two. I may have written widely about it, spoken at a dozen or more lectures and after-dinner events, but I still have only scratched the surface of the culture and the deep, continuous history. I believe that unless one is born there, a partial understanding is the best that can be achieved. Others may have a deeper understanding, but few have committed their knowledge to paper. I have done my best to do so in this chapter.

Outline

In the following, I hope to assist any company or individuals who are about to start or are even in the middle of an outsourcing operation. The assistance will be from real, in-market experience from one who lived in Shanghai for some time. What is presented, however, is only a skim across the surface of Chinese society, as it is so deep and ancient a culture that most Westerners can only guess what is really going on most of the time.

The acronym ISP will be used throughout. This is a Chinese term meaning 'International Support Person' and is used to describe any non-Chinese national who works in China or for a Chinese company. This account does not cover all the issues as I am only aware of the few I have encountered personally, but I hope that those presented are useful to the reader.

Outsourcing into China

A famous Western businessman is reputed to have said that 'one could paper the Great Wall with all the broken Chinese contracts'. This may be harsh or even untrue, but from personal experience of working in the Orient I can understand the feeling. For instance, we discovered that if a deal had been struck by one purchasing agent and they left or moved on, a new deal or price could be struck by the replacement!

However it is fuelled, this economy is running away on an upward curve. This does lead to some behavioural issues which need to be taken into account on an outsourcing project. With many of the people I have to work alongside, the young 20- to 30-something middle-managers in particular have known only China's success as it ascends to the world stage. They have seen only growth in their careers. Take a company like Shanghai General Motors. It has grown its sales by 25 per cent year on year until mid-2008, to become the highest-volume and richest car manufacturer in China. This breeds confident, even arrogant people who have never seen redundancies, downsizing, re-engineering or whatever we call ways of cutting heads. I am not sure they would know how to handle bad times. Their parents might, as they saw plenty.

Technical Problems and Quality Tools

Problems will occur and it is useful to have some techniques with which one is familiar. Avoid presenting these techniques as Japanese in origin, though many of theirs came from the US. Training may need to be given to ask questions in an open fashion and in an unthreatening arena. Interference from the boss may well present itself as a ready-made solution, but that is their prerogative. You then have to manage the situation.

Beware of the temptation to blame a supplier and bend all the evidence towards that end; this happens in the UK too, but I have noticed a strong tendency to do that in China. This may be particularly true if the supplier is not a China-own-brand.

There is a distinct pecking order of suppliers:

• those Chinese-owned and based home-grown companies;
• a joint venture with a big name from the West;
• a joint venture with Japan;
• an imported part.

With problem solving, there is a great difference in learning styles. Part of my job is teaching others quality techniques. When it comes to teaching the Chinese, I have to adapt my teaching style. It is becoming fashionable in China to teach using Western techniques, where it is acceptable to question the teacher (this is not common in China, where learning is often by rote). I could simply tell the students what they needed to know – there would be no questions and no interaction. Some of them described me as a 'good tutor', but they could be just being normally polite Chinese students. Discipline in Chinese schools is exemplary. As with much of our Western society, we have gone too far with the 'rights of the student', with no regard for those trying to keep order and teach. Ask any ex-pat teacher where they would rather teach and you would hear China, because the students want to learn and if they don't the parents will be round to the school finding out why.

Support for Those in Territory – the Role of Personnel

Personnel have a key role to play in supporting what the Chinese call ISPs (International Support Persons). These ISPs are generally experts in a field and are therefore able to command a fairly substantial salary. Their services may well be in short supply and as such could be quite mobile, so the company may well wish to retain them. I was that ISP.

When out in territory, the ISP should be there to use their specialist knowledge to perform the function that they are paid for. Sorting out 'domestic issues' such as living accommodation should be the domain of the local HR function, in order to make their stay as comfortable as possible and keep them out there working, adding value. Worrying about tax affairs, health insurance, transport options and the like should be taken care of for them. In properly set up companies with ISPs, there can be a ratio of one HR person to 20 ISPs.

The support to these ISPs needs to be aware of their needs and culture, preferably having spent some time working in the ISP's country to understand. Sadly, many HR functions are staffed with young girls who have never been anywhere nor have children of their own and cannot understand the needs of the mainly married, older men who do work abroad.

Ideally, the Personnel function should have someone experienced in life; strong, but tough and willing to stand up for the rights of the ISPs, based on a clear set of rules and with a well-written ISP handbook available for all. Before venturing outside the UK or home country, any ISP should clearly understand what will or could happen in territory, the health and safety issues and how to protect themselves. Your Personnel staff should give you this level of support.

Here are a few suggestions based on my own experience of issues likely to be faced by ISPs:

ISP/Personnel checklist
i. *Health*
    a. What injections are required or advisable before leaving the home country?
    b. What medical support is available in territory?
    c. Where does one go for this?
    d. Who pays and how?
    e. What happens in the case of an emergency?
    f. Will the hospital be open on public holidays?
    g. What is in place for optical and dental care?
    h. What free health checks can be given?
    i. What happens in the case of STD (sexually transmitted disease)? (The ex-pat lifestyle makes this almost guaranteed to happen, but it is an uncomfortable question.)
    j. What happens to control excessive alcohol intake? The average Brit abroad is infamous for a lack of control.
ii. *Safety*
    a. What personal protective equipment (PPE) is available in territory?
    b. What is necessary?
    c. How will ISPs travel in territory and is this safe?
    d. If not (see Shanghai taxis or Delhi tuk-tuks), what advice should be given?
    e. How safe are the streets? (Not an issue in China)
    f. What insurance is available?
    g. If testing equipment or products are required in territory, what training or back-up do they need?
iii. *Tax and salary*
    a. ISPs should be no better nor worse off in terms of their tax liability for working abroad.

   b.   Is the salary commensurate with their worth and local costs?
   c.   If they retain a house in the home country, how can they be helped to let it, maintain it or keep it secure?
   d.   What local taxes are payable?
   e.   What reciprocal arrangement with the home tax office is in place?
iv.   *Travel in territory*
   a.   What local bus, train or metro services operate?
   b.   Is there a charge-card to use local transport?
   c.   If the company operates a collection service to pick up local workers, can the ISPs use this? Will they want to?
   d.   What driving licence conditions operate?
   e.   What insurance cover will they have if testing?
v.   *Arrival and housing*
   a.   Before sending anyone out, ensure that from the moment they land, they know where to go at the airport, e.g. taxis to take/avoid, onward rail or bus connections.
   b.   Where will they be staying? Supply them with a large-font address card in English and the local language. Maps are useful, but we found that this just confuses many Chinese drivers!
   c.   Ensure that the hotel is expecting them and processes are in place to have the bill paid by the company.
   d.   For long-term ISPs, have a trusted local person find adequate housing once the worker has had chance to gain a feel for the locality.
   e.   Not everyone will want to sit on a company bus for over an hour to reach the work location every day as we did; do the homework on housing.
   f.   At the end of the assignment, ensure that the process of repatriation is thought through and that there is support for a worker who is now back in an 'alien' culture.
   g.   Also ensure that arrangements for the return of any of their possessions are agreed up front, i.e. before they go out into territory in the first place.
   h.   At a time when a certain global auto manufacturer is cutting its losses (but not executive perks) and ex-pats (some with families) are being left high and dry in territory, there is no shirking individual responsibility. Look after yourself. Always plan for success, but be prepared for disaster.

There are many more issues which need to be covered. Look after your people and make use of their talents.

Cultural Differences – General

'*Vive la différence*', said a wise French person. Thankfully, the West and the East are different. Here are some differences:

- In China, it is every right-minded, up-market Chinese female's aim to prevent her skin from becoming even slightly tarnished by sunlight. Her brolly or parasol will be up at the merest hint of solar warming. This is because a suntan is seen as something that lower-class peasants have through working in the fields.
- In the West, we view a suntan as an outward sign of health, wealth or a visit to a sunnier clime if one is a UK resident. (Although even this only applies since air-travel has been available to the 'masses'. So, as I will hope to show, despite the differences, many views or issues in China are now much as they were, say, 50 years ago in the UK.)
- For a Western product to be copied by a Chinese company is seen in the West as a challenge to copyright law, something almost shameful.
- The Chinese, with an apparent disregard for Western copyright law, see it as an achievement to copy a Patek Philippe watch, or a BMW 4×4. They say 'Look at us; we can achieve similar quality levels'. The fact that the watch or car may only work reliably for a tenth of the time of the original is no shame or problem. It cost less and sold for a fraction of the price – an achievement.
- At the introduction of a new product, it is a case of falling on swords in Japan if there are more than a handful of launch problems.
- In China, launch issues seem to be a complete surprise, but a leader will soon come along and suggest that the problems will be closed soon. And they are. Not solved, just closed.
- In the West, there will be much soul-searching over the problems and in some companies even an element of reaching for the swords that have been unused by the Japanese. A truly brave attempt will be made to solve as many as possible, but even premier European manufacturers will sometimes use customers as product testers.
- When dining, in order to impress Westerners, suppliers, the boss or even subordinates, Chinese colleagues will often select the most bizarre and rare items on the menu. This will often taste like chicken, but be many times the cost (e.g. snake). The Westerner in particular will probably rather have the chicken and use the money to buy more beer, thinking that the host is just showing off and has not really considered Western taste-buds at all, nor our liking for too much beer.
- The lone drinker in a Western bar is viewed at best as a person just wanting a peaceful drink alone to consider the meaning of life. The Chinese view this person as having no friends, but definitely having a drink problem.

These real examples show how we regularly do not understand each other's viewpoints and values. We are different, East to West, and thankfully so. Otherwise we would all be Americans, or some other mélange of cultures.

When managing Chinese workers, reporting to a Chinese superior or just working alongside them, there are many 'rules' which could be written. Then the month or year changes and these are no longer true, such is the pace of change in this great country. All one can be sure of as a '*lao wei*', or foreigner, is that unless one is born in China, one will never fully understand.

A famous man once said that the only thing that the Chinese outsource is Western rock music. Extensive multi-city research by myself and friends has revealed this to be true. This, then, is a business and employment opportunity which has been skilfully exploited by Philippinos. Their innate sense of rhythm and ability to speak Mandarin and English better than most Brits mean that they command the stages of various venues, aping the great purveyors of rock music.

Staring, personal space and privacy

Remember, China is a massive country of 1.4 billion people and as such there is much competition for food, jobs, money, space etc. Every simple task that involves queuing, such as waiting for buses or trains or even looking at exhibits in a gallery, can involve a shoving match which resembles a rugby scrum. Leave a tiny gap between you and the bus or Ming vase and there will be someone taking advantage of your apparent weakness.

The same thing will happen in business – leave a gap and a competitor will move in or a colleague will pop up with some surprise move or action.

Foreigners who are fair or dark of skin will be stared at in public. This is because in some of the less popular Chinese cities with no Terracotta Army or Great Wall to bring in tourists, very few non-Chinese are seen, so a black or white face is a rarity.

Personal space is not appreciated by our hosts. Be prepared to be leaned on or over and have one's belongings picked over, one's shopping basket contents stared at and a book read closely over your shoulder by others. Please do not be offended, they are just being friendly. The time to worry is when one is ignored.

Entertainment

A traditional Beijing Opera may be music to some, my favourite rock music may be noise to others. If you are offered entertainment, try to understand what is on offer, though sometimes it is impossible to refuse without causing offence.

Any acrobatics are amazing, traditional fireworks are like being in a war-zone; after all, they invented them as well as the paper wrappers.

KTV or Karaoke TV remains a favoured pastime of many Chinese and KTV bars can be found in any city, some of which are quite simply huge and packed nightly. A likeable trait of my Oriental friends is their ability to perform with a microphone in their hand, despite not having any talent whatsoever. We British are mostly too reserved unless fuelled by alcohol. If invited, do go as you will probably be familiar with many of the sugary tunes and ballads from the West so popular in China. Therefore you could be a star, as you have an advantage.

I was in Chengdu, Sichuan province, home of the giant pandas and hot food, tramping the streets one night in search of a drink to pass an evening. The four-star hotel had no bar, although it did have an 'Entertainment Centre', a euphemism for a brothel. According to our local colleagues, such is the case in most Chinese hotels. (It is funny how the Rolling Stones were not allowed to sing 'Let's spend the night together' at their Shanghai concert yet brothels are a common facility in Chinese hotels. You could even pull the lyrics to that great song off the internet, but there were security guards ready to pull the plug, if Mick and his mates started one of their most famous songs!) Just be careful, ensure you know where you are going or being taken.

Back in Chengdu, our search for a drink found us down some steps into a musty-smelling, dimly lit room with a few small glass tables, each with ten 'Pins' or bottles of beer on them and two shot glasses. There were 'Happy Christmas' banners and swinging pictures of a beaming Father Christmas hanging around, yet painted onto every table-top and illuminated from below was the legend 'Merry Chrismace' [sic]. (It was April.) There were three of us within – the barman, my boss and me. After a time, the chap's favourite tune came on the computer-generated song-list and he sprang onto a stool, looked full at the screen and gave us a stunning rendition of one of the Commodores' classics. We declined to join in, as the choice of songs included 'Edelweiss', complete with video of the von Trapp family doing their best in the face of a stern Christopher Plummer. Had we been at a works do, we might well have been obliged to pick up the mic. Having a go at KTV is quite important to social bonding in China. Find time to practise before you fly out.

Another social bonding is the humble weed – smoking cigarettes. It is undeniable that my reluctance to burn money has excluded me from otherwise beneficial conversations and befriending opportunities with fellow-smokers. My Chinese boss could be talked to quite openly in the smoking room, whereas in the office proper he was almost cold, as if sticking a glowing stick in his mouth defrosted his cool, impervious nature. Western colleagues who have less regard for their health than I and do smoke confirmed that I was losing out. The risk and choice are yours.

Once we were asked by HR what we would like to do for a team-building event. We replied with the normal 'blokey' sorts of things, such as karting, bowling, drinking, eating or football. Our Chinese Personnel department asked the locals and in no particular order it was sleeping, computer games, shopping or chess. Unaffected by the requests of the teams, HR decided on a badminton match! This was fine; however, it is something of a national pastime for the Chinese and we struggled against formidable opponents.

Eating out

More usual is a Chinese banquet. The country apparently spends more on entertainment at these events than it does per capita on healthcare and the restaurants have to be seen to be believed. As with the KTV establishments, they are often massive, hotel-sized monoliths. A whole book could be written about this subject, with useful coloured pictures of what one might be expected to find on a Chinese table. Space permits only a brief look at this essential but deeply etiquette-ridden activity.

Now we British, or at least those with style, may regard ourselves as knowing stuff about table manners: keeping the elbows tucked in, sitting up straight, not talking with our mouths full. All this superiority goes right out of the restaurant window in the East. New rules on who sits where, how to hold chopsticks, drinking 'games' and knowing when to say '*War hung-bao-le*' ('I am very full', depending upon intonation), when the meal ends, who pays, and a host of other issues surface. No part of a chicken, for example, is wasted and I still struggle to find any nutritional benefit or eating pleasure from consuming their crunchy feet. A duck may well be presented to table with its head lolling on the plate or floating in the broth. You have been warned, as it is hard not to imagine the hapless bird eyeing you up in a moist, accusatory manner. It is worth bearing in mind that any foray into a different culture means that food can be very different from 'meat and two veg'.

Absolutely everywhere in my China travels, I have found my hosts to be unfailingly generous in their feeding of me. They almost kill you with kindness and will often attempt to impress with the most expensive, outrageous dish such as shark's fin (I would refuse that) or snake, whereas I would rather have chicken or a noodle soup. I find English food quite boring in a way after some of the things I have eaten, but it is always good to come home.

It is perfectly acceptable to ask what is on the table, but do not expect an accurate description; this is China after all. The host may not know or be familiar with the English translation. Do not expect it to look like the numbers 32 and 42 you order from Ching Wah down your local high street. What we see in the West is a sweetened-up, sanitized version of the real thing and Chinese guest visitors to our Engineering Centre in the UK cite the lack of 'Proper Food' as the worst aspect of their stay with us. We often employ a proper Chinese chef to pander to their needs. The Brits, however, seem more willing to eat local when in territory than the Chinese who here suffer meat and two veg, although some do express a liking for fish and chips.

If you are at a banquet with a rotating central plate (what a practical idea for socializing, as are chopsticks to increase your reach!) then wait until the food arrives and the host picks up his or her sticks. It is fine at this point to ask for help in holding sticks, the host will appreciate you having a go. There is, however, no lasting shame in asking for more familiar instruments. They will want to laugh at your misfortune; broken-leg humour is as alive in Chengdu, Sichuan Province, as it is in Chipping, Lancashire.

Once over the fight with the sticks, drinking at table is another minefield of behavioural rights and wrongs. It is a metabolic fact that the average Western constitution can process more and stronger alcohol than the average Oriental, but do not judge a book by its cover – I have seen size 6 Chinese girls who would blow away in a Blackpool promenade wind down jugs of German beer from Tsingdao. They seemed fine to me for a couple of hours at least.

Wait until everyone's glass is charged and some food is on the table, when the host will usually tap his (I've never seen a lady do this) glass on the rotating plate. Follow suit and watch over the rim of your glass to see how much is imbibed by the Chinese. Later on, the host or other 'significant individuals' will look to you and invite you to drink one-on-one. Beware this occurring just after your glass has been filled to the brim and theirs is barely wet. This may well be accompanied by the word '*Ganbei!*' This is loosely translated as 'bottoms up' and is an excellent ploy for ensuring that the Westerner is drunk while all remain sober on the Oriental side. We allowed this to happen once only, having learned from our mistake. We then set out to nail the main protagonist of this tactic. He lost.

   Another ploy is 'watch the Westerner smart', much as we would do in taking a newcomer to the delights of Birmingham cuisine by suggesting a balti curry. Sichuan cuisine is famous across China for being chilli-ridden, hot, spicy food. As with sport or hot food, a little conditioning is vital. Start gently and with small quantities and then work up. Once the lips are numb, it is hard to lose any more feeling anyway. We were lucky to be entertained once while in Sichuan by caring, genteel hosts, who divided up the 'hot-pot' (a heated dish sunk into the table centre) into two halves, one for the Western softies and one for real men and women. An occasional dip into the fiery side allowed a slow, but occasionally painful, conditioning of our taste-buds. It would have been churlish to have refused, as the Chinese engineers almost fight to be allowed to go on a business trip to that province.

   On our last night in ChongQing, we had finished the meal (or so we thought) and proclaimed our satisfaction and full bellies, when a 'special dish' was brought in. Significantly, only my manager and I (token foreigners in the 400-seater restaurant) had a dish set down in front of us. All eyes were upon us. Tension and expectation quivered like a jockey's whip at the side of his horse. They nudged each other and grinned. Ever the cool quality engineers, and men of some cultural sensitivity, but also wanting to fuel the atmosphere, we looked at the innocuous small dishes with white noodles, finely chopped green leaves and a chilli-red ring of liquid. We looked at each other and declared that there would be a short intermission while we rested after such a magnificent meal (which we thought was over). Following a suitably dramatic wait, with many knowing glances between waiting-on staff and hosts, we wound the noodles around our sticks, lowered our heads to the food (in approved Chinese style) and slurped away (also in approved style). We raised our heads to an expectant circle of waiting locals, anticipative of a failure to consume without coughing. We declared it to be fine food and downed some more. We were heroes; there were big grins around the table. We were, after all, with a bunch of foundry-men who relish temperature and spice daily. We passed the test thanks to preparation and conditioning.

   It is good manners to appreciate the food put in front of you as a guest. At one factory, the head honcho turned to me (as we have known each other for some time) and asked for my preference, a certain fast fried chicken or Chinese food. He grinned as I selected the latter; this would be better for our health and for the comfort of the other locals around the table. My manager and I would be fine with Chinese fare. It was delivered in an instant (so it was fast) and was suitably simple and tasty. No finger-lickin' was necessary, which was useful as the laptop does not work well with cooking oil on the keys.

   Gifts often come up as an issue – what is right or wrong. This is far too complex for me to understand. It is an accepted form of Chinese business practice to proffer brown envelopes and as a Western businessperson you either accept this or do no business. I have little experience in this – try to talk to someone from a purchasing background if you are concerned about negotiation tactics.

At a lower level, gifts of fruit are always welcome; Chinese streets are full of stalls selling most attractively presented boxed or wrapped oranges in particular. Flowers are as acceptable as they are in the UK but, as in the UK, I am sure there are a whole host of right flowers and wrong blooms to give. Books, chocolate and DVDs go down well.

Prejudices, ABCs and bananas

The UK and indeed every other country is full of stereotypes and prejudices. The Middle Kingdom is no exception. ABC stands for American-born Chinese. These are not seen as real sons and daughters of the Motherland, as are any others born outside its colossal boundaries. Bananas are those who are 'yellow of skin' on the outside, but white on the 'inside'. Be prepared if you are, or work with, one of these characters. Prejudice can be ugly in any language. It can be quite hard for a person whose features are Oriental to be taken seriously by true locals if they do not have the linguistic skills to match their looks.

Amusingly, we had one senior Chinese colleague who fervently believed that any child born outside of the national boundary could naturally speak Mandarin. The same deluded individual also held that Tom Cruise et al. could speak his language as he had seen them do so on TV. An example of the evidence and logic being there for all to see to the contrary, but he believed otherwise.

Questions and tense

It is rare to see a Chinese person irritated by a Westerner asking questions, especially about Chinese culture and customs. There may be areas which it may be wise to circumnavigate, such as Tibet, but ask and one will soon find out if the responder is comfortable or not.

Normal questions are a little more fraught, even the simplest ones. Asking 'Have you done x, y or z?' can elicit the answer you want, which may often be 'Yes'. This can mean 'I don't know'; the responder just wants to sound positive, or does not know. I have a UK colleague who famously says 'No' while nodding, to illustrate the attitude of his Oriental counterparts.

One can ask a simple question, to which one would expect a UK respondent to answer with 'No', such as 'We didn't win the World Cup, did we?' The answer is logically and clearly 'Yes'. This will therefore be a Chinese response and is quite correct. What is expected though is 'No', qualified by some pathetic excuse about 'poor refereeing'. See the problems? If one translates this into a complex technical situation, it is easy to see how confusion on both sides can be perplexing. Always seek clarification and ask the question in another way.

Mandarin does not have tenses the way we have in European languages. They use modifiers to imply that the action is behind or ahead. It is best to ask a question about things having been completed in the past by starting the question with a time reference such as yesterday or last week. That or learn Mandarin. Even learning some Mandarin will earn respect. It is *the* question that Westerners are asked and the answer is normally a qualified 'No'. You can see the interest wane at that point. Even a few words in the local dialect will put a smile on faces, usually because it has been intoned wrongly!

Try not to become irritated if you do not receive the expected or required response. Patience is useful, essential, admired. I have watched go-getting action men who are revered in the UK or the US but who completely turn off Chinese colleagues owing to impatience. Those Westerners who are sensitive to Oriental ways are a pleasure to watch. They allow time for business to unfold and ideas to be formed, opinions heard.

I recall one massive problem with a product on which I worked. We had supplied test-bed information to China some 12 months before a rash of product failures, but still the advice was ignored. One day, the problems stopped coming, the product passed tests and all was well in the garden. None of the locals could be persuaded to tell us what had happened, but we knew. The system was as it should always have been. Patience is a virtue.

In China, possibilities are endless and even when a project looks quite bleak, something changes and the bacon is saved. I heard of one massive pipeline project which was lumbering towards total failure in the time-frame of the contract, with Western managers unable to see a way forward. At the last moment, labour and soldiers from the People's Liberation Army arrived and the line was completed on time. Shouting and humiliation by the Western civil engineers and project managers had been met with disdain.

China is a surprise around every corner. A visit to the Three Gorges Dam project at San Dou Ping would confirm that. Less well known than this massive creation of steel and the most concrete I have ever seen is the Gezhou Dam, also on the Yangtze. This was completed on time by Chinese engineers and labour, completely unaided by the West. It too generates hydro-electric power. China is a real leader in this clean method of power generation, as she needs so much electricity to light up her cities and she has some huge rivers waiting to be tapped.

Currently the longest metro rail system in the world is being laid out in Shanghai. There are already eight lines in place criss-crossing the city and this is the same place that boasts the longest magnetically levitated railway in the world. The journey on this wonder of Sino-German cooperation takes 7 minutes 20 seconds and connects the new airport at Pudong with LongYang Lu, which is useful if one wants to go there, but not if you are expecting a fast connection to the city centre. Even at 431 kph, a taxi is still required at the terminus to go anywhere significant. Plans are afoot, however, to extend the line.

The more one sees of China, the more it seems like Texas, where everything is bigger and better. The Hoover Dam is impressive, but having seen both it and the Three Gorges, I take my hat off to the Orient. I met a sales manager at a top-quality

Chinese supplier in ChongQing, who was travelling to the US shortly after I met him. I told him that if he was asked 'So where are you from, buddy?' by an affable Detroit host and he replied 'ChongQing', this would most likely be followed by the Michigan resident saying 'Never heard of it, boy'. I advised him then to say that it is probably three times bigger than Motor City, USA. I hope he had some sport with that one. Depending on how one draws the boundary and talks of cities or districts, ChongQing on the Yangtze is home to 36 million souls. Having driven through part of it and walked the streets, it is simply huge and overwhelming. How does one even start to imagine how to feed everyone a simple daily rice dish? Somehow it happens.

Nothing worthwhile is easy, from feeding 36 million people to launching a new product; frustration will set in and patience on top of patience is required. Some people are suited to Chinese life and ways, generally the older or calmer individuals. Do not expect normal business rules or logic to be applicable in territory. 'You do not understand China or Chinese ways' may be something thrown at you. It means that they disagree with you, but again we often know better than they appreciate. I repeat again that unless one is born in China, it will always be a mystery.

The Chinese are, with reason, very mistrustful of foreigners. The Olympic torch made it safely onto the Chinese mainland, but its passage around the planet had been marked by some fearful demonstrations. The Games seemed to strengthen Chinese relationships with the West, but they will probably still be very wary of Japan. Nothing short of hatred can describe the attitude towards the Land of the Rising Sun from some Chinese I have talked to. Surprisingly, if one ventures below the People's Heroes Monument at the north end of the riverside Bund in Shanghai, sepia photographs will show a shameful Navy bombardment of the river city by British gun-boats, yet today we are seemingly welcome.

I can understand the Germans being welcome as they brought beer-brewing techniques to Tsingdao on the coast and some interesting Bauhaus architecture to the beer-brewing city and to Anting New Town, again in Shanghai. China has an inexhaustible ability to absorb what it wants of other cultures, but I for one hope that the nation hangs on to its Chinese-ness; it is so appealing. A clown's fast-food restaurant on every Oriental main street would be a tragic loss of local colour and noodles.

Cultural Differences and 'Agreements' – Business

The boss, or leader. Her/his word is law

Now, being an automotive engineer, I have worked for and alongside some fairly good actors, whose meeting theatrics had to be seen to be believed, but in the Orient, the boss's word is law. If she or he decides that tomorrow is Friday, then despite your Western diary and Gregorian calendar showing that Thursday is tomorrow and you know that you haven't quite finished with Wednesday, then Friday it is. As Westerners, we do struggle with having seemingly incontrovertible evidence demonstrating a fact, but then the boss or government speaks and all Chinese are silent. I have witnessed this so many times. For example, despite it being obvious that repeatedly dabbing the throttle is (a) uncomfortable for passengers and (b) fuel-sapping, the average Chinese driver will do this. You thought it was hard to criticize an Englishman's driving. Try it in another language and across a cultural abyss, for such it is behind the wheel.

A colleague of mine, one of the best drivers around a circuit that I know, tried for two solid years to drum into his team how to drive safely and with due regard for tyres, passengers, fuel economy and general wear and tear. He might as well have taught them flower-arranging. They will still venture 'off-road' when an opportunity presents itself and knock a transmission into neutral, coasting out of control downhill.

Witnessing subordinates at a meeting with a very senior local director is fascinating. If the meeting starts on time, with all present who should be, dissent is not welcome in the room. Once he or she has decided on an action, then that is it. As a lone Western voice, not understanding the language, it is extremely difficult, even with a translator. You could well be assured that meetings would be open to all and help will be given but, in reality, this may be just platitudes, as I have experienced.

By way of example, I recall one technical issue with a sensor. This was a standard fit on UK cars, but for some reason, somehow, the Chinese acquired a bill of material which had been 'doctored' by those engineering experts in Finance as a cost-down exercise. As this was cheaper than the production version (due to being short of some costly key components), they gleefully took it as the official list of components required to build a car. We then spent three years fighting to have the parts put back, so that the car would work in an acceptable manner. Up to the point of having a major customer problem, there had been no give over this sensor. Once discovered by the general public, something had to be done to avoid warranty costs and we finally saw sense prevail.

Business practices and common difficulties

Some China experts would advise on dress codes and traits like punctuality at meetings. These issues are changing all the time. In my employer's Engineering Centre, dress is quite relaxed, especially in summer. In winter, despite a comfortable working temperature inside, Brits will be wearing shirts and our local colleagues may still be sporting long-johns, the wearing of which often spreads way beyond spring. It is not unusual to be working with people who never take their coats off, nor the three layers beneath. Spring Festival in February and October's Golden Week signify an almost official change to the way people dress. The men sport leather jackets and dark coats as soon as they return from the latter holiday. The country, being so vast and featuring so many mountains, does have some wide temperature and humidity variations. Hainan Island, for instance, is almost sub-tropical in the south, yet ice-sculptures in northern Harbin city are famous throughout the land. Be prepared for all eventualities.

Punctuality is not something I have observed amongst my Chinese colleagues, unless there is someone fairly senior chairing. Even if punctuality is observed, the meeting at any level will be punctuated by ridiculous mobile ring-tones.

During one year of living in Shanghai, I only ever knew one meeting happen regularly requiring my attendance anyway.

Mobile phones are a feature of our society, but if one wants an uninterrupted meeting, rules will have to be agreed at the outset. Be prepared for this to be an unpopular move. I know of one colleague who did succeed in establishing a meeting start time and 'radio silence'. He had less success with the recording of minutes and actions being apportioned.

Even in fairly well-developed Chinese companies, a reluctance to jump up to the whiteboard and record matters is noticeable. Even if the facility is there (which it often is not), it will most likely be the Westerner with pen in hand. This is useful to present data and try to gain accord. As in any other part of the world, information is power, so sharing data with one's colleagues may not be seen as a good move.

Women in business

Not being of the fair sex I do not pretend to know much about women. A lifetime of in-depth careful research has produced many surprises and some shocks, but I remain optimistic and an eager student. My observation of women in business in China is far more positive than in the UK, and there are more of them. Also, if there is a male/female pair representing a supplier, it is the woman who is often smarter and can speak better English. Mao Tse-Tung declared in his Red Book that 'women hold up half the world'. Now that may have been a ploy to get them on his side and agree to do some fairly awful, hard labour in field and factory, but it is true. In my short 50-year lifetime the chain-manufacturing sweatshops in Birmingham's Black Country were staffed by a large number of women, so we again are little different from China, just doing similar things at different times. Many women occupy senior positions in Chinese companies, which is as it should be.

Owing to female infanticide and the one-child policy, there are vastly fewer Chinese women than men, therefore they have to try harder to be smarter, and regularly succeed. From astute bar-girls on low wages to smartly turned-out businesswomen, they are a force to be reckoned with. There is a much higher ratio of female engineers to male than in the UK, which is no bad thing as 50 per cent of car-driving customers are women.

Working patterns and dates

You may think that the world revolves around its axis to a Gregorian calendar, but in China the Moon is the origin. The lunar calendar dictates seasons and holidays and then the government has the last say. In 2008 there was a plan to change the traditional holidays, easing the load on the country's overburdened transport infrastructure by changing holiday dates. The uncertainty over when was holiday and when was not lasted until the week before the actual dates. This must be borne in mind when trying to do business; it is somewhat fundamental. My director came over to China from the UK for a particular meeting at the request of our Eastern masters and was unaware of the changes. He felt quite silly.

Your Western diary might have 'Chinese holiday' printed on the page, but do check with the locals. One Spring Festival Eve, the office finishing time was set not by the company, but by the army of coach-drivers who ferry the merry throngs to and from various pick-up points in the city to and from work.

Terminal Disease and Preventive Medicine

Terminal disease – comparing Heathrow and Pudong airports

T5 at Heathrow was physically built and ready ahead of time, as was Pudong in Shanghai, but there the similarities end. T5 looked good and equipment trials had taken place successfully. Even the baggage handling handled bags as it was designed to do. However, the following were notable failures:

- The baggage handlers could not gain access to the appropriate car parks to start work.
- The first time that most of them had seen the baggage handling equipment was the day the terminal opened to the public.
- Instead of starting with a few flights into the new terminal, a large number of BA planes landed at the rate of one every 30 seconds.

When ex-motor industry colleagues of mine (who had been involved with the successfully opened terminal building) were finally asked to assist with the mounting issues of passenger delay, they met those responsible for 'air-side' operations and were staggered to find no 'hit-list' of prioritized problems and responsible managers, so they had to start at the beginning. What those at the airport seemed to fail to realize was that processing passengers is much like processing the manufacture of a car, with the input being passengers with bags and the output being bags in a hold and passengers in the cabin. Other issues of a very unionized workforce and belligerence on both sides did not help either. We had dispensed with much of those attitudes in the car industry many years before. One only has to visit Jaguar Cars at Castle Bromwich to see this.

Preventive Chinese medicine

What happened in China at the same time as T5 lurched from disaster to disaster and highly paid people hung on to their jobs? Terminal 2 at Pudong airport in

Shanghai was 'tested' live by 5,000 marauding schoolchildren who were given instructions to act out the part of various types of passengers with their own bags, rucksacks and children's ways of seeing and doing things. This was in addition to the testing completed on the handling equipment using 3,000 suitcases. If you believe the figures, three bags were lost or misdirected due mainly to poor labelling. The target was 5 in every 10,000, so it was met. I remember once travelling through Brussels airport and a sign at Baggage Claim proclaimed that the success rate of matching passenger to bag was 87 per cent! This they seemed proud enough of to post the result in public. This meant that 13 in every 100 people were stuck in the same clothes until the shops opened the next day. In Pudong this would not be tolerated.

Pudong T2 opened slowly, with just a few planes at first and then flights being added at a decent pace. T2 is a delight to travel through. Before any BA or BAA employees send letters to the publisher, I know that London Heathrow Airport is one of the busiest in the world; the principle is what I am promoting here. I have been to both airports enough times to see the difference.

Moral of the story – we can learn from the Chinese. We do not have a monopoly of great ideas in the West. The Great Wall may have been fundamentally weak in concept (bribing gate-guardians ensured a safe passage), but it was built and stands. There are only three 50-metre swimming pools in the UK. How many are in China? Who will find more Olympic medals in the water? Many of the Beijing Olympics arenas or venues were already operational before the Opening Ceremony. Conversely, when my wife and I honeymooned in Canada 25 happy years ago in 1983, the Olympic pool in Montreal from the 1976 games was still unfinished.

The Concept of 'Face'

This is well known as a phenomenon in the West. What is not well known is the true meaning. Much research has been conducted on this issue and still the meaning is unclear. Chinese people will use the fact that we recognize its existence as a 'mask' or 'cloak' behind which they will hide. It is generally accepted not to try to embarrass or force a Chinese person to admit a fault in public, but to do this in private. Open disagreements, especially in front of a superior, can be counter-productive. As with many topics in this chapter, this is another issue which is changing rapidly as the East assimilates Western behaviour. As with many Westerners, it is often best to let the local engineer believe it is their idea when trying to push forward an argument or notion. This gives the local credibility and will not be forgotten by them.

Having face means being highly regarded by one's peers. Face can be given as in the example above or just by giving thanks for a job done. Embarrassment takes it away, as this is essentially insulting them or criticizing in public. This action can invite recrimination if directed at a senior, or ruin further business prospects. It is a mistake to treat anybody as a subordinate, even in fun, especially if their perceived status by others is high. Our sense of British 'fun' can be seen as insincerity, not just by Chinese. One only needs to work with Germans to see this.

I once became so irritated by one senior engineer that I effectively 'showed him the red card', as he was being downright disruptive and argumentative with other members of my team. He did not attend any further meetings with me and only returned to the meeting process when I had returned to the UK. To this day, I remain unsure as to whether I did the right thing or not. Many of the other attendees – people at his level or higher – were happy for me to have done this, but subordinates seemed less happy. I believed he had to be dealt with firmly as he was distracting us from our logical course of action. He was, however, a direct 'plant' by a president on my team. The latter still seems to side with his (cactus) plant's opinions, despite incontrovertible evidence to the contrary.

Evidence, face and being right

This brings in another interesting concept – evidence and believing oneself to be correct. With many British and certainly German people, having good evidence of one's position being correct is often best presented to Chinese people on the quiet, one-to-one. I have seen it dished out quite harshly from very senior people to (in particular) lowly suppliers' representatives in China, but this is not easy for Westerners to pull off, unless they are older, vastly experienced and/or Welsh. An accent from west of the Marches seems to convey something authoritative.

While on the subject, tattoos, being left-handed and having little hair also help as these things are seldom seen on Chinese. I have seen them silence a meeting, eliciting open wonderment as a balding, left-handed colleague rolled his sleeves up to reveal an SAS motif on his arm. The meeting held its breath in respect.

Now back to evidence. I have known it collected and presented to an open forum proving beyond doubt, even to a non-technical interpreter, that a fact was incontrovertible. The 'accused' supplier's representative denied any wrongdoing on his company's part. This he maintained in the face of repeated and more desperately annoyed accusations of lying from my UK colleague. In order to prevent the latter from bursting a blood vessel, the colleague's Chinese manager took him aside and told him that the supplier was not lying, 'Just telling stories'. An important distinction if one is J. K. Rowling, but hard to accept when there are hundreds of bad parts due to this problem.

Much of face-saving and giving is down to common sense and courtesy. If you are negotiating a point or contract, be patient. Some experts would argue that it is inadvisable to argue, especially heatedly, with our Chinese colleagues, but passions rise; this is difficult, especially as they seem to do this to each other from time to time. One will hear more raised voices in China than the UK, but it is often just the way they are with each other and no real offence is given or taken.

Be sensitive to face, and take care to build up relationships; these are important, as is shown in the following account.

Example – being an 'old friend' – relationships

On a tour of suppliers in the west of the 'Middle Kingdom', as China is often known by its people, we found many examples of this. 'We' were two UK engineers and four Chinese colleagues. Only one was sufficiently experienced to know what to ask during some fairly technical visits and detailed project management and quality discussions. He had blisters on his fingers where he had been burnt before on other outsourcing projects. I had worked with him through these and liked and trusted him. He was most useful, pulling on his own experience and backing up myself and the other Brit, who between us had 50+ years of engine experience at work and more before that. Of the other local engineers, two were just months out of education and unlike us had no old bikes or cars in their teen years to tinker with. This is not their fault, just a fact.

Many Chinese assume that everything is more expensive in the West as we are paid so much more. What they do not realize is the high cost of living in the ambulance-chasing, litigation-ridden, safety-mad UK. Interestingly, it is easily possible to acquire a roadworthy car in the UK for a fraction of the cost of a mere number-plate in Shanghai, as these are auctioned to keep some control of the car population. At one point in 2007, the highest price for a licence plate was over $7,000. Hence the difference in practical vehicle knowledge and experience.

Back to using a local to push the point you might be trying to make; with all the evidence on your side, it really is a case of working with the willing. We used my old friend on the trip to convince his less experienced colleagues and the suppliers that issues we were raising were not just us being bullying Westerners, but aimed at achieving a quality product for us all and our Chinese employers. He was worth his weight in gold on the trip. The key was the relationship that he and I had cultivated over the years; I had risen to the status of 'an old friend', a phrase which I spoke to him to cement the bond, so it became a fact in the group. Engineering and psychology; this is a heady mix.

Following our trip, we planned to use this character to support us in responding to the manager of the team who had himself realized that he was in way over his head, both technically and managerially. He had made that most difficult step of admitting his weakness, which is a real strength in any culture, especially China, and stunning in the face of foreigners. It would be almost futile to try, as many Westerners do, to tell the locals what to do and that we always know best.

Imagine a bunch of foreigners coming into your company, most of whom are refugees from a failed UK company. Would you think that they had anything to teach you? The failure of the company in question, MG Rover, was down to a lack of money, the inability to link with a big enough business partner and some rank-poor marketing and product planning, i.e. management. It never fails to amaze me that in the UK we are awash with MBAs and management colleges and courses, yet it is so often the core reason for our failures. Leadership is often in poor supply.

Politics

The Party

Many people ask about the 'Party' and its influence on everyday life. This is an excellent question. My observation is that when a Party meeting was called, the office would empty, except for a few key individuals. These would then be (we assumed) the non-members. There appeared to be no relation between being a Party member and achieving promotion, the same as there seemed to be none between showing competence and climbing the ladder. In this latter respect there is a similarity with the West!

The Party has its own offices in many Chinese companies and these may be labelled as the 'Party' or 'Trade Union' room. There is, of course, plenty of encouragement to join 'for the good of all'. The only way to understand it all is to be born in China. It has been heard that some Westerners have been invited to join, which is fine if one does not intend returning to work in the West, where government departments of certain more paranoid states view such membership very dimly. Ask questions, but be careful not to offend.

Discipline – free market v state control

With such a large country and population, one instrument used for control is the fact that China is under one time zone – Beijing. This is fine if your office is just down the road from the Forbidden City or down the coast in Tianjin, but not so if you are in the far east or west of the country. It might be morning light over the Summer Palace, but back in Tibet, the monks are still in darkness. This is really only an issue if you have operations which are stretched out across the width of the 'Cockerel' (the shape of China on a map). Although one time zone seems crazy, it works, but it is another difficult one for your average European or American.

The government's role in China is all-pervading. I have walked around so many new facilities, funded by I know not whom, which are world-class. Factory buildings and apartment blocks are built speculatively all over China. I have seen many. The people will be moved in and the infrastructure is ready for them. Detractors may opine that it is a shame to remove people from their traditional small Chinese homes, but a French film-maker spent many years first befriending Shanghai families and then seeking their permission to record the destruction of their neighbourhood and way of life since the 1920s. Her initial story angle was that this was a shame; a community about to be dispersed and uprooted from quaint two- and three-storey homes near the river. Once she had been taken into the locals' confidence and they realized that she essentially meant no harm, they convinced her that they would laugh and shout with joy when they were finally out of their damp, cramped tenement housing with cold running water and shared toilets, into new buildings with a guard at the gate, hot water on tap and space.

SGMs (the Self-Governing Municipalities of Beijing, ChongQing, Shanghai and Tianjin), like other big and respected companies, especially in the government-controlled and planned economies receive special plaques which adorn their receptions and meeting rooms, to show that they are good corporate citizens and pay taxes to be reinvested into the local economy (or officials' pockets). In one ChongQing company, I counted 27 on the wall! The road to the plant from the new toll-charged motorway was itself a toll-road and it was so bad that I would have expected them to give me money as a roughed-up traveller. There is some way to go on infrastructure out there in the Yangtze basin.

My own employer staged a huge event where all divisions of the massive company were present and made solemn promises to the mayor of the city to be a good corporate citizen.

Summary

Frustration will be the principal emotion of any foray by a Westerner into the Middle Kingdom, but nothing worthwhile is ever truly easy. Keep your eyes open and ensure your own personal safety – no one else will. Be ready for an amazing adventure; so many new experiences every day will delight, amuse or bemuse you. Be prepared for all eventualities and plan ahead. The ability to do so will set you aside and ahead of those around you. The Chinese have a stereotypical view of British people, in that we are polite, straight people. If you are British, try not to disappoint them.

Part II
Theory and Evidence

Chapter 6

Introduction to Theory and Evidence

Stephanie J. Morgan

The 'outsourcing in practice' chapters demonstrate a broad range of issues that can occur with people, owing to poor negotiating or contract skills, cultural differences, anxiety and bad feelings after transfers, uncertain roles or conflicting demands. Together they bring a wealth of experience to the table, and offer some useful practical advice. They can indicate at first hand how difficult the human aspect of outsourcing can be; however, to really explain in depth why these issues arise, we need theory. Good theories, supported by evidence, can enable us to better understand (and sometimes predict) what may occur in outsourcing in future, and take action to improve the people side in the knowledge that we are more likely to succeed. Individual experience is important, but could be specific to their situation. Of course, by bringing together five practitioners who seem to have experienced similar issues, we are increasing our evidence base, but it is still in need of theory and further evidence to aid explanation.

In this chapter I will outline research on work processes that have some similarities to outsourcing, such as downsizing and mergers, and then highlight the range of theories applicable to the human aspects of outsourcing situations. Finally I will introduce the remaining chapters.

Downsizing and Mergers

The human relations aspects of outsourcing may be informed by research on related organizational change processes such as downsizing and mergers and acquisitions. Indeed, many outsourcing transfers do include an element of downsizing. Much of

The Human Side of Outsourcing: Psychological Theory and Management Practice
Edited by Stephanie J. Morgan

the literature suggests there may be a lasting change in organizational relationships after downsizing, including organizational commitment (Allen, Freeman, Russel, Reizenstein, & Rentz, 2001), job satisfaction and intent to remain (Sweeney & Quirin, 2008). Survivor reactions have been researched from a variety of perspectives (see Brockner, Weisenfeld, Reed, Grover, & Martin, 1993; de Vries & Balazs, 1997). Survivor expressions of organizational resentment have been linked to procedural justice aspects (Konovsky & Brockner, 1993), and justice has been shown to affect post-layoff stress and job insecurity (Sweeney & Quirin, 2008), supporting the view that the management of the transfer process may be crucial. Differences have been found between managers and staff, and between different technical departments (Armstrong-Stassen, 1993), indicating the importance of allowing for a broad range of differences rather than trying to generalize across the board. In one of the few papers on downsizing specific to information systems, Jiang and Klein (2000) indicate that the nature of the downsizing process has a key influence on survivor attitudes and career practices. De Vries and Balazs (1997) discuss the links between downsizing and ideas of employability. The breaking of the psychological contract and the enforcement of shorter-term, limited-security relationships is argued to go against an employee's need for connectedness and affiliation. Others (see Hallier, 2000), while discussing how employees will shift to a more transactional form of relationship after contract violation, focus on the implications of long-term feelings of uncertainty and insecurity which may result from many types of organizational change. The constant change that occurs through outsourcing and downsizing has also been shown to impact on perceptions of psychological contract breach and employee deviance (Chiu & Peng, 2008) and Kallinikos (2009) emphasizes some of the issues around the fragmentation that can occur due to the increasing focus on roles.

In the downsizing literature to date, the main focus has been on single organizations; any impact on dual organizational relationships such as occurs in outsourcing is not understood. For example, whether one organization is blamed, or both, any lasting influence on the individual–organizational relationships is virtually unknown, although our own research indicates that both can be blamed. What can be learnt from this literature is that the experience of outsourcing is likely to be influenced by whether downsizing also occurs, and the extent of perceived justice during the process.

The human effects of mergers and acquisitions have also been studied (see Buono & Bowditch, 1989; Cartwright & Cooper, 1996). Employee reactions are frequently claimed to be responsible for lack of success. Although clear evidence is often lacking, it seems logical that the widespread disruption, job insecurity and stress reported will impact upon performance, and there is increasing evidence that employee resistance will impact on performance (Larsson & Finkelstein, 1999).

Hubbard and Purcell (2001) have argued that employees develop dual expectations during acquisitions, based on concerns for both the individual and the work group. They highlighted employee concerns about where they 'fitted-in' to the new organization and showed how expectations changed during the course of the acquisition. They also indicated that middle managers experienced the process in a different way to staff, having concerns for their own future as well as having to manage staff anxieties. They highlighted the importance of trust, fairness and good communication in developing a new psychological contract with employees, although their case studies showed that a lack of attention was paid to these aspects.

The emphasis on culture clashes in the merger literature may be particularly relevant to outsourcing transfers, as staff from IT departments within a public or private organization may feel a low degree of fit with an organization like a large systems house. However, usually in mergers and acquisitions eventually only one company remains as a focal organization, and the long-term impact may therefore be very different in outsourcing, where a continual relationship needs to be maintained with the previous employer. Similarly, although the brief overview above highlights the importance of group and individual expectations, which should be very relevant to outsourcing transfers, in outsourcing there is the added element of the specific group feeling unwanted. The impact that this may have on future organizational relationships is unknown. Coyle-Shapiro, Morrow, and Kessler (2006) found that perceptions of organizational support from both organizations impacted on affective commitment and service orientation to each (client and contractor), emphasizing the importance of both parties to employee behaviours.

Literature on both downsizing and mergers and acquisitions often uses a bereavement metaphor and focuses on reaction stages. For example, the Kübler-Ross (1969) model includes feelings of disbelief and denial, anger, emotional bargaining and depression, followed by acceptance (see Cartwright & Cooper, 1994). It is proposed that employees may become fixated at an early stage, leading to unproductive behaviour. While there are some problems with stage models, in particular the tendency to focus on 'states' rather than processes, the acceptance of the emotional aspects of the change process may be useful, particularly where uncertainty and loss of control are experienced, such as in outsourcing. Research on emotions in organizations is very limited (Briner, 1999). Kahn (1998) does suggest that emotions underlie the nature of attachments people have to others at work, and definitions of attachment constructs such as commitment usually include an affective element. Donada and Nogatchewsky (2008) carried out a study on the role of emotions in supplier switching, emphasizing how psychological factors moderate the influence of relational and economic aspects. Taking a broader approach linking transitions and attachments may alert us to the role of emotions in outsourcing. However, not enough is known about outsourcing transfers to assess how useful models and metaphors used in the transition literature may be. It may be important to consider more explicitly the transition itself as a key influence on future relationships.

Work Transitions

Outsourcing transfers could be viewed as a new form of work transition. Certainly the relationship between staff and the two organizations concerned is likely to be influenced by the nature of the initial transfer. Indeed, Nicholson (1990) argues that the outcomes of work transitions will depend substantially on prior influences. In a similar way to mergers and acquisitions, the literature on work transitions tends to emphasize stages, viewing role transitions as discrete steps between fixed states. Weiss (1990) suggests that change or transition that involves loss of relationships (which may include distancing from co-workers) may trigger a form of grieving. Recovery stages are similar to those proposed by Kübler-Ross (1969) discussed in the previous section; however, Weiss also discusses recovery processes. These include cognitive acceptance, emotional acceptance and identity change. However, often in transition research little attention is paid to the nature of the transition process (Ashforth, 2001). Bullis and Wackernagel Bach (1989) assessed the importance of turning points and events or episodes during role transitions, and there is evidence that these may be perceived differently at different times in the transition process. It may be helpful, therefore, to assess the specific events and any perceived phases of work transitions that are relevant to outsourcing transfers, to ensure that the context and the temporal nature of the experience are understood.

Transitions can be analysed across a range of dimensions, including the speed at which they occur and the extent of change involved. The literature offers different terms and types of factors that impact upon the transition experience (see Ashforth, 2001; Nicholson, 1990) and some are likely to be more important than others in an outsourcing transition. In terms of key attributes, outsourcing is likely to be a high-magnitude, involuntary, unpredictable and collective form of transition; these aspects are discussed further below. It is also likely that the duration and extent to which the transfer is viewed as socially desirable varies a great deal. Temporally there may be substantial differences. The research suggests that outsourcing transitions can take place within days of an announcement, or can take years (Morgan, 2003). Similarly, the nature and reputation of the company taking over the staff, and the individual perceptions of the desirability of working for that company, will vary.

High-magnitude changes increase the amount of information that employees must gain, and are likely to require greater adaptation, owing to the complexity of the change. Involuntary transitions are often seen as a threat to one's sense of control, and can lead to a loss of a sense of meaning and belonging (Ashforth, 2001). Unpredictable transitions reduce sense-making, and may mean that people spend much energy trying to render the change predictable, through gossip and politicking. Although a collective transition can be helpful in developing meaning and belonging as the group work together to resolve ambiguity and anxiety, most research has been based on voluntary newcomers, socialized by exposure to current 'insiders' and later placing them, often separately, within the existing organization. In outsourcing the collective may find itself rather isolated, with few 'insiders' to help them with sense-making. Furthermore, the involuntary nature of the transfer may impact upon perceptions of, and reactions to, organizational socialization. Brehm (1993) suggests that individuals react against a major decision being made for them by desiring the former situation even more strongly. Being forced to leave one company may make individuals feel a stronger attachment to the former company, and resist the new. These aspects should be taken into account in research on outsourcing.

Although stage models have been criticized for being simplistic, they may be helpful heuristics that facilitate an understanding of temporal changes. A number of models have been produced, some appearing similar to Lewin's (1951) original unfreezing, changing and refreezing (see e.g. Trice & Morand, 1989) and emphasize stages of separation, transition and integration. In outsourcing, the 'unfreezing' or separation may be influenced by how the initial announcement is managed and could be made difficult by the continued contact with the original employer. The changing or transition 'stage' is often characterized by liminality (Turner, 1969), where people are in an unstructured and ambiguous state. The refreezing or integration stage is completed when employees feel they have been fully incorporated into the new role or organization. Whether this final state occurs in much organizational change, and indeed whether it should occur, has been questioned (McLoughlin, 1999). In outsourcing this aspect may be especially problematic as it is likely that staff lack the required level of exposure to the new organization, which might mean that ambiguity remains.

Organizations and individual careers are said to be changing rapidly, with outsourcing just one example of the supposed shift to employability and boundaryless careers. It is argued, therefore, that transition cycles may be a more useful way of trying to understand this type of change (Herriot, Hirsh, & Reilly, 1998; Nicholson, 1990). Phases of preparation, encounter, adjustment and stabilization are posited as cyclical and recursive. Nicholson's (1990) model has the benefit of being processual, to the extent that it allows for recursion and interdependence across phases. Using the model can enable us to consider the transition as shifting experiences through time and allow for the impact of context upon each individual's experience.

Although variables in the transition literature often include individual characteristics and role requirements, there is increasing evidence that organizations are 'strong' situations, minimizing the influence of individual aspects such as dispositions (Saks & Ashforth, 2000). An important area to consider, therefore, when studying organizational transitions, is socialization (Nicholson, 1990).

Organizational Socialization

Louis (1980) defined organizational socialization as 'a process by which an individual comes to appreciate the values, abilities, expected behaviours, and social knowledge essential for assuming an organizational role and for participating as an organization member' (pp. 229–230). In early research there was a tendency to consider employees as passive recipients of organizational attempts to socialize them, mostly based on van Maanen and Schein's (1979) model of institutionalized versus individual tactics (Jones, 1986). More recently there has been an increased focus on the proactive information-seeking and relationship-building tactics that individuals carry out to make sense of the organization and, indeed, interactions between these (Griffin, Colella, & Goparaju, 2000).

Socialization processes are argued to be key to enabling newcomers to become effective members of the organization (Kraimer, 1997). Research on organizational socialization frequently assesses attachment constructs such as commitment and/ or identification as outcomes of socialization (see Bauer, Wolfe Morrison, & Roberts Callister, 1998; Saks & Ashforth, 1997a). There may be some key differences in outsourcing transitions that may impact upon the relationships between socialization and attachment that need clarifying.

First, the transition is not voluntary, which may lead to individuals resisting organizational socialization tactics (Ashforth, 2001). Some have been through downsizing, often during the transfer, which has also been argued to make them less easy to socialize into a new organization (Bauer et al., 1998). Similarly, their expectations, which research suggests are crucial to socialization outcomes (Louis, 1980; Major, Kozlowski, Chao, & Gardner, 1995), may be very different from those of voluntary employees, partly due to the nature of their initial contact with the new organization (generally presentations extolling the virtues of the transfer) and their perceptions of the handling of the change by their previous employer. While this suggests that there may be some similarity between outsourcing and mergers and acquisitions, a key difference is the continued, long-term exposure to the old organization, which may further complicate the situation. Louis (1980) suggested that part of the process of becoming socialized to a new organization was the turning away from old role relationships and experiences, which may be particularly difficult in outsourcing.

Furthermore, the staff are likely to have little exposure to the new organization, and to remain in their original grouping, at least initially. Research suggests that it is particularly difficult to socialize staff from a distance (Wiesenfeld, Raghuram, & Garud, 1999, 2001), with lack of understanding of organizational goals and values being a key issue (Platt & Page, 2001). Although group socialization has been argued to be more effective than organizational level socialization (Saks & Ashforth, 1997a), in outsourcing the group generally move across together. The group therefore consists only of outsiders, making group socialization difficult. Although person–organizational fit has been shown to help with adjustment during socialization (Chatman, 1991), in outsourcing it is rare for selection to take place at all.

It has also been shown that the type of organizational socialization has different effects on the form and nature of attachment, with institutionalized socialization tactics being more positively related to organizational commitment and identification when compared to individualized tactics (Ashforth & Saks 1996). However, much of the research has focused on young employees relatively new to the workplace, and it is possible that more mature and experienced individuals react to socialization tactics differently (Ashforth, 2001).

Kraimer (1997) and Saks and Ashforth (1997b) suggest that the extent and type of organizational socialization will influence the extent and nature of the individual's proactive tactics. In particular, Kraimer hypothesizes that if the 'social' aspects of organizational socialization are individually based (disjunctive and divestiture forms – van Maanen & Schein, 1979), the individuals will be less likely to engage in tactics such as information seeking, modelling etc. It is likely therefore that perceived distance and remoteness from the new organization will reduce the level and range of proactive tactics used by the individuals concerned, reducing further the chances of their becoming socialized.

It is feasible that no socialization is considered necessary in outsourcing, as for some staff 'nothing should change', and the transition has been proposed as a mere change of name on the salary slip (Purcell & Purcell, 1998). Ashforth (2001) suggests that externalized employees may be denied rigorous socialization procedures, although the term 'outsourcing' here is used very broadly. The transferred staff may be considered 'core' rather than 'external' to the systems houses involved, therefore the literature on non-core 'contingent' workers may not be so relevant.

Organizational Commitment

A number of definitions of commitment exist in the literature. Meyer and Herscovitch (2001) typify the frustration felt by researchers at the multiple definitions, levels, and foci of the commitment construct. Distinctions have been made between attitudinal and behavioural commitment, and affective (or moral) versus calculative (side-bet) forms (Barge & Schlueter, 1998; Brown, 1996; Cohen, 1999; Etzioni, 1961; Mowday, Porter, & Steers, 1982; Oliver, 1990). Commitment has been argued to be an important attachment construct due to a range of possible behavioural implications, including continued employment, performance, attendance, and organizational citizenship, although findings are mixed and correlations often low (see Benkhoff, 1997; Meyer & Herscovitch, 2001). Findings are also mixed regarding the links between commitment and resistance to change (Meyer, Allen, & Topolnytsky, 1998). However, commitment to the original organization is likely to be lost quite quickly after an outsourcing announcement, and, unlike most change processes, a second company is involved. It is unclear, therefore, how these links may work in such circumstances.

It is not intended to go into the history of the concept or summarize the huge volume of research (mostly based on questionnaires), as meta-analyses can be found in Mathieu and Zajac (1990) and Meyer (1997). Instead, after a short overview of the bases and foci of commitment, this section will focus on findings that may be particularly relevant to outsourcing transitions.

One of the categorizations used in organizational literature is that of affective, continuance and normative commitment (e.g. Allen & Meyer, 1996; Meyer & Herscovitch, 2001). From an attachment perspective, it has been suggested that affective commitment reflects the strength of the relationship, while continuance commitment reflects duration. It is argued that people stay in an organization because they want to, owing to high affective commitment, because they have to, owing to high continuance commitment, and/or because they ought to, owing to high normative commitment. Meyer and Herscovitch (2001) agree that there are weaknesses in this categorization as affective and normative commitment are often highly correlated and continuance commitment possibly consists of two factors.

They propose a multidimensional model of organizational commitment, based on this categorization, and including a number of antecedents and consequences. This model has the benefit of including other constructs and processes such as socialization, the psychological contract and identity relevance, but is unable to develop the processual nature of commitment, owing to a focus on states. Meyer and Allen (1997) suggest that 'we know relatively little at this point about many of these (process) mechanisms' (p. 109). This may be partly due to the emphasis on cross-sectional studies and issues with measurement, which will be discussed towards the end of this chapter.

Commitment has been shown to be multiple-constituency based; for example, Becker (1992) demonstrated that commitments to top management, supervisor, and work group are all important. Becker and Billings (1993) showed that distinctions between local and global foci, along with differing bases of commitment, had differential relationships with behaviours and outcomes. Distinctions have also been made between, for example, occupational, work, team and organizational commitments (Ellemers, de Gilder, & Van den Heuvel, 1998; Meyer, Allen, & Smith, 1993). McElroy, Morrow, and Laczniak (2001) propose that external organizational commitment, the commitment of an employee towards another organization, may be useful in understanding dual relationships (such as with an employer and client). This model is useful in highlighting a range of factors that may influence an employee's commitment to another organization, including the nature of the interactions and a range of contextual factors. However, in outsourcing the client is an ex-employer, and there may be existing feelings of resentment that impact upon the relationships.

Most research focuses on global organizational commitment, and potential conflicts between foci are mostly ignored in the literature. It is likely that these various attachment foci will be affected in different ways by an outsourcing transition, yet research tends to be based on a minimum number of foci. This is possibly because of the emphasis on measurement – multiple questionnaires for differing foci are off-putting to respondents and have problematic demand characteristics.

It is likely that different foci become more salient after an outsourcing transition. For example, Meyer et al. (1998) suggest that changes in the work environment may lead employees to look beyond the organization and make other forms of commitment more salient. Outsourcing may be a particularly pertinent example of this, as employees begin to realize that the entire nature of their organizational relationships has changed.

IT outsourcing is still a large part of the outsourcing contracts signed. Commitment has been researched specifically within the IT community, as there have been suggestions that personal and job characteristics specific to IT staff may exist. Although the evidence for this is mixed (Couger, 1996), some findings may be relevant to outsourcing. For example, Raghunathan, Raghunathan, and Qiang (1998) suggest that organizational variables, particularly degree of information systems (IS) control and top management support to IS, were correlated with higher levels of organizational commitment. They suggest that this desire for control may not be a realistic expectation for future IS environments. Outsourcing is likely to be viewed as a loss of control, although in principle a transfer to a systems house could indicate an increase in control, but at a different level. Ang and Slaughter (2000) argue that much of the research on IT personnel misses important contextual influences, including changing labour market conditions. Their earlier research on IT outsourcing (Ang & Slaughter, 1998) focused purely on differences between contract staff and permanent employees. Their small-scale study suggests that contract workers have a negative influence on permanent employees, are less trusted and perceived to be lower performers than client staff. They suggested that contract workers were more likely to feel alienated, although their study did not take the relationship with the employing organization into account. Other research contradicts their findings (Jarmon, Paulson, & Rebne, 1998).

Organizational Identification

Mathieu and Zajac (1990) claim that organizational identification is a subdimension of attitudinal organizational commitment, whereas Mowday et al. (1982) suggest that attitudinal commitment is the extent of identification with an organization. Certainly many definitions of commitment include the term 'identification'. The confusion in terminology in both the commitment and identification literature makes evaluating research difficult, as the same term means different things. Scott, Corman, and Cheney (1998) argue that most organizational commitment research actually ignores identification even when including it in a definition. This may be part of the reason why there is so much conceptual confusion. Russo (1998) suggests that organizational commitment is the expression of organizational identification – the latter being the substance and commitment the form.

In 1991, Sass and Canary examined conceptual and operational convergence between the two constructs, and argued that attitudinal commitment and identification have considerable overlap, representing the same attitudes, although they do suggest that identification should be referred to as a process, and commitment as an outcome of that process. However, they do this based on the assumption that operationalizations correspond to their conceptualizations (which it will be argued shortly is rarely the case) and their definition of attitudinal commitment focuses on the 'devotion and loyalty' form (Morrow, 1983). This form, and its associated questionnaire, the Organisational Commitment Questionnaire (OCQ), has been criticized (Brown, 1996; Guest, 1996). Scott et al. (1998) suggest that loyalty is only one dimension of individual relationships with an organization and one could argue that it is a key overlapping area. Elsbach (1999) focuses on the link to the self-concept: identification can be distinguished from commitment because the identification process is linked to one's own identity and the need to enhance one's sense of self. This link is lacking in most of the commitment definitions, with the exception of more recent conceptualizations of affective commitment (Meyer & Herscovitch, 2001). Ashforth and Mael (1996) suggest that identification is likely to be organization specific, whereas commitment may be to more general values and goals which one organization may have, but that other organizations may also share.

This suggests that identification may be a more useful construct to assess when considering attachment to more than one organization.

Definitions of identification itself also vary substantially. Becker, Billings, Eveleth, and Gilbert (1996) suggest that identification occurs when one adopts values and behaviours in order to be associated with someone or something. Rousseau (1998) describes identification as a psychological state where the individual perceives 'self' to be part of a larger whole. Wan-Huggins, Riordan, and Griffeth (1998) argue that individuals can coalesce with organizational values and attitudes without making them a part of their own value system. Some of these distinctions appear to confuse internalization with identification. Furthermore, the distinction between affinity (recognizing that one shares values with the organization) and emulation (changing one's self-concept to enable values to become similar to organizational values) may be important (Pratt, 1998).

In organizational behaviour, identification is researched primarily from two very different perspectives: functionalist mainstream occupational psychology and a generally more interpretive communications approach. The mainstream research tends to view identification as a state, a 'product' of socialization. It tends to be linked very closely to commitment, often confusing the two constructs. The communications field tends to view identification as more of a process, and frequently to argue for a clear distinction between identification and commitment (Cheney, 1983; Sass & Canary, 1991). Organizational identification has been linked to decision making on behalf of the organization, role orientation, motivation and job performance (Cheney, 1983; Pratt, 1998). The first aspect may be particularly pertinent in outsourcing situations, from the point of view of the outsourcing company. It is proposed that individuals gain safety needs, which could be particularly important to them in times of change (Pratt, 1998).

Identification foci and forms

As with commitment, identification is said to develop with a number of possible foci. Van Knippenberg and van Schie (2000) found that work-group identification was correlated more strongly than organizational identification with job satisfaction, involvement and turnover intentions. They suggest that to focus on the organizational level may miss important attachments at work. Barker and Tompkins (1994) suggested that identification to the team may be at the expense of the wider organization and other targets (although analysis of the narratives indicated that this is not the case). Jetten, O'Brien, and Trindall (2002) found links between different foci of identification and suggested that employees with high initial organizational identification were less negative about a proposed change, and more likely to maintain levels of organizational commitment after the change, compared to those identifying with their work group. This suggests that the extent of identification with both team and organization should be assessed when analysing the impact of organizational change.

Russo (1998) analysed differences between organizational and professional identification, and highlighted how the meanings of these may change over time. This emphasizes the issue of assuming that studies from the 1960s and 70s can still inform research in today's workplace – much research assumes that there has been no change in society or in the meanings of constructs.

The above research also suggests that increasing physical separation of employees from the organization may lead to a strain on affective attachments, and indicates that the increase in the number of 'knowledge workers' offers a potential for them to identify more with their profession, both factors that may be relevant to professional forms of outsourcing. It is possible that the experience of being outsourced prompts employees to look elsewhere for identity-based resources.

Links to identity

Self, group and organizational identity have all been shown to influence the processes of identification (Barker & Tompkins, 1994; DiSanza & Bullis, 1999; Pratt & Foreman, 2000; Scott & Lane, 2000). Baumeister and Leary (1995) review evidence in support of a fundamental 'need to belong' linked to the social self as individuals define themselves in terms of their immersion in relationships. Research suggests that perceived organizational identity impacts upon one's sense of self and one's ability to identify. Albert and Whetten (1985) suggest that there are particular times when organizational identity might become particularly salient, including major change. Dutton, Dukerich, and Harquil (1994) propose that the attractiveness of organizational identity may vary with members' length of tenure and intensity of exposure, but that this is likely to change during restructuring. While it is not the aim of this thesis to assess in detail the effect of outsourcing on personal, social or role identities (Ashforth, 2001; Ashforth & Mael, 1996), it will be important to bear in mind the potential influence of the organizational 'identity' of the new employing company while conducting this research. Similarly, some consideration should be given to identity processes and any personal change experienced by employees. This influence also suggests that it will be important to carry out research across a range of companies.

Scott et al. (1998) suggest that identities both shape and are shaped by social interaction, and will shift in importance depending on the situation and context. Berger and Luckman (1966) suggest: 'By the very nature of socialization, subjective identity is a precarious entity. It is dependent upon the individuals' relations with significant others, who may change or disappear' (p. 118). An outsourcing transition is likely to be a key transition time when significant others, to the extent that they exist within the work context, may change or indeed disappear.

The Psychological Contract

One area that is increasingly referred to as a possible attachment construct, and is linked to the other areas discussed so far, is the psychological contract. The popular view of this construct is as an invisible or implicit psychological contract that supplements the formal written employment contract and covers how people think they should be treated (Rousseau, 1995). Studies have shown that perceived breach of the psychological contract is linked to reduced commitment, trust, performance, and citizenship behaviour (Coyle-Shapiro & Kessler, 2002; Robinson & Rousseau, 1994; Robinson & Wolfe Morrison, 2000). In principle, this concept could be of use in assessing organizational change processes, as the changing or breaking of contracts is perhaps more likely to occur.

Millward and Hopkins (1998) argue that the psychological contract is vital in analysing changes in relationships, although they agree that most studies are static, whereas psychological contracting is dynamic and combinatorial. Nelson, Quick, and Joplin (1991) and Payne, Culbertson, Boswell, and Barger (2008) propose that attachments are the foundation for the psychological contracting process, although they point out that the two areas are rarely combined.

The psychological contract has received much research attention, including a Special Issue of the *Journal of Organizational Behavior*; however, the concept is not without its critics (Arnold, 1996, 1997; Guest, 1998a, 1998b). There is particular concern over the potential overlap with existing constructs, and the variation in definitions. The first issue of definition concerns whether the contract is only an individual perception, in the mind of the employee (e.g. Robinson & Rousseau, 1994; Rousseau & McLean Parks, 1993), or whether it concerns the perceptions of both parties (Hendry & Jenkins, 1997; Herriot & Pemberton, 1996, 1997). Rousseau (1995) argues that the potential organizational agents are numerous and that research should focus on the individuals' perceptions, although others (e.g. Herriot & Pemberton, 1997) highlight that this does not enable consideration of the contracting process. This issue impacts upon the scope of the construct, and highlights the difficulty of assessing whom the 'contract' is with. The second main issue surrounding definition concerns how to operationalize the concept (see Anderson & Schalk, 1998; Rousseau & Tijoriwala, 1998). While some studies define the concept as beliefs concerning entitlements, others focus on expectations (returning more to Argyris's original definition (1960) of 'practical and emotional expectations of benefits', e.g. Hendry & Jenkins, 1997). Most of the Rousseau 'school' focus on obligations (e.g. Robinson, Kraatz, & Rousseau, 1994; Rousseau & McLean Parks, 1993; Rousseau & Tijoriwala, 1998) and stress the implicit and unwritten nature of the phenomenon, although Herriot and Pemberton (1997) suggest that differing degrees of explicitness are likely. Research often includes measurements of explicit promises or obligations, and is in danger of making the distinction with written contracts unclear.

As with the commitment and identification literature, there are issues regarding the foci of the psychological contract. In particular, there is concern over the lack of clarity regarding the organizational 'agent'. Issues with anthropomorphizing the organization have been highlighted (Conway, 1999). It is questionable whether employees view all supervisory contacts as 'agents' of the organization. The impact on attachments is likely to differ substantially depending on whether the particular aspect violated is considered important to the individual. It is also unclear whether contract violations occurring at a group or organizational level impact differentially upon the individual. It is possible that contracts are multiple, and operate at different levels. Millward and Hopkins (1998) discuss this possibility. They found that job commitment was more meaningfully related to contractual orientation than organizational commitment. Research also suggests that middle managers' concerns with fulfilling their own contract commitments conflict with and impact upon obligations to subordinates (Hallier & James, 1997). This research highlights the importance of considering multiple agents and multiple levels of analysis in the contract process. If the psychological contract is purely subjective, an individual level of analysis is likely to be appropriate, although more might be gained by developing an understanding from each individual of which foci are important in different contexts. In terms of outsourcing, it is likely that the decision to transfer would be considered by employees as a breach or violation of the contract. However, it is unclear whether the entire organization would be 'blamed' or just the senior managers involved.

There is some evidence that the nature of the psychological contract may change after such a breach (Robinson, 1995), but there is little research on the development of a new contract with the new employer, particularly in involuntary situations.

Research on contract violations (e.g. Robinson & Rousseau, 1994; Robinson & Wolfe Morrison, 2000; Wolfe Morrison & Robinson, 1997) and on the mediating role of trust in this process (Robinson, 1996) may be more likely to offer insight into change processes. However, such studies are limited in number, rarely longitudinal (for exceptions see Robinson et al., 1994; Robinson & Wolfe Morrison, 2000) and with a restrictive range of samples. A broader sample studied by Turnley and Feldman (2000) indicated that unmet expectations and job dissatisfaction partially mediate the relationships between psychological contract violations and certain outcomes. However, as unmet expectations and job dissatisfaction were so highly correlated, it was not possible to develop a definitive causal model. Turnley and Feldman (1999) developed a discrepancy model of psychological contract violation, which suggests that expectations develop through specific promises, perceptions of the organization's culture and practices (including socialization) and idiosyncratic expectations of how the organization operates. An earlier model by Wolfe Morrison and Robinson (1997), while useful in pointing to a range of influencing factors, focuses on the development of violation perception, and cannot inform on how the psychological contract itself develops. Although Nelson et al. (1991) have linked the psychological contract to socialization processes, with the exception of Thomas and Anderson (1998) very little research has taken place linking the two. Chiu and Peng (2008) demonstrate that psychological contract breach positively relates to both interpersonal and organizational deviance, suggesting that serious problems can arise if breach is perceived during outsourcing. However, we have very limited understanding of how contracts develop and change, or of how far the 'contract' is shaped by the organization or by the individual (Conway, 1999; Conway & Briner, 2005).

Rousseau (1995) claims that organizational attachments, and particularly relational contracts, evolve, to a certain extent, by length of tenure and extent of security, although there is little evidence of a direct link between relational contracts and formal contract type (Millward & Brewerton, 1999). In their study, team spirit and identity were considered to be a predictor of relational psychological contracts, although this finding was based on regression analysis with a cross-sectional study, which limits the validity of causal findings. Rousseau (1995) suggests that two factors are critical to the formation of contracts: external messages, including observations of the treatment of others with the same deal, and personal interpretations and dispositions. The recruitment process and early socialization are considered key, although much of the research focuses on MBA graduates, for whom organizational recruitment and socialization may be particularly new and crucial (Ashforth, 2001). Alternatively, graduates may find it easier to accept more transactional contracts (Herriot & Pemberton, 1997). In outsourcing, the initial presentations and early socialization practices may be influential in developing a 'new' psychological contract, but most of the staff involved have a substantial career behind them.

It has been suggested that the psychological contract may play an increasingly important role in helping us to understand contemporary employment relationships (Turnley & Feldman, 2000), and in principle a focus on contract development and negotiation should offer insight into processes of attachment. However, there are some key issues with the psychological contract, in terms of multiple definitions and general lack of clarity about the construct. This may be due to the atheoretical nature of work in this area (Guest, 1998a). Rousseau (1996) argues that psychological contract revisions must be made in specific ways at certain times to facilitate continued commitment, although the impact of organizational interventions is rarely evaluated. In an outsourcing situation employees have in principle suffered a major violation of their psychological contract. They receive very specific interventions and negotiations from their new employer, which may influence their perceptions of new psychological contracts.

Organizational Justice

Extant literature tends to focus on three specific forms of justice perceptions (Cohen-Charash & Spector, 2001). Distributive justice considers perceptions of fairness of outcomes (equity equality and needs). Procedural justice emphasizes the importance of fairness of the methods or procedures used (decision criteria, voice, control of the process), and interactional justice is based on the perceived fairness of the interpersonal treatment received, whether those involved are treated with sensitivity, dignity and respect, and also the nature of the explanations given. Although there have been concerns regarding the distinctions between different forms of justice, a recent meta-analysis suggests that the distinction between these three forms is merited (Cohen-Charash & Spector, 2001). Justice perceptions have been related to a range of work outcomes, including performance, turnover, commitment and cooperative behaviours (for a recent review see Colquitt, Conlon, Wesson, Porter, & Ng, 2001). It is not the purpose of this chapter to review the justice literature, which has been extensively discussed in recent years. However, of specific interest to this research is the repeated finding that good attention to procedural justice concerns can increase perceptions of fairness even if the outcomes are unfavourable. If we assume that, at least initially, staff will view the likely outcome of being forcibly transferred to another organization as unfair, it may be possible that procedural justice will reduce their perceptions of unfairness.

Literature suggests that important aspects of justice perceptions include employee involvement and voice, and perceived empathy, sensitivity and support from management. Justice perceptions might tend to be particularly negative during outsourcing because the change is imposed, and tends to be based on one-way communication by managers who are themselves feeling stressed or distanced owing to their own uncertainty, and senior managers tending to assume that staff are no longer their problem, as they have handed over responsibility to another organization. While there are similarities to other change processes, including mergers, a key difference is that staff generally continue to work for their previous employer, who has become a client.

To summarize, a variety of research in the areas of downsizing, mergers and acquisitions may inform our understanding of outsourcing transitions; however, we argue that there are sufficient differences to warrant further research, in particular the existence of both organizations. There are also a range of theories (and research around them) that can help us, primarily around commitment, identification, organizational justice and the psychological contract. However, there are also theories linked to trust, knowledge sharing and cultural differences that are clearly important, as issues around these have been raised by all of the practitioner chapters.

The remaining chapters focus on these different theoretical aspects. Chapter 8 reminds us that to fully understand anything we need to place it in context. Roy Morgan also reminds us that much of what is said about outsourcing, particularly in the popular press, is based on the need to 'sell' the concept or to position people as successful within the outsourcing sphere. These contextual aspects are vital in reminding us of the influence of our business norms and organization–staff relationships on our attitudes to and interpretations of outsourcing. Brigitte Cobb illustrates issues that can arise owing to cultural differences, primarily focusing on national culture, although (as the mergers and acquisitions literature shows) organizational culture can also have a big impact. To negotiate and manage an outsourcing contract requires trust. Research indicates that trust is particularly problematic over a distance, yet increasingly outsourcing leads to teams of people working at great distances from each other – often to the extent they are 'virtual' in organization. Alex Watts demonstrates clearly the issues that can arise in virtual teams in Chapter 9. Another finding, raised by a number of practitioners, is that after outsourcing transfers, knowledge is lost to the organization, and that during outsourcing contracts, acquiring knowledge from a supplier (or knowledge transfer) can be very difficult. Richard Blakeley completed a literature review on knowledge transfer and together we have outlined the implications of these findings for outsourcing. While these chapters can be applied to most forms of outsourcing, there are some specific issues that arise when people are transferred to an outsourcing supplier. Roy Morgan takes a life-cycle approach to research investigating the experience of being outsourced. Jan Aylsworth gives us a US perspective, in particular considering downsizing, which occurs more frequently than outsourcing transfers in the US. In Chapter 13 I continue the theme of focusing on transitions, and consider the implications for the psychological contract at work, complicated by the existence of two organizations to contract with, the client and the original employer. Finally, in an attempt to understand the different responses we have found to outsourcing transfers, Chapter 14 develops a tentative model, including some suggestions for good management.

References

Albert, S., & Whetten, D. A. (1985). Organizational identity. *Research in Organizational Behavior, 7*, 263–295.

Allen, N. J., & Meyer, J. P. (1996). Affective, continuance and normative commitment to the organization: An examination of construct validity. *Journal of Vocational Behavior, 49*, 252–276.

Allen, T. D., Freeman, D. M., Russel, J. E. A., Reizenstein, R. C., & Rentz, J. (2001). Survivor reactions to organizational downsizing: Does time ease the pain? *Journal of Occupational and Organizational Psychology, 74*(2), 145–164.

Anderson, N., & Schalk, R. (1998). Editorial: The psychological contract in retrospect and prospect. *Journal of Organizational Behavior, 19*, 637–647.

Ang, S., & Slaughter, S. A. (1998). Organizational psychology and performance in IS employment outsourcing and insourcing. *31st Annual International Conference on System Sciences*, Hawaii.

Ang, S., & Slaughter, S. A. (2000). The missing context of information technology personnel: A review and future directions for research. In R. W. Zmud (Ed.), *Framing the domains of IT management: Projecting the future through the past* (pp. 305–327). Cincinnati, OH: Pinnaflex Educational Resources.

Argyris, C. P. (1960). *Understanding organizational behaviour.* Homewood, IL: Dorsey Press.

Armstrong-Stassen, M. (1993). Survivors' reactions to a workforce reduction: A comparison of blue-collar workers and their supervisors. *Canadian Journal of Administrative Sciences, 10*(4), 334–343.

Arnold, J. (1996). The psychological contract: A concept in need of closer scrutiny? *European Journal of Work and Organizational Psychology, 5*(4), 511–520.

Arnold, J. (1997). *Managing careers into the 21st century.* London: Paul Chapman.

Ashforth, B. E. (2001). *Role transitions in organizational life: An identity-based perspective.* Mahwah, NJ: Lawrence Erlbaum.

Ashforth, B. E., & Mael, F. A. (1996). Organizational identity and strategy as a context for the individual. *Advances in Strategic Management, 13*, 19–64.

Ashforth, B. E., & Saks, A. M. (1996). Socialization tactics: Longitudinal effects on newcomer adjustment. *Academy of Management Journal, 39*, 149–178.

Barge, J. K., & Schlueter, D. W. (1998). A critical evaluation of organizational commitment and identification. *Management Communication Quarterly, 2*(1, August), 116–133.

Barker, J. R., & Tompkins, P. K. (1994). Identification in the self-managing organization. *Human Communication Research, 21*(2, December), 223–240.

Bauer, T. N., Wolfe Morrison, E., & Roberts Callister, R. (1998). Organizational socialization: A review and directions for future research. *Research in Personnel and Human Resources Management, 16,* 149–214.

Baumeister, R. F., & Leary, M. R. (1995). The need to belong: Desire for interpersonal attachments as a fundamental human motivation. *Psychological Bulletin, 117*(3), 497–529.

Becker, T. E. (1992). Foci and bases of commitment: Are they distinctions worth making? *Academy of Management Journal, 35,* 232–244.

Becker, T. E., & Billings, R. S. (1993). Profiles of commitment: An empirical test. *Journal of Organizational Behavior, 14,* 177–190.

Becker, T. E., Billings, R. S., Eveleth, D. M., & Gilbert, N. L. (1996). Foci and bases of employee commitment: Implications for job performance. *Academy of Management Journal, 39,* 464–482.

Benkhoff, B. (1997). Ignoring commitment is costly: New approaches establish the missing link between commitment and performance. *Human Relations, 50*(6), 701–726.

Berger, P. L., & Luckman, T. (1966). *The social construction of reality.* New York: Doubleday.

Brehm, J. W. (1993). Control, its loss, and psychological reactance. In G. Weary, F. Gleicher, & K. L. Marsh (Eds.), *Control motivation and social cognition* (pp. 3–30). New York: Srpinger-Verlag.

Briner, R. (1999). The neglect and importance of emotion at work. *European Journal of Work and Organizational Psychology, 8*(3), 323–346.

Brockner, J., Weisenfeld, B. M., Reed, T., Grover, S., & Martin, C. (1993). Interactive effect of job content and context on the reactions of layoff survivors. *Journal of Personality and Social Psychology, 64,* 187–197.

Brown, R. (1996). Organizational commitment: Clarifying the concept and simplifying the existing construct typology. *Journal of Vocational Behavior, 49,* 230–251.

Bullis, C., & Wackernagel Bach, B. (1989). Socialization turning points: An examination of change in organizational identification. *Western Journal of Speech Communication, 53*(Summer).

Buono, A. F., & Bowditch, J. L. (1989). *The human side of mergers and acquisitions.* San Francisco: Jossey-Bass.

Cartwright, S., & Cooper, G. L. (1994). The human effects of mergers and acquisitions. In G. L. Cooper & D. M. Rousseau (Eds.), *Trends in organizational behaviour* (pp. 47–61). Chichester: John Wiley & Sons.

Cartwright, S., & Cooper, G. L. (1996). *Managing mergers, acquisitions, and strategic alliances: Integrating people and cultures* (2nd ed.). Oxford: Butterworth-Heinemann.

Chatman, J. A. (1991). Matching people and organizations: Selection and socialization in public accounting firms. *Administrative Science Quarterly, 36,* 459–484.

Cheney, G. (1983). On the various and changing meanings of organizational membership: A field study of organizational identification. *Communication Monographs, 50*(December), 342–362.

Chiu, S., & Peng, J. (2008). The relationship between psychological contract breach and employee deviance: The moderating role of hostile attributional style. *Journal of Vocational Behaviour, 73,* 426–433.

Cohen, A. (1999). Relationships among five forms of commitment: An empirical assessment. *Journal of Organizational Behavior, 20,* 285–308.

Cohen-Charash, Y., & Spector, P. E. (2001). The role of justice in organizations: A meta-analysis. *Organizational Behavior and Human Decision Processes, 86*(2), 278–321.

Colquitt, J. A., Conlon, D. E., Wesson, M. J., Porter, C. O., & Ng, K. Y. (2001). Justice at the millennium: A meta-analytic path analysis of 20 years of research. *Journal of Applied Psychology*, 86, 425–445.

Conway, N. (1999). *Using the psychological contract to explain attitudinal and behavioural differences between full-time and part-time employees.* London: Birkbeck College.

Conway, N., & Briner, R. (2005). *Understanding psychological contracts at work: A critical evaluation of theory and research.* Oxford: Oxford University Press.

Couger, J. D. (1996). The changing environment for IS professionals: Human resource implications. In M. J. Earl (Ed.), *Information management: The organizational dimension* (pp. 426–435). Oxford: Oxford University Press.

Coyle-Shapiro, J., Morrow, P., & Kessler, I. (2006). Serving two organizations: Exploring the employment relationship of contracted employees. *Human Resource Management*, 45(4), 561–583.

Coyle-Shapiro, J. A. M., & Kessler, I. (2002). Exploring reciprocity through the lens of the psychological contract: Employee and employer perspectives. *European Journal of Work and Organizational Psychology*, 11(1), 69–86.

DiSanza, J. R., & Bullis, C. (1999). Everybody identifies with Smokey the Bear: Employee responses to newsletter identification inducements at the U.S. Forest Service. *Management Communication Quarterly*, 12(3), 347–399.

Donada, C., & Nogatchewsky, G. (2008). Emotions in outsourcing. An empirical study in the hotel industry. *International Journal of Hospitality Management*, in press; doi: 10.1016/j.ijhm.2008.10.005.

Dutton, J. E., Dukerich, J. M., & Harquil, C. V. (1994). Organizational images and member identification. *Administrative Science Quarterly*, 39, 239–263.

Ellemers, N., de Gilder, D., & Van den Heuvel, H. (1998). Career-oriented versus team-oriented commitment and behavior at work. *Journal of Applied Psychology*, 83(5), 717–730.

Elsbach, K. D. (1999). An expanded model of organizational identification. *Research in Organizational Behavior*, 21, 163–200.

Etzioni, A. (1961). *A comparative analysis of complex organizations.* New York: Free Press.

Griffin, A. E. C., Colella, A., & Goparaju, S. (2000). Newcomer and organizational socialization tactics: An interactionist perspective. *Human Resource Management Review*, 10(4), 453–474.

Guest, D. (1996). *Issues in human resource management, MSc. course module.* London: Birkbeck College, University of London.

Guest, D. (1998a). On meaning, metaphor and the psychological contract: A response to Rousseau (1998). *Journal of Organizational Behavior*, 19, 673–677.

Guest, D. E. (1998b). Is the psychological contract worth taking seriously? *Journal of Organizational Behavior*, 19, 649–664.

Hallier, J. (2000). Security abeyance: Coping with the erosion of job conditions and treatment. *British Journal of Management*, 11, 71–89.

Hallier, J., & James, P. (1997). Middle managers and the employee psychological contract: Agency, protection and advancement. *Journal of Management Studies*, 34(5), 703–728.

Hendry, C., & Jenkins, R. (1997). Psychological contracts and new deals. *Human Resource Management Journal*, 7(1), 38–44.

Herriot, P., Hirsh, W., & Reilly, P. (1998). *Trust and transition: Managing today's employment relationship.* Chichester: John Wiley.

Herriot, P., & Pemberton, C. (1996). Contracting careers. *Human Relations*, 49(6), 757–790.

Herriot, P., & Pemberton, C. (1997). Facilitating new deals. *Human Resource Management Journal, 7*(1), 45–56.

Hubbard, N., & Purcell, J. (2001). Managing employee expectations during acquisitions. *Human Resource Management Journal, 11*(2), 17–33.

Jarmon, R., Paulson, A. S., & Rebne, D. (1998). Contractor performance: How good are contingent workers at the professional level? *IEEE Transactions on Engineering Management, 45*(1, February), 11–19.

Jetten, J., O'Brien, A., & Trindall, N. (2002). Changing identity: Predicting adjustment to organizational restructure as a function of subgroup and superordinate identification. *British Journal of Social Psychology, 41*, 281–297.

Jiang, J. J., & Klein, G. (2000). Effects of downsizing policies on IS survivors' attitude and career management. *Information & Management, 38*, 35–45.

Jones, G. R. (1986). Socialization tactics, self efficacy, and newcomers' adjustments to organizations. *Academy of Management Journal, 29*, 262–279.

Kahn, W. A. (1998). Relational systems at work. *Research in Organizational Behavior, 20*, 39–76.

Kallinikos, J. (2009). *Work, human agency and organizational forms: An anatomy of fragmentation.* London: London School of Economics.

Konovsky, M. A., & Brockner, J. (1993). Managing victim and survivor layoff reactions: A procedural justice perspective. In R. Cropanzano (Ed.), *Justice in the workplace: Approaching fairness in human resource management* (pp. 133–153). Hillsdale, NJ: Lawrence Erlbaum Associates.

Kraimer, M. L. (1997). Organizational goals and values: A socialization model. *Human Resource Management Review, 7*(4), 425–447.

Kübler-Ross, E. (1969). *On death and dying.* New York: MacMillan.

Larsson, R., & Finkelstein, S. (1999). Integrating strategic, organizational, and human resource perspectives on mergers and acquisitions: A case survey of synergy realization. *Organization Science, 10*(1, January–February), 1–26.

Lewin, K. (1951). *Field theory* and learning. In D. Cartwright (Ed.), *Field theory in social science: Selected theoretical papers* (pp. 60–86). New York: Harper & Brothers.

Louis, M. R. (1980). Surprise and sense making: What newcomers experience in entering unfamiliar organizational settings. *Administrative Science Quarterly, 25*(June), 226–251.

Major, D. A., Kozlowski, S. W. J., Chao, G. T., & Gardner, P. D. (1995). A longitudinal investigation of newcomer expectations, early socialization outcomes, and the moderating effects of role development factors. *Journal of Applied Psychology, 80*(3), 418–431.

Mathieu, J. E., & Zajac, D. M. (1990). A review and meta-analysis of the antecedents, correlates, and consequences of organizational commitment. *Psychological Bulletin, 108*(2), 171–194.

McElroy, J. C., Morrow, P. C., & Laczniak, R. N. (2001). External organizational commitment. *Human Resource Management Review, 11*, 237–256.

McLoughlin, I. (1999). *Creative technological change: The shaping of technology and organizations.* London: Routledge.

Meyer, J. P. (1997). Organizational commitment. In C. L. Cooper & I. T. Robertson (Eds.), *International review of industrial and organizational psychology* (Vol. 12, pp. 175–228). Chichester: John Wiley & Sons.

Meyer, J. P., & Allen, N. J. (1997). *Commitment in the workplace: Theory, research and application.* Thousand Oaks, CA: Sage.

The Human Side of Outsourcing

Meyer, J. P., Allen, N. J., & Smith, C. A. (1993). Commitment to organizations and occupations: Extension and test of a three-component conceptualization. *Journal of Applied Psychology, 78*(4), 538–551.

Meyer, J. P., Allen, N. J., & Topolnytsky, L. (1998). Commitment in a changing world of work. *Canadian Psychology, 39*(1–2), 83–93.

Meyer, J. P., & Herscovitch, L. (2001). Commitment in the workplace. Toward a general model. *Human Resource Management Review, 11,* 299–326.

Millward, L. J., & Brewerton, P. M. (1999). Contractors and their psychological contracts. *British Journal of Management, 10,* 253–274.

Millward, L. J., & Hopkins, L. J. (1998). Psychological contracts, organizational and job commitment. *Journal of Applied Social Psychology, 28*(16), 1530–1556.

Morgan, S. J. (2003). *Organization attachments in IT outsourcing.* London: University of London.

Morrow, P. C. (1983). *The theory and measurement of work commitment.* Greenwich, CT: JAI Press.

Mowday, R. T., Porter, L. W., & Steers, R. M. (1982). *Employee–organization linkages. The psychology of commitment, absenteeism, and turnover.* New York: Academic Press.

Nelson, D.L., Quick, J.C., & Joplin, J.R. (1991). Psychological contracting and newcomer socialization: An attachment theory foundation. *Journal of Social Behavior and Personality, 6*(7), 55–72.

Nicholson, N. (1990). The transition cycle: Causes, outcomes, processes and forms. In S. Fisher & G. L. Cooper (Eds.), *On the move: The psychology of change and transition* (pp. 83–108). Chichester, John Wiley.

Oliver, N. (1990). Rewards, investments, alternatives and organizational commitment: Empirical evidence and theoretical development. *Journal of Occupational Psychology, 63*(1), 19–31.

Payne, S.C., Culbertson, S.S., Boswell, W.R., & Barger, E.J. (2008). Newcomer psychological contracts and employee socialization activities: Does perceived balance in obligations matter? *Journal of Vocational Behavior, 73,* 465–472.

Platt, R. G., & Page, D. (2001). Managing the virtual team: Critical skills and knowledge for successful performance. In N. J. Johnson (Ed.), *Telecommuting and virtual offices: Issues and opportunities* (pp. 130–147). Hershey, PA: IDEA Group.

Pratt, M. G. (1998). To be or not to be? Central questions in organizational identification. In D. A Whetten & P. C. Godfrey (Eds.), *Identity in organizations: Building theory through conversations* (pp. 171–207). Thousand Oaks, CA: Sage.

Pratt, M. G., & Foreman, P. O. (2000). Classifying managerial responses to multiple organizational identities. *Academy of Management Review, 25*(1), 18–42.

Purcell, K., & Purcell, J. (1998). In-sourcing, outsourcing, and the growth of contingent labour as evidence of flexible employment strategies. *European Journal of Work and Organizational Psychology, 7*(1), 39–59.

Raghunathan, B., Raghunathan, T., & Qiang, T. (1998). An empirical analysis of the organizational commitment of information systems executives. *Omega International Journal of Management Science, 26*(5), 569–580.

Robinson, S. L. (1995). Violation of psychological contracts: Impact on employee attitudes. In L. E. Tetrick & J. Barling (Eds.), *Changing employment relations: Behavioural and social perspectives* (pp. 91–108). Washington, DC: American Psychological Association.

Robinson, S. L. (1996). Trust and breach of the psychological contract. *Administrative Science Quarterly, 41*(December), 574–599.

Robinson, S. L., Kraatz, M. S., & Rousseau, D. M. (1994). Changing obligations and the psychological contract: A longitudinal study. *Academy of Management Journal, 37*(1), 137–152.

Robinson, S. L., & Rousseau, D. M. (1994). Violating the psychological contract: Not the exception but the norm. *Journal of Organizational Behavior, 15*, 245–259.

Robinson, S. L., & Wolfe Morrison, E. (2000). The development of psychological contract breach and violation: A longitudinal study. *Journal of Organizational Behavior, 21*, 525–546.

Rousseau, D. M. (1995). *Psychological contracts in organizations: Understanding written and unwritten agreements.* Thousand Oaks, CA: Sage.

Rousseau, D. M. (1996). Changing the deal while keeping the people. *Academy of Management Executive, 10*(1), 50–59.

Rousseau, D. M. (1998). Why workers still identify with organizations. *Journal of Organizational Behavior, 19*, 217–233.

Rousseau, D. M., & McLean Parks, J. (1993). The contracts of individuals and organizations. *Research in Organizational Behavior, 15*, 1–43.

Rousseau, D. M., & Tijoriwala, S. A. (1998). Assessing psychological contracts: Issues, alternatives and measures. *Journal of Organizational Behavior, 19*, 679–695.

Russo, T. C. (1998). Organizational and professional identification: A case of newspaper journalists. *Management Communication Quarterly, 12*(1, August), 72–111.

Saks, A. M., & Ashforth, B. E. (1997a). Organizational socialization: Making sense of the past and present as a prologue for the future. *Journal of Vocational Behavior, 51*, 234–279.

Saks, A. M., & Ashforth, B. E. (1997b). Socialization tactics and newcomer information acquisition. *International Journal of Selection and Assessment, 5*, 48–61.

Saks, A. M., & Ashforth, B. E. (2000). The role of dispositions, entry stressors, and behavioral plasticity theory in predicting newcomers' adjustment to work. *Journal of Organizational Behavior, 21*, 43–62.

Sass, J. S., & Canary, D. J. (1991). Organizational commitment and identification: An examination of conceptual and operational convergence. *Western Journal of Speech Communication, 55*(Summer), 275–293.

Scott, C. R., Corman, S. R., & Cheney, G. (1998). *Development* of a structurational model of identification in the organization. *Communication Theory, 8*(3), 298–336.

Scott, S. G., & Lane, V. R. (2000). A stakeholder approach to organizational identity. *Academy of Management Review, 25*(1), 43–62.

Sweeney, J. T., & Quirin, J. J. (2008). Accountants as layoff survivors: A research note. *Accounting, Organizations and Society*, doi:10.1016/j.aos.2008.04.005.

Thomas, H. D. C., & Anderson, N. (1998). Changes in newcomers' psychological contracts during organizational socialization: A study of recruits entering the British Army. *Journal of Organizational Behavior, 19*, 745–767.

Trice, H. M., & Morand, D. A. (1989). Rites of passage in work careers. In M. B. Arthur, D. T. Hall, & B. S. Lawrence (Eds.), *Handbook of career theory* (pp. 397–416). Cambridge: Cambridge University Press.

Turner, V. W. (1969). *The ritual process: Structure and anti structure.* Chicago: Aldine.

Turnley, W. H., & Feldman, D. C. (1999). A discrepancy model of psychological contract violations. *Human Resource Management Review, 9*(3), 367–836.

Turnley, W. H., & Feldman, D. C. (2000). Re-examining the effect of psychological contract violations: Unmet expectations and job dissatisfaction as mediators. *Journal of Organizational Behavior, 21*, 25–42.

Van Knippenberg, D., & van Schie, E. C. M. (2000). Foci and correlates of organizational identification. *Journal of Occupational and Organizational Psychology*, *73*(2), 137–148.

Van Maanen, J., & Schein, E. H. (1979). Toward a theory of organizational socialization. In B. M. Staw (Ed.), *Research in organizational behaviour* (Vol. *1*, pp. 209–264). Greenwich: CT: JAI Press.

De Vries, M. F. R., & Balazs, K. (1997). The downside of downsizing. *Human Relations*, *50*(1), 11–50.

Wan-Huggins, V. N., Riordan, C. M., & Griffeth, R. W. (1998). The development and longitudinal test of a model of organizational identification. *Journal of Applied Social Psychology*, *28*(8), 724–749.

Weiss, R. S. (1990). Losses associated with mobility. In S. Fisher & G. L. Cooper (Eds.), *On the move: The psychology of change and transition* (pp. 3–12). Chichester: John Wiley & Sons.

Wiesenfeld, B. M., Raghuram, S., & Garud, R. (1999). Communication patterns as determinants of organizational identification in a virtual organization. *Organization Science*, *10*, 777–790.

Wiesenfeld, B. M., Raghuram, S., & Garud, R. (2001). Organizational identification among virtual workers: The role of need for affiliation and perceived work-based social support. *Journal of Management*, *27*, 213–229.

Wolfe Morrison, E., & Robinson, S. L. (1997). When employees feel betrayed: A model of how psychological contract violation develops. *Academy of Management Review*, *22*(1), 226–256.

Chapter 7

The Context and Narrative of Outsourcing

Royston Morgan

Introduction

A critical review of outsourcing takes as a starting point that as a management practice it is a set of discourses embedded in a wider asymmetric power relationship. Managers, senior executives and consultants reproduce these relationships in an accepted and uncritical way. How the practice is executed and the ways that strategic intent can be expressed are embedded in a particular context where certain patterns of power constrain action and 'takes for granted the historical and political conditions under which managerial priorities are determined and enacted' (Alvesson & Wilmott, 2003). In this chapter we review outsourcing by looking at the narrative and discursive practice that arise during the outsourcing life cycle. We will tease apart the divergent meanings of groups of people and organizational members involved and how they make sense of what is going on, and from their various perspectives how they frame and interpret the events taking place. The purpose of this is to draw attention to the nature of organizations, that they are, in spite of management exhortations to the contrary, not uniform in the way they respond to an outsourcing. They consist of real people who need to legitimize and make sense of what is going on during periods of intense change. They act to preserve status and position in their organization; however, their modes of expression are constrained by an overarching management dialogue that excludes alternative ways of representation, regarding them as illegitimate. This results in a lacuna in our understanding of how organizations 'really' work and respond to change, and ignores the legitimate concerns of people in transition. We construct care for people in organizations as paternalism, a sign of management weakness, and a diversion from the technical and logical process that strategic management has created.

The Human Side of Outsourcing: Psychological Theory and Management Practice
Edited by Stephanie J. Morgan
Copyright © 2009 John Wiley & Sons Ltd.

From our standpoint the narrative of outsourcing can be seen as an extension of a familiar strategic management discourse and, as such, represents a restatement of an asymmetric power relation already existing within organizations. It is a systemic way of talking that allows only a limited view of the right way forward and 'silences and marginalizes others' (ibid.). An outsourcing life cycle is a political bidding process where managers jockey for position and power and attempt to gain some measure of ownership of the prevailing narratives, and in the meantime the people who are moving organizations are left as bystanders. In terms of informing practice we aim to draw out key lessons for practitioners, clients and outsourcers alike, restating the importance of justice, involvement and ethical practice, not only for purely instrumental reasons, but also as it is the right thing to do in an ethical society.

In presenting a critique of the various actors involved during an outsourcing we will first draw on some of the narratives present within an outsourcing cycle in the press, the literature and from our own research. We will point out some of the ubiquitous features of how outsourcing is positioned in the market, how words are shaped and by whom, show how these ways of talking can have a direct effect on how outsourcing is received by the people being outsourced and explain how these ways of talking ignore the legitimate concerns of the main parties involved in such a change process, the outsourcees and the survivors – those who are left behind when the train moves on.

A justification for taking this approach of looking at what people say is that we are often drawn as consultants and managers to examine the way we talk about a management phenomenon as a mechanism for a study of the process itself – using language as a resource for understanding the process. For example, teasing apart what a 'core competency' is as a result of someone using this form of words rather than asking why the person said this thing at all. What is this argument based on, why is it being used in this way, what is its purpose and does it stand up to scrutiny in the way it supports a strategic proposition? These are the important questions. I aim thus to turn the process around, in part by considering what we as managers and consultants are saying, how we sell the outsourcing proposition and what grounds and theories we draw on. What are the assumptions behind what is being said, what is being kept off the agenda, why do we ignore the people dimension and why, when things go wrong, are we locked into a conspiracy of silence?

We propose that this continued repetition of a particular way of constructing outsourcing restates a particular relationship of political and environmental conditions at this specific point in time and does not reflect any fundamental change in post industrial society structure. Outsourcing extends the already instrumental, short-term perspective of management practice in the UK and US. Configuring organizations globally is just an extension of the constant search for new ways of reducing labour cost – and scouring the world for cheap labour and then moving on when the advantage dissipates is a short-term business strategy that in the end leads nowhere. The people being outsourced are the ones at the receiving end of these practices, and the overriding instrumental nature of outsourcing practice focused on labour cost reduction influences their responses and imprints negative expectations of what is about to unfold – expectations that are usually realized.

Do People Matter at All?

Outsourcing is often presented as an objective, neutral and technical process focused on efficiency and opportunity for organizations and sometimes even an opportunity for the people being outsourced:

> Outsourcing is always an opportunity, never a threat … it's not about people taking other people's jobs – it's about freeing people up to maximize their potential. Lord Digby Jones conference address, 2007 cited in Barton (2007)

This speaker then goes on to tell the audience one of those quaint folk stories beloved of management gurus and presenters alike: 'as a child I used to walk past the Longbridge plant every day and saw the security people on the gate … then they were outsourced … and no longer part of the manufacturing industry [but] part of the service industry'. It is not my intention to criticize, but as unintentional as it was, the speaker here demonstrates that he has no idea at all of the disruption caused to a person being outsourced, with powerlessness, loss of identity and loss of worth as typical consequences:

> What I particularly didn't like was that I felt out of control, I didn't feel I had any say in the matter … there was no choice and that was quite worrying. (Female, staff member, private sector)

> [I] was basically OK with the idea … it was all the mucking about changing … it strips you emotionally. (Female, staff member, public sector)

Little account is made in management practice for the complexities of organizational life and precious little insight into how the people within organizations actually react to the dramatic changes about to unfold. What this means is the management of the people intimately involved in the outsourcing process; the people being transitioned are dealt with in a perfunctory manner in most cases. The people are not seen as important or, better said, as not relevant to the process, and even when they are included in the mix it is only to ensure their acquiescence and silent acceptance of the better judgement of those running an organization.

There may indeed be opportunities in an outsourcing but is it always so for the people involved and how do the people directly affected by an outsourcing make sense of what is going on? Why do managers present outsourcing to their people in a particular way, borrowing from a strategic discourse that they have had little part in shaping? Managers and outsourcing commentators restate aphorisms that have little practical value or relevance for the people affected and a whole industry has sprung up of outsourcers and consultants advising clients, all reiterating the same pattern of words and using the same rhetorical devices to persuade, cajole and sell the advantages. They restrict the frame of reference, exclude alternative explanations and define the subject area in order to manage the debate and thereby lead organizations in a controlled direction within their definition of what is organizational success. However, before we turn to addressing these discourses in more detail we must place them within their context, pointing to their emergent nature and the embeddedness of context (Alvesson & Willmott, 1996) and the constraints on managerial behaviour driven by the business environment. We will show how the prevailing practice in outsourcing, especially within the UK and US, extends a way of managing people that is rooted in history and is characterized by an instrumental short-term perspective. This practice carries over the legacy of poor ways of working with people, breaking their identity with, and loyalty to, their organizations, and as a result creates problems of managing change that will take years to repair.

The Context of Outsourcing

In a critical analysis the context of the issue is explored both to aid understanding and to set outsourcing as a practice in its historical context, thereby clarifying how it fits with, and is coherent with, other solutions to the longer-term environmental changes driving organizational structuring. Outsourcing and the way it is practised in North America and the UK is mediated and directed by a culture of short-termism. This short-term view can be traced back to a particular form of capitalism in the UK and US that favoured finance from the capital markets, rather than credit institutions as is the case in leading industrial nations such as Germany, France and Japan. Furthermore, growth by acquisition was favoured over organic growth and business development, which further emphasized a quick-win mentality. The dominance of the financial institutions and their focus on stock market price and shareholder value as critical indicators of success have heavily incentivized managers in the UK and US to focus on cost as a key performance measure and has institutionalized a short-term focus into management practice. There is little room for considered improvements; savings have to be delivered, shareholder value increased, usually within a short period of time or else management changes are engineered. This cultural backdrop, coupled with a rationalist scientist perspective dominant within the US and partly in the UK, has continued a 'Taylorist' management practice, a deskilling, codification and then expropriation of knowledge and skills by management and a focus on short-term financial results at the expense of almost everything else – a position quite different from the rest of Europe and the Far Eastern economies which the US and UK were trying to emulate. It is as if management strategists missed the point when they looked to the East for guidance to explain their own poor performance during the latter decades of the last century.

Outsourcing as a major business change has its origins (along with many other large-scale structuring initiatives) in a confluence of major political and economic contextual influences in the 1980s and early '90s. Well before this time, forms of offshoring were commonplace, especially in electronics manufacture where possession of English was not important for the assembly of mass-produced commodity products, and factories became dotted around the world in areas of cheap, disciplined labour. At that time the author was employed by a major European electronics company doing just that, finding ways to trim a few cents from the direct labour cost of production by shuffling manufacture between factories across the developing world. What occurred during this time was a radical shift in the global economic balance; while the UK and the US had been in long-term relative decline since the Second World War, this was accentuated by the emergence of strong, highly competitive newly industrialized nations (NICS) such as Japan that forced a rethink of corporate strategy.

The predominance of the strong economies in the East and the relative weakness in the major Western nations, coupled with the perceived vulnerability of major corporations to raiders and asset strippers, forced corporations to diversify and de-merge. In the competitive environment there was a view that the advantage enjoyed by the Eastern 'tiger' economies was in part a result of leaner techniques, especially in manufacturing, coupled with a focus on 'time based competition' (Stalk, 1988) and a cultural context that favoured innovation. The view that leaner techniques held the key for the way forward, forced through by financial institutions, led to a widespread pressure on companies to focus on core competencies, loosely defined as those parts of the business making money, and leaner organizational structure. This analysis of the reasons behind Eastern economic success was interpreted in a uniquely Western way such that success meant delaying, breaking up of large corporations and focusing on those aspects of the business that added value without consideration for the integrated nature of organizations. While in part true, the prevailing consensus excluded many of the contextual influences such as involvement, equitable hierarchies, collective social cohesion and a strongly favourable political context that underpinned the success story they were examining. Consequently there was an attempt to transplant the surface-level features of the Eastern experience without the deep structural context – and as a result many of these attempted transplants were rejected.

As a back-story to the above, also occurring during this period was a step change in the delivery of IT, especially around IT infrastructure and networking and the opening up of the real possibility of operating a globally networked corporation. This led to an explosion in growth in networked communications and outsourcing as a potential delivery mechanism for commodity services facilitated by the emerging global communication network. As a corollary of this, a growth of what are now the major outsource consultancies and companies was seen, driven in part by the refocusing of consultancies towards supporting the internal and external coordination tasks that were arising from this revolution (Clark & Fincham, 2002). Managing the new networked value chain became a prime task of organizations and, *inter alia*, the outsourcing consulting market was born.

A final piece of the puzzle that defined the context for the outsourcing revolution was the dominant political ideology during the late 1980s and '90s. Within the UK and US neoconservative liberals were in power, and they constructed their ideology around a non-interventionalist 'laissez faire' role for the state with a focus on individualism, with markets as the prime regulatory mechanism in terms of organizational behaviour. There was little sign of a coherent industrial policy with a belief that the free market could solve everything, whereas the rest of Europe was more circumspect, approaching the problem of competitiveness with a strong protectionist industrial policy with high levels of funding for innovation at its core and an approach that emphasized a multifaceted and well-trained workforce (Rothwell & Dodgson, 1992). The political ideology in the US and UK matched well with shifting economic terrain and acted to further emphasize the focus on efficiency (mainly cost based), and spilt over, especially in the UK, to include the public sector. This led to a wave of privatizations of nationally run organizations, the co-opting of private sector management recipes into the public sector without any regard for differing organizational culture, and a focus on cost savings right across industry and public sector alike. Downsizing, outsourcing and business process re-engineering (BPR) were all aspects of the same process and became watchwords of the day. This powerful political ideology, reinforced by the gurus and business school lecturers of the day, supported this process and brought into vogue a whole plethora of management theories and fads which offered to organizations a new management nirvana of excellence in such troubled times.

Outsourcing as Localized Practice

One feature of the outsourcing market, imprinted on the market as a consequence of the above forces, is the Anglo-Saxon-centric nature of the movement. More than 90 per cent of the outsourcing market in 2007 was driven within the US and UK. In Europe the UK is dominant, with pockets of interest in Germany, Holland and the Nordic region, all areas where the cultural norms of pragmatism and individualism play an important role. As well as consuming countries being culturally centred in the Anglo-Saxon world, provider countries are dominated by English-speaking nations, where English is a first language and there is a plentiful supply of cheap, well-qualified and disciplined personnel easily able to deliver the low-end call-centric services required. In short, the outsourcing market is focused on a limited area created within a favourable cultural and political context, and provision is centred on provider nations that are unified by a source of cheap and pliable labour who can speak a common language.

What this suggests is that the outsourcing market today owes its roots to, and is embedded in, a particular economic and political context that influences how organizational culture and practice in these areas has developed, and may play a part in explaining the differences in practice seen between national states in terms of outsourcing practice and strategy formulation. For example, the focus on individual freedoms (and minimizing the role of the state) and the lauding of 'free enterprise' as inherited within Anglo-Saxon business circles frame strategic practice in outsourcing. As a corollary of this, strategic planning and budgeting processes, embedded as they are within a national context, may be 'culturally peculiar' to Western managerial circles (Whittington, 1993) and the way outsourcing is practised can be seen as a localized issue.

Overall, the way outsourcing is carried out in the US and UK, and in particular the almost total disregard of the people aspects, is not peculiar to outsourcing at all but is an extension of an already prevailing business ethic that regards people as disposable assets and mere factors of production, and takes little account of the importance and influence of people – and as a result cannot manage the process well. Consider the focus on the individual and the rejection of political influence and how this extends to rhetorics such as 'employability' and 'opportunity'. This leaves the problem for the individual to solve and allows employers to abdicate responsibility for developing or training their people and preparing them for transitional change.

> In outsourcing it puts a lot of onus on the individual to carve up their own future, I think that is a bit callous. They have been sheltered if you like, within a company, and to suddenly cut them loose is unfair. (Manager, outsourcer)

> The world is in front of you, explore, when you have found it we will accommodate you ... have done a lot of exploring, lots of promised lands, but it is not just use me, the question is do they really want to use you? (Male, manager, private sector)

No account of wider societal or individual needs is made, training is discretionary and tightly focused, and people in the UK have a limited and narrow skill base making them particularly vulnerable when an outsourcing takes place. All this begs a question whether the aphorism that 'people are our most important asset' has any merit as a management slogan at all – as a staff member told us: 'All HR chit chat is about how people are [an] asset and really need to develop ... reality is they don't.'

The context and setting of outsourcing and how a particular management approach, mainly in the UK and US, interprets its implementation, set outsourcing as an institution and practice very firmly in the traditional short-term financial focus that still frames the way that managers, consultants and even outsourcees talk about what is happening. Outsourcing is a constrained dialogue, operating within bounds, with arguments posed in particular ways that trace their origins across 50 years of practice since the Second World War and could even sit comfortably in a Taylorist world from the turn of the last century. There is a consistency in the way we talk about the people affected by outsourcing, with the low wage, poor skill, and deskilling process that has been in vogue, especially in the UK, during this time: taking no account of their development and simplifying their jobs to the extent that innovation and agency are squeezed out and what remains is 'made fit' to place into the market. Having set the scene we now turn to a slightly different take on the context of outsourcing, moving in from the broad-scale contextual drivers to consider and challenge some of the traditional assumptions of managerial understanding of organizations and give indications of what this means for people during this transition.

Rational Management

The rational theory of management underpinning much of practice in the West assumes that organizations have common goals that are agreed and accepted by all and that a select group of managers have the sole rights to set these goals and sole ability to structure behaviour in ways that further the achievement of them. There is a belief that goals and objectives will be automatically shared right across the organization and that there exists a unitary perspective within an organization that frames all action. If this were in fact the case, organizational members would act in unison in promoting the achievement of organizational objectives in their own way, and resistance to change would be minimal or generated due to a lack of knowledge. A corollary of this perspective is that all forms of organizational resistance can be seen as a symptom of the breakdown of this assumed consensus and overt opposition as irrational behaviour. The management of resistance within such a framework of belief would consist (mainly) of communication protocols designed to align thinking and thus behaviours congruent to the overall direction by an educative process. This normative re-educative process is the cornerstone of most management and consulting practices to manage organizational behaviour. The mechanism being posed is that if only the people within the organization could understand what we are about then they would buy into the whole process.

The micro-political theory of organizations and more critical perspectives take a view that organizations are pluralistic by nature and can be seen as consisting of coalitions of competing groups that share and promote their own group goals over those of the organization. Change is judged and weighed against the extent to which group objectives are affected and, accordingly, individuals respond to change dependent on where they are in both hierarchical and role terms within an organization. The degree of resistance and how it is expressed depends on how individuals or groups judge the effects on them directly, and even though it is possible to ensure compliance and suppress open resistance, such assessments of the adverse effects of change can cause latent resistance issues, including moulding outsource outcomes that can potentially sabotage the change process during and after the transition.

As a result of this process, some groups promote their own goals, attempt to co-opt part of the agenda or propose alternative approaches that suit their own aims at the expense of the superordinate organizational objectives. In the process of judging a major change such as an outsourcing transition, different groups – accountants, line managers, IT staff and outsourcees – will judge the nature and impact of a change on how 'it' affects them at a group and individual level before considering higher-level organizational impacts: 'you move beyond the intellectual broad picture view to the about me concerns' (manager being outsourced). They act in their own self-interest and they resist. How their group's relative position in the organizational pecking order is changed and how their role and responsibilities are affected will be typical concerns for those staying as well as those being outsourced.

What this implies when communicating with those affected by an outsourcing is that the relevance of much of the standard fare is doubtful – producing 'slide-ware' is insufficient. People want their practical concerns to be addressed and are not attentive to higher-order exhortations to change. In summary, a more accurate way of representing an organization is in recognizing that there are diverse interests in organizations 'upholding a plurality in beliefs' (Young, 1989) and that the responses to change by people in an organization come first from an individual and group perspective. Events do not have a fixed meaning to all those affected, different views exist between groups and individuals and over time, and these must be accounted for if there is to be a chance of managing the consequences of change. This means that change management is particularly tricky and a multilevel comprehensive approach is required that addresses the real concerns of people and that can handle emotion and conflict – all of which are areas traditionally avoided in much of HR and change management practice.

A rational approach is adopted during many strategic management processes, with a focus on the technical dimension in order to objectify outsourcing, reduce the role of politics and present outsourcing as an objective process devoid of personality and subjective bias. In the same way as setting a budget is seen as a technical process, outsourcing is posed as a formulaic redistribution of resources across organizations and countries. Often organizations co-opt consultants to support this proposition by posing as role experts to objectively ratify the already agreed outcome and thereby attempt to defuse political action and resistance from those affected by the process by posing a false rationality. By this means, management attempts to pose the outsourcing decision as an end outcome of a rational process as they 'need and desire the mask of objectivity to cover the capriciousness and arbitrariness of corporate life' (Jackall, 1988, p. 144). The decision is driven by market forces outside the control of the organization with almost a suggestion that the whole thing is determined by forces that cannot be resisted and they as managers are following a rational and predetermined course.

This mode of thinking, which reduces the influence of political and human factors, poses outsourcing change as a rational re-educative process. The idea is that if the rationality behind the process can be laid out and explained to people – the market pressures, objectiveness of the financial figures etc. – then people, those being outsourced and their managers, will suddenly have an epiphany and see this great vision before them, ignore their own interests and buy into the whole process. Unfortunately, outsourcing as a practice is a deeply polarizing process, representing an auction of resources to bidders and interest groups, and inevitably becomes a source of conflict and resistance to be managed. Managers who ignore this political dimension do so at risk and must account for and manage power and political implications explicitly if outsourcing processes are to deliver value.

The classical managerial prescriptions that underpin much Western management practice offer a unitary perspective culturally centred within Western managerial theory assuming a normative and neutral approach – ignoring politics and alternative views such as cultural or critical perspectives. The development of an outsourcing strategy can be seen as an exercise of power owned by a restricted elite of managers that reproduces existing organizational relationships and is used in practice as a symbolic and hierarchical resource. It is legitimized by reference to accounting numbers and availability of global resources and underwritten as a vision by a host of consultants and market makers cloaking outsourcing with the accessible clothing of objectivity – removing subjectivity and posing neutral inevitability. This strategic discourse is used as a mechanism for proposing a de-political and objective organizational process. The 'scientific' rationale is achieved by reducing the outsourcing cycle to a technical process supported by a rigorous set of techniques, templates and contracts executed in a predetermined order to deliver a transition plan that flows logically from the business imperatives. However, as we now see, these technical processes are themselves constrained by the closed narratives available.

The Closed Narrative of Outsourcing

The practice and the benefits of outsourcing are described in a constrained way. Those managers and especially senior management who have an exclusive and privileged access to the formulation of strategy express the way forward within a confined area of known and acceptable discursive practices often articulated for them in the form of the accepted managerial recipe of the day. A particular business context is co-opted and used for their own ends in order to legitimize a specific definition of how a problem is to be solved, which excludes other definitions or potential ways forward. These alternative ideas are regarded as attacking not only the legitimacy of the strategy but the legitimacy of the managers themselves. A vision is constructed that offers senior executives an aspirational identity of the forward-looking and modern executive leading from the front at the cutting edge of management practice.

> Those organizations who are against the concept of outsourcing generally tend to be culturally paternal and protective, in the older less innovative industries and dominated by a particular inward-looking style of executive. (Morgan Chambers, 2001)

This type of argument implies that if you are against it then you are too protective of your employees and, if so, you will be unable to reap the benefits of outsourcing. Your people will be unable to grow and realize their potential and see the 'opportunities' because of the overbearing fatherly attentions of this old-fashioned company dominated by a particular inward-looking risk-adverse 'jobsworth' who is serving time until pushed out on early retirement. Paternalism as used here draws on a discourse that re-creates a masculine rhetoric and says something about the roles and responsibilities in a differential power relationship which in its execution re-creates a pattern of dominance and control. There is a presumption of authority that represents a societal-level expression of disciplinary power co-opted for use in an organizational setting. A managerial decision is made that must be accepted, even if it is against the wishes of personnel in the organization, as it is actually in their best interest. This is exactly what is wrong with the outsourcing process; it is in fact reproducing this masculine paternalistic way of working that the author above is railing against. The author lays before us a new management Shangri La, a way to be seen as innovative, forward-looking, strategic and in line for promotion, awards at outsourcing conferences, winners of CEO or CIO of the year, speaking to graduate schools and so on. Little wonder that real management ideas get little air time in the heads of people involved.

This argument is a start of an explanation of why, despite the weight of opinion in some quarters, internal bids and full cost assessment in an outsourcing process are virtually absent. An internal bid is where an internal organization has a chance to structure itself to achieve the benefits (Willcocks, Lacity, & Fitzgerald, 1997). Why also are other alternative structuring opportunities dismissed? The creation of an internal bid can enable an organization to pre-trim the fat in a failing functional group, enable an organization to gain understanding over the department they are thinking of outsourcing, and at the very least help them derive a baseline cost for future negotiations with potential suppliers. Yet despite the evident advantages, very few internal bids are undertaken.

Speaking up, proposing alternatives or appearing to oppose outsourcing by any group or individual is setting forth a view of the strategy that is not permitted as legitimate opposition and is construed as resistance. Certain forms of words or terms are not allowed; they are excluded as not forming part of the acceptable management agenda within an organization undertaking an outsourcing journey. Senior management have bought into an idea of a modern identity and aspirational growth, and cannot allow disturbance of this vision which reifies their position as sole arbiters of strategic direction. The strategic discourse of outsourcing restates their hegemony and re-creates the pattern of power and influence pre-existing in an organization. Neither Personnel nor IT managers dare put forward alternatives, such as an internal bid, as these ideas do not conform to the accepted vision of their superiors and could even be seen as a self-preservation response. Outsourcing, as we saw earlier, is sold as an issue to solve competitive pressures (core competency playing a strong legitimizing discursive role) or to gain access to other competences. Senior managers who have bought into this idea, and have internalized the approach, find their legitimization of the whole process challenged by alternatives which show that the main benefits could be achieved if managers did their jobs properly and managed the IT department or call centre more effectively. This in part is also an attribution of failure in a management process to an external agency by posing poor performance of a function within the firm's boundary as due not to inadequate performance internally (of managers) but to a fundamental organizational mismatch (not core to operations) that can only be solved by moving a part of the organization outside the organizational boundary to people who are posed as inherently more capable as it is their core competence. The solution of outsourcing, redefining the business boundary and getting rid of a problem, is the accepted position. The privileged access that senior management have to the strategy process enables managers to co-opt a particular context to legitimize a restricted definition of the solution to organizational problems but cannot stand outside of their own discourse as their ownership of the process restates their entanglement with it. Raising the idea of potentially delivering cost savings or access to better technology by an alternative mechanism interferes with this internalized discourse and is potentially at dissonance with the current definition of management success (at least in the West) of restructuring, cost reduction and focusing on core competences in order to achieve shareholder value. This is this vision that has been bought and is potentially disturbed should anyone come out with an idea that we could do all these good things anyway if we got our act together – which is in effect what an internal review and bid would do. The rhetoric of outsourcing is congruent with excellence as a discursive practice, non-outsourcers are paternalistic, old-fashioned and by implication failures, and senior managers see the construction of their own identity as 'strategic' in the context of this movement as more important than the performance of the business they manage.

This closed nature continues even after the transition, with senior managers, line managers and outsourcing consultants alike in almost a state of denial that there are problems, or so afraid of revealing issues that they are forced into a stunned silence. In our research on many occasions we have been told, 'do not quote me but' and the interviewee has gone on to describe in detail a transition almost completely destructive, with poor supplier performance, snake-oil consultant salesmen, no benefits achieved and poor relationships with those who have been outsourced to the extent that several of our respondents felt it had gone so badly that they feared for their own position and expected to be fired. This type of process, where acknowledging problems may endanger individual careers, is almost a form of groupthink where there is 'discursive closure' that excludes alternative perspectives and explanations and re-creates in the mind of the managers the justifications that started the whole process.

This extends to influence the way that organizations and wider society regard work organization and, more importantly, legitimizes the sole ownership rights of senior management to the broader strategic agenda. It silences critique not only from within an organization or industry, but also at a broader societal level, removing opposition politically and ensuring a favourable agenda for a continuing 'laissez faire' approach to industrial organization. In a more negative sense, contrary to the proclaimed benefits, a closed discourse actually shuts off innovation, closes off organizational access to the people who actually run the operation and denies the development of true competitive edge. The process can expose companies to the risk of substituting good business development and long-term market growth with short-term cost reduction gained by stripping out the essence of what can set a company apart from the crowd. We now take a closer look at the types of closed narratives and what they achieve for the people involved in outsourcing and show how these are used to construct a unified picture to enrol organizational members and control resistance.

The Currency of Power

The narratives of outsourcing – cost, core competence and flexibility – are used as a currency by the various actors and groups within organizations to enrol or affiliate to the strategic direction and to position themselves both during and after the outsourcing transition. Managers use outsourcing rhetoric to position themselves as competent and to counter ideas that they are not in control of the situation. This use of the correct form of words has more to do with job status, career and employment than the internalization of a management theory. We will consider how line managers and other key functional groups relate to senior management and in what way the exploitation of these narratives enables them to demonstrate both acquiescence and resistance. We close the section by showing in part that these dominant narratives enable a unified picture to be constructed to enrol other key stakeholders – the customers, shareholders and outsourcees – to both organizational and group objectives and reduce resistance.

The Ownership of Competence

The basis of outsourcing and the focus on labour cost is legitimized in the market by appeals to other benefits. As evidence emerges that simplistic savings on primary labour expense is counterbalanced by increased coordination cost (*ex post* transaction cost), especially for offshore contracts, the justification has switched to other potential benefits to maintain market interest. Other resources have been drawn on to justify outsourcing – flexibility, access to new technology and service improvement to name but three – but the most prevalent of justifications for outsourcing is the use of the rhetoric of 'focusing on core competences'. It appears in almost all the literature and management press and in many celebratory accounts of outsourcing deals – so what does focusing on a core competence mean?

The importance of focusing on core competences in the management mindset first arose from a debate about what constituted a firm and in what ways we could explain differential performance and thus the competitive advantage one had over another. One of the explanatory ideas that found resonance in a theoretical sense was the concept of 'core competences'. In this model of the firm, organizations can be considered to be a set of competences that collectively give an organization advantage and form the basis of what an organization is. Within this set of competences, certain of them, owing to a process of specialization or the acquisition of deep tacit knowledge, define an organization's advantage in the market over other competitors – they carry out a process or have knowledge that is qualitatively better than that of their rivals. In this explanation the differences between relative performances between organizations could in part be explained by the degree to which they focused on these core areas of competence, refined and honed them, and were not diverted by peripheral issues. A competence thus can be seen as something that an organization does well and, as a corollary, can add significant value to the end product or process being created. One take on the Japanese advantage, for example, was their 'ability to acquire, control, utilize and commodify technological knowledge ... and assimilate (these) over time is one of the core competencies of individual firms and the industry as a whole' (Harvey, Maclean, & Hayward, 2001,

p. 13) and this core competence underpinned much of the success of their electronics industry.

Prahalad and Hamel (1990) provided the necessary theoretical underpinning for this view. In their seminal work around organizational complexity their core thesis was that an organization can be seen as the binding together of a complex set of organizational abilities. They operationalized a core competence as collective knowledge about how to 'co-ordinate and integrate the multiple technologies required for product design and production' (Prahalad & Hamel, 1990).

They suggested quite clearly that organizational competence is to be found in the whole rather than in parts. This is a system perspective and collectively a set of internal processes may add up to a strategic competence that cannot be outsourced piecemeal. This makes a lot of sense if you think of the functional processes such as IT and logistics which in many organizations are tightly bound and collectively can have a profound effect on organizational performance and can form a core technological performance for many. The main issue with technological competences in particular are that they are accumulated and become 'assimilated over time', are summative and are very difficult to codify in order to outsource without losing the essence of what makes them core. Careless outsourcing can break the linkage between the areas and can cause a valuable competence to be dissipated. Furthermore, owing to the long time needed to really obtain high degrees of competence it will probably not be possible to reconstruct and could mean that such a competence is lost forever:

> You don't just move people out, you move the knowledge; (we) lost control of the people who understood how your business worked. The value of the business knowledge gets lost in companies … it is not valued. (Male manager)

> the other interesting thing that comes out of all this is that the skill set gets moved out of the company into the outsourcer and then they (the company) go and back-fill, they have been busily sort of quietly recruiting people that have got the skills to check on what we are doing basically. (Male outsourcee)

The same argument applies when disaggregating an organization into functionally separate entities without considering the consequences of how they work together. However, for the purpose of this argument the core competency aspect of organizations has been interpreted and co-opted by managers too simplistically, assuming that it is an objective and singular concept without understanding its embedded nature. Accordingly, they do not realize that taking an organization apart without appreciating the integrated nature of competence will lead to loss of competitive advantage. The focus on core competence in current practice misses its essential collective characteristic and as a result potentially destroys it.

Without knowing what an organization's competence is, outsourcing, far from being a philosopher's stone for 'turning assets into gold', risks doing the opposite in turning it into lead. Cultural orientation towards technology and the structuring of organizations vary greatly across countries and may underlie the differences in technology use and ultimately business competence. This factor alone may explain in a clearer way the differences in relative competitiveness rather than the core competence rhetoric. It is the nurturing and development of competence that is key, not the competence itself. The way that core competence is used to justify and then cut out part of the business with a view that we can then focus on that which is key to our survival presupposes that we know what is 'core' and that we have the wherewithal and ability to focus on and fine-tune 'it' from day one after the outsourcing.

Rhetoric in Use

The use of a focus on core competence or an increase in flexibility from an outsourcing appeals to mid-level managers or organizations with a mainly operational focus. We saw earlier that core competences as a concept is perhaps poorly understood but offers to mid-tier managers at least the opportunity to move the agenda on to other aspects of business performance. The movement of non-core assets and people 'off balance sheet' to an expense budget at reduced cost enables us to focus on our core competences, our added value services, as there is a least the possibility that we are no longer distracted by these troublesome issues we cannot manage. By some such story mid-tier managers can demonstrate to senior managers that they understand the strategic imperative while simultaneously positioning themselves for the new situation post outsourcing. Participation in a strategic discourse is something that managers aspirationally want to do but they rarely do so in practice, as 'seeing the big picture', 'strategic intent', 'focusing on core' are part of this discursive set that they need to articulate to gain trust and affiliation at senior levels. By such co-opting of selective parts of the rhetoric of outsourcing managers can position themselves and protect their status and position which can be eroded as a consequence of the change taking place. In a slightly different way, operational managers, by appeals to core competency, access to new technology and flexibility, can stake a claim to these benefits and begin the process of re-crafting a new position.

There is, however, a fundamental tension at the heart of the core competency debate and the ability of organizations to shift attention and resources towards focusing on 'it' as a strategy. This is the idea that competences are embedded in the organization in the processes, the culture and people within it; their tacit knowledge and experience make up the organization's core competency and as a consequence it is something the organization is, rather than has as an identifiable artefact we can control. Specialization and deep learning characterize a competence, expert performance can take years to realize and describing this at very high level as a 'marketing' or 'R&D' core competence does not do it justice. There is an assumption that it is something that top strategic management has an unchallenged right to access and can control and configure at will, and that is the real problem; with this type of deep characteristic its make-up can hardly be touched – and when control is applied it dissipates.

Stable systems or processes that are commodities can be outsourced provided we understand that the basis of their stability is due to the accumulated experience of operation (possibly over many years) and that this experience must be available in an ongoing manner or else there is a certainty of deterioration in performance:

> The actual performance of the people here has gone down a lot – level of service definitely much worse ... a big problem a few weeks ago, something seriously wrong, cost the customer a lot of money. I am convinced that in the old days (they) would not have shrugged their shoulders and said so-and-so will sort it out in the morning. (Male, manager)

In one of our research contacts in the finance sector the outsource company had a 'work at home Friday' policy that coincided with a year-end close. How the outsourcer got away with that we have no idea, but what it meant was that no one was present at the client site when the IT services failed during the close routines on a Friday and great panic broke out. The importance of the problem was completely lost on the supplier and all the staff refused to change to new work patterns. Stable services often have organizational slack which is stripped out to achieve promised savings. We are then relying on 'good will' from the supplier unless we have accounted for this in the contract. The basis of stability also includes the organizational learning that has been acquired in how to manage a crisis situation and recover quickly when things go wrong or to do that bit extra when the pressure is on and demonstrate good citizenship behaviours. It is these features of organizational behaviour that are most at risk of being lost by careless outsourcing of stable commodity services or when we ignore the people dimension in outsourcing.

A Discourse of Exclusion

In a cultural sense the use of the term 'non-core' immediately excludes that non-core group from the culture of the organization even if they continue to work at the same site doing the same tasks with the same people as before. The core competence rhetoric tells people to whom it is directed that they are peripheral to the organization's success. By such means they are moved from being a primary to a secondary labour resource in the minds of the organization and those remaining within it. People become detached from the original organization by a social process of exclusion and are initially left neither with the old company nor yet attached to the new company as socialization has yet to take place. They become almost suspended and liminal between the two organizations:

> When the letter comes you know you are to go and then there are the little grievances with the people staying. When you are going you also know they are staying. (Public, staff, female)

> We were the same people doing exactly the same job sat in the same building ... but were treated differently. (Private, staff, female)

The patterns of rules, vocabulary and ways of working deemed to be successful in solving organizational problems and into which people are inducted during the course of their work become redundant as a way of coping with the organizational demands. A whole new set of procedures has to be learnt and the culture of the receiving organization internalized. In order to do this the outsourcing company has to put in place processes to assimilate new people quite quickly – something which is sometimes neglected:

> Little socialization, no opportunities outlined, no increases in salary, all these things were dampened down ... we were told we had to do a job and we would do it in the same way as before. (Private, staff, male)

Particularly in the case where work is to be performed on the site of the client at the old location, socialization with the new company can be stunted or non-existent. Outsourcing organizations cannot wash their hands of this issue and state that this is the vendor problem alone. Notwithstanding the fact that morally the people have given sometimes years of loyal service, it is in the interests of the outsourcer to ensure that this process goes well and that the service provided does not suffer. A proper transition plan must be in place, jointly run by both HR organizations, to avoid long-term destructive behaviour or else there will be problems: 'the whole organization stinks, the management is crap, and I feel very badly about all this'.

After a while the first generation of outsourcees become replaced, assimilated or move on to be replaced by a new cohort grinding out the same job as before but without the attachment to the organization. These who have never worked for, nor had a link with, the client company do not share its culture or shared values and are not party to its goals. They provide service as per the contract and no more – cutting the delivery to meet the cost savings target and acting as a group apart. A core competence acts to draw a bound around a group and exclude others. It unifies them in a common purpose and enables people to identify with the organization. Stating that what they do is 'non-core' devalues their contribution and cuts right at the heart of their identity, breaking the identification with and loyalty to the organization – people need to feel valued and that they add value. Outsource vendors have to do much more to sell themselves as a potential employer to create in the minds of their new employees a vision of a new identity – and thus enable them to let go and move on. Sadly, there is little evidence that this lesson has been understood; we do not value people for their contribution but regard them as an expense, and having a wait-and-see attitude on behalf of the receiving organization is not helpful. Having considered core competences we now turn to some of these issues around cost, exploring how objective it really is, who owns the cost picture and why, and to what extent the allocation of cost is a political act used for making decisions within tight bounds that reduces people to cost elements and supports the depersonalization of the outsource process.

The Politics of Cost

For financial managers the key enrolment narrative is the one of cost reduction and is by far the most dominant theme in all areas of the outsourcing life cycle. Even when other justifications, such as the enabling of flexibility, are used, it is almost always predicated by 'this flexibility can lead to efficiency savings'. The whole basis of outsourcing, driven as it is by a short-term view of a company's performance in the market, forces a focus on cost reduction as a key criterion of organization success. The latter point is extended to the public sector in the UK where cost performance is seen as critical; this stark reality is tempered by appeals to the value-for-money rhetoric. Dominated as the agenda in the UK and US is by cost performance and the strong influence of short-term thinking, it is of little surprise that finance as a role has colonized the strategic agenda of outsourcing, with performance measured against the very narrow criterion of cost and calls for bottom-line results the key decision imperative.

This aspect of technically framing the outsourcing issue as an accounting exercise and the co-opting of accountants makes it possible to pose the question of outsourcing as an extension of common sense (Power, Laughlin, & Cooper, 2003) that does not require much elaboration or explanation. It supports a rational objective basis for a decision that is invulnerable to scrutiny and defines the reality within which the decision will be made. The approach disguises the fact that the allocation of cost elements is a political process – the budget itself is hostage to management fighting over allocation and in its final form freezes the political relationships at a point in time. The definition of cost is a contingent matter; what is included or excluded becomes a matter of debate and depends on what is required to support the decision or what will look good on the balance sheet. This accountancy process cloaks the decision making in an organization with the veneer of objectivity and symbolically ratifies the outsourcing process, and accordingly explains the main reasons for the use of the cost-reduction, bottom-line rhetoric to co-opt accountants as the dominant constituency in US and UK organizations. What this means is that, despite exhortations to the contrary, the purchase of outsourcing services is based on cost and when that advantage disappears – so will the market.

While it is still possible to generate savings as a result of transferring operations to lower-wage-cost areas, a process that was under way for many years in the consumer electronics industry, evidence from the field shows that increased coordination and compliance cost often outpaces the direct labour cost reductions. 'The little white lie of outsourcing is that it is a silver bullet guaranteed to lower costs … instead costs often increase and headaches multiply because outsourcing is under managed and poorly monitored' (Lepak & Snell, 1998, pp. 220–221). Our argument is that one of the reasons that outsourcing holds so many hidden costs is the refusal to consider human aspects. People manage negotiations and contracts and these *ex post* costs are often not clearly understood at the outset.

The make or buy option at the heart of the outsourcing decision is consistent with the resource-based view of the firm and transaction cost institutional economics (Williamson, 1981). The decision to place an activity under market governance is determined by whether a resource (people or process) is needed or is critical to the core process – whether it contributes to the added value of the product or service delivered. By such a process, moving cost to 'off balance sheet' defines the boundary of the firm. Congruent with this view is that the choice can be made when the costs of placing the resource into the market is cheaper than running or managing it internally – when the costs (risk, overhead as well as direct cost) are reduced by market placement. In the transaction cost economics model (ibid.) a make or buy decision, whether to keep a process in-house, under hierarchical governance, or under market governance, is made on the basis of where the costs of doing so are minimized. Fundamental to this model is that managers act to minimize transaction costs, in contrast to the profit-maximizing assumption of classical economics, and there is equilibrium between market and in-house management in cost terms at the boundary of the firm.

The decision whether to go to the market or keep in-house is informed by two behavioural assumptions: bounded rationality, which tells us that we always make decisions, sign contracts and negotiate based on a limited set of knowledge and cognitive resources we can assign to a problem; and opportunism. Opportunism constrains a perfect process as people and groups in organizations tend to pursue goals in their own interests over that of the super-ordinate organization's objectives. Williamson also describes the principles of organization design, hierarchical decomposition, divisional forms of structure, externality, which can be likened to the opportunism of vendors, and finally asset specificity. This latter principle is particularly important in technological transitions. Specificity results from the process of specialization of equipment, people or processes or the integration of different technologies and is an aspect of the development of core competence. When this happens, the assets or people have little value outside of the specific process concerned and cannot be used outside of the narrow confines of the specialization, and in governance terms are far better managed in-house.

In an outsourcing transition from the transaction cost perspective, managers act to source from the market those products or services where it is cheaper to carry them out in cost terms, be that onshore or offshore. Transaction cost includes all elements of the management, risk and overhead costs as well as the direct cost. The first checkpoint here is that most organizations in practice have no idea what a particular internal function, such as IT, actually costs them in order to be able to carry out a comparison with an external supplier. Furthermore, where costs are found, this is done by simply taking the budget or broad-brush cost pictures, which are often self-created realities supporting an already taken decision. This evident lack of knowledge and the unwillingness to find out, for both the internal costs and the available market offering, in a reasonably thorough way, point to the nature of bounded rationality and the closed nature of the strategic discourse. Managers may wish to act rationally in making a market choice but are constrained by imperfect knowledge and a constrained dialogue. Opportunism also plays a role here, as managers have favourite suppliers and close off alternative ways of structuring and achieving the same ends as it does not their suit personal objectives. This last point finds resonance with a management theory dominated at the highest levels by a singular perspective that does not permit alternative discourses to be aired.

Where technology changes and specificity reduces, such as in desktop utility or payroll services, we can imagine that this can be placed more efficiently with the market, especially in a shared service environment. But where there are issues in high specificity in areas where the embeddedness of IT and logistics or service delivery are apparent, these areas are best kept in-house.

Thus, even if we accept that a cost-based resource view of an organization offers an explanation of the structure of boundaries and how they change over time, it can be seen that the way in which this approach is applied in outsourcing can lead to problems, especially when considering the environmental changes and technological advances. What may have seemed logical at the start of an outsourcing can be quickly bypassed by advances and the process of specialization that occurs during the relationship. High-specificity asset and service provision created by a supplier may make it difficult to switch (or offer) to another client and in such a situation either party may be tempted to start opportunistic behaviour, demanding either steep cost reductions or price hikes – in the case of a total supply outsource the client would be at severe risk of such effects. A key to understanding the evolution of the relationship between supplier and client is this process of service specialization that occurs as the relationship deepens and the supplier learns how to provide the specific service demanded at the required service level. In pure transaction cost terms the specialization causes the specificity to increase and such a service should be brought back in-house, something that in practice is difficult to do.

The problem with an approach that says we outsource an asset or process to the market in those cases where the specificity is low (it is a commodity) and it is cheaper is that it pre-supposes that we have knowledge in our organizations of those factors: we know our cost structure well, we know what really makes it tick and we have some idea of what a core competence really is. Technological factors such as the cumulative nature of competence over time and the process of specialization may mean that some aspects of technology or highly specific process competences should never be outsourced. Understanding competence, true cost and the embeddedness of technology is a key task or else there is a real chance of fragmenting and losing the essence of what makes an organization successful. Lack of will, bounded rationality, imperfect knowledge and decisions made against deadlines set by people distant from the process, and a reliance on partner rhetoric cause the problem. It is even fanciful to believe that an outsourcing consultancy will be able to back-fill this knowledge given that the required information is embedded deep within the client organizational culture and business processes. The way around this is to be thorough in the appraisal of the organization and clarifying what the outsourcing is to achieve, together with a careful assessment of what the organization is about – a process unlikely given the short-term superficial approach demanded by key stakeholders.

The Capture of Value

Sourcing from the market means placing a service in the hands of a third-party provider on the basis that the service can be rendered more effectively by the third party and more efficiently in cost terms. A lot is heard in outsourcing discussions about partnership and other sorts of rhetoric intended to construct the deal in terms that minimize the purchaser–supplier divide, but basically both parties have to be clear in their own minds that a business relation is being formed that proposes an exchange of money for services rendered, and talk of partnerships serves to obfuscate this. We must be clear in understanding an outsourcing company's main objectives in taking on a major outsourcing contract. As well as gaining a margin on the services it is also to gain unfettered access to the market channel represented by the organization resources taken over, and be able to lock out effective competition and enjoy sole supplier rights.

This aspect of sole supplier increases the cost risk in two ways: first, from eliminating the internal departments currently carrying out the performance; and second, the normal competitors in the market are also closed out, which effectively negates the whole market mechanism. Furthermore, while it is possible to negotiate a good contract *ex ante*, the process of specialization exposes the client to *ex post* transaction cost risk, the policing of the contract that becomes necessary after a few years of contract execution. After a period of time the supplier of a service has a great advantage over the client: the original people move and the tacit knowledge and best practice become embedded on the supplier side while it is lost from the client operation. This process changes the balance of power between the organizations, favouring the supplier which can spread its own risk amongst other clients, something the outsource client cannot.

The rhetoric of partnership is the rhetoric of power and is about ensuring a continuous privileged access to the client's assets and locking out the opposition. It is wheeled out by account managers when there is even the slightest whiff of a competitive bid. Sole sourcing is about ownership and is the process of channel management, converting what was a complex selling process into a simple one – from a situation where all projects have to be bid and won to a simple selling process; while cheaper as far as the supplier is concerned, this carries with it the risk of sub-optimal procurement for the client in both cost and service performance. In summary, it is cheaper to win business from an existing locked-in client than having to go to the market constantly and win new business, so it is in the interests of the supplier to lock and subordinate a client and processes to the supplier's will, and this is the source of the partner rhetoric heard of so often in the market.

The Asset Management of People

'People are our most important asset' is a proclamation often given by companies even as they arrange an outsourcing contract – what do they mean by people as assets? What is surprising when looking at outsourcing as a management practice is the lack of any real attention to the main actors in the drama – the people being outsourced. Often they are introduced into the arena as 'functions', 'factors of production', 'non-core' to operations or working on 'non-added-value processes' in the eyes of the market. Outsourcing is presented as something that is happening to employees, to other groups of people, abstracted and made remote from our own experience of work. Little is said of them as people with aspirations and real needs to perform in society and to be of value to their employers. The way we talk about people in the context of outsourcing says a lot about how we as managers attempt to minimize their (our employees') humanity and reify them as objects that can be unemotionally moved from one company to another at our will and not seen as individuals – this making it possible for us to not confront our own fears of dealing with them as people. Often this is done to minimize the barriers to taking action against them. The choice of words and the context in which they are used enable managers to reduce their own affective responses and to objectify the people concerned by posing seemingly neutral ways of talking about those really affected by the decisions being made about them. Just as in war we speak of sneak attacks from an enemy as against pre-emptive strikes by our own forces, the outsourcing world is littered with such phrases in order to, as it were, reduce the moral impact of what we are attempting to do. We talk of downsizing/rightsizing against compulsory redundancies or dismissals, focusing on core competences as a nod to half-understood theory rather than getting rid of a function we do not know how to manage, and so on, all to mask what is going on, in an attempt to cloak poor management practice with a veneer of de-personalized objectivity. Outsourcing is something that happens to someone else – at least in the minds of presenters at conferences.

This is accentuated by the role played by finance in attaching cost to people and supports a traditional role of the subjugation of people as disposable items, removing the barriers between them and tangible assets like machines by using the same measure for both. Leading consulting practices, most of the big players coming from an audit or financial background, use their privileged access to the board to frame strategic issues in a way that is constrained by their own cultural and role vocabulary – the words of finance. In other words, problems and issues facing a company are always posed internally by powerful role groups and by the support they call in to advise them in financial balance sheet terms, framing the problem with a very narrow range of language with the singular purpose of justification. There are also other aspects at play, as the need for large consultancies to gain access to boards that can justify and agree their large fees forces them to use language in a particular way and adapt the structuring of problems to match a hidden but agreed business language to maintain the client relationship. Consultants in such a context act to create and consume their own advice. It is as if leading members of organizations, stock market advisers and consultants are discussing this strategic issue using only a limited set of the business language available, constrained by the overall logic of the prevailing strategic environment that permits a single solution. But by such means, problems and advice offered are constrained in terms that the client understands and wishes to hear, reducing the issue of outsourcing for both consultant and client alike to one of a purely technical nature, objectified by financial figures and suitably sanitized of the people involved.

Disciplinary HR and the Management of Resistance

To label people as a resource connotes a positive feeling of nurturing and growth. HRM functions in order to advance a particular notion of personal growth, improved opportunities and entrepreneurial individualism prevalent in Western industrial circles. The power exercised by HRM is not via explicit authoritative or line control but unobtrusively by the creation of controls and procedures (such as the disciplinary manual or contract of employment) and the management of the disciplinary organization. The ways in which HRM is practised in an institutional context ensure that the dominant group's definition of reality becomes the accepted and unchallenged norm and way of working. One of HRM's roles is to disable resistance, reduce the potential for meaningful discussion and ensure that alternative approaches and innovation are stillborn – this reduces the voice of organizational stakeholders and does not give outsourcees and managers any liberty to pose alternative measures of success. Their role is to moderate their own responses and discipline themselves within narrow bounds in an outsourcing cycle. Thus they are the arbiters in a disciplinary organization and restate their own subordination by an affirmation of the rhetoric of outsourcing. The mainstream discursive practice around outsourcing is thus used as a powerful rhetorical device used to frame issues and enhances a particular instrumental view of organizational behaviour, constraining meaning within very narrow bounds.

HRM has traditionally had a subordinate role in organizations and in practice owns no substantive part of the strategic discourse. In other times 'personnel management' was seen as unreliable and not trusted as a senior management partner, sometimes appearing to be overly sympathetic to personnel concerns – brought about perhaps by their daily interactions with unions and personnel. In order to gain position HR professionals will often co-opt the dominant rhetoric of the day, gaining access to the seats of power in an organization, demonstrating affiliation and commercial understanding, appearing integrated with senior management (Legg, 1994) and attempting to gain lost trust. This acts to exclude any alternative approaches and means that transitional issues are ineffectively managed. People in organizations (especially in the public sector) still regard HR as their interface into the organization. Pensions, holidays and the possible future roles and jobs that outsourcees may be forced to take are concerns that must be addressed, and the domain expertise is expected to reside within the HRM function. However, in order to maintain affiliation, answers to these types of questions are framed in a particular way, supporting the overall direction and acting to minimize conflict and resistance. So opportunities for growth, to work elsewhere, are typical ways of justifying the outsourcing transition. In such a way a particular meaning is transmitted and maintained and opposition disciplined. But as a corollary, stock answers are given to people being outsourced that in no way satisfy their needs and the answers are not to be had from the receiving HRM function either: 'by and large HR people have got their hearts in the right place, but the follow through is not there – they make the right noises to win the bid but actually no one seems to care much'.

This aspect of the need to maintain and internalize a strategic discourse to maintain position and to deliver compliance frames the way they have to act with those being let go and those remaining; an advocate's role is out of bounds and is replaced by the need to manage meaning. This means that in many of the outsourcing deals we reviewed, the potentially important role of HR was stunted and ill formed. In an outsourcing, those being outsourced (or even let go) need personally relevant timely support to cope with and make sense of what is going on – a need that should be well provided for by HR but in many cases they are disconnected. As our research revealed, there is limited HR engagement, perfunctory performance and restricted discourse which demonstrated not only poor appreciation of the human side of outsourcing but the subordinate role of HR in this process – reduced to reiteration of core competence aphorisms and 'it will be all right on the night' epithets.

The Full Circle

Outsourcing in its many guises is a form of work structuring that is here to stay and we must learn how to do it well. We have argued that it is not anything really new in terms of management practice but it can be seen as just an extension of the general trend towards globalization and the fragmentation of work experience. The way outsourcing is practised forms part of a dominant management discourse in the Western economies that is based around an instrumental short-term focus where a rational and unitary practice is bound by a common vocabulary that takes no account of the political dynamics of organizations and the people aspects of outsourcing.

This discourse is a set of rhetorics that allows the different groups of players within an organization to exercise a knowledge power relationship with each other as they compete to gain hegemony or to demonstrate affiliation. The concept is not fixed either, as organizational members oscillate or switch between the various forms of interpretation of what is going on dependent on what suits them at a particular moment in time. The purpose of the rhetorics of cost, focus on core competence or flexibility is to unify management and to present a common front to those whom they need to control. A barrier to opposition is constructed of so-called objective truth supported symbolically by an accounting vision ratified by cost pictures that are apparently invulnerable to scrutiny. On the downside, the way that outsourcing is practised excludes alternative solutions, as the creation and internalization of a particular truth of business excellence precludes other, just as relevant, ways of improving performance. It allows managers to attribute organizational failings outside of their own practice and onto the people being outsourced, suggesting that their work is of lesser value, non-core and thus suitable for outplacement by this discourse of exclusion.

Senior managers, managers, outsourcing vendors and consultants alike are bound together in a web of a particular business truth that constrains the practice of outsourcing along instrumental lines. The outsourcing press, the literature and practitioners re-create and consume a particular form of discourse that constantly restates a way of working that de-personalizes the people aspects, removes emotion and reduces people to factors of production, cost elements and resources to be deployed at will. This closure acts to block access to the innovation available in organizations and reduces the ability to manage people effectively through the outsourcing transition. As practitioners we need to see through our self-constructed barriers to explore the realities of the issues around competitive advantage and competence and use the market wisely when we need to. Thinking through the strategic aspects and the process of outsourcing is a key task. Putting together a managed process to decide on the direction and then engaging all the stakeholders to shape the direction is necessary – and when we need to manage the outsourcing of people we must do so ethically.

It is surprising how few companies realize that when the dust has settled and the deal done the people involved will still be working for the organization in some capacity. It is simply not true that you can 'wash your hands' of your people as it is 'someone else's problem now'. These are the people, whether survivors or outsourced, who will greet your internal and external customers every day of the week in the real moments of truth in customer relationships. You disturb their loyalty or negate their expertise of how the business really runs at risk. Compliance can always be achieved but latent resistance is not avoided with an instrumental approach and there will come a time for payback – something that several major outsource clients have found to their cost. The key words are not 'communicate, communicate, communicate' but 'involvement, involvement, involvement'. People will respect managers who demonstrate fair and equitable practice and spell it out as it is – evidence shows that resistance is reduced when people are treated fairly. Managing people openly and with ethical practice has clear business logic behind it, and so doing puts people management at the heart of outsourcing and as a corollary increases the chances of its success.

References

Alvesson, M., & Willmott, H. (1996). *Making sense of management: A critical introduction.* London: Sage.

Alvesson, M., & Wilmott, H. (2003). *Studying management critically.* London: Sage.

Barton, A. (2007). Outsourcing: UK ahead of game. *Supply Management*, 1 November.

Clark, T., & Fincham, R. (2002). *Critical consulting – new perspectives on the management advice industry.* Oxford: Blackwell.

Harvey, C., Maclean, M., & Hayward, A. (2001). From knowledge dependence to knowledge creation: Industrial growth and the technological advance of the Japanese electronics industry. *Journal of Industrial History*, 4(2), 1–23.

Jackall, R. (1988). *Moral mazes: The world of corporate managers.* New York: Oxford University Press.

Legg, K. (1994). *On knowledge, business consultants and the selling of TQM.* Lancaster: University of Lancaster.

Lepak, D., & Snell, S. A. (1998). Virtual HR: Strategic human resource management in the 21st century. *Human Resource Management Review*, 8(3), 215–234.

Morgan Chambers. (2001). *Outsourcing in the FTSE 100: The definitive study. Episode One: The UK PLC.* CW360.com

Power, M., Laughlin, R., & Cooper, D. (2003). Accounting and critical theory. In M. Alvesson & H. Willmott (Eds.), *Studying management critically* (pp. 132–156). London: Sage.

Prahalad, C. K., & Hamel, G. (1990). The core competence of the corporation. *Harvard Business Review*, May–June, 79–91.

Rothwell, R., & Dodgson, M. (1992). European technological policy evolution: Convergence towards SMEs and regional technological transfer. *Technovation*, 12(4), 223–238.

Stalk, G. (1988). Time – the next source of competitive advantage. In D. Mercer (Ed.), *Managing the external environment* (pp. 215–232). Newbury Park, CA: Sage.

Whittington, R. (1993). *What is strategy and does it matter?* London: Routledge.

Willcocks, L., Lacity, M., & Fitzgerald, G. (1997). IT outsourcing in Europe and the USA: Assessment issues. In L. Wilcocks, D. Feeny, & G. Islei (Eds.), *Managing IT as a strategic resource* (pp. 306–338). London: McGraw-Hill.

Williamson, O. E. (1981). The modern corporation: Origins, evolution, attributes. *Journal of Economic Literature*, 19, 1537–1568.

Young, E. (1989). On the naming of the rose: Interests and multiple meanings as elements of organizational culture. *Organizational Studies*, 10(2), 187–206.

Chapter 8

Cultural Differences in Outsourcing

Brigitte Cobb

Introduction

Research on outsourcing has been mostly concerned with the commercial aspects of the change rather than the human dimension. Where research has been done on the human side of outsourcing, it has tended to be around the impact of outsourcing on individuals themselves and the psychological issues of losing their employment or being transferred to an outsourcer. The day-to-day experiences of staff performing work in an environment spanning national or organizational cultures have not been widely examined. This chapter discusses theory and concepts which can help us understand how cultural differences between firms and nations can be best managed and negotiated at the onset and most importantly during the life of the outsource contract.

What Is Meant by Culture?

The first thing to do when writing about culture, with the aim of offering practical advice on how potential impact can be mitigated and managed, is to ensure that the reader has a very good understanding of what is actually meant by the concept, and is in a position to relate what is being proposed and discussed to his or her experience. In fact, this is actually true of any text where culture is discussed, whether theoretical or practical, and most research papers will start by stating the

The Human Side of Outsourcing: Psychological Theory and Management Practice
Edited by Stephanie J. Morgan
Copyright © 2009 John Wiley & Sons Ltd.

lack of an agreed definition in academic circles and will set the scene as to what they mean in the context of their paper. We will therefore start by providing a generic definition of culture illustrated by everyday examples which we will then look to develop further and position in the context of outsourcing.

For the purpose of this chapter, culture, whether national, organizational or professional, is understood to be the values and assumptions shared by a group of individuals bound by their belonging to a nation, an organization or a profession – a sort of secret code guiding what behaviours will be acceptable or 'the way we do things around here'. In essence, culture is a system including values, norms and priorities that are common to the members of a nation and will guide how they act with people from their own country; a 'design for living' for a people (Hofstede, 1991; Kroeber & Kluckhohn 1952). Although the previous sentence refers to national culture, the same is true of organizational culture, and definitions found in the literature all gravitate towards the idea of shared group meaning and of the 'glue that holds an organization together' (Smircich, 1983). In the case of professional culture, not much attention has been paid to the concept by scholars; however; when discussed, it is defined in a similar manner but refers to shared norms and values for a particular profession.

Where does culture come from and how is culture created? Many researchers (Hofstede, 1991; Berger & Luckmann, 1967; Terpstra & David, 1991) believe that national culture is learnt from a person's first social interactions with their family, with friends and teachers at school and at play. For example, the rules associated with table manners in English society are taught in early life by the parents to their children who are expected to hold the knife in their right hand and the fork in their left hand all the way through the meal, without putting the cutlery down or switching from hand to hand. There is even a particular movement required for peas which must be slipped onto the back of the fork. This complex set of rules is alien to most North Americans, who will switch their knife and fork around depending on whether they are eating or cutting, will put the knife down when eating and more than likely sweep the peas with the fork if not stab them. Should a North American child find their way to an English table, they would undoubtedly get some frowns and be considered lacking in manners, while the English child attending a meal with an American family would probably raise a few smiles. In any case, whatever the reaction may be, neither child would be displaying the 'culturally accepted' behaviour and might, at the extreme, stand to be 'rejected' by the group.

In a similar fashion to national culture, the norms that bind organizational culture and professional culture will also be 'learnt'; the difference is likely to be on how strongly these will guide the behaviours or expectations of individuals, which, in our opinion, will largely depend on the length of time an individual has worked for a particular organization or practised their profession, and also on their personality type, most specifically their adaptability and flexibility, as in some cases individuals will be very quick to adapt to a new organization, particularly if they have selected one that is a good fit with their personal values. To illustrate this point and to gain a better understanding of some dimensions of organizational culture that may differ from company to company, consider how decisions are made (by whom and at what level), attitude to risk (risk aversion or risk takers), where power comes from (senior management or experts), who the heroes are, how 'errors' are viewed (as ways to learn or with deep frowns), what the symbols are (the company car, the last coat on the rack) and what myths and legends tend to stick around for a long time.

In the case of professional culture, norms and values will have been learnt during professional education and training and through interactions with other members of the profession (Van Maanen & Barley, 1984; Jordan, 1990). An example would be the legal profession where focus is on attention to detail, on assessing risk and developing mitigation against it, which often creates risk aversion, a critical mind and challenges when there is a need to rise above the detail and make a decision based on trust rather than analysis.

The aspects discussed above do not form a comprehensive list and there are models of cultural dimensions available, providing a framework for understanding the differences between nations, organizations or professions. The models from Hall (1976), Hofstede (1980, 1991) and Handy (1999) are amongst the better known. These models are, however, criticized and Straub, Loch, Evaristo, Karahanna, and Srite (2002) discuss the difficulty in using such high-level dimensions in organizational research and analysis because individuals from the same country will undoubtedly also be influenced by the culture of the various sub-groups to which they belong; for example, their membership in professional, organizational, ethnic, religious and other sub-groups, making the requirement for analysis highly multidimensional. In our opinion, models such as Hofstede's and Handy's are useful when wanting to start bringing to the fore the characteristics of a culture but should not be considered comprehensive and one should always be ready to build upon them, using one's own judgement and analytical skills.

One last point to make about culture is that once it is learnt, it becomes unconscious and will be invisible to the uninitiated. The consequences are that an organization may have a written-down strategy, mission statement, operational policies and a clear hierarchy to guide their direction and decisions but none of this will be relevant if all the 'hidden' elements of culture (the politics, group dynamics, attitudes and behaviours) are unsupportive. In reality, it is the culture rather than the written policies and standards that will truly define the organization. The consequences of this are far-reaching for any initiative that involves a group coming into contact with a culture different from its own. Firstly, it means a period of adaptation and secondly, a high possibility for conflict and confusion, which in business terms can be translated as a time of low productivity.

Overview of the Impact of Culture Types on Outsourcing

Bearing the above definitions and examples in mind, we can now start to look at how the different types of culture may impact outsourcing, which as a business model presents the complexity of disparate groups with their particular 'ways of doing things' coming together to deliver a product or, more and more these days, a service. These will be groups of individuals who are likely to have spent little time getting to know each other before they start interacting (depending on the model) and will be burdened with high expectations: high productivity at a lower cost or the provision of specialist skills. So that the reader can form a good idea of what is meant by outsourcing models, we will first give a high-level view of the impact of culture types on different outsourcing models. Specific dimensions of culture will be considered later as these apply across culture types and across models.

The first type of culture and the one that automatically springs to mind when thinking of the impact of cultural differences is that of national culture. This type of culture will come into play in the model referred to as business process offshoring. The practice of offshoring, that is, of producing goods in a country different from the home country, is not new and most people will remember the shift of automobile production from North America to Japan in the 1980s and several other waves in sectors such as steel, shipbuilding, textiles and consumer goods. What is different in the most recent wave of offshoring is that now companies are not offshoring material goods, they are offshoring services. Carmel and Tija (2005) identifies six factors responsible for the latest offshoring wave: globalization of trade in services, business-friendly climate, wage differentials, growth of offshore labour pool, lower telecommunication costs and software commoditization. What this means in practice is that policies more favourable towards doing business across borders, coupled with technological advances (mainly cheap networks) and the availability of an educated and cheap resource pool, have led to companies looking for ever-lower production costs and to sending more and more process or service-type work offshore. What originally started out as the offshoring of IT services (e.g. software development and support) quickly moved to mean more and more services (e.g. HR, accounting and call centres), referred to as IT-enabled services, and even more recently the offshoring of knowledge-type activities (e.g. research and legal support). According to IDC (a well-known market research firm), the worldwide market for offshore outsourcing will reach US$70 billion by 2008.

For the purpose of our first example, we will refer to a company located in England (EnglishCo) which has entered into an outsourcing contract with a company located in India (IndiaCo). In this case, the cultural differences will come into play when the employees from EnglishCo liaise with the employees from IndiaCo, for example providing business requirements for the development of a particular piece of software or monitoring the delivery of a project or task. The staff from EnglishCo and the staff from IndiaCo will have attitudes, expectations and assumptions based on what is socially acceptable in their own culture; the challenges will come when there are differences and these are not made explicit and visible – as a reminder, culture is largely unconscious. For example, one culture may see speaking up on a conference call as the way to get things done and expressing needs and wants, while another culture may see speaking up as rude and may prefer to wait for the call leader to ask them to speak. It is easy to see how the group waiting to be called to speak may end up saying very little if the call leader is unaware of this practice and how some critical questions may remain unanswered or conflict and confusion may ensue. Cultural differences related to someone's country of origin may affect both sides' ability to make joint decisions, their understanding of the requirements and therefore the quality of delivery, and their ability to work together and negotiate and agree solutions, leading potentially to reduced productivity, late delivery and even rework. The challenges will be further compounded by the complexity of the task and the number of interactions required to complete it (the number of times both sides will need to come together to achieve the end goal). Taken in the context of the main goal of outsourcing, which is usually around cost savings, it is easy to see how culture may impact an organization's ability to reap the promised benefits and even add costs. This is probably why many outsourcing contracts are said to have not yielded the expected benefits and even to have added cost (Deloitte, 2005).

The second type of culture to consider is organizational culture. The impact of organizational culture may exist in isolation but may also compound the challenges in the above example if the culture of EnglishCo is very different from that of IndiaCo. For our next example, we will look at two organizations operating in the same country in order to reduce the number of variables. To illustrate the challenges that organizational culture may bring to the outsourcing model, we will look at OldCo, a company with a hierarchical structure where decisions are made after careful consideration by a limited number of high-ranking individuals. Consider Tom, a member of staff from the IT Department of OldCo, who is transferred to NewCo under TUPE. NewCo is a specialist IT firm structured mostly in project teams where decisions are made by the teams and will only be escalated to senior management when there is a serious impact on budget or resources, or when the team cannot agree a way forward. How would Tom learn how decisions are made? How would Tom be perceived by his new colleagues when he sits and waits for senior managers to make a decision? How comfortable would Tom feel moving from a highly structured to a more flexible environment? What if Tom has been with OldCo for 10 years? What if OldCo has transferred 50 people like Tom across to NewCo? It is easy to see the challenges that the different cultures will create, particularly if a number of staff are transferred together rather than one individual. If only Tom comes across, once surrounded by new ways of behaving he may adapt quite quickly, but if 50 individuals transfer then it will take longer to adapt as they will probably keep the old ways of working alive within their group, either because this is more comfortable or simply because they still have an allegiance to OldCo. The culture clash between the staff that transfer across and the staff in NewCo will affect productivity, either because of confusion of expectations or because of loss of motivation, but also could hinder decision making and the employees' ability to form relationships with their new colleagues.

The third type of culture to look at is professional culture. In this case, the impact may be positive and may actually lessen the cultural differences brought by nation or organization. Some researchers argue that the professional culture of certain employees mitigates national differences (Cougar, Adelsberger, Borovits, Zviran, & Motiwalla, 1990). If we go back to our offshoring example, a group of software developers from the US and a group of software developers from India may actually interact well, as they are likely to share the same technical language and similar ways of approaching tasks (software development methodologies work across borders). Cougar et al. found that they will share other values, for example a desire to work on their own rather than to have a high level of social interaction. All of which will potentially lessen the impact of organizational and national culture.

What Is the Definition of Success in the Context of Culture, Outsourcing and Business?

Now that we have a good understanding of what constitutes culture and a high-level summary has been provided to illustrate how culture impacts outsourcing, let's look at some key performance indicators of commercial success and how these can be adversely impacted by culture in an outsourcing arrangement.

In order to succeed in business, a company must be in a position to offer the type of experience that its customers will want to re-create. Several studies aimed at uncovering what characteristics yield the highest degree of customer satisfaction and brand loyalty found employee behaviour to be key (McEwan & Buckingham, 2001) and that the 'person-to-person experience' was twice as important in driving satisfaction as any other factor (Julian, 2006). It is interesting to consider this performance indicator in the context of outsourcing arrangements where there is a clash of national cultures and of organizational cultures. Two case studies are presented below to illustrate this point.

In the first case study, Bank X, in an effort to cut cost and follow the trend, outsources its UK customer support function to a call centre in India. Bank X prides itself on being the 'local' bank, on providing a service that feels like it is coming from a small company with offices in the neighbourhood rather than from a large global corporation. This is the experience it wishes its customers to have and is part of the bank's branding. It is not clear what training the Indian customer advisers go through, but one customer from Bank X based in London reported that when they put a call through and asked the adviser whether they should present themselves to the Jubilee Place branch, the adviser did not know what they were asking. The customer then clarified by stating 'Jubilee Place in Docklands', which also drew a blank. In our opinion, this example illustrates that the customer adviser was lacking in local knowledge, which contradicted the brand value of being a 'local' bank and adversely impacted the experience of the customer. It was certainly obvious to our customer that they were not phoning someone local. Clearly, in this case, training on geography could have helped; however, it may not be possible to train on more subtle aspects of culture which could also be picked up by customers.

In the second case, imagine a hospital where the aim is to make people healthy and their experience during recovery as comfortable as possible. Now consider what happens when senior management of the hospital outsources the catering function to a provider that is only concerned with cutting cost and providing food as cheaply as possible. This happened in an NHS hospital where one of our interviewees worked. They told us that the outsourcing deal was not successful and that in the end the contract was cancelled and renewed with another food provider who this time had similar values. Although the aim of the second contract remained to cut cost, the values of the provider included the notion of 'health' and the new meals were aligned with what one would expect to eat in order to get better. It is also important to look at the experience of the staff transferred under TUPE in the first contract. The values of the employees were very much centred on providing good care to the patients, these values having been imparted by their first employer. The staff were very unhappy in the first transfer, as the focus on cheap food prevented them from delivering the service they believed in. This contributed to the failure of the contract, with conflict erupting on a regular basis. The employees are much happier now that they work for the second provider where their, the provider's and the client's values are aligned.

In addition to creating the experience sought by customers, an organization must also consistently meet their expectations. According to Mosley (2007), 'consistency' is a key component of successful brand management. In our opinion, achieving this goal is not easy at the best of times but will be even more difficult to attain if an organization has entered into one or several outsource contracts. The complexity brought by the outsourcing element lies with ensuring that all services are 'joined up' – in essence, that the customer is getting the level of service they expect from the start to the end of their interaction with the company and that this occurs irrespective of whether they are dealing with the organization itself or with the outsource provider.

One of our interviewees related an experience which illustrates this point quite well and demonstrates not only a break of service but also what we could call a break in 'culture'. Having been recently involved in a car accident, our interviewee raised a claim with their car insurer, phoning during the day. They were put through to a call centre in the north of England and received what they considered a good service. A day later, they placed a follow-up call to the company to raise a query on their claim, this time during the evening. As this was after six o'clock in the evening, they were put through to a call centre offshore. Our interviewee reported that although the agent was polite and helpful, it felt as if they were dealing with 'a different organization'. The service our interviewee received was inefficient: the agent's knowledge was lacking and they had to refer to a superior several times, they did not have access to the information they required and it took quite a while and some discussion for the customer to be in a position to complete the transaction. The interviewee reported that they did not enjoy their experience and became worried that the second call centre was not truly part of the organization they had paid to provide them with a service.

Competitive advantage and performance also come from organizations delivering their services or products to market on time, on budget and according to certain specifications. It is very common nowadays for a part of the production process of a service or a product to be the responsibility of an outsource provider, creating a dependency. In *Offshoring Information Technology* (2005), Carmel and Tija discuss the impact of the low-context/high-context cultural difference on the deadlines set for two 8-month-long software development projects. The case study, entitled 'Why the project was late: cultural miscommunication in an India-American collaboration', relates the experience of two teams: the American team leading the project and the team of their Indian outsource provider. The low-context cultural dimension was first identified by Hall (1966) and describes the predisposition of a culture, in this case the American culture, to be direct and openly state their needs and expectations (low-context) versus a very different approach in the Indian culture, where the tendency is to be implicit and to assume that the American partner will read between the lines (high-context). The story, in essence, relates how the Indian team had stressed the fact that they were working very hard to meet deadlines, detailing in several emails the long hours spent on the project, and how the American team had assumed that since no direct request was made for additional resources, all must be well and the project must be on track. As it turned out, both projects encountered significant delays and it took a while for the American team to realize that there was an issue.

The low-context/high-context dimension is part of a culture model designed by Hofstede (1991) and is also referred to as a cultural orientation. Hofstede (1991) and Hall (1966) were the first to attempt to define cultural orientations. Table 8.1 presents a brief overview of some cultural orientations that could also have an impact on a company's performance in the context of outsourcing (as discussed previously, culture models are useful but should not be considered comprehensive).

Gurung and Prater (2006), in one of the rare studies on IT outsourcing, virtual teams and culture, say that managing cultural differences becomes a key factor for successful outsourcing and by extension commercial success. They specify that although the importance of culture is widely cited in the information systems literature and it has been noted that managing virtual teams across culture is a daunting task, there has been few efforts to include the cultural dimension to research. When studies mention culture, they fail to stress its importance. Anawati and Craig (2006) describe culture as one of the key issues of modern project management as well as a significant challenge for virtual teams (although both parties in the outsourced arrangement may not be considered to be 'teams', the forces at play are similar). They postulate that the greater the cultural distance between two countries, the more difficult it will be to interface. When studying the impact of technology, Zack (1993) found that the more shared context between the members of the team, the less important the richness of the technology. What this proposes for the purpose of this chapter is that the more cultural differences (and the less shared context), the richer the technology will need to be to support communication; less in common makes communication more difficult and better technological support is required to compensate. This idea will be explored later on when we discuss how cultural challenges can be best mitigated.

We have looked at some customer-related aspects of commercial success: being able to create brand loyalty, consistently meeting customers' expectations or delivering services on time; but what about less tangible 'value-add' differentiators such as an organization's ability to learn from its mistakes, a propensity for continuous

Table 8.1 Selected cultural dimensions and potential areas of impact

Dimensions	Definition	Areas of impact
Power orientation	High – autocratic style of management	High – unlikely to disagree with managers, will be less direct in discussions, more comfortable with autocratic decision-making styles
	Low – participatory and consultative style of management	Low – will want to be involved in decisions, will be direct in discussions which could be misconstrued arrogance, will expect others to be direct
Individualism vs. collectivism	Individualism – focused on the needs of the individual	Individualism – less focus on relationships, assertive, will require high level of personal freedom
	Collectivism – focused on the needs of the group	Collectivism – will put the group first, will expect time off for family events, will put a lot of effort into developing relationships
Uncertainty avoidance	High – uncomfortable with ambiguity	High – will not like rules to be broken, will not leave job even if dissatisfied, will like structure and plans
	Low – comfortable with ambiguity	Low – will be more innovative, more flexible
Future orientation	High – delayed gratification	High – will favour long-term outlooks and plans
	Low – past or present focused	Low – will look for more instant satisfaction of material needs
Time orientation	High – time is linear	High – deadlines are clear and respected, meetings start on time
	Low – time is elastic	Low – deadlines are flexible, meeting times are indicative
Communication orientation	High – message is explicit	High – listens for how something is said rather than what is said, reads between the lines
	Low – message is implicit	Low – listens for what is said rather than how it is said, expects directness and clarity
Performance orientation	High – values performance, believes they are in control	High – values training, development, results, assertiveness, competitiveness and materialism
	Low – values societal and family relationships	Low – values societal and family relationships, loyalty, harmony, integrity; comfortable with ambiguity

Source: table based on information from House et al. (2004).

improvement, a customer-focused workforce or, even more basic, an organization's ability to innovate? These dimensions when discussed outside of this chapter are related to organizational culture and, as readers will know, difficult to measure and to embed; however, the link between them and organizational performance is accepted. A study by Deloitte (2005) illustrates how outsource providers failed to deliver in areas identified by customers as their reason for outsourcing, thus creating an underperforming culture for the parts of the organization under their control – consequently affecting the customers' ability to develop a high-performing culture across the whole 'network' (by network we understand the sum of in-house and outsourced services) and lessening their ability to succeed (see Table 8.2).

The survey from Deloitte raises an additional cultural challenge posed by outsourcing in that the decision to outsource by an organization was found to impact

Table 8.2 Outsourcing supplier performance and likely impact on organizational culture

Customers' rationale for outsourcing	*Deloitte's findings*	*Impact on organizational culture and performance*
Best practice/ quality/ innovation	31% of participants stated that vendors became complacent once contracts were in place.	– Direct impact on customers, issues of quality of service or product. – Lack of drive around continuous improvement and innovation.
Flexibility/capacity/ scalability	Outsourcing adds a level of rigidity because contracts are binding and vendors may choose not to accommodate last-minute changes or requests.	– Rigidity of service provision unlikely to support the development of customer-focused behaviours if every additional request has to be evaluated. – Limits an organization's ability to reinvent itself and improve.
Access to high-calibre labour	1 in 5 participants experienced greater than expected vendor employee turnover and realized that the knowledge base they had paid for was fleeting.	– Developing a lasting 'joined-up' culture will be very difficult.
Lack of expertise in-house	44% of participants indicated that their vendors did not have the capabilities to provide the expected level of quality and cost savings, resulting in the participants' decision to bring operations back in-house.	– Direct impact on customers, issues of quality of service or product. – Desired injection of skills and expertise unavailable, compromising ability to innovate.

Source: first two columns based on Deloitte Consulting LLP (2005), p. 5.

organizational 'cohesion' by creating political and cultural challenges amongst the organization's workforce:

- One in four participants reported to have struggled with internal politics and conflicts surrounding their outsourcing decisions.
- Forty per cent of participants faced some significant issues around the realignment of roles and responsibilities and mentioned that 'Managers who were trained to run day-to-day operations now need to learn to manage results and vendors'.

The survey concludes by stating that outsourcing has the potential to create tremendous resistance inside an organization, which should not be underestimated. To add to the roles and responsibility issue, it is also worth mentioning that an organization's culture may be at odds with the concept of outsourcing without anyone realizing it, thus sending mixed messages to employees. Consider the example of an organization that is supportive of people starting at the bottom, for example a 'legend' embedded in the culture could be the story of the chief executive who started in the mail room or as a tea boy. What happens when the mail room is outsourced? Can the organization realistically continue promoting the story and does it then need to clarify where it stands in terms of career paths and in-house promotion?

Originally outsourcing was mostly based on the principle that an organization should focus its resources and energy on core activities and should look to outsource non-core activities to another organization that specializes in that particular area, for example human resources management or information technology. From a purist point of view, this argument makes sense as it would allow for the development of a high degree of specialism on both sides. The complexity in our opinion comes from the fact that organizations are not machines that can be easily broken into separate pieces; they are in fact the sum of their parts. So, while it may seem logical to think that the IT department can be completely separated, in practice, there are a myriad of grey areas:

- An IT system is a tool to automate a business process (a particular task/activity). When it comes to automating industry-specific processes, can an outsource provider have enough understanding of an organization's processes and of its industry context to develop the right solution?
- Are the boundaries between IT and the rest of the organization really that clear cut? The development of an enterprise system requires a good understanding of the infrastructure that will end up supporting it. Can an outsourced development team offshore really understand the limitation of the organization's internal network?
- A user that requires IT support will often need as much 'process' information as 'system' information; they will need to understand the way they must do something (steps, information they must provide, expected outputs) as well as which button to press. Support staff will therefore require a good understanding of the

Table 8.3 High-level outsourcing/cultural differences impact model

Type of service	Scope	Skill Level	Location	Proximity
Client facing Service provider staff may not have embraced the brand values of the organization they are contracted to, which could impact customer loyalty and perception Or they may have embraced the values too much, which may affect their loyalty to their employer (service provider) and reduce revenue opportunities (i.e. why should I charge for this additional service?)	**Self-contained (Catering, Mail Room)** Easier to define, measure and control outcome as service is 'whole' May be difficult to align culture of service provider team with organization; sub-culture may develop Potential issue with 'boundaries'; where does our loyalty lie? May underestimate 'value add' to organizational culture before outsource and create an impact on organizational performance	**Highly skilled (Pharmacy Dept of Hospital, Legal Research)** Professional culture may lessen impact Service provider staff likely to focus on contracted service rather than value add, which may impact the organizational culture, particularly the propensity to innovate and to improve organization-wide Outsourced service may be perceived as desirable jobs by people who remain in organization and yield resentment There may be knowledge-sharing issues between the service provider staff and the rest of the organization	**On site (Pharmacy, Catering, Reception, Mail Room)** Direct impact on customer and on organization; essential that staff are clear on boundaries with respect to cultural values and loyalty Creates confusion in outsourced function: who do I work for? what ways of working should I adopt? what is the behaviour expected here? May be difficult to create this level of 'split in personality' Creates confusion in organization which may affect relationships: should we invite them to the Christmas party?	

Challenges

	Back Office	Part of process (Pharmacy, Account Payable)	Low Skill (Reception, Mail Room)	Off site – onshore (Call Centre)	Offshore (Call Centre)
Challenges	Service provider staff may see the link between the service they provide and the brand even less (more remote than client-facing team)	The more hand-offs, the more potential for miscommunication, conflict, etc. The more dependencies, the more opportunities for delays to overall delivery Quality of delivery of service and product issues	May impact career path value; e.g. 'start at the bottom' Service provider staff may struggle to understand work context and lend allegiance to the company they provide the service to rather than their employer, lessening revenue opportunities. Will be worse if there is no critical mass; e.g. one or two receptionists in one organization Higher staff turnover – impacts ability to address issues longer term Service underrated; may not been seen as worth investing in addressing cultural issues	Virtual team issues around distance, communication and relationship Organizational culture 'cohesion' issues	Same issues as off site – onshore but also includes additional impact of national culture impact, language, etc.

Source: author's own.

'context': what the system is for, what process it is automating, etc. Can an out-source provider realistically understand the context pertaining to an industry significantly different from its own?

• Well-implemented IT systems provide a competitive advantage. Is it therefore core or non-core?

As a conclusion to this topic, we would like to stress that before moving into an outsource arrangement an organization would be well advised to get a thorough understanding of which aspects of its culture are responsible for its success, as it may be that what looks like non-core on the surface may actually be an important component of its ability to differentiate itself from others. And since culture is hidden, it may simply be doing away with an essential component of its identity.

The Different Dimensions of Outsourcing – a Model

At this stage, much content has been covered and several ideas introduced. In order to help the reader form a good picture of what has been discussed to date and to embed the learning, we would like to introduce a high-level model which can be used to understand as well as summarize how certain properties of an outsource arrangement may create a 'cultural' challenge (Table 8.3).

What should organizations do to ensure that cultural challenges
are addressed and their outsourcing contracts stand
more chance of succeeding?

According to Gartner, a well-known IT research provider, the global outsourcing market will grow by 8.1 per cent in 2008. This statistic is interesting given the challenges raised by some studies on how mixed results have ensued from the practice (Deloitte, 2005). The continuation in trend may have to do with the fact that the market is maturing and best practice is becoming more well known and more widely adopted. Unfortunately, when it comes to applying lessons learnt, it is our view that culture is one of the areas that is still mostly left to chance and where organizations would benefit from investing in understanding and actively managing the risks to their outsource contract. As we have seen, culture can have a significant impact on an organization. This statement is supported by Hofstede (1991), who believes that national culture is so strong that it is responsible for 50 per cent of the differences in managers' belief systems and how this will guide their behaviour and attitude.

The advice below is aimed at providing managers with ways of lessening the impact of cultural differences on the outsource relationship; however, in some cases, the advice can also be applied to the contract in general.

Being clear on why you wish to outsource and making sure this is for the right reasons

It is essential that an organization is clear on why it wishes to outsource and that the rationale is sound. We will first look at the reasons for outsourcing, which, while not specifically related to culture, must be identified so that communication can be used to gain employee commitment and lessen the impact of some of the challenges identified earlier in the model.

Good reasons for outsourcing, according to Tadelis (2007), include negotiating a cost-effective deal, increasing the focus on core activities inside an organization by outsourcing non-core activities, and having access to capacity outside the company. To this we would add having access to a level of skills and knowledge which is not present in the organization. Bad reasons for outsourcing include getting rid of a problem area by transferring it to someone else as well as following the 'fad' without assessing if the model is right for the organization or the area under consideration.

From a cultural impact perspective, being clear will help gain support for the model inside the organization, lessening the potential for conflict and sabotage by disgruntled employees. Outsourcing is a major change for an organization and it is important that the messages around the reasons for adopting the model are clear, make sense and explain why this is necessary so that employees are willing to make the sacrifices they will need to make when adopting the new ways of working. The communications should also clarify what will change, how it will change and what this will mean to the organization and its people. This could be as a recipient of the outsourced service, as someone who will need to interface with the service to do their job, as the person who manages the relationship or contract but also as someone whose role and responsibilities will change. It would be counterproductive to say to a manager that outsourcing some administrative tasks will allow them to spend more time on revenue-generating activities (e.g. sales) without ensuring first that the manager is happy to become more sales focused and also feels they have the skills to move into a different role.

In our experience, the main challenge around clarity is that since outsourcing deals generally include redundancies and transfers, there is by default a tendency to be secretive around the initiative. Additionally, the negativity surrounding redundancies and transfers and the fear of resistance and conflict will lead many managers to communicate less than they normally would and to shy away from managing issues. In our view, it is paramount that the message is communicated inside the organization in a clear, unambiguous and timely fashion so that employees understand the consequences, how their work will change as a result and the organization's level of resolve.

Making sure employees are ready for the new model

Outsourcing, like any major change, will mean different ways of working for individuals and even changes in roles and responsibilities. This change is identified by

Shi (2007) as a key risk; he says that outsourcing will mean changes to tasks, processes, structures and systems and will more than likely create disorganization, disorientation and clashes of IT and management systems. Clear communication will go some way to securing buy-in but resistance will undoubtedly arise from employees being unsure whether they are in a position to work with the new model; for example, that they have the right skills to undertake their new role or that they will be able to work with staff that belong to a different organization and who may even be located in a different country and be from a different culture. There may also be uncertainty on how they should behave when coming into contact with colleagues who used to work for their organization but have now been transferred to that of the service provider.

Successfully transitioning from one model to another will obviously involve actively managing change, which is not the focus of this chapter. The point we would like to make is that as part of the overall change management plans and activities, it would be advisable to ensure that cultural impact is assessed and mitigated. In the same way that an employee will need to know how to use a specific system or process when interfacing with an offshore provider, they would also benefit from being aware of potential cultural differences and how these can be lessened.

Ideally, a cultural assessment of the organization and of the outsource provider should be done before the actual contract is signed. This would allow the organization to decide whether the provider is enough of a match in terms of organizational culture, but also to identify differences and potential areas of conflict. The assessment could be used to run workshops with the employees on both sides to raise their awareness of the impact of cultural differences (both national and organizational) and equip them with techniques to lessen the impact.

The challenge here is that since outsourcing is usually about saving money, there may be a reluctance to invest in what will be seen as the 'softer' side of outsourcing. Our advice is to adopt a pragmatic approach by, for example, focusing the work on managers rather than all employees or by selecting an outsource provider that already trains its staff in cultural differences between nations. One of our interviewees identified the need for managers to be 'on board' as a key success factor, particularly when outsourcing low-skilled activities. Focusing on managers would also help in areas of high turnover or where employees may struggle to understand concepts such as culture. In this instance, the managers are likely to be more of a constant and can be used to act as 'change agents' at the onset of the change, but also ongoing, when for example issues arise or new employees join the organization.

As discussed previously, culture is complex and models of culture dimensions, although useful, are unlikely to be complete. The significance of this fact is that it will be impossible to identify all the cultural differences that pertain to two organizations and may impact their interactions. Our belief is that the most significant differences should come out of any assessment as they will be the most obvious. Additionally, the act of raising awareness among managers and staff and training them in dealing with the most significant differences will alert them to the possibility of other differences and educate them in ways to lessen the impact or resolve issues.

Being sure that what you consider non-core really is non-core

As discussed previously, it is entirely possible that what on first look appears non-core could possibly be an integral part of what gives an organization a competitive edge. We will use a slightly obvious example to illustrate this point. Consider our private hospital organization which prides itself on providing high-quality care to patients. When evaluating core and non-core services, senior management in the hospital assesses the catering function to be a 'support' service as, inherently, it is non-clinical. It is easy to see that what is being overlooked is that part of the patient's experience will include what they eat when staying at the hospital. Additionally, there is a strong link with the quality of the food being related to recovery. As discussed previously, should the outsource provider's value be on cost rather than quality, then the experience of the customer would be adversely affected. In this example, an area that is considered non-core actually directly affects the customers' experience and influences future decisions to do business with the company.

The purpose of this discussion is not to dissuade organizations from outsourcing anything that may have an impact on their customers. The advice is to be aware of the different facets of a service and to conduct a thorough analysis of what elements of this service actually support the success of the organization and to make sure that this differentiator remains in the outsourcing contract. For example, it may be that an outsource provider actually supplies a much higher quality of meals for a fraction of the price because they have access to better-quality food at a lower cost (they buy in bulk) and their staff development practices are more focused (this is core to them so they invest in training). In this instance, the experience of the customer would actually be better than if the catering function had remained under the management of the hospital.

In addition to the product, in this case the food, there is also a need to ensure that the staff that come into contact with an organization's customers are in a position to deliver the level of service expected and desired. Some outsource providers treat staff as a commodity, particularly employees they have inherited from a second transfer. The recommendation here is to make sure that the culture of the outsource provider promotes good people management and development practices to ensure that staff are motivated to perform to meet expectations.

Making sure that customer satisfaction and quality are measured, not just the number of transactions performed

Every outsourcing contract will include service level agreements and key performance indicators to measure the quality of the service provided. Contracts will also often include service credits and service debits to reward or penalize the provider. It is important that this performance management framework is actually designed to measure what is important and work to the organization's advantage. Expanding on our catering example, it may for example be interesting to measure how many meals are prepared by the provider to ensure that demand is satisfied; however, given that in this case there is a direct impact on customers, it would be more appropriate to conduct customer surveys on the quality of the service and product they received from the catering function. Was the food at the right temperature? Was it delivered on time? Organizations must resist the tendency to measure everything and focus on what will actually matter from their customers' point of view.

Accepting that there will be cultural differences and looking to reduce the possibility of them arising

An additional and valuable approach is to look to reduce the possibility of cultural differences arising in the first place. In his tips for good outsourcing, Tadelis (2007) mentions that companies should not outsource a problem and should look to have a very well-defined contract in terms of expectations, responsibilities, activities and outcome. In our view, these two pieces of advice go hand in hand as a problem area is one that is unlikely to be streamlined, efficient and well defined, making it very difficult to set boundaries in a contract and in practice. A simple, well-defined service provision where each side's responsibilities and expectations are set at the onset will go a long way to lessen confusion and misunderstanding, and although cultural differences may still have an impact, the level of clarity should help reduce the intensity.

When streamlining business processes, an organization could also look to reduce the hand-offs (the points of contact). It is obvious that the more interactions there are between the organization and the service provider, the more chances there will be of cultures colliding. Lessen the number of points where they interact and the situations that may give rise to misunderstanding will also reduce. This is important across the board but particularly for business process offshoring where the issue of distance compounds the impact of cultural differences. In essence, organizations must make it as easy as possible for the provider to succeed by providing a clear, simple and efficient process to follow and by reducing the number of times that the two organizations will have to depend on one another for the delivery of the overall service. A reduction in the number of hand-offs may also have the additional benefit of improving efficiency and speeding up delivery.

When improving processes, organizations should look at using technology to further eliminate the need for human interaction by, for example, automating manual tasks (this will also reduce the need to outsource that part of the process and the ongoing cost) or to provide structure to tasks that cannot be fully automated or require human input. For example, information could be captured in a structured fashion via a form rather than be provided as free text in an email, reducing the need to go back and forth for missing information and providing pro-forma answers to some questions. An additional example could be using remote technology to allow the customer service operative to access a customer's computer and see for themselves the error messages being generated by a particular piece of software. The entire business process offshoring industry was made possible by technology. Organizations would be advised to leverage the infrastructure as much as they possibly can.

Lastly, in our opinion, the better the relationship between two people, the less likely confusion and conflict will arise. When outsourcing, organizations should make sure that the messages are positive and that the outsource provider is seen as a valuable contributor to the organization's success. If possible, an organization should devise mechanisms that will support staff on both sides in developing good relationships. In an ideal world, this would be face to face but it is not impossible to achieve success in this area by providing good supporting tools, for example web cams to see each other's faces, instant messaging to create good instant links, good telephone lines, speedy and efficient networks, and systems that support the processes well rather than hinder them and reduce distance rather than increase it.

Conclusion

Historically, linear, rational and logical approaches to business and management have been favoured by managers rather than more random, systematic and complex approaches, since the outcome of one is more predictable and tangible than the outcome of the other. For example, when negotiating with an outsource provider, it is far easier to focus on what services are on offer, how much they will cost and how many employees will transfer over than on the value-add of a non-core service or the impact of culture. What this has meant in practice is that even where there is acceptance that culture has an impact, activities to manage the issues have not been forthcoming, either because they were seen as too difficult to quantify or simply because they did not fit with what is considered a hard-core business deal. In our view, this is not helped by the practice of having the procurement function lead outsourcing deals as the focus will be on price and negotiation rather than managing the human element. Additionally, it is likely that negotiations will be conducted with the outsource provider's commercial team and contact with the people who will actually provide the service may not happen until after the contract is signed, thus limiting an organization's ability to see the culture of the provider early on.

We hope that this chapter will go some way to promote a better understanding of what is meant by culture in the context of outsourcing and to provide a practical approach to identifying and reducing its impact on the success of outsourcing arrangements. We would also like to reiterate words of caution mentioned several times in the text: because culture is a constantly evolving form, it is impossible to provide a comprehensive and finite model to identify and address the issues it poses. In our view, the skills that need to be developed are more around awareness, namely an understanding of potential areas of conflict so that new ones can be quickly identified; as well as some familiarity with methods that can be used to lessen the impact or a desire to search for solutions. Obviously, this is an approach that does not sit in the linear, predictable and rational school of thought and should be led by a multifunctional team, suitably trained.

References

Anawati, D., & Craig, A. (2006). Behavioural adaptation within cross-cultural virtual teams. *IEEE Transactions on Professional Communication*, *49*(1), 44–56.

Berger, P. L., & Luckmann, T. (1967). *The social construction of reality: A treatise in the sociology of knowledge*. London: The Penguin Press.

Carmel, E., & Tija, P. (2005). *Offshoring information technology*. Cambridge: Cambridge University Press.

Cougar, J. D., Adelsberger, H., Borovits, I., Zviran, M., & Motiwalla, J. (1990). Commonalities in motivating environments for programmer/analysts in Austria, Israel, Singapore, and the USA. *Information and Management*, *18*, 41–46.

Deloitte Consulting LLP (2005). *Calling a change in the outsourcing market*. New York: Author.

Gurung, A., & Prater, E. (2006). A research framework for the impact of cultural-differences on IT outsourcing. *Journal of Global Information Technology*, *9*(1), 24–42.

Hall, E. T. (1966). *The hidden dimension*. New York: Doubleday.

Hall, E. T. (1976). *Beyond culture*. New York: Doubleday.

Handy, C. (1999). *Understanding organizations* (4th ed.). London: Penguin Books.

Hofstede, G. (1980). *Culture's consequences: International differences in work-related values*. Beverly Hills, CA: Sage.

Hofstede, G. (1991). *Cultures and organizations: Software of the mind*. London: McGraw Hill.

House, R. J., Hanges, P. J., Javidan, M., Dorfman, P. W., & Gupta, V. (Eds.). (2004). *Culture, leadership and organizations: The Globe Study of 62 societies*. Thousand Oaks, CA: Sage.

Jordan, A.T. (1990). *Organizational culture and culture change: A case study. Studies in Third World Societies*, *42*, 209–226.

Julian, C. (2006). *What top performing retailers know about satisfying customers: Experience is key*. New York: IBM Institute for Business Value.

Kroeber, A. L., & Kluckhohn, C. (1952). *Culture: A critical review of concepts and definitions*. Cambridge, MA: Massachusetts Papers, Peabody Museum.

McEwan, B., & Buckingham, G. (2001). Make a marquee. *People Management*, 17 May, 40–44.

Mosley, R. W. (2007). Customer experience, organizational culture and the employer brand, *Journal of Brand Management*, *15*(2), 123–134.

Shi, Y. (2007). Today's solution and tomorrow's problem: The business process outsourcing risk management puzzle. *California Management Review*, *49*(3), 27–44.

Smircich, L. (1983). Concepts of culture and organizational analysis. *Administrative Science Quarterly*, *28*, 339–358.

Straub, D., Loch, K., Evaristo, R. O., Karahanna, E., & Srite, M. (2002). Towards a theory based measurement of culture. *Journal of Global Information Management*, *10*(1), 13–23.

Tadelis, S. (2007). The innovative organization: Creating value through outsourcing. *California Management Review*, *50*(1), 261–277.

Terpstra, V., & David, K. (1991). *The cultural environment of international business* (3rd ed.). Cincinnati, OH: South-Western Publishing.

Van Maanen, J., & Barley, S. R. (1984). Occupational communities: Culture and control in organizations. *Research in Organizational Behavior*, *6*, 287–365.

Zack, M. H. (1993). Interactivity and communication mode choice in ongoing management groups. *Information Systems Research*, *4*(3), 207–239.

Chapter 9

Establishing Trust in Virtual Teams

Alex Watts

Introduction

'Nobody is going to listen to what you say,' he assured me. 'People are seldom interested in the actual content of a speech. They simply want to learn from your tone and gestures and expressions whether or not you are an honest man.' (Advice given to Kurt Vonnegut and recounted in *Wampeters, Foma & Granfalloons*, 1974 p. 17)

We take for granted how we build relationships at work by spontaneously dropping by someone's desk to ask a question, by socializing after work, by gossiping either at the coffee machine or while we are waiting for a meeting to start. We take for granted how we make decisions about people by watching how they behave in the office. We take for granted that we can see from someone's facial expression that they don't understand something or their voice is saying 'Yes' but their body language is saying 'No'. How do we cope when we can't do these things?

One of the implications of global outsourcing or insourcing is that a worker may have co-workers, customers or suppliers who are located hundreds or even thousands of miles away. Often these distant 'virtual team' workers need to collaborate closely on project work or to deliver business-as-usual services. This chapter describes how people build relationships at a distance from the other team members and how they decide whether their distant colleagues are trustworthy.

I interviewed 10 senior managers, all of whom have several years' experience of managing teams in this situation to deliver high-value IT and building construction projects. What I discovered is that these managers do different things when they are

The Human Side of Outsourcing: Psychological Theory and Management Practice
Edited by Stephanie J. Morgan
Copyright © 2009 John Wiley & Sons Ltd.

establishing the team relationship from the things that they do after the team relationship has been established. During the early stages of team building, people present themselves as trustworthy, trusting and competent and observe the other team members closely to decide how to approach the relationship. Body language, facial expressions and office behaviour are at least as important as the words that people say. Unsurprisingly, these managers emphasize the importance of face-to-face meetings when establishing these relationships.

In this chapter, I explain what virtual teams are, their relevance for outsourcing, some of the challenges they face and why trust is important for them. I describe five different ways of looking at trust in working relationships. I profile the managers that I interviewed and explain how I conducted the research. I then describe the strategies that these managers use to establish trust, using both my words and the words of the managers themselves. I summarize the two-stage process that the managers follow when building working relationships with the distant members of the virtual team and how they decide whether the other team members are trustworthy. I then explain why the two-stage process works the way that it does. Finally I suggest some limitations of this research and summarize its implications for existing project management techniques and for managers of virtual teams.

What Is a Virtual Team?

A virtual team is a group of people who work together and are dependent upon each other but who work in separate geographical locations and cannot easily meet each other face to face. Therefore the primary characteristic of a virtual team is that it is dispersed and team members need to travel significant distances in order to meet face to face. Two further characteristics of virtual teams follow from this. The first is that the team workers use technology to communicate in situations where they would normally communicate face to face. In order to communicate electronically, they may use asynchronous technology such as email and chat or synchronous technology such as telephone calls, teleconferences and video conferences. The other characteristic of virtual teams is team diversity. The reason that a team is split across several locations is often because the team needs to include people from different organizations or from different countries or from different professions or people who have different roles within the team. Virtual teams are diverse because they incorporate different organizational cultures, different national cultures and customs and the needs of different professions and job roles. One important role difference is that of customer and supplier.

Cohen and Bailey (1997) divided teams into four types. These are work teams, project teams, parallel teams and management teams. All of these can be virtual teams. The research in this chapter will focus on project teams. Such teams are set up for a limited period of time and are therefore temporary. However, some of the teams described by the interviewees in this research had qualities of work teams or management teams as well as project teams.

The Relevance of Virtual Teams for Outsourcing

In high-value technology projects such as those described in this research, the relationship between organizations can be complex. There is often a web of customer–supplier relationships where a customer may be supplied by insourcers or outsourcers or both. A specific group will often be simultaneously a supplier to some groups and a customer for others. These sophisticated relationships have developed because they enable high-quality projects and services to be delivered rapidly, flexibly and cost effectively. Technological advances have made these working arrangements possible. Global differentials in the availability, cost and quality of labour mean that it is often beneficial to outsource to an organization in another country or to set up an insourcing department in a foreign country. In order to obtain the optimal skill set for a complex project that requires a range of specialist skills it may be necessary to outsource to organizations in several different countries. This web of customer–supplier, insourcer–outsourcer relationships is often achieved by setting up global virtual teams. These are virtual project teams formed to deliver a specific objective and then disbanded. However, they can also be one or more virtual work teams providing an ongoing service to a remote customer.

Hoegl, Ernst, and Proserpio (2007) suggest a definition of virtual teams based on 'whether it is problematic to arrange spontaneous face to face meetings'. This defines virtual teams in terms of a specific outcome that is a challenge for team working. It broadens the domain of virtual teams by considering reasons other than travel why it is difficult for teams to meet face to face. It may be that the other team members are too busy to meet or that they wish to avoid taking on other tasks in addition to their usual responsibilities. Under this definition, other insourcing or outsourcing relationships may experience the same challenges and issues that are described in this chapter for dispersed virtual teams, even though those team members may be working in the same country or city and could in principle meet face to face on a regular basis.

The Challenges of Working in a Virtual Project Team

The interviewees in this research described the challenges they have experienced when working in virtual teams. The challenge they mentioned most often was the difficulty of having to communicate electronically rather than face to face. They also pointed out that holding a face-to-face meeting incurs a high cost in terms of both time and money owing to the travel that is required. They said that time zone differences were especially problematic when the working hours of team members in different countries have a limited overlap or no overlap at all. They said that it was necessary to be sensitive to the organizational culture of the groups with whom they were working in order to build relationships with people from that organization. They made a similar point that extra thought and effort were required when a team member did not share a first language with other team members or where team members from other national cultures had different customs and behaviours. The interviewees believed that implementing a consistent project governance and communication process was particularly important to the success of a virtual team. Many of these topics are covered elsewhere in the literature on virtual teams (see Axtell, Fleck, & Turner, 2004; Gibson & Cohen, 2003).

The academic literature on virtual teams discusses difficulties with team conflict, team cohesion and knowledge sharing in virtual teams. Burke's (2006) list of the primary causes of conflict in organizations all occur in virtual project teams. They are globalization, employee diversity, constant pressure, rapid change, less managerial oversight, increased complexity of work and reliance on email to replace face-to-face contact. Hinds and Bailey (2003) distinguished between three types of conflict and found that task conflict can sometimes be beneficial to virtual team performance because it makes the team consider more alternatives, but affective conflict and process conflict always have a negative impact. The reliance on email and telephone rather than face-to-face communication in dispersed teams can produce exaggerated impressions of other virtual team members owing to a lack of interpersonal cues. These can have a negative impact on group identity (Axtell et al., 2004). Rosen, Furst, and Blackburn (2007) found that diversity of national cultures reduced knowledge sharing, although Haas (2006) found that a team with the correct mix of diverse nationalities applied knowledge better than single-nationality teams. Olson and Olson's (2000) research ascertained that some of the things that make it more difficult for team members to work remotely from each other are that they cannot observe whether the others are present and they cannot determine their mental state. Cramton (2001) found that virtual team members were not aware of the work pressures, personal circumstances of other team members or the reasons why they were silent. Because of this, it was difficult to be confident that a decision had been agreed by all members of the virtual team and remote workers were unfairly blamed when things went wrong because the team members at a different location were not aware that those workers did not have control over the situation. Cramton's paper provides an in-depth discussion of this topic and its relationship to attribution theory.

While containing a few potentially positive effects, the overall impression is that working in virtual teams is more difficult than working in face-to-face teams, especially in terms of the costs involved, communication and interpersonal relationships.

The Importance of Establishing Trust in Virtual Teams

The intended direction of this research was to examine the ways in which managers evaluate the trustworthiness of others in the extreme situation of virtual project teams. However, the managers that I interviewed steered the research in a different direction. When asked how they assessed the commitment of another organization, in most cases they began by explaining their strategies for building strong personal relationships. One of the managers opened up the interview with these comments:

Interviewee 5: The first thing for me, if I am dealing with something that is (on) the other side of the world, is (to) get over to the other side of the world (and) spend some time to actually build relationships, understand mindsets, culture, understand some of the people, put names to faces and actually press the flesh. I think that is job number one because I think from that point on you feel rapport (and) even though you are dealing then five thousand miles away from each other by phone, by email, by whatever medium, you have got that seed of a relationship that you can build on.

The interviewees also described how they monitored and evaluated the behaviour of the other members of the team to determine whether those individuals were trustworthy. This monitoring was split into two distinct stages. The first stage of monitoring occurred at the same time that they were building relationships and focused primarily on the competence of the other team members but also on early indications of openness and commitment. The second stage of monitoring occurred after the team members began to deliver plans, designs and other deliverables to the rest of the virtual team.

The interviewees talked about the fact that they are willing to accept deficiencies and disappointments in an alliance as long as the other team members are motivated to make the relationship work and meet threshold levels of competence and commitment. Over and above this, they described how they actively encourage other team members to say 'No' or encourage them to provide pessimistic work estimates rather than deliver the work late or fail to deliver at all. Most of the managers stressed the value of openness and transparency between members of the virtual team. All these behaviours are risky strategies. They involve the risk of being let down by another team member and the risk of reprisals as a result of being open and honest about one's failures. As we will see, the reason that the managers incur these risks is because they usually produce significantly better working relationships.

Five Viewpoints on Trust

There are five viewpoints about trust that help to explain the interviewees' descriptions of their trust relationships in virtual teams. I will summarize these five viewpoints to create a context for the discussion of the interviewees' comments and for linking their comments to some of the topics within the academic literature on trust. It is outside the scope of this chapter to provide a full treatment of these viewpoints or to explore the many other complementary and contrasting writings about trust.

The 'Bounded Rationality' view of trust (Good, 1988) proposes that we do not calculate in advance all the risks involved in trusting a particular person or organization in a specific situation but instead we adopt a simple strategy in all cases. These simple strategies are sometimes referred to as 'rules of thumb'. An example of bounded rationality is to initially trust everyone, even if some individuals occasionally prove to be untrustworthy.

In contrast, the 'integrative' model of trust (Mayer, Davis, & Schoorman, 1995) implies unbounded rationality where trusting behaviour is based on a calculation of the trustworthiness of the others and the risks involved in trusting them. This model differentiates three factors of trustworthiness. The first, 'benevolence', is the extent to which one party is believed to want to do good to the other party and it implies that the parties have a mutual attachment to each other. The second, 'ability', is trustworthiness that is based on a party's skill, competence or influence within a specific area of expertise. The third, 'integrity', is trustworthiness that is based on consistency of a party's past actions, a good reputation and especially whether the party keeps their word and does what they say that they will do.

The 'initial trust' model (McKnight, Cummings, & Chervany, 1998) incorporates much of the integrative model but also introduces things that people do in the early stages of a relationship that increase or decrease a trustor's confidence in the trustworthiness of the trustee. These include noticing subtle tell-tale behaviours as part of a first impression that give rise to 'gut feelings' about the other person. They also include small actions taken by one party to assure themselves that the situation is under their control. For example, the trustor may attempt to influence the other party in some way and, if successful, this increases the trustor's confidence in the potential for the relationship to be successful. The model proposes that institutional factors such as regulations, guarantees and legal recourse increase the likelihood of trusting behaviour. It asserts that trustors will tend to look for clues that confirm their belief rather than disconfirming clues. Both the integrative model and initial trust model consider 'trusting dispositions', that is, whether some people are more likely to be trusting than others.

The 'swift trust' model (Meyerson, Weick, & Kramer, 1996) describes trust that must develop quickly to support a short-term enterprise. It is based on the interdependence of group members where the mutual fate of the larger group is dependent on the behaviour of individuals and subgroups. It assumes that there is one person or group who has the ultimate power to hire and fire the other team members. It assumes that parties will act in a way that maintains their personal reputations in order to safeguard their future employment prospects. It proposes that the swiftly formed relationships require a good understanding of the roles of the parties involved in the enterprise and that trust can be more rapid when it is role based. Swift trust proposes that 'there is less emphasis on feeling, commitment and exchange and more on action, cognition, the nature of the network and labour pool and avoidance of personal disclosure, contextual cues, modest dependency and heavy absorption in the task'. Swift trust is effectively the same thing as network governance (Jones, Hesterley, & Borgatti, 1997), where demand uncertainty encourages relationships involving aggregations of autonomous groups who work together in outsourcing and subcontracting arrangements. Reputation is important for these groups and network governance predicts that repeated personal contacts across organizational boundaries discourage behaviour that seeks an advantage from a single transaction.

'Social trust' (Gambetta, 1988) is a label that I have given to Gambetta's viewpoint in order to differentiate it from the others. In Gambetta's words, social trust involves the appearance of trusting blindly 'not because we do not want to know how untrustworthy others are, but simply because the alternatives are worse' (p. 223). One implication of this viewpoint is that someone must make the first move in order to nurture trust in a relationship. Another implication is that trust is an efficient and pleasant way of organizing relationships and without it relationships require more effort and are less satisfying. Allowing distrust to develop is one of the 'alternatives that are worse'. Distrust may be hard to dislodge and have a negative effect on a relationship. In this vein, Gambetta suggests that coercion reduces trust. It disposes of mutual trust by introducing asymmetry and promotes power and resentment. In effect trust is depleted through disuse, rather than use and may increase through use. Social trust requires the person who initiates the relationship to temporarily suspend their assessment of the trustworthiness of the other people in the relationship. Gambetta proposes that the other person 'will be well disposed towards us if we make the right move' (p. 228) and 'if trust is not unconditionally bestowed, it may generate a greater sense of responsibility at the receiving end' (p. 234). In other words, if you have expectations of another person in a new relationship and you act as if you believe that they will fulfil those expectations then that person will often become committed both to meeting your expectations and to their relationship with you. Social trust is explicitly excluded by the authors of the integrative and initial trust models and the feeling and commitment aspects of the trust relationship are explicitly excluded by the authors of swift trust. However, it can be argued that the product of social trust is the benevolent trust that is described in the integrative model. Social trust is consistent with Good's (1988) observation from studies involving games where people competed under different conditions. He noticed that the greater the communication between players during the game then the greater the likelihood of a mutually beneficial outcome. Jones and George (1998) propose something similar to social trust that describes the evolution of unconditional trust within teams. One of their proposals is that unconditional trust is necessary before it is possible to communicate tacit knowledge. Tacit knowledge is knowledge that is 'difficult and extremely time consuming to translate into standards or procedures or to explain to people who are not involved in the interactions themselves' (p. 543). Social trust or unconditional trust may therefore be attractive to virtual team workers because it facilitates the communication of tacit knowledge between team members when they are performing knowledge-intensive work. Imparting tacit knowledge is relevant in most outsourcing situations, including those where staff are transferred under a TUPE arrangement as well as more temporary arrangements.

In order to understand the comments made by the interviewees and how trust is established in virtual teams, it is necessary to consider both bounded and unbounded rationality, benevolence, ability, integrity, methods of rapidly developing confidence in the other members of the virtual team, the interdependent fate of the members of the virtual team and the social costs and benefits of making the first move in a trusting relationship.

Introduction to the Research

The purpose of this research was to document the strategies used by managers to determine the trustworthiness of others when working in global virtual teams. The research was 'exploratory', which means that the intention was simply to provide possible explanations for the strategies described in the interviews rather than to prove a hypothesis. It was 'within subject' research, which means that it examined common themes from the interviews and the chronological sequence of events.

My own background includes more than 25 years' IT consulting experience in software development and quality assurance as well as a Master's-level education in Organizational Behaviour. I work for one of the major outsourcing companies in the UK. I have worked in virtual teams on many occasions and observed their successes and failures at first hand.

I interviewed managers with significant experience of working in virtual project teams. The interviewees were senior managers who managed a team of junior managers and had several years' experience working on virtual team projects which regularly have budgets of tens or hundreds of millions of pounds (GBP). Most of the managers were involved in multiple projects and had relationships with more than 10 groups in their own country and more than 10 groups in foreign countries. The groups in their own countries were often located hundreds of miles away from each other. In two instances the manager only had one or two foreign relationships but these were relationships that had a large impact on the projects for which the manager was responsible. The virtual team relationships included customers, insourcers, outsourcers or a combination of all three. The managers' organizations included a high-technology architectural consultancy, an architect who manages global construction projects, a financial institution, two IT services organizations and two IT consultancies. For three of the organizations I interviewed two managers and for the other four organizations I interviewed one manager. One of the managers was based in North America, one in India, three in Germany and the other five in the UK. All of the interviews were conducted in English and this was not the first language for four of the managers. Three of the managers were women. Four of the interviews were conducted face to face and six were conducted by telephone. All interviews lasted approximately 60 minutes. Table 9.1 summarizes each interviewee's business, primary work location and whether their primary role within virtual teams is a customer or a supplier.

The size of the managers' organizations ranged from 40 to over a hundred thousand employees. In most cases, the managers worked in teams that interacted with several tens of different groups and often more than half these groups were located

Table 9.1 Interviewee roles, businesses and work locations

Interviewee	Primary team role	Business	Primary work location
1	Customer	Financial institution	UK
2	Supplier	IT consultancy	UK
3	Customer	Financial institution	UK
4	Supplier	IT consultancy	India
5	Customer	IT services	UK
6	Supplier	IT services	UK
7	Supplier	Architectural consultancy	Germany
8	Supplier	IT consultancy	North America
9	Supplier	Architectural consultancy	Germany
10	Supplier	Architect	Germany

in a foreign country. Typically the managers worked on several projects simultaneously but the intensity of each individual virtual team relationship varied depending on the stage of each project and the role of the manager's team on that project.

The interviews were semi-structured. I created a predefined list of questions that covered the topics from the swift trust paper. The questions were open questions and I tried not to give the interviewee any indication that I was expecting a specific answer. I varied the questions a little in the interviews depending on the time available, the direction the interview was taking and whether the interviewee had already discussed a subject before I reached the question on that subject. However, I always asked the following questions and these generally stimulated the interviewees to describe their strategies for establishing trust:

- How do you assess the commitment of another organization?
- What do you do if you are unsure whether to trust another organization?
- In general, how would you expect a trustworthy organization to behave?
- What do you think makes the difference as to whether your employer is trusted or not?

I transcribed the interviews and analysed them using template analysis to identify the main themes from the interviews.

In the quotes from the interviews throughout this chapter, I have tried to give a sense of the volume of similar comments. I have also noted which interviewee made each comment in order to give a sense of the number of interviewees with similar opinions. In many cases there were even more comments in the same vein which have been excluded because they are not easily understood out of context or simply to restrict the length of this chapter.

Most of the interview quotes used in this chapter did not contain references to specific people or organizations. In order to maintain confidentiality for those that did, references to the managers' organizations have been changed to 'your employer' and any names have been changed to fictitious people or organizations.

Trust Strategies

There were clear trends in the way that the managers establish trust. First, they actively engage with the other team members to present themselves, respond to the presentations of others and build personal relationships. Second, the interviewees believe that a face-to-face meeting is by far the most effective way of building trust, especially in the initial stages of a relationship, and will sometimes travel thousands of miles for meetings that last a few days or even a few hours. Third, the interviewees obtain an impression of the other team members based on both explicit statements from team members and implicit body language, facial reactions and office behaviour. This impression was often described as a 'gut feeling' about the trustworthiness of the other team members. Fourth, the interviewees consider that openness and transparency between team members are key factors in building trust and therefore they set an example by being open and transparent themselves and expressed a desire to remove the barriers that prevent people from communicating bad news. Fifth, the strategy of many interviewees is to assume that the other team members are trustworthy until proven otherwise. Sixth, the interviewees monitor the behaviour of the other team members, especially with regard to their ability, integrity, commitment and responsiveness, as a verification of their trustworthiness. Seventh, the interviewees were clear that their trust relationships with other members of the team are separate from the legal contractual relationship and that too much focus on the legal contract can undermine trust.

The passages that follow describe these seven aspects in more detail, drawing on comments from the managers that were interviewed. Since this is a book chapter rather than a magazine article, I have been allowed to include several comments on each topic. The similarities between the comments from different managers are striking but each manager also describes a unique perspective. I hope that including several comments in each section will assist the reader both to achieve a deeper understanding of the shared meanings and to find a description that accords with their own individual perspective.

Actively building relationships

The quotes below are examples where the interviewees described the importance of building relationships when establishing trust. This is effectively the creation of benevolent trust between the members of the virtual team. It is also associated with higher motivation and doing more than is absolutely necessary.

Interviewee 2: I interviewed him and he got the job and he came to the UK and spent three weeks with me and that was for many reasons. One was to see whether we had that ability to work together to deliver some unbelievably unrealistic targets. (Another was to see) whether he was competent. (Another was to see) whether he knew his stuff. He sold me a dream and told me how he could do it that made me believe in him and (he) backed it up with some technical justifications. And, you know, he had done prep as well. He had made a little demo to show me how it would work. He'd done his work up front. So when he went back to India and said to me 'I'll send you the plan of how I am going to deliver', I had already bought into him at that point. He hadn't delivered me anything.

Interviewee 3: When I look at a new supplier relationship and I am looking at a few right now. There are a few things that I look at particularly. It's more the people aspect than whether they have the right skills and whether they are the right size at this point in time. Those are important. But the important bit is 'will they stress that extra mile?'

Interviewee 5: It is getting that relationship right in my book. It's a people thing. If the people gel you can do a lot of the stuff that goes on between companies. If the people don't gel, you don't get the trust, it doesn't happen.

Interviewee 6: If you are in a meeting with somebody and seeing them on a regular basis then you can start to pick up on a lot of those things.
Alex: When you say 'pick up on', what do you mean? Are you saying that it is quicker to build trust?
Interviewee 6: Yes because you have multiple interactions. The more interactions there are in any form then the quicker it happens. Or else it doesn't happen because you clarify your position much more easily and earlier.

Interviewee 10: Usually, we try to have in each team, at least a third of the team, people that we know well, we have experience with, (and) we know they work well. The others we interview or usually they come recommended by someone that we know well who has worked with them already. ... (and later on) ...
Alex: How important is building personal relationships in terms of getting the job done?
Interviewee 10: Very important because in the end motivation come through personal relationships, giving and taking, calling in debts. I mean it's human and without a personal relationship, you don't get the best out of people. What you shouldn't forget is that if you lead a design team, a lot of people do their best because they like you or they like the job or the way that you run the job. Motivation is often favours. They do it for you and that has to do with a personal relationship.

One of the interviewees described how he emphasized to his staff the overriding importance of getting people to like you when developing trust:

Interviewee 2: (For) 90 per cent of what we do (it) doesn't really matter about the quality of our delivery. It's about our relationship with the client. We did struggle for quite a while at WestCo to get a reputation in there and it changed when Bill went in there and was given that role and responsibility, not because Bill is awesome because he is not. I said to him when he joined last year: 'You've got two months to build a relationship with these people. I am less concerned about what you do for delivery. I am more concerned that these guys like you because the more they like you, the more they can live with your mistakes.' They have still got issues with what Bill does and the way that he does things but because they have bought into him and they like him they have a bit of loyalty to him as well as him to them. Because that trust is there (then) they kind of can deal with this. I always believe that 90 per cent of what we have to do is to have that right relationship with the client. I think that there is many a project we have done where we have gone in and done a sh*t-hot job but not built that relationship and we have actually been crucified for what we did. We have had a hard time about it.

The following quotes are examples of the virtual team members presenting themselves as non-threatening, respectful and committed to joint goals as part of the process of developing trusting relationships with other members of the team.

Interviewee 3: My style always has been to go seek help. I have never yet asked a supplier or told a supplier to do a certain thing in terms of saying 'this is your job, this is what you've got to do'. So it's also how you do the approaching in terms of saying 'I need some more help here' because you have got to show respect.

Interviewee 4: You need to appreciate and inform and make him understand that 'Your commitment is my commitment.' 'That is how we are going ahead.' 'This is my plan to achieve this.' 'These are the milestones that need to be completed and to achieve this milestone, I am going to monitor this way.'

Interviewee 6: Certainly in the beginning there was quite a lot of mistrust because they really felt that that was it. That we were going to take over and it would be our processes rather than theirs. That's not how we have done it, we've worked together. It's not perfect now and it will take longer than the 18 months that we have been at it. It's getting better.
Alex: How did you go about that? Establish that relationship.
Interviewee 6: I got on a plane [resigned laugh] and went to see the manager of the department who would be my peer I guess. Trying to understand their role and go through how I saw my team's role and then try to build that down to the next level of people.

Interviewee 7: In the first meeting you are more listening how it works and the best thing is to always show your own commitment. You present 'this is what we want to achieve with this job'.

Interviewee 8: You need to have a face-to-face (meeting) when there are multiple people and depending on the seniority of the person. If it's the CEO then you would not want to do a call. The hierarchy of the people also matters and if there are multiple people from the client side in the room then you also want to be there in person out of sheer respect. You need to respect their time. If there are senior execs that have gathered together in a room to give you time then you want to be there in person.

Interviewee 9: We want to make clear, and to underline, that we are being supportive rather than dictating what we are doing here. The informal discussion and the informal presentation of our work support this idea.

The next quotes are examples where the interviewees actively encouraged the other members of the virtual team to present their goals and aspirations as part of a two-way process of building trust.

Interviewee 8: If I have lost an engagement it has been because we haven't been able to connect with the people. Unless you meet the business and personal goals of every individual who is a key stakeholder on the client side then you cannot win the deal.

Interviewee 9: I have an initial design (workshop) in August and there will be many people both from the university and from the city. They have sent me bios and they have sent me websites where the city describes their sustainability goals. That's something that I have got to prepare for. I want to know roughly who is there and what the technical goals are so that I can relate them to what I am talking about.
Alex: What is your objective in doing that preparation?
Interviewee 9: The first objective is that I don't say anything which is contradictory to their goals. Or if I do this then I do this deliberately. I don't want to run into a situation where I am not well informed. The other thing is that I want to get an idea about the positions of the people who are going to attend. I don't want to step on anybody's toes unnecessarily. I don't want to find out whether these are nice people or not. I want to find out their responsibilities.

Interviewee 10: You cannot force anybody to do something that they don't want to do. It's very tiresome. Therefore we try to find people where we have the feeling that they are on board, that for them it is a very special thing.

Finally, one of the interviewees explicitly stated that the early stages of establishing trust were limited to the trustworthiness factors of benevolence and ability and that integrity is assessed later on in the relationship when each party starts monitoring the behaviour of the other:

Interviewee 2: The chatter on the stairways and up the lift sometimes is the most important thing that you ever do because it is building that connection. I try to find out from people what their interest is, what they like, things that you can always get them to relate to you with. You know. Competency. Build-the-Relationship.

(Is there) anything else that I really care about? If you know what you are talking about you can build a relationship. What else is there? ... (and later on) ...

Alex: In your previous comment you said that 'being there when they need you' was important. I think that is different from competency and from building a relationship.

Interviewee 2: But I think that comes after. You can't walk into a room with someone and they instantly know that you are going to support them. That is how the relationship evolves. From the first contact it is having that ability to get that rapport but also to be able to show that you can deliver. After that the development of that relationship has to evolve so that they know that you are the man for them.

Face-to-face contact

Every interviewee talked about the need for members of virtual teams to meet face to face. I had a sense that the enthusiasm for face-to-face meetings was as much an urge to socialize as well as the more rational explanations about the importance of non-verbal communication that were given in the interviews. Below are some of the quotes about the need for face-to-face contact:

Interviewee 2: (When the virtual team is spread across different locations) the bit that I miss about us all being together is the body language, being able to look at someone in the eye, the ability to understand how the other person is really feeling. All the stuff you have to read from body language or vibes or little comments or even being able to go up to someone and put your arm on their shoulder and say let's go for a cigarette, let's go for a beer. You can't do that.

Interviewee 3: One of the important things about outsourcing, whether it is off-shoring or nearshoring, all of that. It's always important to frequently see the whites of the eyes for the key people who you depend on. At all levels of management we are more dependent on our staff than our own ability to grow in the organization. Just extend that to the supplier organization and then think about who you will hire, how you will behave with them, how you will treat them.

Interviewee 5: If you are just dealing with (people on) the telephone you don't get the right connection, you don't get a sense of being able to read people and if you are just doing it by phone without that context of how they are behaving, what their mannerisms are (then) I think that it is very easy to pick up the wrong messages. So that is why I would always go for face to face to initiate and build that relationship from that point on.

Interviewee 6: Well, I like to meet people face to face if I can. That is not always possible when you work in an organization that is spread right across the world. So if I can't meet them face to face then I will ideally do video conferencing and at the worst really it is a telephone call. Just to try to introduce yourself, talk through the roles, what we are all talking about.

Alex: You said before that for some projects you hold every second meeting face to face. Is that true for the whole of your organization?

Interviewee 7: Not every second (meeting) but our experience (is) that you cannot do a project only on video conferences. It is not working. And only on phone calls it does not work. You need personal meetings.

Interviewee 9: It is very important to have a first meeting where we build up relationships. I think it is essential because I have been in many video conferences and telephone conferences where you have not met people before and what you always miss is the tone in between what they say. If you know people then you can put a face to what they say and you know what they mean when they say something.

Alex: Can you build up personal relations over the telephone and video conference?

Interviewee 10: No. You can maintain them but you cannot build them up.

Despite many comments about the costs and inconveniences of travel when working in virtual teams, the interviews contained many examples where team members recounted travelling very long distances at the drop of a hat in order to meet someone face to face. Here are a few of those comments:

Interviewee 5: We don't hesitate to put people on a plane to go over there because I have a fundamental belief that they can achieve more in three days' face-to-face dialogue looking at people across the table, talking the talk, than we would achieve in probably three weeks trying to achieve it anywhere else.

Interviewee 7: It's totally different to be with someone in a room or communicate by phone or by video conference. We have a lot of jobs now with offices from the west coast (of the USA) which means that they start working when we go home normally. And you have a 13-hour flight to go there so you are trying to minimize the trips. But we still do every second meeting by video conference and every second meeting in person.

Interviewee 8: If I am looking at an outcome that is critical to change the nature of the process or something like that then that I would do(a) face-to-face (meeting). I would not leave it to a call. I have flown half way across the world to have a one-hour meeting because the outcome of that meeting was extremely critical for me and that would be a game-changer if the outcome was negative for me and the entire deal could get scuttled or it could have a negative impact across the entire process. You can do a much better 'convincing' job sitting in front of the person eyeball to eyeball than you can do on a telephone.

As other researchers have observed (see Olson & Olson, 2000; Gibson & Cohen, 2004), informal social activities tend to occur before and after face-to-face meetings and do not occur around teleconferences and video conferences. These activities assist the development of personal relationships and benevolent trust. Here are some examples from the interviews that describe the importance of informal interactions:

Interviewee 4: When I go for any personal meeting, I reach (the meeting) five minutes early. It's important to talk about how the day was and other non-business factors and to know how the person is and then go ahead and have the business discussion. That makes a lot of difference.

Interviewee 6: If you could then you would do everything face to face just because you have got that relationship built. You can talk about all sorts of things rather than just straight business which we tend not to do if you are on a video conference call. You can try to do it but it is not the same. Just sat in a room and having a cup of coffee before you have your meeting or whatever.

As well as regular short-term travel by members of virtual teams, some of the interviewees described longer-term arrangements for collocating members of virtual teams:

Interviewee 2: We always put somebody with the client. When we do a straight offshore engagement with anybody we always have somebody with the client in the UK even if it is just one person because that is the direction of focus (to whom the) client gives their comments or questions or moans and groans.

Alex: What's the thinking behind that co-location approach?
Interviewee 5: It goes back to maintaining communication. Making sure that we are as joined up as we can be and avoiding the disconnects or at least minimizing those as best we can. There is a one-team concept here. Even though we are different organizations and have different corporate goals and objectives, there is something that is bringing together two organizations to deliver something. The two things are so interdependent that we can't do this in isolation. We have got to do it together.

Alex: When you are doing all the things that you have described over the last few minutes, do you have to send people from one country to another to meet people face to face?
Interviewee 8: All the time. All the time. Not internally so much but clients for sure. Alternatively we will fly to a common place and create a war room and get all of them together. The way that I like to do it is to get the key folks who are the leaders of individual teams from different countries. Initially for the first few days I would get them in a room together to get them to bond together so that they can all understand who each one is and what each other's strengths are and what

each one's role is. However, many times it is not humanly or economically possible to do this because it is a very expensive exercise.

A number of interviewees commented that face-to-face communication was most important at the start of a virtual team relationship, although it still occurs throughout the duration of the relationship:

Interviewee 1: It is very much easier to build up relationships and trust when you are face to face with someone rather than being completely remote from them all the time. But I think that once you have that initial interaction then it does not really make that much difference location wise.

Alex: Why is it the face-to-face contact that is the most important?
Interviewee 8: It is all about building a relationship and I think that people need to invest in the relationship initially. If the client is in a particular city then you have to fly to that city and sit in front of the client for a few days and build that rapport and connect with that person. Look into his or her eyes and make sure that you can trust them. After that, when you are connecting back in terms of calling up and things like that, if there is no responsiveness then you have not really been able to build a relationship. You cannot keep calling up and leaving voice mails and nobody calls you back. So until the time that you are confident that you will get a call back then I don't think that you can get away from a face-to-face. I am putting it very simplistically but this is all based on my personal experiences. You wouldn't stop doing face-to-face completely until you actually win the engagement but you can slowly fade off.

Interviewee 9: For this project that we are doing in North America now. The high-rise building that we've worked on for the last three years. It was basically one meeting and all other meetings we could have done by video conference.
Alex: So did you do all the other meetings by video conference?
Interviewee 9: No. I did one meeting by video conference but there were 30 or 40 people over the other side. And I figured out that if the group of people is too big on the other side then it becomes useless. I think that you can have a very productive video conference where there are two or three people on each side and you connect to two or three locations. (There should be) a maximum of maybe 10 people.

Interviewee 10: I would say that two out of three meetings you can do by video conferencing but the third meeting has to be in person. You cannot really read people over video conferencing so the crucial meetings have to be in person.
Alex: Is that every third meeting all the way through the project or at some point can you stop having face-to-face meetings?
Interviewee 10: No you can't really stop because if you are involved to the end and then you do quality control, you pick the colours and all this stuff. You need

face-to-face meetings for this to convince the client that this colour is right. In my opinion, there is no way to stop face-to-face meetings entirely but whilst you meet in the beginning face to face once a month at least, towards the end it is once every two or three months.

Two of the interviewees commented that telephone and video communication is more effective after face-to-face relationships have been established. This is consistent with the findings of Takeuchi and Nagao (1993, reported in Kasper-Fuehrer & Ashkanasy, 2001). It is also consistent with the fact that most of the interviewees were motivated to start their long-distance relationships with face-to-face meetings:

Interviewee 9: We have built up a very personal relationship (with these people). So when we are now in video and telephone conferences and they say something then we know exactly what they mean with it and what their intent is behind what they say. Whether it is ironic or whether they want to force something. We have a very clear picture about the meaning behind what they say which we don't have when we don't know the people.

Interviewee 10: Once you have built a relationship with people, you can keep it up on the telephone or video conference.

The interviewees were consistent in their views about what types of meeting needed to be held face to face and about when face-to-face meetings were not necessary. They thought that meetings benefited from being face to face if the meeting made important decisions, if it was a creative meeting that involved intense collaboration and communication of tacit knowledge or if the purpose of the meeting was to resolve a problem. If the purpose of a meeting was to present information or to monitor the progress of the project tasks then a teleconference or a video conference was adequate. The following comments are typical of those made in the interviews. This is consistent with the extensive research described in the paper by Olson and Olson (2000).

Alex: So why would you go for face to face rather telephone call or video conference?
Interviewee 7: Because it is so easy to squeeze out of a conflict on the phone or even in a video conference and you don't feel the atmosphere of the other person, not even in a video conference.

Interviewee 8: I think that when you have a face-to-face (meeting), it is more vocal, it is more ideas and brainstorming and you want to have a dialogue. The phone can work very well when you are going through a presentation or going through numbers or something like that where things are more black and white. A face-to-face dialogue allows you to discuss something more abstract when you want to have a dialogue with the individuals.

Interviewee 9: (A face-to-face meeting) is always one of the first meetings so that we (can) build up the relationship with the other team members and of course position ourselves. I think that it is also important for creative design meetings and the other situation is when things become difficult. When we have a different opinion from other team members and things start to become nasty then that is a time when people have to sit together.

Interviewee 10: Let's say you are trying to coordinate with a mechanical engineer over the telephone or video. If you are not face to face they just tell you 'that is how it has to be' but when you sit there over a drawing and really discuss stuff you find out that actually it doesn't have to be that way, it is just easiest for them.

First impressions and gut feelings

Several of the interviewees talked about experiencing a 'gut feeling' about a person before they knew enough about that person or their organization to make a fully informed judgement about their trustworthiness. Some interviewees report that the 'gut feeling' often occurs after a matter of minutes. One of the implications of this is that trust develops between individuals as a precursor to trust between organizations.

Alex: How long do you need to build up that face-to-face relationship and what sort of situations do you need to be in? Is it an hour's meeting?
Interviewee 1: Could be. It could be as simple as that. Yeah. (It) could be even just a few minutes. It all depends upon the people and the situation.

Interviewee 2: I'm quite quick at making the decision on the people I work with. I don't usually find I'm wrong in terms of the first impression I make. Honestly, I think that I usually make my decision in ten minutes.

Interviewee 6: Once you have started working with people you get an instinct about whether you can trust them or not and but you can't rely on that, you do need facts to try and understand it. You have an instinctive feeling anyway and I don't know what it is that says 'yes I can trust this person. I think that I can trust this person' and then you evaluate against that statement or 'I feel uncomfortable with this person, I need to set some criteria and assess whether I am right or wrong'. There is a certain element of that up front.

Interviewee 9: If I meet them in person, (and) mostly it is not about (the) organization it is about (the) people, I would say within minutes I probably know whether I can trust them or not. Even though it is not scientific and it is more a gut feeling. But I have been right on most occasions. ... (and later on) ...

Let's put it this way. Whenever I come back from such a meeting and I have said 'I have a bad feeling and I think it is going to become a difficult job' then most of the times it has ended up being difficult.

Interviewee 10: Usually it takes a month to six weeks until we get a feeling, and often it is just gut feeling, you think that you can connect with them or not. It is more about the individuals that you are going to work with than the organization.

Openness and transparency

The phrase 'openness and transparency' was mentioned regularly during the interviews. Most interviewees believe that these factors are key element for establishing trust. The quotes below indicate this:

Interviewee 4: Maintaining the transparency of the situation is very important. Saying 'this is something that is required which is why I am doing it. I hope that you are fine with it.'

Interviewee 5: It has to be open. It has to have a culture of openness. It has to not just pay lip service to that. It needs to be lived and breathed. It needs people who are prepared to work with others to make things happen. So collaboration rather than conflict. It is a bit of a cliché but I think openness is probably the main word for me. The moment that you start disappearing into your own dark corners then that is a clear sign that the trust that may have existed actually doesn't exist or you haven't built that right level of trust in the first place.

Alex: Is it as simple as that they keep their word?
Interviewee 9: Yes. And that they are always honest with it even if we don't like what they say. I don't have a problem with that but I want to deal with a situation that is completely honest and frank in our relationship.

Some interviewees believed that secrecy damages both trust and reputations:

Alex: And when you get individuals that are untrustworthy. What is it about them that makes them untrustworthy?
Interviewee 6: It is not delivering on their commitments but potentially hiding it in many ways. People will hide that they are not going to deliver and that makes it far worse. Everybody doesn't deliver on some occasions and there are usually valid reasons. There are people who will hide things from you just so (that) you carry on thinking that it is ok and then it hits you big time.

Alex: If other team members keep things secret or if you changed your approach and kept certain things secret, what effect would that have, do you think?

Interviewee 9: I think that you would lose your reputation and people would start not to trust you any more. That is exactly what I mean with politics. When people want to influence a project in a certain direction, what they tend to do is keep secrets and they exchange their secrets with only a few specific people. That tends to split the teams into groups which work against each other and this is never beneficial within a team.

It isn't just a case of expecting openness and transparency, many of the interviewees went out of their way to find ways to encourage others to be to be open and transparent:

Interviewee 3: You look at other IT departments that support you. It is always better to show the first level of transparency yourself and to see who engages.

Interviewee 5: They are a proud bunch and they don't like to admit failure. They don't like to say 'No' and they don't like necessarily to open their arms to people to come and join in and make it happen. So the first challenge is to shift the playing field to a place where there is that openness.

Many of the interviewees would rather be warned about upcoming problems and would rather a partner said 'No' than fail to deliver. An implication of this is that openness and transparency are more important when there are problems than when things are going well. Saying 'Yes' and then failing to deliver undermines trust:

Interviewee 1: If the other one is up front and says we can't do it or whatever then I would have a lot more respect and trust for them.

Alex: In general how would you expect a trustworthy organization to behave?
Interviewee 2: That is a hard one. I suppose it is no different to how I deal with anyone, I just like honesty, openness, transparency. I don't care if it's going to deliver late. At the end of the day I just want to know that so that I can manage it. What I hate about SystemsCo, and it's just a prime example, is that they don't tell you half what is going on and so when they deliver plans (then) you just never believe in it. I don't think (that) they are a trustworthy organization. I just want them to come and tell me as it is. In fact I want them to be a little bit negative because then you can manage it, you can manage expectations. So to me you have got to be open, you have got to be honest. I really try to make everything transparent (with) nothing to hide, because at the end of the day if I am missing something and someone finds it then the next day it is only going to be better. Just let them see everything.

Interviewee 5: I have dealt a lot with organizations where culturally they don't like saying 'No' and the first battle you need to overcome is getting them to a point where 'No' is an acceptable answer.

Interviewee 8: In one of the countries that we work in people say 'Yes' all the time to everything and 'Yes' means 'I will do this but when I will do it and when it gets delivered is not the Yes'.

As well as advocating the value of saying 'No', the interviewees described the importance of acknowledging one's own deficiencies and accepting deficiencies of others for establishing trust:

Interviewee 3: If there is openness and transparency on both sides about what are the successes, challenges, common goals for life then it kind of keeps working on. Then there is also a subtle acceptance of each others deficiencies because I think that is more important.

Interviewee 5: The world's not a perfect place. Not everything happens as you would expect in this organization with some of the scale of the deals that we are doing. But again, the one thing that struck me coming into the organization is the willingness to say 'OK we have got that wrong'. First of all the willingness to make a decision and make something happen and secondly (instead of) debating and not getting up and doing something when something doesn't go to plan then the focus of attention is on (the) resolution of that issue and an engagement process with the client about 'OK it ain't gone right, how are we going to fix it, this is what we are prepared to do, now let's go forward from that'.

Interviewee 6: We all have things that don't go right in the project-world but it is then being able to work through (it) to come to an agreed approach.

Interviewee 7: So what we are trying to do is to put it on the table and say 'Guys, we have a problem, we have to solve this' and without blaming anyone. This is what we are facing. All of us are facing. You can always try and do it in a moderate way and say 'this is not to blame anybody but to get it into the conversation because we are still at the point where we can solve it'.

The assumption of trustworthiness

Several of the interviewees explicitly stated that their strategy was to assume that their partners were trustworthy until proven otherwise. This is similar to Gambetta's proposition that it is rewarding to behave as if one trusted the other person.

Interviewee 1: If it's the first meeting (then) it's very hard to assess (another organization) and my tendency is to trust rather than distrust.

Interviewee 2: I think that I always have the expectation when I work with any organization that they are going to help (and that) they're going to obey and we are going to work together. So I am never really unsure whether I am going to trust them or not because I always go in there open minded. I think it is what develops after that where I lose trust or faith. I don't think that I have ever been unsure about trusting an organization.

Interviewee 3: To start with you go with implicit trust in terms of saying 'I am bringing this person in and they are going to be in my organization and he is going to play my game'.

Interviewee 4: I feel that you need to trust to start with (in) the relationship and trust with the business. You have to keep trust somewhere. But the first management principle which I believe in is you have to prepare for the worst. You need to plan the thing, monitor and then control. The second is that you always have to have a backup. You need to work towards the worst, thinking that everything is fine but you have to plan the thing properly.

Interviewee 5: I don't start from the point of view of distrust. I will start from the opposite of that scale and we will work from that point to a point whereby either we will confirm or validate that that is a sound judgement or wait from them to demonstrate that that was a bit of a stupid assumption to make and deal with that issue at that point in time. So I start from a place that everybody is good.

Monitoring the behaviour of other members of the virtual team

Competence was mentioned several times as an important factor that is monitored in virtual team relationships. It was not discussed as much as other factors. Maybe this is because competence is more black and white compared to behaviours such as commitment and keeping your word which require more interpretation.

Interviewee 2: It is always that baseline where (if) I think that someone is clearly not competent (then) I struggle to deal with (them).

Interviewee 5: The point that you mentioned about capability is also a valid one because you may like somebody but they may not be capable of doing what you are asking them to do. That gives rise to a different issue.

Interviewee 8: First of all the client has to buy you professionally. If you are incompetent or if you cannot have a meaningful, professional, businesslike dialogue with the client or if you are not good at your art then obviously the client is not going to respect you. So the first fundamental is to know your art and to be able to demonstrate that credibly. Your credibility is based on your performance and what you do in terms of the work. And then everything else follows. If that basic foundation is not there then you will never be able to build anything.

Even more interviewees mentioned the fact that they monitored the commitment of their partners:

Interviewee 1: It's not just about the failure or non-delivery it's about all the interactions in between as well. If someone is really committed to it they'll be talking
to you a lot more regularly. (If) they are not really interested or not committed
(then) you struggle to get hold of them and they don't return your calls et cetera.
You do tend to pick that up quite quickly. And if they miss one (of the) first
deliverables (then) it doesn't necessarily mean that they are going to miss the
others but you just get that sort of gut feel fairly early on.
Alex: And why is it that some groups are more trustworthy than others?
Interviewee 1: Track record. And it's also about their attitude and behaviours. Some
areas have got a real can do attitude and will do anything to help you. They go
outside their boundaries. Whereas other areas will just sort of resist. It's their
nature. ... (and later on) ...
Alex: How long does it take you to tell whether another organization is trustworthy
or not?
Interviewee 1: You get sort of the gut feel for it pretty quickly and it tends to be
about the first non-deliverable (or) failures on their commitment.

Interviewee 3: If you try (to) figure out the commitment of any organization, it (is)
how much skin that either party has in the game in terms of making it a success.

Alex: What do you think makes the difference as to whether your employer is
trusted of not?
Interviewee 6: [Pause] Delivery.
Alex: Can you expand on what you mean by delivery?
Interviewee 6: Yeah. Delivery on promises. If the project goes live on time. If the
quality is good. If I can see you working for me. You may not achieve everything
you say but I can see that there is an absolute desire to achieve what you are
saying. Also that the management of the organization is involved and understands what's going on.

Interviewee 7: Typically we discuss it with the client and by a certain set of questions we want to find out how far he is ready to go. Typically you decide out of
your gut feeling and the impression you get out of these discussions that they
really want to go for it or (whether) it's only words.

Interviewee 8: Those are the three simple measurements for me. Are they committing the best people to the deal right from the top, are they giving the right
amount of time and assets from that organization and commercially are they
doing the right things for us to win the deal.

Monitoring whether a partner keeps their word and does what they say that they
are going to do was mentioned on many occasions:

Alex: What do you think makes the difference as to whether your employer is trusted or not?

Interviewee 1: It comes down to people. Are people doing what they say they will do?

Alex: Is it all down to that or are there other factors as well?

Interviewee 1: There possibly are some other factors. It all pretty much comes down to that. I am just trying to think of an example where it wouldn't be. I can't think of anything offhand.

Interviewee 5: I think delivery is a key one for me. Being a pretty task-focused individual. It is a sure way to end up in a different place from where I am, if you fail to do what you say you are going to do roughly when you say that you are going to do it.

Alex: So presumably a trustworthy organization would do what they say that they are going to do? Is there anything else that a trustworthy organization would do?

Interviewee 6: They would not just deliver it but do it in a quality fashion. It is no good delivering something that does not work. It doesn't just need to be on time but it has to work in the way that we have talked about it.

Alex: How would you expect a trustworthy organization to behave?

Interviewee 9: With many clients we have never had a contract. When I know that I can fully trust a handshake from this person, that's the kind of behaviour that I expect.

The interviewees also used the responsiveness of their partners as an indication of trustworthiness:

Interviewee 1: I would be looking for very fast follow-up on actions. So generally something back to say 'this is what we are gonna do'.

Interviewee 2: I asked them for a plan, a detailed plan of how (they were) going to deliver it and I did not get that plan for three weeks and their comment to me was 'trust me (interviewee) I'll do it'. I said 'I'm not being funny mate but I need something a bit more than that because I need to know what is going on'.

The interviewees used governance (both formal and informal) and risk management as part of their monitoring of the trust relationship and the trustworthiness of others:

Interviewee 2: I always look out for those vibes on the project. That is my yardstick. Are my key people communicating with me and talking to me telling me what is going on and telling me the secret bits that I shouldn't know about? If that dries up then I know that there is maybe other conversations going on.

Interviewee 3: What makes it a little easier holistically is that we have got strong vendor management that is layered across and they are the key focal point. It is actually driven by a little bit by perception but a large amount (by) metrics. I think that metrics is what helps in terms of driving that. There are clear indications based on all of that (regarding) who we should work with and who we should not work with based on our strategic direction.

Interviewee 6: If I got an uncertain feeling then I would put more checkpoints in. You might call something amber and I might call it red. That's OK. That might just be your interpretation of the scale. By having that conversation we might actually agree that we are both right because we are both (of) the same opinion of it, it is just that my own organizational rules says that it becomes red and yours are saying its amber.

The interviewees were aware that monitoring is a two-way street and maintaining trust also involves being sensitive to the other members of the virtual team who are monitoring them:

Alex: That actually leads me onto my other question. It's about how you tell that the relationship that you have had for a period of time has broken down.
Interviewee 2: Well, I have never got to that point, that's because I think so far that, one, we've done a good job and secondly because I am always constantly on the lookout for the tiniest little indicators.

Interviewee 6: (Our clients) all have some level of distrust. They are bound to. They are paying us a lot of money for our services and they want them right and I can completely understand that. I can't think on one yet that hasn't really looked at us and checked us out and made sure that we do exactly what they would anticipate from us. But the level will vary dramatically, there will be some that are just like 'Hmm that is not quite what I expected' but when you have talked it through it is like '(this is) what it is you were expecting and (this is) what were we expecting to do' and actually that is where the issue is. And then it goes away and then something else happens. With others it's a bigger issue.

Interviewee 8: Ultimately you need to realize that when the client gives you an engagement then in some sense he is putting his credibility on the line. He has chosen you based on all the promises and commitments that you have made and he is putting his neck on the block internally. If the project goes foul then people will say 'you chose them and you have to suffer the consequences'.

For some interviewees, monitoring could be described as a four-way street. Each party monitors the other but also monitors their own behaviour and reputation to ensure that they don't do anything to tarnish that reputation and appear untrustworthy:

Alex: When you are using a network approach, what is it that is special about the people you go to that allows you to do that?

Interviewee 1: We've got mutual respect and trust. So they would know that I don't do this all the time. And so if I went to talk to them then there is obviously a reason for it and I will know that they will not fob me off. They will listen so there is mutual understanding and trust.

Alex: Does trust ever break down within the organization?

Interviewee 1: All the time. [Laughs]

Alex: OK. So in what way does it?

Interviewee 1: There is the fear culture in the organization. And if you escalate too many times (about a) non-deliverable (or) complain about it or whatever (then) you lose that trust and respect. It does happen all the time.

Interviewee 3: I have seen relationships go south with suppliers because as a financial institution (that) is not in the IT services sector, we need to be very clear where our skills are and where the supplier organization's skills are. What tends to happen is (that) where there is a large organization dealing with a very small supplier organization and if the intensity of the relationship increases (then) you have a tendency to kind of cross the line to try and manage the business. That is a dangerous game to play because that is not your core skill.

The way that contracts influence trust

The consistent view from the interviewees was that, at best, legal contracts are irrelevant to establishing trust and, if handled badly, contracts can undermine trust. For example, the contract cannot regulate things like motivation, good communication and giving the benefit of the doubt.

Interviewee 3: First and foremost, you never outsource a problem. So if you think that you are outsourcing something because it is a problem, it will always remain a problem. Second, in any scenario you never wave the big 'C' and the big 'S', 'I'm the client and you're the supplier'. The moment that you go down that route it's a negative spiral in my mind because if you are not able to have a content-driven conversation (then) you can keep waving the client flag at them and they will keep waving the supplier flag at you (but) the relationship (will go) in a different direction where you don't get the best out of (it).

Interviewee 10: The contract is nothing more than the written form of the mutual expectations. It regulates the fee, the scope and the way that you do it. But for example, you can't write in the contract that we want above normal engagement or that you do your very best to do an outstanding project for us. That's nonsense because you can't sue someone for that because that is all relative and non-defined.

On several occasions the interviewees commented that reference to a contract was a bad sign and generally indicated that trust had broken down:

Alex: We have talked about you not trusting another outside organization, do you get into a situation the other way round where another organization doesn't trust your employer?
Interviewee 1: Uh huh m. [affirmative]
Alex: And what do they tend to do?
Interviewee 1: You get all the sort of push-backs. No desire to help and no desire to go that extra mile. They'll hide behind contract.

Interviewee 3: When I meet with new suppliers or even existing suppliers, my basic point to them is, 'If I have the ability to call you at any point in time with any challenge I have that is not related to you and you can do the same then that is a good working model (and) a good relationship'. The day we move into a space where we sit round a table and say 'the contract says this and let's talk about what our services are' then that is the day that it starts crumbling.

Alex: So how important is the legal contract then?
Interviewee 9: It is important to get into the country when you are working in the USA. It is not important at all for our working relationships. We have many projects where we never ever had a contract except for a three-line email.
Alex: So how often do you have to go back to the contract?
Interviewee 9: Whenever we go back to the contract, it is always a bad sign. With regard to payment, of course, you go back to the contract and look at what is described in the contract in detail. Other than that I would say normally never.

Interviewee 10: The contract itself is only important if something goes wrong. It regulates the working relationship, but you don't usually look at it again unless there is a problem because you have regulated everything and you have it in your head.

A few interviewees mentioned that the contract negotiations at the start of a relationship have the potential to create distrust if they are not handled carefully:

Interviewee 5: The moment that you get into commercials, there is always an element of distrust that creeps in at that point in time because you are always second guessing 'so why is that person asking that question?' 'why is he going down that route?' My strategy around that is to try to avoid getting into the nitty-gritty dispute-type discussion. I have always played the role (of) 'let those boys over there worry about all that lot. I'm over here and I just need to get this job done'.

Interviewee 10: Most clients make the mistake that they do these 60-page contracts which is total nonsense. The best contract is less than 10 or 12 pages. It just regulates the scope, the payment, the expenses, confidentiality clauses, who's involved in the project and (for what) period. Nothing else needs to be in the contract and long contracts usually create mistrust because you are discussing, at the beginning, eventualities that hopefully will never happen. The contract is not the important thing. The negotiation of the contract is a very good way to come to know each other and to understand what all parties involved expect out of this project.

When trust breaks down

A number of the interviewees talked about situations where trust had broken down. In many cases they gave the impression that it was not possible to reinstate trust. It is not clear whether this was because they had already invested their best efforts to build trust and failed or because there is something about distrust that is difficult to dislodge. The word 'professional' was often used to describe their reaction to a relationship that had deteriorated in this way. The interviewees' comments indicated that benevolent trust does not exist in these situations and the motivation to do more than is absolutely necessary has been lost.

Alex: When that happens, when trust has broken down with an external organization, how do you deal with that?

Interviewee 1: On a very professional basis. You lose that personal relationship (and it becomes) just very professional.

Alex: What do you mean professional in that circumstance?

Interviewee 1: Well, it's making no assumptions around anything and setting everything out really clearly. This is our scope, this is your scope.

Interviewee 2: I know that there are lots of people in that company that are good and I like and I would rely on them. I don't trust the company and I think that is based on my first interactions with them. So I do kind of bear a grudge a bit.

Interviewee 3: In that particular instance we had a few management changes at our end with people coming in who were not used to that model. So they drove the operating model in a way that was different from that which we originally emphasized. That took the operating model into a different space where they suddenly clamped up. They suddenly went into a shell and decided that that their organization wanted to deal with it in a pure supplier/client relationship. Kind of throw things at us and expect things back. So they moved to that operating model and that fundamentally shook the foundation of that relationship and it went to a stage where it was not recoverable.

Interviewee 9: What he does all the time is to give a counterpart to everybody he does not know very well. In this way there is always a competitive situation within the team because he cannot judge our work. This gives him security in front of his client. It is an unhappy situation. It is not very common and is not a lot of fun to deal with.

Alex: So how do you approach that? How do you deal with that situation?

Interviewee 9: I deal with it at a professional level. That is not the way that we normally react. I draw a clear line. We provide our work and we try to do solid work but nothing more.

A Two-Stage Process for Establishing Trust

A consistent picture has emerged from this research of a two-stage process for establishing trust in virtual teams. The two-stage process is summarized in Table 9.2.

During the first trust stage, virtual team members initiate situations where they can develop personal relationships with the other team members. They assume that the other team members are trustworthy at this stage. They collect information about the goals and personal characteristics of the team members in order to facilitate this relationship building. They also present themselves as competent and committed to the team activities and they monitor the competence and commitment of the others. A typical example of commitment is willingness to 'go that extra mile' by doing more than is absolutely necessary for the benefit of the other team members. Much of the information about the other team members is collected by observing their non-verbal communication. The interviewees believe that it is especially important that the interactions during this stage are carried out face to face. At some point during the first stage the team members may make a quick decision about whether they will continue with the relationship and, if they don't, then they end the relationship and do not proceed to the second stage. In many cases the decision to move to the second stage will be taken by others in the organizations and the team members will have no choice but to proceed. However, it is always

Table 9.2 Key characteristics of the two-stage process for establishing trust

	Stage One	*Stage Two*
Basis of trust	Benevolence Ability Commitment	Commitment Integrity Responsiveness
Typical behaviours	Assume trustworthiness Initiate relationships Present oneself	Communicate targets Implement project governance Monitor the work of others
Typical outcomes	Personal relationships	Reputation
Face-to-face contact	Non-verbal communication and social activity are crucial	Non-verbal communication and social activity are less crucial
Openness and transparency	Openness and transparency are very important	Openness and transparency are very important
Legal contracts	Coercive legal contracts may undermine trust	A focus on legal contracts indicates that trust has broken down

Source: author's own.

beneficial to build the personal relationships and assess the competence and commitment of the others since this will establish benevolence-based trust, ability-based trust and commitment-based trust, which will make the second stage more effective.

During the second trust stage the team members start exchanging the products of their work. They monitor the work and the behaviour of the other team members. Specifically, they monitor their integrity, commitment and responsiveness. They use formal and informal project governance as a matter of course as part of the monitoring process. They are aware that they are being monitored by the other team members and present themselves in a way that maintains both their own reputation and the personal relationships that they developed during the first stage. They prefer that interactions during this stage are carried out face to face. However, face-to-face contact is less important than it was during the first stage. If they become unhappy with the integrity, commitment or responsiveness of the other team members then they will typically do two things. First, they will increase project governance in order to simultaneously verify their negative assessment and also communicate specific targets to the other team members so that they can be in no doubt of what is expected of them. They may also do more relationship building in order to improve the relationship. If the unsatisfactory behaviour cannot be rectified then they will restrict their activities and efforts to their minimum obligations and the relationship may eventually be terminated by one or other party. The effective operation of the virtual team depends upon the maintenance of the benevolence-based trust, ability-based trust and commitment-based trust from the first stage and the successful development of integrity-based trust and responsiveness-based trust during the second stage.

The openness and transparency of the members of the virtual team are a success factor in both the first and the second stage of the relationship.

If a legal contract is created at all then this will be done at the end of the first stage or the beginning of the second stage. The contract is a risk management activity carried out by the organizations involved and is, at best, irrelevant to the quality of the trust that is achieved and the team relationship and, at worst, it can have a negative on the team relationship by introducing distrust.

One implication of the two-stage process is that although the first stage is not necessarily a prerequisite for the second stage, it creates the conditions for a pleasant, efficient and motivated working relationship with the other virtual team members. Since assessments of trustworthiness during the first stage are based on observing non-verbal communication then the first trust stage is likely to be a greater challenge for virtual teams than collocated teams because face-to-face contact and opportunities to observe non-verbal communication are limited.

Discussion of the Two-Stage Process

In this section I will discuss the two stages with reference to the interviews and the five trust viewpoints.

The first trust stage is explained by the social trust, initial trust and bounded rationality viewpoints. The social trust and bounded rationality approaches are evident in the way that the team members initiate relationship-building activities and make the assumption that the other team members are trustworthy until proven otherwise. They take this approach because they need to develop benevolent trust quickly in order to foster team cohesion and collaboration at an early stage in the lifetime of the team. The initial trust approach is indicated by the fact that the first activity that the team members engage in is to communicate their own ability and commitment and observe how the other team members react to this. If they react positively then the team members develop confidence that everything is under control and the relationship is likely to be successful. The team members test each other by discussing real or hypothetical situations and then assessing how well the other team members understand and react to these communications. This is where non-verbal communication is important since it allows honest misunderstandings as well as intentional deceit to be detected using cues such as body language, facial expressions and office behaviour. The outcome will often be a rapid 'gut feeling' about the trustworthiness of the other team members. Face-to-face communication is important during this stage for several reasons. First, it provides non-work opportunities for building personal relationships that contribute to benevolent trust. These include social communication before and after meetings, at the coffee machine and after work which help the team members to discover common interests and become comfortable with each other. Second, face-to-face meetings are the only way to observe body language, facial expressions and organizational behaviour. Consistent with the findings of Olson and Olson (2000), the interviewees believe that current video-conferencing technology does not provide sufficient detail to discern non-verbal communication. The latter is essential in order to make rapid assessments of trustworthiness based on bounded rationality. Third, face-to-face meetings are important for the communication of tacit knowledge in two ways. They facilitate the development of benevolent trust which in turn encourages the communication of tacit knowledge. They also directly transmit tacit knowledge through styles of collaborative work that are only possible when people are collocated. At the end of the first stage the team members may have the opportunity to decide whether to proceed to the second stage. This decision will be based on bounded rationality.

Swift trust is not usually relevant to the first trust stage for virtual teams. Virtual team members are often unknown to each other or are imposed by senior people within their organizations. Therefore the selection of team members based on their reputation is not the norm. However, it does sometimes occur and, where it does, the swift trust viewpoint will be relevant to deciding whether a team member is trustworthy based on their reputation.

The second trust stage is explained by the integrative trust and the swift trust viewpoints. The bounded rationality of the first stage gives way to unbounded rationality during the second stage as the team members exchange the products of their work and increasingly observe specific instances of each other's work behaviour. The team members mostly monitor integrity, commitment and responsiveness. Ability is not explicitly monitored during the second stage but it is implicit in noting whether a team member does what they say they are going to do. As predicted by the integrative trust viewpoint, since the team members have much more information about the other team members they start to calculate the relationship risks based on their observations. They collect information about these risks using formal and informal project governance techniques such as communicating the likelihood that problems will occur on a task (e.g. red, amber and green), comparing the planned and actual dates for project activities, collecting a variety of metrics about the project and the contributions of each of the team members and paying attention to changes in the openness of the other team members. When the governance indicates that there aren't any problems, this contributes to the perceived trustworthiness of the other team members. Even if team members never work with each other again, a good reputation is still valuable because it determines how someone is treated on the current project. As predicted by the swift trust viewpoint, the interviewees are motivated to maintain their reputation. A bad reputation will make the situation difficult for a team member in several ways. First, the other team members may well ask them to provide additional governance information and participate in more governance activities. Second, the benevolent trust with the other team members may deteriorate, therefore they will lose the advantages of benevolent trust and working with the other team members will become more difficult. Third, other team members may expel the team member from the project or alternatively may leave the project themselves. The interviewees described not only how they monitor the behaviour of other teams but also how they monitor their own behaviour in order to ensure that they can rectify the situation quickly if there are early indications that their team is losing its reputation. Face-to-face communication is important in the second stage for subtly different reasons than it was important in the first stage. First, face-to-face communication is important when the team members need to rebuild benevolent trust if it has deteriorated because the team has lost its reputation, or where there are new team members or for any other reason. These activities are typically less frequent than during the first stage. Second, face-to-face communication is important for observing non-verbal communication in order to detect early indicators that a team is losing its reputation. These signs will not necessarily be made explicit nor be easily apparent in emails or on the telephone. Third, as in the first stage, face-to-face meetings are more effective for communicating tacit knowledge. This explanation is consistent with the comments in the interviews that face-to-face communication is more important in the early than in the late stages of a project. The interviewees described how virtual teams persevered with unsatisfactory team relationships by behaving 'professionally'. A decision to terminate a relationship was not taken lightly owing to the costs involved. Ironically, one of the few reasons that a legal contract contributes to the longevity of a team relationship is because it increases the legal and reputation costs of terminating that relationship.

It is interesting that the five trust viewpoints do not reference openness and transparency, although these characteristics were mentioned as important trust enablers in most of the interviews. Swift trust even includes 'avoidance of personal disclosure', which is the opposite of openness and transparency. Being open and transparent and not being open and transparent both incur risks. In order to be open and transparent a team must make themselves potentially vulnerable to opportunistic behaviour from the other teams. However, if a team is not open and transparent they may still be vulnerable because a lack of openness and transparency will inhibit the development of benevolent trust with the other teams. Consistent with the social trust and bounded rationality viewpoints, the interviewees advocated developing the habit of openness and transparency despite the risk of vulnerability because 'the alternatives were worse', since they believed that the lack of openness and transparency inhibits the development of trust and may inspire distrust.

The only viewpoint that addresses legal contracts is initial trust. This proposes that legal contracts will increase the likelihood of trusting behaviour. The interviews do not support this proposal for virtual team relationships and some interview comments indicate exactly the opposite. They suggest that legal contracts introduce the possibility of ulterior motives which make the team members feel more vulnerable and this undermines their trust in the other team members. If a legal contract becomes an instrument of coercion then these interview comments are consistent with the social trust viewpoint that coercion undermines mutual trust because one party in the relationship imposes their power over the others. From the evidence of the interviews, one of the positive effects of a legal contract is to maintain a working relationship when trust between the team members has broken down.

The only trustworthiness factors described in the integrative trust viewpoint are benevolence, ability and integrity. I have added the trustworthiness factors commitment and responsiveness since these were regularly mentioned in the interviews and I think that they are useful additions. However, benevolence is qualitatively different from the other four trustworthiness factors. Benevolence is effectively an affective outcome produced by social trust activities whereas ability, integrity, commitment and responsiveness are characteristics and behaviours that are monitored in the trust relationship.

There are several possible motivations for trusting behaviours. The managers' objectives may have been commercial, task orientated, related to maintaining personal status or centred on the job satisfaction of the project team. The content of the interviews shows that the managers consistently followed the two-stage process regardless of their motivation.

Some Limitations of This Research

Some of the managers that were interviewed were personal contacts of mine and I was introduced to others by either the first set of interviewees or other personal contacts. Therefore the comments from the interviews may be influenced by the type of people that I know and find interesting. The comments may not be typical of all managers of virtual teams. Also, a set of interviews with only 10 people is considered a small number, even for qualitative research of this type, and further interviews might have produced a wider range of evidence. I chose to interview senior managers because I correctly anticipated that these would have a good overview of virtual team relationships and a broad awareness of the problems of virtual team working. However, interviews with more junior staff that do the detailed project work might provide different perspectives on the ways that trust is established. A different set of questions may also stimulate different comments.

The interviewees all work on high-technology projects either in IT or in building construction. Virtual team working in these industries is already substantial and continues to increase; however, the working practices of these industries are specialist and members of these virtual teams are predominantly knowledge workers. The findings from this research may not be applicable to virtual project teams in other industries or to other types of virtual teams such as virtual work teams or virtual management teams.

In some research projects, interviews are analysed by more than one person in order to remove personal biases from the analysis and contribute alternative interpretations of the statements that are made. The interviews used in this chapter were only analysed by myself, partly because no one else was available and partly in order to protect the confidentiality of the interviewees. As the research analyst, it was I who decided that the meaning behind statement 1 from person A was the same as statement 2 from person B. It is certainly possible to draw different and alternative conclusions from the interviews. One of the reasons that I have included so many interview comments in this chapter is to allow the reader to draw their own conclusions.

The brief descriptions of the five viewpoints only scratches the surface of the academic papers from which they are derived. There is also a large body of work about trust generally and trust in virtual teams specifically that is not referenced in this chapter. It would have required several books to cover this subject fully.

Some Unanswered Questions About Stage One

A further limitation of this research is that it leaves some unanswered questions about Stage One of the two-stage process. First, what aspects of Stage One have the greatest influence on the outcome of the project? Is it behaving as if one trusts the other team members? Is it being open and transparent? Is it actively portraying oneself as capable and committed? Is it reading people's hidden thoughts and feelings by observing their non-verbal communication? Is it necessary for team members to demonstrate all the Stage One characteristics in order to develop benevolent trust? Are some characteristics more important than others? Are they all equally important and have a cumulative effect? Are some more important in one situation while others are more important in a different situation? Second, to what extent do Stage One behaviours need to be reciprocated? Is it sufficient for a single person in a virtual team to demonstrate Stage One characteristics in order to trigger benevolent trust? Is it necessary that at least one person in each of the constituent groups that make up the virtual team demonstrates Stage One characteristics? Is it necessary that high-status and influential team members demonstrate Stage One characteristics? The third set of questions appertains to the mechanism by which Stage One behaviours trigger benevolent trust and foster successful projects. Gambetta (1988) suggests some answers to this but these warrant further discussion. Do Stage One behaviours promote a set of group norms within a team that encourages the team members to give-and-take rather than hide behind legal contracts? Do they reduce fears of opportunistic behaviour by other members of the team and allow team members to forego costly defensive behaviours and therefore, quite simply, make the project easier to implement? Do they enhance project success by improving communication and the dissemination of tacit knowledge? Answers to these questions would assist the development of techniques for developing trust in team relationships.

The implications for project management techniques

Formal project management techniques, such as Prince2, fail to address some aspects of the two-stage process. They provide structured techniques for implementing most of Stage Two but almost none for Stage One (see Table 9.2). However, the managers interviewed for this research believe that the Stage One techniques are equally necessary in order to achieve an effective virtual team and a successful project. Some organizations might consider that acting as if one assumes that the other team members are trustworthy and being open and transparent are naïve and risky project management strategies. They might also consider that a legal contract which specifies the actions to be taken in every eventuality and takes advantage of the stronger position in a relationship (e.g. owing to a customer's purchasing power) demonstrates a responsible approach and due diligence. However, the managers interviewed for this chapter consider that team relationships that are based *purely* on project governance and legal constraints have a higher risk of failure and that establishing benevolent trust greatly increases the likelihood of sound team relationships and successful projects. It is clear from the interviews that experienced team managers begin projects with activities designed to develop benevolent trust. However, the techniques for building trust are informal and communicated by word of mouth. Maybe the time has come to acknowledge the importance of Stage One activities and provide formal training in skills such as observing non-verbal communication, acting as if one trusted the other members of the team, and in demonstrating openness and transparency? Maybe it is time to manage trust relationships as rigorously as the governance aspects of projects? In my experience of working on virtual team projects, the amount of trust that exists between a customer and their supplier(s) is a key project success factor. Even when projects succeed despite low-trust relationships, they invariably take longer and cost more than projects that exhibit high trust.

The Implications for Managers

This research has a number of implications for managers working in outsourcing situations that involve virtual teams. In these situations, organizations often rely too much on the details in the contract which, as I have shown, can debilitate working relationships. In my outsourcing work I regularly need to remind managers that 'projects run on trust' and that, in most cases, the only way to resolve a difficult situation is to boost the amount of trust between the constituent groups and especially between customers and suppliers. The implications are listed below.

1. Demonstrating behaviours that promote trusting relationships will increase the likelihood that a virtual team project will be successful. These trust-building behaviours include acting as if the other team members are trustworthy, being sincerely open and transparent in one's dealings, paying as much attention to non-verbal communication as to what people actually say and actively presenting oneself as capable and committed. These actions will have maximum effect if they are started as soon as the virtual team is established.

2. Traditional project management techniques (e.g. Prince2) are important in virtual teams and allow team members to communicate targets, implement project governance and monitor the work of the other team members. However, these should not be allowed to overshadow the trust-building activities, especially during the early stages of the virtual team.

3. The skills required to promote trusting relationships may be different from the skills required to implement traditional project management techniques. This should be considered when staffing a virtual team.

4. Face-to-face meetings are critical for virtual team success and for building trusting relationships. A major reason for this is that face-to-face meetings facilitate the observation of body language, facial expressions and other non-verbal communication which indicates people's otherwise hidden thoughts and feelings. Another reason is that they facilitate informal social activities. This is the reason why virtual team workers travel so far and so frequently to meet their counterparts. The video-conferencing technology used by virtual teams was considered inadequate for observing non-verbal communication by the managers who were interviewed. Further research is required both to understand what aspects of non-verbal communication are most important for establishing trust in virtual teams and to develop video-conferencing technology that can support this.

5. Creative activities, decision making and problem-solving meetings derive most benefit when the participants are face to face. Meetings that present information and review status are just as effective via teleconferences and video conferences as they are face to face.

6. Trust develops between individuals as a precursor to trust between organizations. Creating the conditions that enable trust to develop between individuals

will increase the likelihood that a virtual team will be successful and will promote strong relationships between organizations.

7. Demonstrating and encouraging openness and transparency is critical to trust building within virtual teams and therefore the success of those teams. In order to achieve openness and transparency it is necessary to demonstrate a reasonable tolerance of mistakes and to refrain from opportunistic behaviour. It seems likely that an organization where there is fear of opportunistic behaviour from others or where there is a blame culture will find it difficult to develop trust within virtual teams.

8. Coercive legalistic behaviour undermines trust within virtual teams. Too much reliance on legal contracts for project governance increases the likelihood that trust will break down in a virtual team. However, when trust is absent from virtual team relationships, the legal contract contributes to the success of the virtual team activities by increasing the legal and reputation costs of terminating a relationship.

References

Axtell, C. M., Fleck, S. J., & Turner, N. (2004). Virtual teams: Collaborating across distance. In C. Cooper & I. Robertson (Eds.), *International review of industrial and organizational psychology* (pp. 205–248). Chichester: John Wiley & Sons.

Burke, W. W. (2006). Conflict in organizations. In M. Deutsch, P. T. Coleman, & E. C. Marcus (Eds.), *The handbook of conflict resolution: Theory and practice* (2nd ed.) (pp. 781–804). San Francisco: Jossey-Bass.

Cohen, S. G., & Bailey, D. E. (1997). What makes teams work: Group effectiveness research from the shop floor to the executive suite. *Journal of Management, 23*(3), 239–290.

Cramton, C. D. (2001). The mutual knowledge problem and its consequences for dispersed collaboration. *Organization Science, 12*(3), 346–371.

Gambetta, D. (1988). Can we trust trust? In D. Gambetta (Ed.), *Trust. Making and breaking cooperative relations* (pp. 213–237). Oxford: Blackwell.

Gibson, Christina B., & Cohen, Susan G. (Eds.). (2003). *Virtual teams that work. Creating conditions for virtual team effectiveness*. San Francisco: Jossey-Bass.

Good, D. (1988). Individuals, interpersonal relations, and trust. In D. Gambetta (Ed.), *Trust. Making and breaking cooperative relations* (pp. 31–48). Oxford: Blackwell.

Haas, M. R. (2006). Acquiring and applying knowledge in transnational teams: The roles of cosmopolitans and locals. *Organization Science, 17*(3), 367–384.

Hinds, P. J., & Bailey, D. E. (2003). Out of sight, out of sync: Understanding conflict in distributed teams. *Organization Science, 14*(6), 615–632.

Hoegl, M., Ernst, H., & Proserpio, L. (2007). How teamwork matters more as team member dispersion increases. *Journal of Product Innovation Management, 24*(2), 156–165.

Jones, C., Hesterley, W. S., & Borgatti, S. P. (1997). A general theory of network governance: Exchange conditions and social mechanisms. *Academy of Management Review, 22*(4), 911–945.

Jones, G. R., & George, J. M. (1998). The experience and evolution of trust: Implications for cooperation and teamwork. *Academy of Management Review, 23*(3), 531–546.

Kasper-Fuehrer, E. C., & Ashkanasy, N. M. (2001). Communicating trustworthiness and building trust in interorganizational virtual organizations. *Journal of Management, 27,* 235–245.

Mayer, R. C., Davis, J. H., & Schoorman, F. D. (1995). An integrative model of organizational trust. *Academy of Management Review, 20*(3), 709–734.

McKnight, D. H, Cummings, L. L., & Chervany, N. L. (1998). Initial trust formation in new organizational relationships. *Academy of Management Review, 23*(3), 473–490.

Meyerson, D., Weick, K. E., & Kramer, R. M. (1996). Swift trust and temporary groups. In R. M. Kramer & T. R. Tyler (Eds.), *Trust in organizations. Frontiers of theory and research* (pp. 166–195). London: Sage.

Olson, G. M., & Olson, J. S. (2000). Distance matters. *Human–Computer Interaction, 15,* 139–178.

Rosen, B., Furst, S., & Blackburn, R. (2007). Overcoming barriers to knowledge sharing in virtual teams. *Organizational Dynamics, 36*(3), 259–273.

Vonnegut, K., Jr. (1974). *Wampeters, forma & granfalloons.* London: Jonathan Cape.

Further Reading

All the references above are worth a read, especially the Olson and Olson paper for a description of research into the differences between face-to-face and electronic communication and the Axtell, Fleck, and Turner paper for an excellent summary of virtual team research up to 2004.

Gambetta, Diego (Ed.). (1988). *Trust. Making and breaking cooperative relations.* Oxford: Blackwell.

This is out of print and it is difficult to obtain original copies. However, a scanned copy of the book can be can be downloaded as a pdf document from Diego Gambetta's website at www.nuff.ox.ac.uk or Google 'Diego Gambetta'.

Chapter 10

Knowledge Transfer and Knowledge Sharing

Richard Blakeley and Stephanie J. Morgan

One of the problems discussed many times by clients involved in outsourcing contracts is the perception that knowledge is lost to the outsourcing supplier after a transfer, or is not gained during outsourcing contracts. Very little academic research has been carried out to gain insight into how knowledge can be retained (nor indeed into how much is actually lost). It makes sense that people who have been transferred into another organization may decide to withhold knowledge, given that their own knowledge may be the main reason they are valuable. Similarly, new people coming into an outsourcing contract may find it hard to gain new knowledge, or may feel that their own knowledge should be primarily used by the supplier rather than the client. In this chapter one of us (Richard Blakeley) gives an overview of the literature on knowledge transfer and between us we assess how this may inform the people side of outsourcing.

This literature review will start by defining knowledge transfer and sharing and associated behaviours and its importance as an issue for study. It will then consider current literature with regard to determinants and barriers to individual participation in knowledge sharing. The review will also consider work with regard to practices that may have an effect upon knowledge-sharing behaviour, such as collaborative working practices, leadership, managerial support, supervision and procedural justice, and consider further practices that may be studied for their effect on knowledge-sharing behaviour. The review considers literature on the broader organizational factors that may affect knowledge-sharing behaviour, such as sub-unit behaviour and restructuring. This review touches upon how national cultures may influence knowledge-sharing behaviours. Finally, some potential issues arising for outsourcing contracts are discussed.

The Human Side of Outsourcing: Psychological Theory and Management Practice
Edited by Stephanie J. Morgan
Copyright © 2009 John Wiley & Sons Ltd.

Leidner defines 'knowledge' as the possession of insights, understanding plus practical know-how (Leidner, 2003). This definition is a useful starting point, but there still remain questions that the field of organizational psychology has not adequately addressed in its literature. For example, how is knowledge categorized or measured in a meaningful way? What are the most precious or essential forms of knowledge and what are the benefits or costs of being in possession of that knowledge?

The field of knowledge management has become important because of increased global competition which has led to organizations looking at better ways to manage knowledge as a source of competitive advantage. A key challenge within knowledge management is for organizations to collect knowledge that individuals hold so that it is not lost should they move on, and for the whole organization to benefit from access to that knowledge. In outsourcing, knowledge can be lost during staff transfers, or difficult to acquire in-house during ongoing contracts.

Key activities with regard to knowledge management include 'knowledge transfer' and 'knowledge sharing' which, as Renzl (2006) observes, are used interchangeably. Renzl defines knowledge transfer as the transmission of knowledge directly from source to recipient. Knowledge sharing emphasizes the collective character of knowledge that emerges from interaction between individuals and groups. However, in both transfer and sharing, the individual chooses within certain constraints and limitations (e.g. supervision, contractual obligations etc.) when to do so and to what extent and it is the question of how to maximize the input of individuals and the reasons why they may or not do so that has become of so much interest. Much of the enquiry has been with regard to knowledge sharing, because this has a broader potential and it is less understood than transfer between individuals.

Two recent studies advance understanding of the 'determinants' and 'behavioural intention formation' in individuals with regard to knowledge sharing.

Cabrera, Collins, and Salgado (2006) hypothesized that aspects of personality, including agreeableness, conscientiousness, openness to experience, value-based commitment and self-efficacy (Bandura, 1986), have a positive correlation with knowledge sharing. They also hypothesized that individuals enjoying high autonomy (e.g. Hackman & Oldham: job characteristics model, 1976), expecting intrinsic and extrinsic rewards (expectancy theory, Vroom, 1964), perceived support from colleagues and positive perceptions of the quality and accessibility of knowledge management systems would strongly correlate with knowledge-sharing behaviour. The references to Bandura, Hackman and Oldham, and Vroom show that Cabrera et al. consider theories of motivation to have applicability in the knowledge-sharing field.

In a self-report survey of 372 people working in Spain for a large multinational, Cabrera et al. (2006) found significant correlations between knowledge sharing and self-efficacy, openness to experience, and perceived support from colleagues and supervisors. Further, less significant relationships were identified between knowledge sharing and organizational commitment, job autonomy, positive perceptions regarding the availability and quality of knowledge management systems and perception of positive reward. Many of these aspects change during outsourcing transfers, or are less easy to modify when using outsourced suppliers, leading to possible issues with knowledge sharing.

Bock, Zimud, Kim, and Lee (2005) hypothesized that intention to knowledge share is affected by attitudes, rewards, reciprocal relationships, self-worth and 'subjective (group) norms'. Their research was undertaken by means of a field survey of 154 managers in 27 Korean organizations and found that subjective norms and organizational climate affect individual attitudes to knowledge sharing and that anticipated reciprocal relationships and self-worth affect intention to undertake knowledge share. However, 'extrinsic' rewards were found to have a negative influence over intention to knowledge share.

The hypotheses in both of the studies are on face value, a useful field of enquiry that should be undertaken more widely in different industries, size of companies and cultures, and different methodologies should be tried to develop more understanding of individual determinants of knowledge-sharing behaviour. The results of these studies do not have universal application. However, Cabrera et al. perhaps capture something of Western corporate and 'individualistic' attitudes to knowledge sharing, whereas Bock et al. capture something of Eastern 'collectivist' attitudes to knowledge sharing: this point perhaps being best illustrated by the differing findings regarding reward as an individual motivator. Again, these findings should be borne in mind, particularly when offshoring.

Both studies explain what the determinants of behaviour are, but they do not explore in any detail why these behaviours have developed, other than Bock et al.'s reference to the theory of reasoned action, which suggests that individuals consider all the information available to them regarding the consequence of an action (i.e. knowledge sharing) and take action based on what they perceive to be the best way forward. This theory may appear too general to be of any real value, but as Cabrera and Cabrera (2005) observe, the theory of reasoned action suggests that 'in order to influence intentions to share knowledge, one must first identify the factors that affect people's attitudes towards sharing and their perception of norms for sharing' (p. 721).

Cabrera and Cabrera offer potential theoretical development in terms of knowledge-sharing behaviour through adaptation of social capital theory, social dilemma theory and social exchange theory (ibid., pp. 721–724). Social capital theory would suggest that workers choose interpersonal relationships to facilitate knowledge sharing. Social dilemma theory would suggest that an individual makes a rational choice to share information for the collective good of an organization, having weighed up the social dilemma of whether to contribute to the organization's knowledge or to 'free ride'. Social exchange theory would suggest that individuals regulate their interactions (i.e. knowledge sharing) with individuals based on a self-interested analysis of the costs and benefits of doing so. All of these theories are interesting and insightful and should be put to the test through further research.

There has been research into negative individual behavioural intention to sharing knowledge, which may be considered to be 'barriers'. Bordia, Irmer, and Abusal (2006) conducted research in 'evaluation apprehension' and its relationship to the perceived benefits of knowledge sharing and the intention to share knowledge.

Evaluation apprehension was defined by Rosenberg as a 'person's active anxiety toned concern' (Rosenberg, 1969) that their actions may be evaluated negatively, i.e. knowledge shared may not be valued, appreciated or reflect well on the individual. Social exchange theory was used as a framework to examine the apprehension evaluation and perceived benefits of knowledge sharing and the intention to knowledge share in two contexts: (1) an interpersonal transfer of information and (2) transfer of information to a database.

The results of their research using questionnaire returns from 119 employees in a 'knowledge intensive' multinational consultancy firm show a negative association between 'evaluation apprehension' in both the interpersonal and database contexts, though evaluation apprehension is higher and knowledge share lower on a database.

There is perhaps more research to be done regarding the personal experience of both transferring knowledge from person to person and sharing via web-based and database media. An interpersonal conversation by which knowledge is transferred is temporary in nature and therefore may be perceived to represent less effort expended and less risk to an individual's reputation than committing something to documentation, which more permanently captures someone's ideas and know-how, may take more time and may be discredited by increased exposure. Similar themes are discussed by Dickerson and Kemeny (2004), who have identified stronger 'stress responses' in situations where an individual is unable to control the size of its audience.

In contrast, Birgit Renzl's (2006) working hypothesis was that knowledge documentation and the fear of losing one's unique value mediated the link between trust and knowledge sharing within and between teams. Using a sample of two companies, one in the utilities sector and the other in software consulting, Renzl received returns on self-administered questionnaires from 133 in the first company (utilities) and 68 in the second company (software). The sample was taken from knowledge-intensive project teams and headquarters-based employees, respectively.

The results supported the hypothesis and revealed that trust in management had a positive impact on knowledge sharing, but trust had a negative impact on the mediating fear of losing one's unique value. Further, it was found that trust had a positive impact on the mediator of knowledge development, but fear of losing one's unique value had a negative effect on knowledge sharing within and between teams. The research found that knowledge documentation had a positive impact on sharing within and between teams. This suggests that in outsourcing contracts it will be important to facilitate trust in teams (see Chapter 9) and action will need to be taken to ensure that knowledge is clearly documented. However, issues still remain.

Renzl has adopted a definition of trust as 'faith in the trustworthiness of others' (Cook & Wall, 1980), related to trust grounded in emotional bonds between individuals involving mutual care and concern. However, levels of trust are arguably subject to change over time and perhaps a longitudinal study on an organizational level that measures knowledge sharing against measures of 'trust' within management–employee relationships would reveal more.

Both Renzl (2006) and Bordia et al. (2006) identify emotional barriers to knowledge sharing, but at a highly conceptual level that is hard to break down into everyday language. Further, there is a lack of specificity regarding the level, type, volume and quality of the knowledge being discussed. It may have been useful to have tested for self-efficacy and personal worth as competing variables to shed light on the apprehension regarding the value placed on knowledge in the company and the fear of losing one's unique value by making personal knowledge available to other people. There is perhaps something to be considered in terms of the dynamic and changing nature of knowledge and the way in which individuals evaluate their personal knowledge in that context.

Some of the knowledge-sharing literature considers the effect that management style and organizational practice can have on knowledge-sharing culture. Jen Te Yang (2007) undertook an empirical exploration of how 'collaboration', defined as 'mutually sharing norms of behaviour', affects knowledge-sharing behaviour. Knowledge sharing was measured by a 15-item scale which incorporated the scales developed by Yang (2004) and Sveiby and Simons (2001). Collaboration was measured by use of their measure of organizational culture, which has a collaboration component. The survey of employees working at all levels in nine international tourist hotels in Taiwan found a strong and positive relationship between collaboration and the effectiveness of knowledge sharing, particularly between lower-level workers in the organizations.

Using the same sample, Jen Te Yang's research also collected data on how certain types of leadership role affect knowledge sharing. This found strong correlations between facilitator, mentor, innovator and broker roles and knowledge sharing. These are all roles that could be associated with the view that managers and leaders should concentrate their efforts on team development, in order to increase knowledge at the disposal of an organization.

Te Yang's research is important because of the sheer size of the sample and the development of measures of knowledge sharing on an organizational level. As a cross-section of this particular Taiwanese industry at present, it presents a strong picture of a culture with a highly developed style of organizational learning and knowledge management.

However, Te Yang's key findings would not appear to have universal application and may be particular to Taiwanese culture and the structure of the hotel industry. For example, a key finding, that there was a negative correlation between a supervisory style of leadership and knowledge sharing, is not supported by King and Marks Junior's study of knowledge sharing within a US military organization (King & Marks, 2008). This research found that supervisory control had significant impact on frequency and effort. Further, the research found that 'perceived organizational support', defined as 'global beliefs concerning the extent to which the organization values their contributions and cares about their wellbeing' (Eisenberger, Huntington, Hutchison, & Sowa, 1986), had little effect on knowledge-sharing activity. Therefore, like Bock et al.'s study (2005), Te Yang's research in Eastern cultures may not have general applicability to Western organizations. Again, in outsourcing situations these two cultures are often working together, so differences in approaches to knowledge sharing may have an impact on the success of the outsourcing, and on the amount of knowledge shared between organizations.

Kim and Mauborgne (1998) consider the importance of 'procedural justice' in determining knowledge-sharing behaviour. Procedural justice is defined as 'the extent to which the dynamics of the decision making process are judged to be fair'. There are three criteria within organizational justice: engagement (individual input to decision making), explanation (individual understands the reasoning behind the decision) and clarity of expectation (managers have a firm idea of what is expected of them). In line with other procedural justice research, which has found individuals more willing to cooperate voluntarily with others and management initiatives, Kim and Mauborgne develop propositions that perceived procedural justice will have:

- positive effect on attitudes of trust and commitment;
- positive effect on idea and knowledge sharing;
- positive effect on performance (via attitudes of trust and commitment and idea and knowledge sharing).

Further, they propose that perceived violation of fair process will:

- induce emotional anger, intellectual discontent, the hoarding of ideas, counter effort behaviours, and have a negative effect on performance.

Kim and Mauborgne found support for their propositions through two rounds of unstructured interviews with senior managers in eight participating companies. Further, they developed a theory of 'intellectual and emotional recognition' explaining the results, which suggests that where individuals feel that their 'intellectual and emotional worth' is met by an employer, they demonstrate a willingness to cooperate with others, whether it is in their self-interest or not.

Kim and Mauborgne's propositions and theory have some intuitive appeal, particularly as justice has been shown to be a crucial concept across a wide range of organizational issues. However, on the basis that they provide no information about the industry or size of the organizations studied, no conclusions can be drawn regarding the validity or applicability of the study.

Despite the questions that I have about Kim and Mauborgne's and Jen Te Yang's research, they have opened up an important area of research with regard to management practice and its effect on knowledge sharing. Cabrera and Cabrera have recently listed management practices that may foster a knowledge-sharing culture (Cabrera & Cabrera, 2005), warranting further enquiry. These good practices include aspects of work design, training, performance appraisal, compensation, culture and technology (see Cabrera & Cabrera, 2005, p. 724). Several of these areas have been touched upon in knowledge-sharing research, including the culture of caring, fairness, perceived support and technology to enhance existing social networks, but there is considerably more research to be done. Their table is a very useful tool for guiding future research in practices related to knowledge sharing.

Dorothy E. Leidner (2003) and Georg Von Krogh et al. (Krogh, Roos, & Hoerem, 1996) make observations regarding structural issues in organizations and knowledge sharing. Leidner observes that organizational sub-units present a big challenge to the development of electronic repositories of knowledge. This is because sub-units fear the loss of the 'dependency relationship' that senior managers may have on their particular knowledge (Leidner, 1992): a concept close to Renzl's suggestion that individuals fear losing their unique value. These issues of 'ownership' of knowledge have led to the failure of executive information systems and decision support systems in the past. Hence, there has been a move towards new systems based on web technology, which return control of information content to organizational sub-units. The issues of control of knowledge in 'team orientated' cultures and the interaction between people and the different forms of technology and how that affects knowledge-sharing behaviour is very interesting and is worthy of further research. Again, what happens to knowledge sharing when the team consists of people from client- and supplier-based organizations is not fully understood, but the research suggests that it may be problematic.

Von Krogh et al. consider what happens to knowledge management at times of 'corporate divestiture', one of the many forms of restructuring of an organization that include merger, acquisition, leveraged management buyout, internal venturing, divestitures and, more recently, outsourcing.

Von Krogh et al. use an analogy of the human body's 'neural system' to describe how knowledge is transferred through an organization, i.e. each part of an organization contributes to corporate memory, thereby influencing a firm's actions and responses to the environment. Organizational memory is acquired, stored and retrieved through (1) knowledge tied to key individuals, (2) physical archives, (3) corporate culture of learning and transmitting knowledge, (4) knowledge embedded in organizational processes and (5) organizational structure. Further, each unit of organization stores and retrieves knowledge from other units to solve specific problems or perform tasks.

Von Krogh et al. then explore the possible effect of corporate divestiture through the use of the 'phantom limb' analogy. Just like the 'phantom limb' that amputees continue to feel, corporate divestiture is seen as analogous to amputation of a corporate part. The negative effects of the 'phantom limb' can reduce knowledge transfer from the departed unit of organization, thus weakening the corporate memory. The extent of the negative effects of the organization being a problem for the organization depends upon the importance of the former business unit to the organization.

Von Krogh et al.'s analogy is negative but relevant for corporate divestiture. The positive effect of a restructure in terms of knowledge sharing and transfer is not considered here. However, it is an interesting area for the knowledge management field and warrants research. The effect on the parent organization of other forms of restructuring as listed above, particularly outsourcing, would be useful.

Conclusion

The literature suggests a range of potential issues for outsourcing contracts. In particular, the loss of corporate memory when departments are divested, or transferred, in an outsourcing deal can be very problematic as time goes by, especially when the deal needs renegotiating or there is a desire to bring work back in-house. Although this chapter highlights that there may be individual differences in approaches to knowledge sharing, organizations are 'strong environments' which will influence the level of sharing. Justice perceptions have been shown to be linked to knowledge transfer, and justice is often embedded in the organizational culture. Justice is also problematic during outsourcing transfers, when unless the transfer is handled very sensitively the people involved will perceive injustice (as shown in other chapters) and are very likely to reduce knowledge sharing. Another important aspect to consider is the potential for cultural differences in approaches to knowledge transfer, which are likely to be based on both national and organizational cultural variations. Our key advice would be to be aware of the potential loss of knowledge and take appropriate action, be aware of the importance of justice while doing this, and be aware of potential differences in approach by organization and country. Such awareness should enable open discussion to set standards, documentation of knowledge where appropriate, and perceptions of justice to reduce the risk of refusal to share. That old saying, 'knowledge is power', is just as true in outsourcing as any other form of business!

References

Bandura, A. (1986). *Social foundations of thought and action: A social cognitive theory.* Englewood Cliffs, NJ: Prentice-Hall.

Bock, G. W., Zimud, R. W., Kim, Y. G., & Lee, J. N. (2005). Behavioural intention formation in knowledge sharing: Examining the roles of extrinsic motivators, social psychological forces and organizational climate. *MIS Quarterly, 29,* March, 87–112.

Bordia, P., Irmer, B. E., & Abusal, D. (2006). *Differences* in sharing knowledge interpersonally and via databases: The role of evaluation apprehension and perceived benefits. *European Journal of Work and Organizational Psychology, 15*(3), 262–280.

Cabrera, A., Collins, W. C., & Salgado, J. F. (2006). Determinants of individual engagement in knowledge sharing. *International Journal of Human Resource Management,* February, 245–264.

Cabrera, E. F., & Cabrera, A. (2005). Fostering knowledge sharing through people management practices. *International Journal of Human Resource Management, 16*(5), 720–735.

Cook, J., & Wall, T. (1980). New work attitude measures of trust, organizational commitment and personal need non-fulfilment. *Journal of Occupational Psychology, 53,* 39–52.

Dickerson, S., & Kemeny, M. E. (2004). Acute stressors and cortisol responses: A theoretical integration and synthesis of laboratory research. *Psychological Bulletin, 130*(3), 355–391.

Eisenberger, R., Huntington, R., Hutchison, S., & Sowa, D. (1986). Perceived organizational support. *Journal of Applied Psychology, 71*(3), 500–507.

Hackman, J. R., & Oldham, G. R. (1976). Motivation through the design of work: Test of a theory. *Organizational Behavior and Human Performance, 16*, 250–279.

Kim, W. C., & Mauborgne, R. (1998). Procedural justice, strategic decision making and the knowledge economy. *Strategic Management Journal, 19*, 323–338.

King, W. R., & Marks, P. V. (2008). Motivating knowledge sharing through a knowledge management system. *Omega, 36*(1), 131–146.

Krogh, G. V., Roos, J., & Hoerem, T. (1996). Restructuring: Avoiding the phantom limb effect. In G. V. Krogh & J. Roos (Eds.), *Managing knowledge: Perspectives on cooperation and competition* (pp. 137–154). London: Sage.

Leidner, D. E. (1992). *Reasons for EIS failure: An analysis by phase of development.* Working Paper. Waco, TX: Baylor University.

Leidner, D. E. (2003). The information technology-organizational culture relationship. In R. D. Galliers & D. E. Leidner (Eds.), *Strategic information management: Challenges and strategies in managing information systems* (pp. 523–550). Oxford: Butterworth-Heinemann.

Renzl, B. (2006). Trust in management and knowledge sharing: The mediating effects of fear and knowledge documentation. *Omega, 36*, 206–220.

Rosenberg, M. J. (1969). The conditions of evaluation apprehension. In R. Rosenthal & R. L. Rosnow (Eds.), *Artifact in behavioural research* (pp. 279–349). New York: Academic Press.

Sveiby, K. E., & Simons, R. (2001). Collaborative climate and effectiveness of knowledge work – an empirical study. *Journal of Knowledge Management, 6*(5), 420–433.

Vroom, V. (1964). *Work and motivation.* New York: Wiley.

Yang, J. T. (2004). Job-related knowledge sharing: Comparative case studies. *Journal of Knowledge Management, 8*(3), 118–126.

Yang, J. T. (2007). Knowledge sharing: Investigating appropriate leadership roles and collaborative culture. *Tourism Management, 28*(2), 530–543.

Chapter 11

The Experience of Outsourcing Transfers – A Life-Cycle Approach

Royston Morgan

Introduction

Outsourcing is a mature business process, with not only a continuing high number of contracts signed, but also an increased activity in re-contracting as the original agreements come up for renewal, as well as a large number of clients bringing outsourced work back in-house. This latter trend of 'backsourcing' is driven in part by an increasing worry that outsourcing is not bringing the expected benefits. This is supported by surveys that are uncovering high levels of dissatisfaction (Deloitte, 2005) amongst organizations using outsourcing as a structuring tool. This dissatisfaction may be partly due to a lack of appreciation of the complexities of the business change being undertaken that must account for the many facets of outsourcing, especially around stakeholder management, resistance and the people who must be transitioned successfully to make the whole thing work. Before concentrating on the people aspects in detail we will first clarify different types of outsourcing, and then discuss the outsource life cycle from a processual point of view, relating this to the life cycle as experienced by the staff, and as a result draw out the issues raised by each stage of the outsourcing journey. We will conclude that the people aspects of outsourcing are only lightly considered in current management practice and that a much more holistic approach is needed for the management of the people aspects. It is our view that this failure to consider the people in outsourcing in part explains many of the failings, problems of resistance and the apparent difficulties in achieving the benefits that this business process promises.

A key criterion for a definition of outsourcing, and the particular focus in this chapter, will be that the process includes a transfer of staff to the third party while still requiring them to carry out more or less the same work for their previous

The Human Side of Outsourcing: Psychological Theory and Management Practice
Edited by Stephanie J. Morgan

employer. This can be compared with more general forms of subcontracting, where outside companies carry out work for a client, supplementing in-house resource with their own staff or providing in effect the finished product using their own resource. In our view this should not be called outsourcing but contracting, as there are substantial differences. In this chapter the main thrust of the discussion is the people in transition between organizations, looking at the ways they cope and make sense of the situation as they move between the two performing the same work, sometimes even within the same social setting, but with a different employer paying their salaries.

In this chapter we will distinguish outsourcing from other types of external sourcing, by using a definition that emphasizes the delegation or handing over to a third party of all or part of the technical, process and human resources of an organization, which includes management responsibility for transferred staff (Morgan, 2002). Thus in this chapter we look only at outsourcing that involves a transfer of people from one company (OldCo) to the service provider (NewCo) and the people factors that must be accounted for during this transition.

We turn now to a discussion of different forms and stages of outsourcing, their implications for the overall transition process, and focus in more detail as we go through each stage of the life cycle in turn, focusing on the people aspects. Figure 11.1 indicates the importance of the stages of scoping, preparation and evaluation, negotiation and selection, transition, maturity and re-scoping, and this model will act as a framework for the discussion that follows.

The Forms of Outsourcing

There are a variety of models of outsourcing that relate the type of service to the form of the relationship with the supplier. Cullen, Seddon, and Willcocks (2005) is a particularly useful framework that outlines seven key attributes, around scope, supplier grouping, financial scale, pricing framework, duration, resource ownership and commercial relationship. To simplify the argument here, we emphasize differences between full versus selective, single or multi-vendor, the process to be outsourced, and the scale and duration of the contract.

Full outsourcing is found when a complete function or department is outsourced and handed over to one or more suppliers. Selective outsourcing occurs when a specific function is outsourced, such as the payroll function in HR. There are also differences between single, dual and multi-vendor outsourcing, with obvious coordination and contractual complexities to be addressed as the number of vendors involved increases. The area to be considered for outsourcing will also impact on the process. There are differences in risk in outsourcing cleaning services compared to functions with high specificity and complexity, such as some parts of IT or human resource management. In general, simpler, easy-to-define services carry lower risk – although this will vary by organization. Our work has shown that even in cases where a service can be classified as simple, and apparently risk free, the

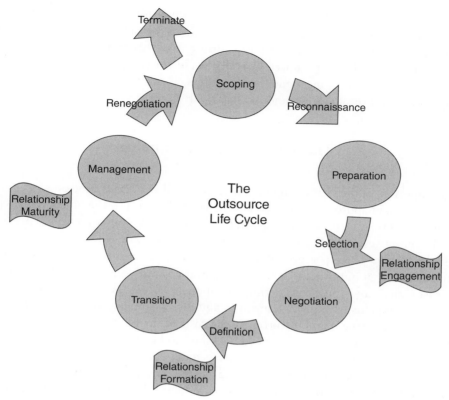

Figure 11.1 Life-cycle stages

removal of that task from the overall structure can have adverse consequences for change. The removal of cleaning staff from the control of ward managers to a more central operation in the UK has led to a deterioration in service and an increase in hospital infection rates as aspects of control and identity that had previously maintained performance have been broken. The scale of the project is also important, not just in terms of value and number of people involved, but also whether multinational operations are included. Extra management effort and time will be needed to construct a workable contract and these hidden long-term costs in monitoring supplier performance for any international suppliers often negates the immediate direct labour cost savings. There are also regulatory aspects such as data confidentiality and security that must be accounted for. Outsourcers cannot 'outsource' their liability for these important areas. Finally, outsourcing varies by timescale, with some contracts being signed for relatively short periods, two years for example, and others extending for 10 or even 20 years. Clearly, the longer the timescale, the more certainty there will be a need for flexibility and for contractual changes, as over such a long timescale, spanning possibly an economic cycle, changes in the business model may result in the original business case being invalidated. However, short contracts carry their own problems, particularly around stabilizing the change, building trust and managing human factors. Calling for too short a contractual timescale, as some authors have suggested, is almost certainly a mistake and does not allow time for suppliers to establish a firm grip of the services or for personnel to adapt to the new circumstances. Overall, the ideal sweet spot seems to be around five to seven years: any longer and the outsourcing is overtaken by economic events; any shorter and the change cannot be stabilized.

The Rationale for Outsourcing

It is important at the start of an outsourcing discussion to determine on what basis this is the right approach and to establish a clear view of how the outsourcing will fit into the broad thrust of the organizational strategy. A clear consensus is needed of the objectives and a thorough review of the options available that may achieve the same ends. There is a prevailing logic, sustained by outsourcing vendors and consultants, that outsourcing is the only solution to organizational problems such as cost management. Just considering the rationale for whether or not to outsource can be an impetus to improve a function and increase understanding and control. If you can understand and then control the costs of the function and clarify where it fits into your business, an informed decision can be made about whether or not to outsource. Furthermore, an open management discussion and a strategic consideration by a broad constituency of management and stakeholders can add to the legitimacy and fairness of the whole process, reducing the chances of resistance and premature failure. There are some good examples where access to high-quality management skills and advanced new technology can happen, but this is not automatic and has to be planned for – an outsourcing is the beginning of such a process, not its end outcome. Some organizations have found an improvement in service quality, especially when the supplier has learnt the business and really understands the client-specific needs, but this will take time to mature. An outsourcing creates a mutual dependency that builds a business relation of high specificity and risk that extends over time and demands a solid relationship between the parties and trust based on delivered performance. There are also situations where economies of scale can be found, and where outsourcing can increase the future flexibility of an enterprise, especially around the area of shared services. However, an increasing number of contracts are being brought back in-house (Deloitte, 2005), or departments being rebuilt, and in IT, outsourcing over half of these processes have poor or mixed outcomes (Cullen et al., 2005), which suggests that there are some problems to be addressed.

The Hidden Costs in the Life Cycle

One of the problems in realizing benefit potential from outsourcing is the *ex post* 'hidden' costs that occur at each phase of the life cycle. It takes time and skill to develop benchmarks, learn how to manage an outsourcer and negotiate with suppliers, and these *ex post* costs can all add dramatically to the expense of managing an outsourcing and swamp savings if not managed carefully. The transition can also involve a lot of disruption, a slowdown in reaction time and flexibility owing to prolonged supplier learning, and the time invested in managing relationships. The time and effort spent on supplier relationships can vary – surveys show that some senior managers feel the relationship can be adversarial, with almost continual fighting over objectives and contract interpretation. The cosy relationship with an internal department changes, as each 'extra' service carries a service cost that will result in heated discussions. Trust (or lack of it) has been shown to be a key element in outsourcing; the development of trust takes time and can be difficult as overarching goals are often not shared or defined so that there is understanding of where the parties are coming from. These 'hidden' costs increase with the number of suppliers or vendors that have to be managed, particularly if vendors are managed individually rather than through a prime supplier. Experience in outsourcing can reduce these management cost pressures but not completely, and there will always be a substantial element of management effort needed to control the service delivery of suppliers. The management of an internal department will be 'swapped' for the management of an external supplier and a whole new set of competences will have to be learnt. It is not the case that the disposal of a troublesome department will allow focus on other areas of the business without cost, and suppliers will need possibly more management attention to ensure the effectiveness of service delivery. There are also issues regarding the level of control over the activity. Using the market for control of a service can never give as much leverage as using 'hierarchy' when swift action is needed in a crisis.

Vendor search and selection is another of the hidden costs of outsourcing (see Barthelemy, 2001). However, investment at this stage can reduce other costs and help to avoid problems later in the life cycle. Trust needs to be developed early and is built upon reputation, repeated interactions, communication and 'courtship' and, at the highest level, joint goals and shared values (Shapiro, Sheppard, & Cheraskin, 1992). Hidden costs here include the learning curve required for the vendor and the general disruption caused during the transfer. During a transition, particularly where there are feelings of resentment owing to poor people management, service can effectively fail and this needs to be planned for. As already highlighted, there are management costs for the client and often development and recruitment costs to ensure that the right skills are in place to manage the transition successfully. Paying attention to the entire life-cycle cost will help control the escalation of these costs and risks but the extra cost to do this and to manage the end-to-end process effectively must be factored in at an early stage. Under-resourcing a major outsourcing is not advisable. The extent to which the strengths or weaknesses of outsourcing can be balanced depends in large part on having a clear understanding of what needs to be achieved from an outcome and an awareness of the circumstances that will influence success – as well as the capability to evaluate the outsourcing decision objectively based on facts.

Life-Cycle Stages in Outsourcing

Most managers understand the concept of the product life cycle as applied to outsourcing. Outsourcing can be viewed as a form of service-based 'product' flowing through the life-cycle stages moderated by the continuous iterative nature of the process as the form of the service is shaped during contracting and the early stages of delivery. Although there may be peaks and troughs in terms of the lifetime value of outsourcing contracts that are important from a financial perspective, a more important consideration is the different stages that each outsource process goes through and how this impacts the people affected. Unfortunately, many organizations consider only the initial search for a vendor and handling of the procurement process when considering outsourcing, forgetting the longer-term factors such as people management, imagining that once the deal is done it is no longer their concern – which is a grave mistake that lies at the heart of most outsourcing horror stories. Even if you think the people were at the core of the original problem, their transition must be carefully planned. Thinking through the transition of the people who will actually still be delivering the service in the new world order, and how their needs and aspirations change during the outsourcing life cycle, is a key task for organizations wishing to be successful in this change process.

While some models have been developed for specific forms of outsourcing that allow for different stages, most of these miss out important steps. For example, Khanna and New (2006) propose that HR planning during outsourcing should move from analysis/evaluation, contract negotiation, and transition to stabilization/improvement. They do allow for a return path in their model, but there is little discussion of changes after the stabilization phase. George (2005) suggests stages of selecting the vendor, preparing the contract, outsourcing management, and termination. However, we believe that it is vital to ensure that the activity to be outsourced has been fully scoped in detail, and efficiency savings made first, before deciding to outsource. We therefore recommend the stages of scoping, preparation, negotiation and selection, transition, maturity, and re-scoping – using these six stages will enable each important aspect of the outsourcing life cycle to be given full attention.

There are also issues regarding the people life-cycle processes, an aspect often forgotten in the management literature. If you are talking of transferring staff to the vendor, and/or imposing redundancies, this will have a major impact upon all the staff. Often they will perceive that you are transferring them because they were underperforming and unwanted. There are also issues around the differences to their contract, and a major change in the nature of their work relationships. Particularly if the contract with the supplier is short term, their work position has become very similar to that of a contractor. Even if they decide to transfer permanently to the supplier, it is likely that they will have to adapt to a very different way of working. The psychological contract – their perception that if they worked well there would be some concern for their welfare – has been broken. Although some suggest that staff have to go through various stages of shock, protest, despair and

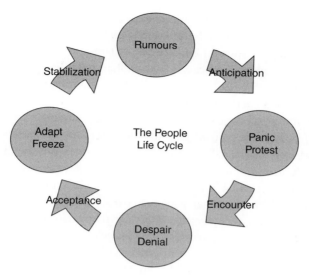

Figure 11.2 People life cycle

mourning, there is evidence that events, particularly how the situation is managed, can make a real difference and mediate the worst effects of this process.

Staff doubts and concerns are likely to make an impact on the performance of the function, both in the long and short term. Research indicates that the very nature of outsourcing contracts, including the need to continue working for the original employer, and often to remain on a contract that matches that of their original employment, does impact upon the way staff evaluate their situation, and influences their performance. In our work on outsourcing transition we have shown that even up to two or three years after the initial transfer staff are still finding relationships with their old and new employer difficult and feel that they need to monitor the situation with their old employer closely.

To highlight the experience of staff during the stages, throughout the discussion we will use findings and interviews from our own research that show the parallel emotional experiences undergone by people, the 'people life cycle': the preparation, encounter, adjustment and stabilization effects as shown in Figure 11.2. We will now assess the key considerations for each stage. Where in the text we have quoted from our own findings, company names are not used and we refer to OldCo and NewCo to mean the original and receiving company, respectively.

The Outsourcing Stage: Scoping

In this stage, the outsourcing strategy is formulated, the core activities of the organization identified, and the areas considered for outsourcing sketched out. It will be important to work through the rationale for outsourcing in detail, and assess the risks involved (Osei-Bryson & Ngwenyama, 2006). In most cases research has shown that the major reasons for considering outsourcing are the need to cut costs and/or get a better grip on a process. However, handing over an activity that is not efficient succeeds only in handing excess profit to the outsource vendor. It is far better to ensure that all activities are evaluated, processes improved and excess cost reduced before handing over to a third party. Indeed, it has been known for vendors to walk away from certain outsourcing tenders once they realize there is no slack. At an outsource conference the author attended, a vendor spokesperson, when asked for a view on companies that did make efficiency savings prior to an outsourcing, responded by saying that 'there has to be a win–win' and 'that sort of approach does not help', which suggests that available cost slack is exactly what was expected from this supplier's side to make this work for them. However, if a supplier still feels that it is worth continuing based on the knowledge that slack has already been taken, this is OK as they are likely to be the type of supplier experienced enough to able to make even more improvements and go beyond the simple options.

The full range of alternative options to outsourcing should be considered, not to avoid the issue, but to really clarify the improvement objectives – most of the savings, if that is all that is required, may be achievable by routine good management practice. Furthermore, do not mistake the option of outsourcing as the business problem itself that needs to be addressed. The symptom (high costs in IT, for example) may be just a result of a much wider systemic problem in the organization that needs to be tackled. Apart from keeping in-house, and setting up an external division or shared services, there are other options available. These include joint ventures, alliances, and bringing in management changes to enhance knowledge and increase efficiency. The use of flexible working, improved performance management and regular review of projects can also assist. HR should be involved as soon as possible, as they can be critical in addressing the performance management aspects. In some circumstances it may be helpful to encourage the internal department under threat of outsourcing to propose an internal bid. This should be handled sensitively but may encourage further efficiencies and perceptions of fairness and justice – at the very least it will deliver a grounded baseline of your costs.

Some organizations try to hide from their staff that they are considering outsourcing – this is unlikely to be a good strategy as the rumour mill is very efficient at making things sound much worse than they are. 'Well, it all started just as rumours, which is the worst thing I think … we were uncertain for a long time.' People have a strong need to make sense of situations and will make up information rather than feel they do not know, and opinion leaders will construct a different reality that will fill the void of disinformation. It should be obvious that from the first meeting on the subject the secret will be out.

Reduce the rumours by making clear statements and giving people the opportunity to discuss the impact on their individual situations. If they are being given the chance to demonstrate their own effectiveness, this should be emphasized as a good thing, giving them some element of agency over their own destiny and allowing the process to be rationalized. Timing is everything in both scoping and the next stage, preparation. Some organizations in the public sector in the UK take years to carry through an outsourcing, with a resultant loss in motivation for the staff – as one public sector worker pointed out:

> Morale went through the floor, over the last six years, it took six years … and in the end we couldn't get any lower. Your pride in working for the old industry had gone and you were just grateful that you still had a job and you got a payslip at the end of the month, and you weren't bothered about going to work anymore, nobody gave a damn, including the bosses. (Public sector staff)

However, pushing through an outsource transition too quickly can also have its problems, for example in terms of the organization not being ready and the impact on the staff involved:

> Because everything that I had set up and done just stopped, and we weren't told it was going to be stopped, now if I had been given warnings that is was all going to grind to a halt suddenly, I could have done things to manage people's expectations … but we were presented with this but were not presented with an alternative. (Private sector manager)

Another participant in our research highlighted how too much speed leaves people feeling confused – their department was set up as a separate organization and then almost immediately outsourced:

> Suddenly we were a separate organization and then we were joining within NewCo, that bit I felt was very quick; I mean we didn't really understand what was happening at that time. (Public sector staff)

While this discussion is a little like 'Goldilocks and the Three Bears', the discussion should be around getting the organization to a state where it is ready for the change and taking the time to do so is necessary to ensure success. It is tricky, sometimes a decision has to be made and action taken, but where it can be used careful planning and allowing enough time to 'move' can pay dividends in long-term change acceptance.

The Outsourcing Stage: Preparation

The first stage will give the information to work through a preparation phase, where baselines are measured and evaluation criteria developed. Here the remaining stages must be considered in far more detail. How will the contract be negotiated and will outside help be needed? On what basis will the best vendor be selected; if not just on cost, what evaluation criteria will be used? The risks here include not fully understanding what is being achieved by outsourcing, not fully scoping the activity, and not employing (or developing) the right skills for managing the future contracts. HR departments should be encouraged to develop clear plans here for the transfer of staff, before negotiation has even started.

In developing transition plans do not assume that all staff will be resistant to the change – many IT staff in traditional bureaucratic organizations may feel that a move will be of benefit to their careers:

> I think the way that IT in general is going in the civil service (with) the tendency towards outsourcing, there's not going to be that many IT jobs *per se* left. So I thought if I wanted to stay in that arena then the obvious thing to do was to get out. (Public sector staff)

Some people will even volunteer to be moved so that they will be transferred, which may give those who are very resistant an opportunity to stay with you, although it must be said that this can cause more problems than it solves if the outsourcing transition is seen as optional. Whatever the situation, do not assume that those resistant to the move are just 'stick-in-the-muds' who will not be needed following the transition – often their scepticism comes from deep understanding of the business process. A concern frequently expressed to us was the potential loss of knowledge and the weakening connection between the organization and its former staff that can result from an outsourcing process – these 'stick-in-the-muds' may be just the people needed to help with supplier management and provide organizational continuity.

In this preparation stage it will be important to reflect upon potential future changes in the organization; in many organizations reconstruction and refinements are ongoing, but even in those that appear relatively stable, some attempts at 'future state visioning' should be made, where the future structure of the organization is envisaged and constructed in its market context 5 or 10 years hence in order to define, *inter alia*, the required form of governance and control needed. The objectives for the outsourcing must be clear, consistent and reasonable, and these should be reviewed in light of what the organization will look like. Objectives such as cost reduction, refreshing technology, and increasing service may not be internally consistent. Determine the key driver, and include it openly in the tender documents – the supplier will then be able to pitch the proposal answering the objectives and the chances of a successful deal will be increased. 'Sign off' internally and agree the rationale that is driving the process forward and then use this as the underpinning for the business case.

Consideration should be given to all elements of the outsourcing area under consideration and the type of contract that will be required. Cullen et al. (2005), as we saw earlier, suggest seven key attributes for consideration: scope, supplier grouping, financial scale, pricing framework, duration, resource ownership and commercial relationship. Although aimed specifically at IT outsourcing, these aspects are likely to be relevant for all types of market sourcing. We would also suggest that inclusion of 'staffing' and 'technology' (not just for IT outsourcing) is essential, as these two areas are of vital importance and prone to rapid change. Do not assume that the best staff from the supplier will be made available or that the remaining staff can be retained. Often the best will leave altogether, the highly skilled redeployed and not so skilled staff brought in to carry out the routinized tasks to a level dictated by the precise service requirement to realize the potential cost savings.

The Outsourcing Stage: Negotiation and Selection

Then comes the negotiation and selection stage, where due diligence is conducted, service level agreements outlined and selection of supplier(s) made. The selection should be based on clear criteria – some companies have chosen purely on price, only to regret this later. Linked to these activities are the important areas of relationship and contract development. We have shown in our work that the type of relationship developed with the supplier can be critical to success. An adversarial purchase–supplier relationship at the start imprints a way of working that can have poor long-term consequences for the total process and can lead to a spiral of poor outcomes that ends in premature closure. Similarly, a poorly negotiated or clumsily defined contract can spell disaster.

Complementarity, strategic and cultural fit are important selection criteria for a vendor – the vendor must be an organization with which you and your people can work. Furthermore, the selection process must ensure that there is a broad fit in terms of size and geography between the parties. If an organization is a large blue-chip organization it is of little use outsourcing to a garage operation – and the opposite is true for a small company outsourcing to an IBM. Research has shown that the overall potential for benefit from this process comes from the joint leverage between parties that are broadly comparable in size and culture – asymmetric partnerships have a higher failure rate. Furthermore, collaborative integrative models increase the value that can be achieved and this increased value can more than cover the increased overhead of the outsourcing management.

Planning and strong management are also essential prerequisites for a successful outsourcing process. It must be understood that the vendor does this for a living – often the vendor sales team have been doing this for years. In many organizations the managers running the project will do this once in their entire careers – assume that training and support are needed to carry out this task. Alternatively, hire good (sceptical) consultants to manage the contracting – although expensive, this will be cheaper than a potential disaster resulting from an outsourcing contract crafted by amateurs. It is vital to plan the capacities of the client team that will be creating and then managing the outsourcing process. In a large bid the job is full time and often key members of the customer bid team will also have a day job to contend with. Time pressure can act in the vendor's favour, so do not be put under pressure by either party's optimistic time schedules and risk the skipping of important details. Research the vendor carefully; details of outsourcing troubles are rarely reported, there is a conspiracy of silence and vendors are likely to give references only for success stories. Contact your industry association to get the inside story and make time for detailed evaluation of vendor client references. Often even competitors will give an inside line; one of our clients in the banking sector was told quite bluntly not to touch a certain large-scale outsource vendor – he chose to ignore this advice, with career-damaging consequences when it went horribly wrong. A well-run processing department turned into a basket case in six months! Accordingly, interviewing past clients with the vendor not present will be the most reliable method to assess vendor suitability. No serious industry-level vendor will have problems with this.

If the outsourcing involves multiple nationalities, or offshoring is being considered, bear in mind the cultural differences in negotiation practice. Hofstede's (1983) dimensions have been shown to be useful for understanding these differences (see also Chapter 8), and cross-cultural training or specific consultant help may be required to enable those negotiating to be fully effective. Differences have been found also in negotiating and decision-making style (Taplin, 2005), and, for example, in how outsourcing success is achieved – particularly between Western and Eastern cultures (see Samaddar & Kadiyala, 2006). There is evidence (Niederman, 2005) that organizations can learn from a limited first exposure to a multicultural contract, and thereby reduce problems for future contracts. Even within one country there are differences in organizational culture that need to be considered, and staff will need priming on how to understand and cope with this.

Many of the discussions we held focused around the differences in organizational culture that outsourcees experience. This becomes more apparent over time, although some of our research subjects had not become adjusted even by the time the 'maturity' stage of the contract had arrived. It is likely that the change in culture and the need to gain an understanding of new ways of progressing one's career within a system house (in the IT examples) cause confusion and need to be learnt. Particularly in the public sector, the career progression routes differ greatly from those in the private sector and position in the organization depends very much on seniority and service length rather than expertise *per se*. It is this adjustment that must be made by newly outsourced staff that can take time. Cultural difference can also extend to the visible artefacts and modes of working that can sometimes be expressed in a form of cultural shock:

> I don't think they tend to communicate, because we have been to two of their meetings and when you go in they are all like robot people. They all dress the same … they are all walking round with cups of coffee … they all sat at their desks and not communicating with their colleagues … we were hoping they were going to communicate with us, maybe that is a bit naïve … they are just working away munching their sandwiches. (Public sector staff)

This can also cause problems for those retained to negotiate or manage the outsource contract – a number have highlighted real problems in dealing with 'the other' when norms and assumptions around speed and professionalism cause issues.

The ongoing management of the outsourcing contract and the process may be at risk if the cultural differences are great. In one former public sector outsource provider in the UK the public sector ethos continued into the way contracts were managed with some of their major banking clients, to the extent that clashes occurred when public sector work practices were grafted onto a dynamic free-flowing environment (in this case a 'work at home on Friday' agreement). This difference between behaviours in differing organizational cultures needs to be understood, especially when offshoring in multinational contexts.

One aspect of the acquisition of new cultural norms is the certainty (or not) that the people being outsourced are actually going to a specific vendor – in several of our research organizations (especially in the public sector) the end selection had (a) taken an inordinate amount of time and (b) 'flip flopped' between several potential suppliers. Staff find it extremely stressful to be told that they are moving to one company and then informed that they will be transferred elsewhere, and although not always avoidable it will be important to recognize that this is an issue for those being transferred. If a change is made, the people being outsourced will need to break the proto-attachment they will have already built with the original choice and start again with the new one. They will need more time to prepare for the transfer, and their own preparation stage means that they must be able to gather information about their future employer. Their expectations will be created here as to how this is all going to work – so allow presentations from the vendor, give time for staff to study documentation and facilitate them searching around to find as much information as possible about the new situation. During this stage of the process employees need to make sense of the situation and start the process of identification and rationalization. Furthermore, allowing a period of adjustment will also demonstrate fairness and care for their future which, as well as paying dividends in the future, is the correct way to treat employees making a difficult transition.

The Outsourcing Stage: Transition

As we move through the transition stage the contract will be actually interpreted and the relationships – good or bad – become established. It is vital here to 'start the way you mean to go on', and set up clear processes for communication and monitoring. Also of importance is the need to retain management and staff who will be needed to manage the outsource vendor. Care must be taken to design the internal organization correctly, and allow some flexibility and slack capacity. The transition team should work closely with the vendor and ensure that the governance structure and staffing transfers are in place. Extra time should be allowed for facilitating the staff transition, as often concerns emerge and are felt a while after the transfer has started, especially if the contract was completed quickly. HR should not assume that the vendor organization is communicating fully to staff; this is often not the case or, if done, is confined to perfunctory efforts. The client organization should also not assume that HR is not needed after the transfer. This is most certainly not the case. There is evidence that HR work becomes more complex owing to the need to assist with managing a dispersed workforce. It is recommended that the transition team should be composed of peer roles between the client and the vendor and should explicitly include the HR function.

Staff will take the transition period extremely seriously and expect HR to discuss this in much more detail than, for example, the specifics of individual contracts. They will want their individual situations to be taken into account and global generic approaches will be insufficient. People assume, especially in the public sector, that HR has a functional role in supporting them through the transition and it is seen as the entry point into the organization for all matters related to their personal circumstances. It cannot be assumed, if the supplier says that individual interviews will be held, that this is sufficient or that things will be handled well. Often these are superficial and skim over important and relevant facts. As one of our participants put it, about these types of interviews: 'That was crap, the personnel interviews were to tell us about being TUPE'd, took our bank details and gave us fuel cards.' What staff actually want is a discussion about their emotional and personal needs, job security and future changes to them. Another staffing issue to be particularly careful of is the clarity of the roles for staff being transferred and those remaining. Many staff remaining behind after an outsourcing do not seem to understand the new relationship, particularly the contractual nature of the work with former colleagues. In our research organizations there were often misunderstandings and conflicts with the managers of staff still contacting outsourced personnel to give instructions or to ask old colleagues for favours.

Promises made during discussions between those being outsourced and the managers and HR personnel representing the outsourcing organizations assume a critical role for people evaluating the potential outcome for themselves as a result of the transfer. Promises cover a wide range, from minor issues like the future location of work to quite serious issues such as how much downsizing will take place following the transition. They are often used as a form of assurance that, very often, is not within the remit of the manager to give and only serve to raise unrealistic expectations and future feelings of resentment when they cannot be honoured. Promises are made to diffuse a difficult and emotional moment and the manager's equivalent of an 'it will be all right on the night' platitude serves no real purpose other than to moderate the manager's own affective response and should not be used. One German-based manager discussed how promises became an issue when he had to downsize the organization, having earlier been assured by NewCo that this would not be necessary:

> As soon as I announced that we were going to close, it was a two-step approach, closed seven last year, finalized during summertime, and starting September last year I announced the closure of another five locations. So people have been somehow shocked as well, especially they have said, 'what you have promised us when we joined NewCo was not true'. (Private sector manager)

Promises become an issue when they are broken, as they often are. Downsizing is a particularly sensitive matter, and promises of this type will assume great importance for staff being outsourced. In the example above, the manager was trying to make sense of and legitimize his actions when he was making promises to staff that he was unsure about. He was paid a bonus based on how many staff he brought across, yet was fully aware that redundancies would be needed later, and whether this bonus got in the way of truthfully answering his staff's questions about redundancy is a moot point. Other transferred managers were unable to make explicit promises to staff because they were as much in the dark themselves. This suggests that managers have an additional burden of sense-making, in that they are partly responsible for the way staff understand a situation and cannot fulfil this task from a position of ignorance. Promises, or not making promises, is an important consideration – organizations need to be clear what the outsource client and the vendor can really promise staff during an outsourcing transition, as it is in reality probably very little.

The Outsourcing Stage: Maturity

Not all contracts reach this stage, although ideally organizations should be aiming for some type of stability, as this is often the most fruitful time when knowledge acquisition and relationship-specific investment start to take effect (Goo, Kishore, Nam, Rao, & Song, 2007). An important point to remember is that as the activities settle down and the mature stage is reached, the contract will need renegotiating, and possibly the relationships as well. This needs careful handling, and is likely to cause upheaval between client and the vendor as well as with staff concerned. Even if the situation appears stable, HR should regularly assess the skills and make-up of the outsourced workforce, and assess whether any key staff have been lost to the vendor or elsewhere. The *ex post* cost of monitoring, bargaining, and generally managing the vendor should be taken into account right from the start. There is evidence that companies with smaller contracts need to set aside a greater percentage of the total outsourcing cost to management time that can easily outweigh process cost improvements (Barthelemy, 2001). Very small contracts may not be worthwhile once these costs are taken into account.

In outsourcing transitions the transferred staff continue to have a relationship with the original employing organization. They carry out their work for what is now their 'client' and reminders of their old relationships remain and are constantly reinforced. In many cases they leave work on one day and turn up the next under a new contract to carry out exactly the same task as before. In a merger or acquisition, it is also possible that the old company no longer exists as a separate entity, further exaggerating the initial feelings of loss and confusion felt in such circumstances, although in this case the actual 'demise' of the former company does allow them to 'get over it' much more quickly. Reminders of the old relationship, the feelings of loss and resentment about what has occurred, will result in a process of distancing and reduced affiliation between the person outsourced and the previous employer. This can be expressed in behaviours sometimes not conducive to good performance, such as uncooperativeness, coolness, slowness in performance and so on, and although this is undesirable it must be understood as a natural part of the transition process and managed accordingly.

Maturity – letting go

The continuing relationship with the client company following transfer and into the mature stage of the outsourcing process causes specific problems with 'letting go' and moving forward with a new job. It was clear throughout our outsourcing research that OldCo was ever present in participants' minds; discussions with our interviewees often highlighted worsening relationship problems. This demonstrated an apparent unresolved conflict and that latent resistance was occurring, pointing to an incomplete transference process. Some, however, do move across and attach quickly to their new situation and one participant who was clearly identified with NewCo gave a very brief discursive account of her relationship with the 'client', suggesting that it for her at least the relationship was not an ongoing concern and no deep psychological engagement was felt or sought.

In a number of cases, discussions centred around meetings with OldCo people, former colleagues, where disputes around aspects of the formal contract engendered arguments. Demanding work outside of the contract, assuming that former relationships were intact and discussions around the needed payment for these services produced questions of flexibility – a discursive vehicle often used for asking for the service for free. Finally, the replacing of staff in roles in the areas that had been outsourced provided a rich area of dispute – not surprisingly, this replacing (whether perception or reality) left a 'bitter taste' in the mouth, as expressed by one of our participants from the IT sector:

> They have actually replaced my old group and probably doubled it. Interviewer: How do you feel about that? … very aggrieved … we knew that was going to happen … I am not saying we are turning it around now … not in a vindictive way at all, we are in a commercial environment, and so if the OldCo department require something that is not part of the contract, we say fine, we will do it, here is the bill. Interviewer: Do you enjoy that? Manager: Yes, I do. [laughs]

This participant, and others who highlighted the issue, stress that they are not being vindictive, positioning themselves as 'fair' people. However, it is clear that making the client 'pay' can be a pleasurable activity in these circumstances and represents an expression of resistance to the whole outsourcing process. At another level, the act of replacement of former roles serves to reinforce systems of belief that support feelings of inadequacy and fuels resentment against the old organization and feelings of injustice for the whole process that is reified in bitterness as to why they were singled out. While such bitterness may help with distancing, the continued exposure to OldCo seems to make it hard for some staff to make any 'closure' on the relationships. Those who are more attached to NewCo discussed more positively their ability to charge OldCo for work, to take the 'commercial' view. The act of taking NewCo's position and the role of a NewCo person who must charge for additional work will reinforce one's sense of belonging to NewCo and help with the distancing. This means in practical terms that the transition to the new organization, which is often simplistic and instrumentally managed by many outsourcers, needs to be supplemented by directed induction into the new organization, the new ways of working and culture, and such behaviours as we see here reinforced to enable a closer identification with NewCo and the promotion of psychological distance from OldCo.

A further aspect of the transference process is a duality, a dissonance, that occurs when newly outsourced managers and staff find themselves 'taking the part' of the old client, siding with the client implicitly against their new employer, and attempting to connect with the old organization by agreeing that NewCo are as bad as 'we all' thought. All these behaviours prevent connection between the staff and NewCo, generating confusion and underpinning nostalgia for the old ways of working and engendering poor engagement and performance. The following excerpt from our work in the public sector is from a participant who has just been promoted within NewCo and illustrates that even when briefing his team on the commercial realities of the new situation he finds himself drawn back to 'seeing their point of view':

> … I have had to say to a couple of people you are NewCo staff now and you have to actually have to look at it that way, and things are different … and some of them have a job to get used to that, they're thinking OldCo all the time. (But) it is difficult … I came up with something last week in one of the meetings and I thought afterwards I am actually speaking, from an OldCo point of view, and not NewCo.

He begins by explaining how the others in the team find it difficult, then goes on to confess that he himself still thinks from the OldCo viewpoint. During his interview, he suggested that he is finding it easier to integrate into NewCo because of his promotion, as he meets more NewCo people now, outside of the outsourced site, yet still finds his role in meetings difficult, sometimes drifting into being an advocate of OldCo's position. The confusion in this example, stressing that little has changed yet a different way of thinking is needed, is typical in an outsourcing process. A few are proud that they have changed their 'mindsets', but others will struggle. As in the above example, some suggest that whenever they were in meetings, either with the client or about the client, they would have switches in role awareness. They would suddenly realize that they needed to 'change hats' and at times felt guilty whichever position they took and felt caught in the middle between two companies, unclear which side to take.

This lack of closure, role confusion and sense of negative history are very different from working on a client site as part of a normal consulting engagement, which *inter alia* many IT consultants do, where any relationship is formed from new. In our work on outsourcing, the relationships were always predicated on a previous long-term work history and although the impact on potential new relationships with NewCo is unclear, it makes a shift of identity more complex and opens up the possibility of stunted transfer. This demonstrates poor attachment, reduction of the image of the new employer and not letting go the previous role. It brings with it the potential for reduced performance and is a sign of unresolved conflict that must be explicitly addressed by a programme of induction and mentoring. Following on from 'taking the part' of the client, an interesting aspect for some was the need to trade on the old relations and affiliation, and attempt to reconstruct a previous relationship to make ongoing work practice easier:

> They know you have an OldCo background and that is why you were there, but you see them go 'oh my god' more NewCo people ... the OldCo perception of NewCo is that they are just awful, and it's only the fact we trade a bit on that we did used to be OldCo people that we are 'all right' then, 'you are not all bad'. (Public sector staff)

This is a particularly dangerous route as currency in the form of service leniency may be demanded by OldCo colleagues as a precondition for affiliation – a feature we have seen on many occasions in our consulting work. On the other hand, others, although finding this trading useful, thought it was potentially problematic. There is uncertainty regarding whether the OldCo colleagues are being fair in assuming they want to 'rejoin' the group and 'play their games'; as this participant suggests, he could have felt aggrieved:

> ... initially I am just a representative of NewCo, start talking to them about how I actually transferred over, from the OldCo, (but) in most cases the attitude changes. Interviewer: In what way? Participant: Oh really, that's interesting; it's almost then as though I am a colleague. Interviewer: So you become like, a member again ... That's interesting ... what sort of an impact does it have on you, that suddenly they feel you are one of them? Participant: How can I put this, if I had sold my soul lock stock and barrel to NewCo and felt a part of that organization I think I would probably feel a little bit aggrieved.

This participant lacked identification with both parties, yet elsewhere he indicates that, just like other participants, he felt the need to belong to something, even if for a short while. We interviewed this research subject a second time at around six months into the transfer where he expressed strong disappointment that the new company had 'failed' to integrate him. The use of strategies to seek affiliation and reduce conflict may temporarily help staff to feel they belong to the old organization again. This need to seek reassurance and to 'ground' the employee in a previous life appears to be particularly important to those who still do not feel any strong sense of attachment to the new organization. Especially during the early stages of a transition where experience of NewCo is limited, no visible change in work practice, rhythm and location has occurred; outsourced staff seek security in old truths and certainties. This transient shift into an old company 'affiliation' has the potential to be used as a tactical device by these participants to express resistance and can result in a failure to focus on the new objectives driven by the commercial realities of their current situation. It is an area where performance can be materially affected unless addressed by a strong programme of induction.

Maturity – maintaining relationships over time

One feature that continues the bond with the previous organization in a practical sense in the UK is the nature of the TUPE contract. TUPE is a legal framework which gives some element of protection during an outsourcing transition to the employees affected. The UK has had such a framework in place since 1981 and in the European Union at large since 2001 (EU, 2001; see also HMSO, 2006). At a basic level the framework protects employees' employment rights to such things as salary, pensions and redundancy benefits as set down in the contract of employment, which must be transferred to the receiving company in the case of an outsourcing. In most cases, the formal employment contract of outsourced staff is transferred, maintaining the key terms and conditions, including the right to the same salary increases as staff still in OldCo. However, to gain these increases requires monitoring. This need to focus on their employment contract, to 'keep an eye on' the situation back at OldCo, connects them to their previous employment on a long-term basis and forces them to maintain relationships with OldCo. Even if OldCo was no longer the direct 'client' and they had been moved on to other sites, their contract status was felt to impact upon their standing in NewCo – their colleagues thinking of them as not fully integrated.

To remain on a TUPE or 'mirror' contract means that all salary increases that would have been received at OldCo are mapped onto increases at NewCo. While this should perhaps in principle be automatic, many outsourced personnel say that they 'find out' that increases had happened in OldCo but that NewCo had not been informed. This led to the need to monitor OldCo closely and in some cases ask for support from OldCo union representatives or HR. This activity drove them to maintain an awareness of OldCo and there was concern that this sort of keeping an eye on the situation would need to continue for many years. Some suggested that OldCo had clearly thought that 'dumping them meant the end of it' and participants felt that OldCo still had residual responsibilities for their outsourced staff even after the transition; as one public sector worker put it: 'The commitment that the exporting organization has, for want of a better term, doesn't end at the day of transfer … we have experienced a number of problems with pay, and things like that.' The use of the term 'commitment' is interesting, as it highlights how long-term commitment is also considered to be important and continuous long after the outsourcing transition is completed. People become more aware of this retained responsibility, and outsourced personnel held the view that OldCo had 'thought' they were no longer involved with the transferred staff but in fact they were. This seemed to generate further irritation and in some ways sadness, and was held up as yet another example of the poor management of the transfer and the lack of clear processes in place.

This seemed to make some participants feel unwanted, perhaps increasing their sense of distance and storing up long-term resentment – as one manager said:

> … we thought that being on mirror terms, any pay increase that the OldCo got, we
> would automatically get … but somehow the communication broke down, and we

didn't get last year's pay rise, we didn't kick up too much of a fuss about it because it is quite normal for a pay rise to drag on, but when it got to October/November and nobody had said anything, we started probing … it came as a total surprise to Human Resources that there had been a pay rise, and we haven't been asked to give you a pay rise, you must talk to the union.

Something participants had understood to be automatic had just not happened. This is significant for them because it is likely to hit their pockets, and leave them feeling forgotten by both parties. Furthermore, in the above example the manager was told by NewCo's personnel management to deal directly with the OldCo union, again increasing the level of contact and making the psychological transfer to NewCo difficult (and making a mockery of NewCo's personnel management system). This causes problems, especially when OldCo is no longer a client. One of our case study interviewees had recently moved to work on another client site when contacted for the follow-up interview. This was a full two years and three months after the transfer, and the first thing mentioned was how upset she was about difficulties around a salary increase that had taken place in OldCo that was not forthcoming, suggesting that NewCo was also to blame for not monitoring the situation and pointing to incomplete personnel management processes.

Maturity – making the final move

The full transfer to a NewCo contract and the 'giving up' of the TUPE protection means that some key decisions have to be faced, a decision 'event' which for many was extremely hard due to the likely financial losses related to signing on to a NewCo contract. In one case, over £250,000 was at stake in the total package when pension, redundancy and other fringe benefits were taken into account. We found increased anxiety and discussion in our interviews, particularly from respondents over six months into the transfer process. For some this led to anxiety, for others it was clear that they needed to 'lose the baggage', for example:

> Interviewer: … so you have moved across to their terms and conditions, was it done to show loyalty or some other reason? … Participant: Well, not really to show my loyalty, it was more a case of well, I have been working here for 18 months, nearly two years now, what is the point of staying on the same OldCo contract if we are not OldCo … because you have to keep track of what is going on in OldCo to make sure you get the same rewards that OldCo are giving their staff, so any annual increments and anything like that, you have to make sure it applies to your salary scale, and things are changing and I thought this is really silly.

The suggestion that to move across is not only sensible but almost 'giving up' and accepting the inevitable could be an indication of the powerlessness that many participants emphasized. Although it is suggested here that this is not done to show loyalty, it is hoped that changing the contract type will reduce the need to constantly monitor OldCo, and perhaps help with a form of closure to the event of being outsourced. However, for some of the longer-serving participants, a move across to the standard contract would mean a substantial loss of benefit, and only a few felt the need to remove the old ties badly enough to accept this.

The decision to stay on the old contract, for financial reasons, was made more difficult by the fact that remaining on a mirror contract left them feeling as if they were 'second class' citizens and can in addition create a bad atmosphere amongst work colleagues:

> … my practice group manager often mentions that I am not on NewCo terms, he shouldn't, but he does … but I am not going to make any move until they make a reasonable offer. I think it would be good to move over, but not just for the sake of it. Participant: they say it doesn't make any difference to them, about how you get treated … Participant: It does when you are on the work floor.

He went on to illustrate how the contract status impacted upon his relationships with his manager and his colleagues, and how he often had to explain that he was on different terms. This is likely to continually remind him and those around him that he is 'different'. Remaining on an OldCo mirror contract is therefore likely to make a shift of identification to NewCo more complex, as one remains in the category of an OldCo transferee and could be regarded as not transferring psychologically either. For example, the public sector respondent below suggested that his contract status was the reason for his not being given the responsibility he had previously enjoyed at OldCo:

> So I expected rather more authority and accountability on the finance side, but then I guess it is not normal company practice to give that to people coming in on mirror terms, at an early stage, I can understand why that might not be true, but I certainly find myself not able to make the same level of decision I would have been able to do at OldCo. (Public sector manager)

According to good company practice, the contract type should make no difference, but for the individuals concerned, the perception is otherwise. If one has lost status or is seen as 'second class', it is likely to make it difficult to feel a full member of the organization and could lead to dis-identification and poor performance. While, strictly speaking, the 'choice' of type of contract becomes theirs, the financial losses in terms of pensions and redundancy mean that some feel there is little choice in practice. While not advocating an end to the TUPE protection or that people should be forced to switch contracts, we wish to point out the issues involved and to make employers from both sides aware of these potential problems so that action can be taken to avoid poor HR practice in this area.

The Outsourcing Stage: Re-Scoping

If an organization finds itself at this stage of the process where there needs to be a return to the stage of scoping, and reassessing strategy, this is where the effectiveness of the outsourcing transition is felt. If a backsourcing is needed, for example, an assessment of how many staff will return to your organization – and how many of them will do so willingly – will be needed. This is linked to how the transfer process went in the initial stages, so it is vital to have thought this through early on and planned for this eventuality. Changing suppliers not only has obvious contractual and switching cost risks (Whitten & Wakefield, 2006), but also staffing implications. Organizations will have to work together to assess which staff will stay with the original company (NewCo) and which will transfer to the new organization (NewCo2 or OldCo). Remember that the better staff will have the most choice here. Some may have already transferred fully to the vendor and moved on, and may be particularly hard to attract back into the organization. There have been situations where the best staff were transferred to the vendor and moved on to different client sites, therefore losing any possibility of re-engagement altogether. This eventuality should be considered and discussed during the early stages, to avoid excessive loss of knowledge. However, staff do have the freedom to work where they wish, so it will be important not only to ensure that the contract offers protection, but also that the staff have been treated well enough during the transition process that they still wish to work for the organization again.

Re-scoping – return to sender?

The impact on outsourced staff of the prospect of a contract renegotiation, back-sourcing or even the moving of the service to a new service provider is to increase anxiety and feelings of uncertainty. We noticed this particularly in outsource trans-actions that were closing in on the final years of the running contract. For some the anxiety is increased by the reality (or rumour) of outsourcing contract renegotia-tions, making them very aware of the tenuous nature of their relations with both companies, and that the move was not permanent. The attachment to the new company becomes questioned, as does the relationship with the old, resulting in those affected being detached and floating between organizations in a sea of uncer-tainty. To find that their transfer status was under discussion, again, after such a relatively short time with a new company comes as shock. When discussing the latest contract negotiations this manager suggested:

> That's the problem OldCo would have, I mean a lot of staff would not want to go back, a lot of senior staff in NewCo, who have come in from elsewhere, no way would they go to the OldCo, so, if you took the whole organization and tried to put it back with the OldCo there would be a flurry of activity and people disappearing over the horizon.

This 'flurry' was emphasized to be due to bad feeling from the transfer, and the strong feelings generated due to perceptions of poor treatment. There were also hints that managers had become accustomed to the more flexible 'culture' of a private company, and would not wish to rejoin the bureaucracy of the public sector. Although he suggested that it would be mainly the managers that would be concerned with such a move, staff in similar circumstances also expressed concern that there may be yet another change of employer. For some this was their first full realization that the contract of employment they held was subject to the discussions of senior executives in OldCo. A small number of the participants said that it made little difference to them, with one participant suggesting that staying on the mirror contract would make this return easier:

> … because I am on the mirror terms, and as long as I can keep those same terms and conditions I don't feel that anything really changes for me, not really … if I was standard I would feel very worried, I mean, you are with NewCo and if somebody else comes in, will they want you, what sort of interests, it's moneymaking and if your job isn't going to make that much money they might decide that they don't want that part.

However, the holding of a security net such as a 'mirror contract' did not entirely reduce the impact of a return as this was tempered in this case by the realization that the whole service area was likely to be put back out to tender:

> I think that would start to be a bit worrying, because there is talk of if NewCo did pull out maybe it wouldn't be handed straight back into the government, it would be put out to more tenders and then who would we go with then?

A way in which some seemed to make sense of this anxiety, and find some sort of stability, was in the idea that the job itself needed to be done, and it wouldn't matter for whom they were working. There were indications that some were far from happy with that, but were trying to be positive; for example, this staff member said while discussing the renegotiation of the contract: 'Well, apart from not knowing who I would work for, obviously the job would have to carry on.' Note how this manager (who comes over in the interview as primarily 'job involved' and not terribly worried about who he is working for) still adds that NewCo have stressed they want a long-term contract. A comment shortly afterwards indicates again that he would like to feel comfortable about his future but balances that with some reality testing. Many, however, found the thought of going back to OldCo abhorrent: 'I wouldn't want to go back, not at all.' This has serious implications for any company wishing to 'backsource'. Even some of those participants who were having difficulty integrating with NewCo still suggested that they would be happy to further their careers with NewCo. While there were clear anxieties about what role they might have in the future, with many saying they were not impressed with 'being told not to worry, there were always places for people with talent,' another said: 'I would actually look to move on within NewCo providing something was there.' Many of our research subjects returned a number of times to the issue of future roles, and showed concern that there might not be a place for them in NewCo in the future. Similarly, they were anxious that there may be no role left either in OldCo. This perception was exacerbated by the view that OldCo was 'back-filling' (taking staff on in their old roles). Role theory suggests that if identification with an organization is low, the role may become a more important focus (Ashforth, 2001). However, the emphasis on role may work both ways; the perception that one's future role in an organization is unclear or uncertain is likely to reduce organizational identification as well as increase anxiety and reduce commitment.

Differences in organizational culture also become more apparent over time, although some can at least become adjusted by the time the 'maturity' stage of the contract is reached. The change in culture and the need to gain an understanding of new ways of progressing one's career within a systems house is a difficult process and increases anxiety about future roles. Problems with having lost a 'network' and not being sure of how to move on within the new organization are common concerns. Some were anxious that their expertise was with OldCo systems that may not be recognized or required elsewhere and while there was a shift to considering future roles outside the confines of the OldCo remit, anxiety and uncertainty become prevalent.

This analysis highlights the importance of understanding differences in staff concerns across the life cycle, maintaining communications with staff who have been transferred, and of keeping to the contract, ensuring that any salary increases, for example, are managed automatically. This would reduce the need for transferred staff to continually monitor the situation and also retains perceptions of fairness, which may be important if the original employer needs to backsource. If new employees are brought in to help manage contracts or handle unexpected work following on from the transfer, it will be useful to communicate the rationale behind this to the outsourced staff. This should reduce ill-feeling, again hopefully reducing the risk of retaliation, and maintain a good relationship should the original employer need to bring staff back in-house.

Conclusion

Our work has shown that many outsourced personnel maintain a connection with the former organization that extends well beyond the initial years of the transition. Our research participants were constantly reminded of the existence of the previous organization and their past relationship with it in sometimes negative ways. This lack of closure makes it more difficult to transfer fully psychologically to their new employer. We saw in many companies only a small number of personnel that could be classed as fully transferred as evidenced by a clearly articulated identification with the new company, NewCo. We found that significant numbers of outsourced staff had maintained an attachment to the previous employer, taking 'their part', acting as 'advocates' for OldCo and lacking a meaningful engagement with their new organization. Many seemed to be not really 'attached' to either company, a form of liminality, caught in the middle, drifting and confused. The contract status and the way the rules have to be applied force continued negotiations with old employers, acting as a form of anchor to the old organization and maintaining a bond that was difficult to sever. There were signs of dis-identification from OldCo, but it was rarely total, with many realizing that they did not 'belong' anymore but unable to forget or break with the past and maintaining nostalgia for times past.

Outsourcing needs to be seen as a long-term process that develops iteratively through a number of stages: scoping, preparation, negotiation and selection, transition, maturity and re-scoping. These stages need to be considered in depth even before the initial scoping of the possibilities starts and especially during the preparation stage and development of the contract. Staff will also proceed through different stages, with many experiencing anxiety and often re-experiencing that anxiety as contracts are renegotiated. The special nature of outsourcing, where personnel are required to continue working for their old employer, means that their reactions should be taken into account when preparing and moving through the life cycle. In the end the same staff will be carrying out the service just as before, often in the same location, for the former organization. Managers cannot assume that once the outsourcing dust has settled their responsibility ends. Increasingly departments have to be rebuilt and people backsourced and in practice a relationship needs to be maintained with former staff long after the initial change. A poor, clumsily handled outsourcing can generate latent resistance and conflict that will persist for many years after the initial transition. This latent resistance may result in hostile feelings for the former organization and underpin a poor service provision that may ultimately impinge on a company's overall position and ability to react to market and contextual forces.

References

Ashforth, B. E. (2001). *Role transitions in organizational life: An identity-based perspective.* Hillsdale, NJ: Lawrence Erlbaum.

Barthelemy, J. (2001). The hidden costs of IT outsourcing. *MIT Sloan Management Review,* Spring, 60–69.

Cullen, S., Seddon, P. B., & Willcocks, L. P. (2005). IT outsourcing configuration: Research into defining and designing outsourcing arrangements. *Journal of Strategic Information Systems, 14,* 357–387.

Deloitte. (2005). Survey by Deloitte Consulting. *Computing,* 28 April.

EU (2001). *Council Directive 2001/23/EC of 12 March 2001 on the approximation of the laws of the Member States relating to the safeguarding of employees' rights in the event of transfers of undertakings, businesses or parts of undertakings or businesses.*

George, B. (2005). Innovation in information systems education – III Sourcing management – a course in the information systems curriculum. *Communications of the AIS, 15*(19), 331–342.

Goo, J., Kishore, R., Nam, K., Rao, H. R., & Song, Y. (2007). An investigation of factors that influence the duration of IT outsourcing relationships. *Decision Support Systems, 42*(4), 2107–2125.

HMSO (2006). *The Transfer of Undertakings (Protection of Employment) Regulations 2006. Statutory Instrument 2006 No. 246.* London: HMSO.

Hofstede, G. (1983). The cultural relativity of organizational practices and theories. *Journal of International Business, Fall,* 75–89.

Khanna, S., & New, J. R. (2006). An HR planning model for outsourcing. *Human Resource Planning, 28*(4), 37–43.

Morgan, S. J. (2002). *Is outsourcing the answer for IT and HR functions?* Paper to the National Housing Federation Conference.

Niederman, F. (2005). International business and MIS approaches to multinational organizational research: The cases of knowledge transfer and IT workforce outsourcing. *Journal of International Management, 11,* 187–200.

Osei-Bryson, K. M., & Ngwenyama, O. K. (2006). Managing risks in information systems outsourcing: An approach to analyzing outsourcing risks and structuring incentive contracts. *European Journal of Operational Research, 174*(1), 245–264.

Samaddar, S., & Kadiyala, S. (2006). Information systems outsourcing: Replicating an existing framework in a different cultural context. *Journal of Operations Management, 24*(6), 910–931.

Shapiro, D. L., Sheppard, B. H., & Cheraskin, L. (1992). Business on a handshake. *Negotiation Journal, 8*(4), 365–377.

Taplin, R. (2005). *Risk management and innovation in Japan, Britain and the United States.* Abingdon: Routledge.

Whitten, D., & Wakefield, R. L. (2006). Measuring switching costs in IT outsourcing services. *Journal of Strategic Information Systems, 15,* 219–248.

Chapter 12

Downsizing, Stress and Forgiveness: A US Perspective

Jan Aylsworth

Introduction

Bruce (identities are being disguised), a 31-year-old graphic designer, recently learned that his position and others like it will be eliminated in two months. The work he now does in-house will be outsourced and also offshored, with a few positions created internally to coordinate the new arrangement. Bruce wasn't surprised at the announcement. 'We all just kind of knew that would happen,' he says. 'I just thought we might have longer – till the end of the year maybe.' Bruce applied for one of the new coordinating positions and is actually relieved that he was turned down. 'We learned after the fact that if they offer you that position and you don't accept it, you lose your severance package,' he says.

Overall, Bruce understands the need for the decision to outsource, and he's impressed with the company's willingness to 'work with' employees who want to leave now without having their severance benefits affected. But in the meantime, morale in the workplace is very low.

'It's terrible,' he says. 'Everyone is afraid they're going to be next. I've heard through the grapevine that even my boss is already looking for another job. Some people are hoping to stay long enough to lock in their retirement benefits … The quality of work hasn't been affected yet … not that I've seen anyway, but I think our customer service is going to be much colder. It's just a sinking ship, really.'

From a US perspective, 'being outsourced' does happen in the same way that it occurs in the UK – that is, employees are offered a position with a third-party vendor in lieu of losing their jobs. However, differences in labour law between the UK and US have contributed to some important distinctions regarding outsourcing, who it affects and how it unfolds.

The Human Side of Outsourcing: Psychological Theory and Management Practice
Edited by Stephanie J. Morgan

Here, we will not address UK law, specifically, because it has already been covered in other chapters. Instead, we will focus on generalizable consequences from a work-stress perspective that encompasses personality variables as well as individual and organizational interventions. Although US employees can 'be outsourced' as they are in the UK, a more common scenario may be the circumstances illustrated by Bruce's experience. In the US, employees do not have legislative protection against losing their jobs due to outsourcing. In addition, employees not protected contractually have been unsuccessful in attempting to block outsourcing-driven job loss or obtain compensation because of it (Scott, 2007).

US labour law and government statistics help colour in this picture. In 2004, job loss due to outsourcing accounted for 2.5 per cent of total job loss, the equivalent of 4,633 workers (Scott, 2007). By 2015, 3.4 million US jobs are projected to be lost due to offshoring. Affected positions include telemarketers, accountants, software engineers, chief technology officers, programmers, hardware engineers, computer scientists, systems analysts and even government workers. The reason: cost savings due to large salary differential. Still another and more frequent occurrence is the loss of one's job due to 'being downsized', a phenomenon whose human side will be explored in this chapter. The term 'laid off' is sometimes used to mean the same thing both in the UK and US, while being 'made redundant' is a familiar term in the UK but not in the US.

Personal experience is not subject to independent verification; but 30 years of watching and experiencing what happens in the US employment context perhaps counts for something. I know more people who have been downsized than I can name from memory, but I only know personally of a few people who have lost their jobs due to their work being outsourced. I know only one person who has 'been outsourced' to a third-party vendor.

In the US, job-holders are employed 'at will', which means that, with some exceptions, either they or their employer can legally end the employment relationship at any time, for any reason, or for no reason at all (Muhl, 2001). Exceptions can exist – for example, contractually as with union workers who are covered by collective bargaining agreements. In addition, courts of law have recognized three broad exceptions to at-will doctrine, but those exceptions are not uniform from state to state and are delivered by judicial remedy rather than legislative protection (Muhl, 2001). Judicial remedy is also a resort for individuals who believe their job termination to be in violation of federal law. Title VII of the Civil Rights Act of 1964 prohibits employment discrimination based on race, colour, religion, sex and national origin (US Equal Employment Opportunity Commission, 1964). The Age Discrimination Employment Act of 1967 prohibits employment discrimination against persons who are 40 or older (US Equal Employment Opportunity Commission, 1967). For this reason, attorneys advise employers to be particularly meticulous with documentation when terminating the employment of individuals in those groups.

At least two other considerations are relevant for outsourcing/downsizing enactments in the US. First, the Worker Adjustment and Retraining (WARN) Act of 1998 requires some employers to provide at least 60 days' notice for certain plant closings and mass layoffs (Scott, 2007). A second and less-clear issue is the employee–independent contractor transition. Again this comes from personal knowledge. In the past, it wasn't unusual to hear of a downsized employee transitioning immediately to working for the same employer as an independent consultant. In fact, that has been my own experience. However, more recently, some companies are enforcing a minimum time-period moratorium that must pass before former employees can consult as independent contractors. Attempts to track down the basis for this change have led to a review of the Sarbanes–Oxley Act of 2002 (One Hundred Seventh Congress, 2002) and the Internal Revenue Service's Independent Contractor versus Employee guidelines (Internal Revenue Service, Department of the Treasury, 2008). Neither document addresses the employee–independent contractor transition, specifically, so we cannot be helpful here in offering a rationale for this change.

Being Downsized

The academic psychology, sociology and economics literature offers numerous and conflicting definitions of what it means 'to downsize', but they are not congruent with what it means to 'be downsized'. One definition suggests that the act of downsizing is broad enough to include the elimination of jobs through attrition or even retirement (Freeman & Cameron, 1993); yet, this writer, at least, has never heard the experience of 'being downsized' described as having any sort of voluntary component. Nor could any reference be found in the peer-reviewed academic literature.

While the term 'laid off' is also used as synonymous with being downsized, at least in the US, it implies that the work-loss may only be temporary. 'Laid-off' employees are sometimes called back to work if the employers' economic circumstances improve. In fact, the US Department of Labor uses the term 'lay-off' in that way, specifying that an extended mass layoff, for example, must be of at least 31 days. In that sense, being 'laid-off' does not always have the permanence associated with 'being downsized'.

Characterizations in the academic literature suggest that 'being downsized' is 'involuntary', that it is a 'permanent layoff' and that the employee was not terminated 'for cause'. Since downsizing has been widely attributed to a company's need to remain globally competitive, we can attach the idea that the act was necessary on behalf of the organization. So, in the absence of being able to find a precise definition of 'being downsized', we offer one here: 'being downsized' means that 'one's employment relationship has been involuntarily and permanently terminated for reasons other than cause – with the implied or expressed idea that the action is necessary for the greater good of the organization'.

Despite the finality of being downsized, some rather unusual former employee–employer relationships can develop. One of them is a phenomenon that we will refer to as an 'employee–consultant' transition.

Almost 18 years ago, Bill, a 56-year-old mechanical draftsman, reported to work one morning, knowing that it was to be a downsizing day. The word was out that there would be cuts, but he'd been told confidentially that he was 'safe'. So Bill was quite surprised when a higher-up called him in, handed him a severance cheque and told him he was no longer employed there. Bill refused the severance cheque and, instead, decided to retire, knowing he was eligible for those benefits as an alternative. Only a few weeks passed before he was contacted by a former supervisor and asked to return as a subcontractor. It seems that Bill had unique competencies that the organization still needed. Now 74 years old, Bill continues to report to work four days a week.

Understanding the Individual's Experience

Bill's experience illustrates why it's important to understand how individuals experience being downsized. By 'individual', we not only refer to the targets of these phenomena but also to two other groups: those who observe it as 'survivors' and those who act as 'executioners' by delivering the bad news on behalf of the organization (Kets de Vries, 1997). At least three bodies of theory are relevant: organizational justice, the psychological contract and stress.

Organizational justice theory

Essentially, justice theory addresses perceptions of fairness and may be useful in exploring how employees experience differing outcomes of organizational change – outcomes that include being downsized, as well as surviving it – or perhaps, even being the party that executes it. The larger idea of organizational justice can be divided into sub-constructs, typically 'distributive', 'procedural' and 'interactional' justice (e.g. Cropanzano, Byrne, Bobocel, & Rupp, 2001). Here – from the perspective of the targeted downsized individual – we present very general descriptions.

- 'Distributive' justice as 'what happened to whom'. It's outcome-oriented. Who lost their job versus who did not? Did someone less deserving fare better than someone more deserving? How equitable was the severance package? Did anyone lose their retirement benefits?
- 'Procedural' justice refers to perceptions of 'how' the change was enacted. Were headcount reduction decisions based on tenure with the organization, occupational competence or some blend of the two? Did the organization develop a well-thought-out plan before proceeding or plunge in haphazardly? Was anyone really in charge?
- 'Interactional' justice brings in the human component. Were people treated with compassion? Was the gravity of their personal loss acknowledged? Was the notification delivered privately, or were people called as a group into a room and asked to find their name on a list?

All three types, anchored in power and politics, are reflected in Vivian's experience of being downsized. Four years ago, the 46-year-old department director was informed quite unexpectedly that her position was being eliminated. She had been with the firm for 21 years, regularly working 55 to 65 hours a week. A month earlier, she had received a very favourable performance review – and, in fact, had earned a bonus for her work.

'We all knew the business was looking for ways to reduce costs; but from an objective perspective, I wasn't the best choice to step aside because I still had a great deal to contribute,' she says. Vivian recalls that the woman who broke the news to her had commented a few weeks prior, 'You're an excellent administrator. You've got two advanced degrees. There's no way they're going to let you go.'

Vivian's personal theory: 'I think I ticked off the president. We were on opposite sides of an issue … I think that she perceived me as fighting her and may have thought that I went over her head, which I didn't … But here was an opportunity where someone had to go, and it was convenient for it to be me.'

From procedural and interactional perspectives, Vivian believes that the manager who informed her of the decision tried to do it fairly and professionally but might have been able to pre-empt the decision if she'd tried harder. The following week, Vivian's former employer released an email stating that Vivian had resigned to pursue other opportunities. Vivian was the only employee downsized that day; but since then, all of the key individuals involved in her event have also left the firm voluntarily or been downsized themselves, including the president.

Perceptions of justice affect survivors, too – and, for that reason, they have important implications for organizational commitment and organizational citizenship. 'Organizational commitment' can be understood as a bond that links the individual to the organization (Mathieu & Zajac, 1990). Facets of organizational commitment are 'continuance' commitment, which refers to an individual's 'need' to remain with an organization – that is, whether the benefits of staying outweigh the costs of leaving. 'Affective' commitment refers to an individual's 'desire' to remain with an organization and brings in ideas of attitudes and emotional attachment (Hopkins & Weathington, 2006). Affective commitment has been associated with work-performance variables that benefit the organization but are not necessarily associated with continuance commitment (Allen & Meyer, 1996; in Marchiori & Henkin, 2004). 'Organizational citizenship' is one of these variables (Marchiori & Henkin, 2004). 'Organizational citizenship' refers to behaviours and efforts that go above and beyond those required by the job.

Downsizing profoundly affects employees who are left behind (Luthans & Sommer, 1999; in Hopkins & Weathington, 2006) – and those effects extend to perceptions of justice. For example, Hopkins and Weathington found a direct and positive relationship between procedural justice and affective commitment among survivors of downsizing. Brockner, Wiesenfeld, and Martin (1995; in Hopkins & Weathington, 2006) emphasize that the future success of an organization is determined by those who survive. All of this implies that organizations should be quite concerned about perceptions of justice during downsizing – not only for humanitarian reasons – but also with regard to future impact on the organization.

Psychological contract theory

Many writers have offered definitions of the psychological contract, presented here as 'people's unconscious expectations of an organization to respond to their psychological needs and support their psychological defenses in exchange for meeting the organization's unstated needs' (Rousseau, 1995; in Kalimo, Taris, & Schaufeli, 2003, p. 92). It's sort of a quid pro quo, which in pre-downsizing days was represented by the idea that employment security was a taken-for-granted payoff for doing a good job.

'Breach', essentially, is the idea that one party – either the employee or the organization – failed to fulfil the obligations implicit in the agreement. It's different from organizational justice theory but still related. For example, in a study of 165 employees from a variety of organizational settings, Kickul, Neuman, Parker, and Finkl (2001) found that anti-citizenship behaviour was higher following a psychological contract breach when both procedural and interactional justice were low.

Herriot and Pemberton (1996) present a model of how they believe that the psychological contract is continuously renegotiated over time, alluding to Rousseau's (1990) distinction between 'transactional' versus 'relational' contracts. 'Transactional' contracts involve the employee and employer trading a work-related behaviour for a perceived reward – for example, services in exchange for compensation. However, 'relational' contracts imply mutual commitment – for example, the exchange of loyalty and commitment for some minimum-time expectation of employment. Using the term 'equity' rather than justice, they suggest that fulfilment of a transactional psychological contract may be linked to distributive justice, while fulfilment of a relational contract may focus more on procedural justice. They hypothesize that relational contracts, whether fulfilled or broken, involve much stronger emotions than transactional contracts. After breach of a relational contract, they propose, employees may feel dishonoured, inequitably treated and cut off from the organization that may have met their needs for affiliative satisfaction. Feelings of anger, mistrust and grief are not unexpected.

As Vivian illustrates, those who have been downsized as well as their surviving co-workers have been found to experience a mourning process similar to bereavement (e.g. Kübler-Ross, 1969; in Kets de Vries, 1997).

> Vivian reports that of all the negative feelings she addressed after being downsized, grief is the only one that she still struggles with.
>
> 'Initially, I was just shocked,' she said. 'I could not believe that it had actually happened because I did not see it coming.' Some time later, anger came into play, as Vivian often found herself thinking, 'This isn't fair.'
>
> But her grief has been re-experienced at different points in different ways, emerging as something of a delayed reaction.
>
> 'I liked the people I worked with, and I was loyal to that organization,' she said. 'I loved what I did. It called to my heart, and I was good at it.'

The academic literature is abundant with characterizations of downsizing as a breach of the psychological contract. For example, Kalimo et al. (2003, p. 93) say that downsizing is 'a one-sided renegotiation' of the psychological contract. Amundson, Borgen, Jordan, and Erlebach (2004) write that employees perceive breach of the psychological contract the very moment that an organization announces its intent to downsize. This applies to those who lose their jobs as well as to survivors. Kalimo et al. (2003) explain that survivors experience a 'double-deterioration' of the psychological contract. They view the loss of their colleagues' jobs as a breach of their own contract while also coping with increased workload (Greenglass, Burke, & Moore, 2003). Regarding those still employed, others have used the terms 'survivor sickness' (Noer, 1993; in Kets de Vries, 1997) and 'survivor syndrome' (Cascio, 1993). Also relevant for survivors, Herriot and Pemberton (1996) suggest that broken relational contracts may prompt a psychological contract renegotiation that's purely transactional.

Stress and coping

A fascinating study by Kets de Vries (1997) featured 200 open-ended interviews with individuals impacted by downsizing. He classified interviewees as 'victims', those who lost their jobs; 'survivors', those who kept their jobs but saw co-workers lose theirs; and 'executioners', those charged with delivering the bad news. Among victims, he distilled four coping types: (1) the 'adaptable', who move on to new jobs and may eventually view themselves as better off; (2) those who 'do a Gauguin (the artist)', making major life-changes, perhaps in pursuit of a long-held dream; (3) the 'depressed', who become stuck in a mourning process, possibly remaining unemployed or contemplating suicide; and (4) the antagonistic, the subset that experiences violent impulses towards former employers and even outward aggression, sometimes inflicted upon family members.

The experience of survivors, according to Kets de Vries, is consistent with previous research in which those who remained 'usually perceive a significant and lasting change in their relationship to the organization' and 'after an initial upsurge in productivity, often settle into a state of fearful expectancy' (Kets de Vries, 1997, p. 13). As a defence mechanism, it's likely that they will distance themselves either from the victims or the organization, or they may address perceptions of inequity by convincing themselves that those who were downsized deserved it.

Executioners were a varied group, but having to conduct the downsizing left an 'indelible imprint' on each of them. Always present was the idea of '*lex talionis*', otherwise commonly expressed as 'an eye for an eye' or the idea that what one does to others will be done to oneself. Here, Kets de Vries also found four types of executive/executioner coping styles: (1) the compulsive/ritualistic executive focused on the process, trying to implement it perfectly and with fairness, although feelings were not mentioned; (2) the abrasive executive who scapegoated the victims, setting the stage for strong counterproductive attitudes among survivors; (3) the dissociative executives, who viewed themselves as spectators carrying out the process and could not experience emotions about the event; (4) alexithymic/anhedonic executives, many of whom had repeatedly engaged in the process of downsizing. Their ability to feel emotions became diminished, and in some cases they developed a communication disorder called 'alexithymia'.

A look at the human side of downsizing needs to push beyond what individuals experience and examine what the consequences have been on organizations themselves, as well as what the implications are for the global, macro employment context. Neither characterizations nor evidence seems to support the idea that downsizing benefits the organization as intended. Morgan (1997) writes that there is no such thing as unilateral power in a complex system and that organizations don't exist as separate from their environments.

Descriptively, downsizing has been characterized as a cancer in organizational life (Kraemer, 2001) and has also been called a 'morally contentious' but normal business practice that is now the major trend of our era (Orlando, 1999).

Downsizing: A Historical View

We should back-track just a bit here and note that downsizing, which began as a trend in the US, has been documented at least since the late 1970s (Arroba, 1979) and into the early 1980s (Cascio, 1993). It quickly gained momentum (Kets de Vries, 1997), and by the end of the 1980s it had become intrinsic in American culture (Cascio, 2004). Early on, downsizing was characterized as a white-collar phenomenon (e.g. Cascio, 1993) as opposed to the familiar loss of blue-collar manufacturing jobs. Invoking the term 'cutback democracy', Kets de Vries (1997) writes that downsizing took white-collar workers completely by surprise. Middle-managers were particularly affected, accounting for 17 per cent of all dismissals from 1989 to 1991 but only 4 to 8 per cent of the workforce (Cascio, 1993).

By the 1990s, a 'downsizing-is-effective' social construction had become embedded in the employment context (McKinley, Zhao, & Rust, 2000), having spread through a cognitive process known as 'schema-packing'. McKinley et al. contend that the construct developed in the absence of evidence to support improved financial or technical performance. In fact, a decline in organizational performance following downsizing was reported (e.g. De Meuse, Bergmann, Vanderheiden, & Roraff, 2004). In their longitudinal analysis of Fortune 100 companies that downsized from 1989 through 1996, De Meuse et al. were able to determine that financial recovery did finally occur – but only after a healing period of several years.

Cascio (1993), Kets de Vries (1997) and De Meuse et al. (2004) are firmly in agreement that downsizing can only be effective within a larger process designed to deliver positive systemic transformation. Yet, that may not be happening. McKinley et al. (2000, p. 229) claim that downsizing has become so institutionalized that managers 'have begun to lose sight of their own agency'. They further contend that the trend is no longer motivated by declining organizational performance.

Organizations that downsize have been reported to experience backlash in a variety of forms. Damage to a business's reputation may play out in increased recruitment difficulties (Zyglidopoulos, 2003) along with erosion of sustainable competitive advantage (e.g. Fombrun, 1996; in Zyglidopoulos, 2003). Large reductions in customer satisfaction (Fornell, Johnson, Anderson, Cha, & Everitt, 1996) have also been found, possibly due to reduced trust and commitment from surviving employees (Farrell, 2003). Downsizing can also lead to reduced organizational commitment, trust and morale (Armstrong-Stassen, 2001), reduced loyalty and feelings of security (Campbell-Jamison, Worrall, & Cooper, 2001), disruption of employees' adaptability due to the disruption of informal communication networks (Fisher & White, 2000), increased role ambiguity and intent to quit (Moore, Grunberg, & Greenberg, 2004).

As for the macro environment, we know that downsizing is now global (e.g. Kets de Vries, 1997; Leana & Ivancevich, 1987) and it is changing cultures. Ahmadjian (2001) writes that in Japan, downsizing has deinstitutionalized the entrenched norm of permanent employment. This shift in a collectivist society where the work organization is seen as an extension of the family (Morgan, 1997) is seismic.

Career forms are changing as well in ways that emphasize the decline of the traditional organizational career (Briscoe, Hall, & De Muth, 2006). Instead, the focus is turning to career forms in which individuals assume greater responsibility for their own employability. How all of this will continue to play out at the macro level is heavy with organizational, societal and global implications. As Kanter (1989) points out, how well people are channelled into jobs affects the productive output of a society as well as its competitiveness in a global economy.

Negative Health Outcomes

Concerns about illness after being downsized deserve to be taken seriously – especially cardiovascular effects and depression – for both victims and survivors. Moore (2004) and others reported higher levels of health problems, including depression, among workers whose companies had downsized. In a four-year study, Vahtera (2004) and others found that major downsizing was associated with an increase in absence due to illness among permanent but not temporary employees. In addition, the extent of downsizing was associated with cardiovascular mortality among survivors. In a sample of unemployed men, deaths due to cardiovascular dysfunction were more than three times expected levels (Cobb & Kasl, 1977; in Leana & Ivancevich, 1987). Depression is also a concern among the unemployed (e.g. Sartorius & Ban, 1986; in Kets de Vries, 1997).

Concurrent with scholarly evidence for illness after downsizing, the victims seem to be aware of the connection on an intuitive level, as illustrated further by Bill, our 74-year-old fired–retired–rehired–consulting draftsman.

The day that Bill was fired and retired within the same 24-hour period makes for a confusing story. As the events of the day unfolded and various co-workers heard of his dismissal, Bill also learned that a colleague, a vice president, was trying to intervene on his behalf. In everyday language, the experience might be described as 'stressful' – not only for Bill, but for his wife, Jean. He called her several times, each time with a new detail as circumstances continued to play out.

He recalls: 'The last time I phoned her, I said, "If I have a heart attack, you sue these (expletive deleted)."'

Important questions surface here. What theories might explain the connection between stressful life events and ill health? What do we mean by 'stress'? Why do some people become ill when stress is experienced while others do not? What can organizations and individuals do to mitigate the health-negating effects of downsizing-related stress? Must health concerns for the individual and financial concerns for the organization be mutually exclusive – or can both be pursued synergistically?

Studying these and related questions requires a critical approach that embraces and integrates psychology, biology and physiology. According to Bandura (2001), psychology is exceptionally suited to provide an appropriate framework. In a world being transformed by technology and globalization, he writes, 'the field of psychology should be articulating a broad vision of human beings not a reductive fragmentary one'.

Bluntly put, stress is a mess to define. The word today, as used in popular commentary, originated within Hans Selye's (1976) general adaptation syndrome (GAS). It survives in the academic literature, but there is no widely agreed definition for it; and in fact, it's sometimes used without definition as though none were necessary.

A full review of the stress theory literature is beyond the scope of this chapter, but a basic presentation and comparison with contemporary research will help make the case for virtuous organizational behaviour. Even though the GAS is pretty much sitting on empty these days, it 'remains an obligatory passage point for the understanding of medicine' (Viner, 1999), and its central ideas have striking parallels in contemporary stress research.

Terminology

Based on observations from his experiments with rats, Selye defined 'stress' as 'a non-specific response by the body to any demand'. He chose 'stressor' to signify the causative agent – for example, heat, cold, poison or frustration. Years after the nomenclature had become accepted, he said that he should have labelled the causative agent as 'stress' and the response as 'the strain reaction'. Interestingly, some researchers today prefer the latter nomenclature (e.g. Lepine, Podsakoff, & Lepine, 2005). Word choice aside, being fired from one's job (Holmes & Masuda, 1974) and job insecurity (Sverke, Hellgren, & Näswall, 2002) are well recognized as stressors, which legitimizes stress as a relevant consideration when organizations outsource or downsize their employees.

Non-Specificity

Selye's notion of 'non-specificity' refers not to symptoms or specific hormonal responses, but, ironically, to a quite specific three-phase pattern that he observed consistently regardless of whatever non-immediately lethal insult he inflicted on his rats. The three-phase response consisted of: (1) an alarm reaction, marked by acute manifestations that represented the direct effects of the stressor on the body. Through an unknown mediator, an alarm signal was said to travel directly from the injured target area to the pituitary gland; (2) resistance or adaptation, during which physiological responses returned to normal due to mobilization of the body's defence mechanisms; (3) exhaustion, the final surrender, characterized by death and brought on by either prolonged or heightened exposure to the stressor. During the exhaustion phase, adaptation occurred briefly; but soon the animal lost its acquired resistance and died. Selye maintained that virtually every organ and chemical constituent of the body was involved in the GAS and that, through a process of wear and tear, the weakest channel wore out first, leading to 'diseases of adaptation' and, eventually, to death. Though Selye invoked the idea of non-specificity to refer to this pattern, he also characterized a non-specific change as 'one that affects all, or most, parts of a system without selectivity'. Statements of this nature have exposed the non-specificity claim to vulnerability, as various stressors at differing magnitudes have been followed by differing hormonal responses (Pacak et al., 1998). Pacak suggests that each stressor is associated with a specific neurochemical and neuroendocrine response.

Adaptation Energy as Finite

Selye (1976) used the term 'adaptation energy' to refer to the resource that was spent and eventually used up as the body cycles through recurring episodes of alarm and resistance before reaching exhaustion. He said that the most fundamental gap in stress research was not knowing what this 'mysterious quantity' was and cautioned that it be spent wisely because its capacity appeared to be the primary determinant of the length of the human lifespan. Clearly, this latter idea is more supposing than empirical, but the possibility that it might have been intuitively on target merits a look at whether contemporary physiologic theory supports the idea. Turns out, it just might.

In 1961, anatomy researcher Leonard Hayflick published a now-classic paper (Hayflick & Moorhead, 1961) describing experiments in which human embryonic cells in culture demonstrated a maximum average of 50 cell divisions before entering a period of senescence. Once reaching senescence, the cells survived for a while in a latent state but could no longer divide. Writing more than 30 years later, Hayflick (1996) commented that the number 50 might or might not be coincidental since the number 40 was believed to represent the doublings required for a fertilized egg to produce a full-grown human adult. This cell-division observation has since become known as 'the Hayflick limit', and it is now regarded as a fundamental characteristic of the longevity of a species (Yegorov & Zelenin, 2003). Hayflick also acknowledged the work of other researchers, who proposed that telomeres, which are protective caps at the ends of chromosomes, might represent something of a cellular clock. With successive divisions in vitro, telomeres become shorter and shorter.

Telomere research now extends to a concept called 'stress-induced premature senescence (SIPS)' in which telomere-shortening and senescence are induced in culture when human cells are exposed to subcytotoxic stresses (Toussaint et al., 2002). SIPS is believed to contribute to ageing and also to act a defence mechanism against cancer (Chen & Goligorsky, 2006). Those effects may seem opposite; but when telomeres in cancerous cells do not shorten, those cells continue to divide, become immortal and spread (Hertzog, 2006). Telomeres are believed to be maintained by an enzyme called 'telomerase', which is normally repressed (Yegorov & Zelenin, 2003) but for some reason becomes reactivated in cancerous cells (Yegorov & Zelenin, 2003). The cancer/telomerase connection is not so relevant for a discussion of stress-related illness, but it's important to point it out because it illustrates the complexity of senescence and steers the reader away from concluding that senescence is undesirable. Rather, the salient question is whether stress as it is perceived or experienced by an individual might be associated with SIPS at the cellular level and, thus, might hasten the onset of illness or premature ageing. Thus, we do have a modern-day concept that parallels Selye's belief in adaptative energy as finite.

In a first-of-its-kind study, Epel (2004) and colleagues set out to investigate the hypothesis that stress impacts health by modulating the rate of cellular ageing. Their subjects were two groups of women, a control group with a biologically healthy child and an experimental group with a chronically ill child. The women completed self-report measures of perceived stress and also had their telomeres, their telomerase activity and cellular oxidative stress measured. As expected, the mothers with chronically ill children did report higher levels of perceived stress; however, as a group, they were not different from the control mothers in telomere length, telomerase activity or oxidative stress. Epel and colleagues surmised that duration of stress might reveal differences, and that proved to be the case. Combining all mothers and dividing them into quartiles, they found significant correlations between perceived stress and all three markers of cellular ageing. That is, there appeared to be a continuum upon which telomere length was related to perceived stress in both caregivers and controls. But most interestingly, in the experimental group, they found that the length of time spent as a caregiver correlated positively with shorter telomere length, lower telomerase activity and greater oxidative stress. Further, they estimated that women who perceived the highest levels of stress had telomere shortening equal to at least one decade of additional ageing versus women with the lowest stress levels. They affirmed the idea that telomere length can be a biomarker of a cell's true age and called for further research, including longitudinal work.

If the telomere–psychological stress connection continues to find support, organizations will need to think ethically about the relationship between organizationally introduced stressors and workers' coping abilities. Employees will need to consider whether the stressors they are willing to accept today may be shortening their telomeres tomorrow. Perhaps the idea of being health-conscious will one day extend to protecting our telomeres.

Good versus Bad Stress

Selye distinguished between harmful 'distress' and non-harmful 'eustress', which he described as a beneficial feeling of pleasure and fulfilment that uses very little adaptation energy (Miller, 2003). He claimed that both eustress and distress elicited the non-specific response and that even eustress cannot be maintained indefinitely. His advice was to utilize one's finite adaptation energy on eustress and not squander it on distress. Since Selye's experiments on rats do not appear to have exposed them to anything that might be described as eustress, we can only conclude that eustress comes from Selye the philosopher, not Selye the scientist. However, the idea of eustress has informed stress and health research. It is also consistent with concepts central to the emerging field of positive psychology, and a recent characterization of workplace stimuli as 'challenge stressors' versus 'hindrance stressors'.

As an instrument that measures stress and health risk, the Social Readjustment Rating Scale (Holmes & Masuda, 1974) builds on the idea that the degree of change required to adapt to a stressor – rather than whether the stressor is good or bad – is the determinant of illness risk. The scale ranks 43 life occurrences, weighted according to how much change they require relative to getting married. Values beyond a certain threshold correlate with the likelihood of becoming ill. Despite criticism, the SRRS has been widely used and has held up under systemic reassessment as 'a useful tool for stress researchers and practitioners' (Scully, Tosi, & Banning, 2000). To account for cultural and societal changes since the SRRS's introduction, Scully et al. revalidated and re-weighted the items. Interestingly, 'fired at work', originally the eighth-highest stressor, dropped to 13th in rank order. With 'death of a spouse' remaining highest at 100, 'getting fired' dropped from 47 to 34 in weighting. Perhaps 'getting fired' in the 1970s carried different stress perceptions than being involuntarily downsized in the 21st century.

The field of positive psychology describes positive feelings as arising from the exercise of one's personal strengths and virtues (Seligman, 2002). 'Flow', which seems to be a reasonable surrogate for 'eustress', is the state in which that happens. Named and investigated by social sciences professor Mihaly Csikszentmihalyi, 'flow' refers to 'a state of gratification that we enter when we feel completely engaged in what we are doing' (Seligman, 2002, p. 113). It occurs without conscious thought or feeling and, according to Seligman, is said to occur when the challenges one faces mesh perfectly with one's abilities to meet them. Cavanaugh, Boswell, Roehling, and Boudreau (2000) directly parallel the eustress–distress dichotomy with their 'challenge' versus 'hindrance' stressor distinction. Hindrance stressors 'involve excessive or undesirable constraints that interfere with or hinder an individual's ability to achieve valued goals'. They produce 'distress', while 'challenge' stressors are viewed as 'pressure-laden and stressful, but well worth the discomfort involved'. They produce 'eustress', which creates feelings of fulfilment or achievement. Cavanaugh et al. found that self-reported challenge stress was significantly positively related to job satisfaction and significantly negatively related to job search. On the other hand, hindrance-related stress was positively related to job search and voluntary turnover. Cavanaugh et al. noted valid reasons why their results might not generalize. Nevertheless, Lepine et al. (2005) reported meta-analysis results suggesting that, given the resources that organizations devote to stress management practices, stress research could benefit by distinguishing between challenge and hindrance stressors.

Status of the Theory

Acknowledging that not everyone agreed with his non-specific theory of stress, Selye wrote that 'the more someone sticks out his neck above the masses, the more he is likely to attract the eyes of snipers' (Selye, 1976, p. 282). He also distinguished between a 'sterile' theory, which 'does not lend itself to experimental verification', and a 'wrong' theory, which can still be highly useful if it helps fill important gaps in knowledge. John Russell, editor-in-chief of the journal *Stress*, suggests that Selye's theory still has guiding value and that 'non-specific' should be considered 'that component of stress that is not yet understood in contemporary terms' (Russell, 2007). He also stated what he believes to be the next frontier in stress research: 'identifying developmental and molecular genetic origins of inter-individual variations in susceptibility to stressors, which have the prospect of enabling better coping with stress' (Russell, 2007, p. 1). So, even though Selye's theory did not prosper in the way he hoped it would, it has proven useful and still provides a comprehensive framework for examining concepts from contemporary stress research.

Stress, Coping and Personality Variables

Personality variables, that is, the individual ways in which people differ from one another, offer a way to study and try to understand who becomes sick and who doesn't in response to stressors, including those that are work-related. Grant and Langan-Fox (2007) write that understanding traits as vulnerability factors is an important focus of research because stress is a widespread and growing organizational problem for which intervention and prevention are imperative.

When personality variables are used in stress research, the aim is often to take a slice-out-of-time, cross-sectional look and examine whether the variable mediates or moderates, rather than causes, an outcome. The distinction between mediate and moderate may seem subtle, but it's important. A mediator variable changes the relationship between a stressor and an outcome. That is, the mediating variable B changes the effect of A on C in a linear way (Baron & Kenny, 1986). A relationship of that sort suggests that a mediating variable might directly buffer or even exacerbate the response associated with a particular stressor. With moderation, the relationship is indirect. A and B merely coexist, each with its own path to C. Thus, a moderating personality variable coexisting with the stressor, but not affecting it directly, would have a multiplicative effect en route to C. As moderators, personality variables could have more generalized, global effects since they would imply some underlying characteristic that's present independent of the stressor. It's also important here to re-emphasize that we are referring to association rather than cause and effect. Longitudinal work, which measures relationships between variables at multiple intervals, is necessary to support cause and effect.

Rather than approaching stress as a linear injury–response phenomenon, Gruen, Folkman and Lazarus (1988) adopt a stress–strain model. They write that stress, in the context of stress and health, is best regarded as a complex system of variables. Some of those variables are environmental, while others are personal. They view the extent to which a stressor is harmful as being dependent on a variety of factors, including the meaning that the individual attaches to it and his or her resources for dealing with it. They elaborate that individual vulnerability can be influenced by 'stable and aversive environmental conditions' and from 'stable properties of the person' (Gruen et al., 1988, p. 759).

However, the word 'stable' here can be problematic in describing personality variables because trait stability is not irrefutable, especially among the variables that have been associated with ineffective coping and stress-related health outcomes. An additional issue is whether a variable is a trait or a state, in which case it might be a target for change leading to outcome improvement.

The following personality variables illustrate this complexity.

Hardiness

Reporting results of a study involving mid- and upper-level executives at a public utility company, Kobasa (1979) introduced the concept of 'hardiness'. It described those who did not become ill when exposed to high levels of stress. She found that hardy executives had four personality 'conditioners' in common: (1) a stronger commitment to self, (2) an attitude of vigorousness towards their environment, (3) a sense of meaningfulness, and (4) an internal locus of control. She also acknowledged one of Selye's more subtle points, the observation that there are mediating factors which somehow deflect the harmful impact of stressors. We find a parallel to the idea of hardiness in Seligman's writing. Before championing the field of positive psychology, Seligman contributed the stimulus–response concept of 'learned helplessness' (Seligman & Maier, 1967). The animals he studied 'learned' to be 'helpless'. They stopped trying to avoid being shocked after learning that they could not prevent it from happening. In his book *Authentic Happiness* (Seligman, 2002), he mentions those experiments in the context of 'embarrassing findings' that changed his thinking about what was going on. He writes that not all of the animals became helpless. 'One out of three never gives, up, no matter what we do,' he explains, 'while one of eight is helpless to begin with.' Extending the concept to humans, he asks, 'What is it about some people that imparts buffering strength, making them invulnerable to helplessness? What is it about other people that makes them collapse at the first inkling of trouble?' (Seligman, 2002, p. 23).

Locus of control

Essentially, locus of control refers to whether an individual attributes outcomes to his or her own efforts (internal locus) or to chance or powerful others (external locus) (Rotter & Mulry, 1965). Having an external locus might seem to offer value in identifying individuals particularly susceptible to illness after being outsourced or downsized because it has been associated with higher perceptions of stress (Anderson, 1977) as well as a host of other ill-sounding characteristics, including negative affect, hostility and depression (Basgall & Snyder, 1988). However, external locus may also have value as a defensive mechanism (Davis & Davis, 1972).

Locus of control is not the best mediator or moderator candidate for stress and illness research because it's a slippery variable that's becoming even more so. Rotter himself said that it was neither a stable trait nor a typology. Further, an external shift has been reported after negative life events (Doherty, 1983; Doherty & Baldwin, 1985) and time periods characterized by loss of control (Twenge, Zhang, & Im, 2004); however, shifts in externality may only be temporary (Wendland, 1973). Disadvantaged populations have also been reported to show greater externality than less disadvantaged groups (e.g. Graves, 1961; in Battle & Rotter, 1963). A further distinction is that at its external pole, locus of control seems to be morphing into important distinctions between the chance-externality and powerful-others locus (Levenson, 1972), which Rotter himself acknowledged.

If locus of control has value as a research variable for organizations, perhaps it may serve as a group or organizational pulse that could be taken at intervals to assess whether external shifts occur during times of change. Given the depression–external locus association, an external shift might indicate an opportunity to offer stress-alleviating interventions.

Self-efficacy

Self-efficacy is not a trait; it is a belief – specifically a learned belief that one can successfully execute the behaviour required to produce a desired outcome (Bandura, 1977). It is derived from mastery of subjectively threatening but relatively safe experiences; and, theoretically, it 'acknowledges the physiologically strengthening effects of mastery over stressors' (Bandura, 2001). In fact, stress experienced while gaining mastery has been associated with beneficial immune system markers (Wiedenfeld et al., 1990). According to Bandura, 'Resilient self-efficacy provides the needed staying power' to function when faced with the adversities of daily life (Bandura, 2001, p. 21). So, at least the possibility exists that development of self-efficacy might exert some sort of buffering effect against work-related stressors and illness. However, self-efficacy is situation-specific and can also be generalizable, so it's reasonable to ask whether a generalized self-efficacy would confer resilience after being outsourced or downsized. Bandura emphasizes that people do have self-regulatory influence in creating supportive environments for themselves. They do things that help them manage their stressors, and transform threatening environments into benign ones (Bandura, 2001).

With regard to acknowledging work-related stressors, organizations have opportunities to both hinder and help employees develop self-efficacy. Bandura (2002) writes that occupational stress occurs when people don't believe they possess the efficacy needed to meet the demands of a task or when they become plateaued in careers that don't make use of or allow for enhancement of their skills. A particular concern is ongoing, aversive occupational stress that doesn't allow the individual an opportunity to develop coping self-efficacy (Wiedenfeld et al., 1990). Long-term job insecurity, whether it's associated with the threat of being outsourced or downsized, or actually having been outsourced or downsized on multiple occasions, could fit that description.

Negative affect

'Affect' is basically 'mood', from the perspective of the individual experiencing it – but sometimes also referring to what the observer sees, for example mood as indicated by facial expression. For general discussion purposes, positive and negative affect can be thought of as being in a good mood and bad mood, respectively, although they are distinct and not necessarily opposites. To illustrate, Watson, Clark, and Tellegen (1988) explain that negative affect is 'a general dimension of subjective distress and unpleasurable engagement that subsumes a variety of aversive mood states, including anger, contempt, disgust, guilt, fear and nervousness'. High negative affect is not the same as low positive affect, which they describe as 'characterized by sadness and lethargy' (Watson et al., 1988, p. 1063). However, both have been suggested to be major features of depression and anxiety (e.g. Tellegen, 1985; in Watson et al., 1988). Negative affect has also been recognized to co-occur with chronic stress (Folkman & Moskowitz, 2000), precipitate problem behaviour in individuals with low self-efficacy (Love, Ollendick, Johnson, & Schlezinger, 1985; in Bandura, 2001) and to be associated with psychosomatic symptoms, anxiety, poor role adjustment and worries (Costa & McCrae, 1980). It is also related to two other potentially illness-predisposing personality variables: neuroticism and Type D personality.

Neuroticism

Neuroticism is one of the five personality traits comprising the NEO Five Factor Model (McCrae & Costa, 2007), also referred to as 'the NEO Five' or 'the Big Five'. The other traits are extraversion, openness to experience, agreeableness and conscientiousness. Neuroticism is characterized by feelings of anxiety, angry hostility, depression and vulnerability (McCrae & Costa, 2007). It is also associated with negative affect (Deneve & Cooper, 1998).

Theoretically the Big Five are considered as biologically determined, inborn traits that are not influenced by the environment (McCrae et al., 2000). However, two asides are worth noting. First, although the traits are considered endogenous, they are not stable throughout the course of a lifetime. Rather, they tend to change in predictable ways, displaying what is referred to as 'intrinsic maturation'. For example, neuroticism evidences a period of decline from age 18 to 30 and again sometime after age 30. Second, although the traits may be intractable, they do not define one's destiny because how an individual adapts to his or her environment is culturally conditioned and involves social adaptation (McCrae et al., 2000).

The connection between neuroticism and stress is worrisome. McCrae and Costa (1986) report that individuals high in neuroticism are prone to using coping mechanisms that are generally perceived to be ineffective. These mechanisms include increased use of hostile reaction, escapist fantasy, self-blame, sedation, withdrawal, wishful thinking, passivity and indecisiveness. Further characteristics of neuroticism are poorer outcomes and a negative association with well-being (McCrae & Costa, 1986). In addition, support exists for the argument that the relationship between neuroticism and stress can be generalized to life at work, including higher job-related stress (Grant & Langan-Fox, 2007). Concern may be particularly warranted for older workers who are unemployed. Creed and Watson (2003) reported higher mean levels of neuroticism among unemployed workers older than 55 compared with two younger groups whose means were almost identical with one another. Mean neuroticism was highest for women over 55. Neuroticism was the most important predictor for all subjects but more so for the mature group. Whether such findings might generalize to outsourced or downsized individuals is unknown. Bühler and Land (2003) note that individuals with a neurotic personality conform to behaviour norms much of the time, displaying neurotic behaviour primarily in stress situations. If this is the case, then individuals high in neuroticism might be among those at greatest health risk when experiencing involuntary job loss or other change.

Type D personality

Type D for 'distressed' is the new frontier in stress-related personality–cardiovascular research – and it is a compelling one. Associations between Type D personality and various populations of cardiac patients have been overwhelmingly supported in the academic literature (Song & Son, 2008) since the concept's originator, Johan

Denollet of Tilburg University in the Netherlands, first began publishing his findings (Denollet, 1991).

Song identified and reviewed 28 studies with the dual aim of examining the relationship between Type D personality and cardiovascular disease and suggesting future research directions. The following conclusions were recognized: (1) Type D personality is associated with increased morbidity and mortality in patients with established cardiovascular disease; (2) Type D patients are at increased risk for impaired quality of life; (3) they seem to benefit less than non-Type Ds from medical and invasive interventions; (4) the need is urgent to adopt a personality approach in order to optimize how patients at risk for stress-related cardiac events are identified.

Contextually, Type D can be considered as the successor to Type A behaviour (Miller, 2005), which has contributed greatly to stress–cardiac research but remains controversial (de Fruyt & Denollet, 2002) and has been associated with inconsistent findings (Pedersen & Denollet, 2003). Type A was described as a behaviour pattern rather than a personality type (Rosenman et al., 1967). It was suggested as a pattern of traits, including 'a drive to accomplish many poorly defined things, a love of competition, a proclivity for recognition and advancement, habitual time-urgent behaviour, acceleration of physical and mental activity, and intense concentration and alertness' (Dembroski & Czajkowski, 1989; in Ganster, Schaubroeck, Sime, & Mayes, 1991, p. 144).

Type D personality refers to individuals who have negative affectivity (NA) and repressive coping (REP) (Denollet, 1991), also known as 'social inhibition (SI)' (de Fruyt & Denollet, 2002). Negative affect has been described in a previous section as a mood that encompasses aversive emotional states, including anger, contempt, disgust, guilt, fear and nervousness. REP refers to a tendency to inhibit the expression of distress and emotions (Denollet et al., 1996). Both NA and SI have been reported to correlate positively with neuroticism at (0.74) and (0.50), respectively (de Fruyt & Denollet, 2002). Type D incidence among groups from the general population has been reported at 21 per cent (Denollet, 2005) to 38.5 per cent (Williams et al., 2008; Grande et al., 2003). The Denollet (2005) study also found Type D personality among 28 per cent of coronary heart patients and 53 per cent of individuals with hypertension. Grande (2003) and others reported Type D at 25 per cent in coronary heart disease patients and 62 per cent in psychosomatic patients. Denollet et al. (1996) found that, among both men and women, an association between Type D and mortality was still present 6 to 10 years later among cardiac patients.

Although the bulk of Type D studies have been conducted among Flemish cardiac disease patients, at least two investigations – both conducted in Poland – have investigated Type D with regard to the workplace. Ogińiska-Bulik (2006) found that Type D individuals among psychiatrists and nurses perceived their workplace as more stressful than non-Type Ds. These healthcare professionals also showed more symptoms of mental health disorders as well as a higher level of burnout in the form of emotional exhaustion and lower personal accomplishment. In a study of firefighters assigned to fire brigade life-saving units, Type D personality was associated with coping strategies that increased the intensity of post-traumatic stress disorder (PTSD) symptoms, intrusion in general and hyperarousal in particular (Ogińiska-Bulik & Langer, 2007).

Investigative work has also focused on associating Type D with physiological pathologies. Whitehead, Perkins-Porras, Strike, and Magid (2007) found a relationship between variations in the cortisol awakening response (CAR) in Type D survivors of acute cardiac events. They concluded that a disruption of the hypothalamic-pituitary-adrenocortical (HPA) axis function might be involved, contributing to future cardiac ill health through heightened inflammatory responses. This association is also consistent with Selye's (1976) original work in rats. In humans, immune system dysfunction is also implicated by associations between Type D personality and higher levels of a pro-inflammatory cytokine called 'tumour necrosis factor-alpha' (Conraads et al., 2006; Denollet, Vrints, & Conraads, 2007). Cytokines are produced as an immune system response, and they are predictors of mortality in chronic heart failure (Denollet et al., 2003).

Interventions

As long as downsizing and outsourcing continue to exist, organizations and individuals will deal with the consequences. Implications for individuals and organizations differ, though they are ultimately interrelated.

For those who have lost their jobs, forgiveness and positive psychology may have something to offer.

> In retrospect, being downsized was a blessing for Bev and for her family, 'but you don't see it at the time,' she says. After 17 years with the same organization, the 47-year-old wife and mother of four lost her director-level job as part of a group downsizing two years ago.
>
> 'They take you into their office; and in less than 30 minutes, you're out the door,' she explains. 'You can't even go back and say goodbye to your employees. It makes you feel like a criminal. It's so demeaning that it's unreal.'
>
> During the weeks and months that followed, Bev experienced emotional numbness, ongoing nausea, loss of appetite and weight loss as well as feelings of hurt and betrayal. In spite of financial fears, she was relieved to be away from the stress of her employment environment, and her husband and children were happy to have more of her time.
>
> The family cut back on expenses, and Bev found part-time employment. 'Being downsized was a good way of getting me out of an environment that I didn't have the strength to leave on my own,' she reflects. 'Financially, I've learned to live on practically nothing; and it's amazing to think back about all of the money I piddled away while receiving a pay check.'
>
> Bev says that although she will always feel some hurt because of how she was treated personally, she has forgiven the organization as well as any

individuals who played a role in her job loss. 'Forgiving and getting rid of the anger, I think, created in me a clean heart,' she says. 'I had to lose the anger and bitterness in order to open up room to appreciate the goodness of everyone and everything in my life. I'm actually grateful.'

Forgiveness

Consistent with the idea of 'forgiveness' now emerging in the secular academic literature, we present 'forgiveness' as 'neutralized unforgiveness', an idea that does not necessarily include the cultivation of positive feelings towards one's transgressor (e.g. Wade & Worthington, 2003). Strelan and Covic (2006, p. 1076) have proposed a new definition of 'forgiveness' as 'the process of neutralizing a stressor that has resulted from a perception of an interpersonal hurt'.

Individual outcomes associated with being downsized and being in the state of unforgiveness share a long list of negative emotions as well as increased risk of cardiovascular disease (e.g. Cook, Cummings, Bartley, & Shaper, 1982; in Leana & Ivancevich, 1987; Witvliet, Ludwig, & Vander Laan, 2001) and depression (Moore et al., 2004; Thompson et al., 2005). From a health-stressor perspective, neutralizing negative feelings may suffice. For the individual who perceives being harmed, the cultivation of positive feelings towards the transgressor may not be necessary in order to derive healthful effects. Neutralization of negative feelings may be enough. According to McCullough (1998, p. 1660) and colleagues, 'any variable that helps people modulate hostility might be an important facilitator of physical health'.

Charlotte van Oyen Witvliet of Hope College in Holland, Michigan in the US is leading exciting work in this area. She and her colleagues have measured differences in physiological effects that occur when people imagine real-life offences, rehearse hurtful memories and nurse grudges instead of cultivating empathy and imagining forgiveness (Witvliet et al., 2001). They found that unforgiving thoughts led to more aversive reactions, including heart rate increases and blood pressure changes, and the heart rate effects persisted into the recovery period. An interesting detail is that even though neutralized unforgiveness may be a sufficient endpoint, positive emotions, particularly empathy directed towards the offender, may be essential during the process of forgiveness (Worthington, 1998; in Witvliet et al., 2001). For example, the victim of a transgression might try to imagine an occasion when he or she asked for and received forgiveness. He or she might also try to understand how the transgressor felt leading up to the transgression and empathize on that basis.

A question that complicates the idea of forgiveness after downsizing is the issue of whom or what is to be the target of forgiveness. Enright and Zell (1989; in Thompson et al. 2005) have stated that people forgive only other people, not situations. However, Thompson and colleagues have described forgiveness of situations and developed scales that measure dispositional forgiveness toward oneself, others and situations. They suggest that the personality variable of dispositional forgiveness might help people reframe transgressions in a way that eliminates the negative 'thoughts, feelings, or behaviours about the transgression, transgressor, and associated outcomes' (Thompson et al., 2005, p. 351). Also with regard to the object of forgiveness, who or what represents the organization in the mind of the victim is unknown. Scholarly attention to this question seems to be missing, yet there is an implicit difference between forgiving an organization versus forgiving a situation or individuals. Nothing more than personal conversation is necessary to reveal that downsized individuals may forgive the organization that downsized them but still harbour unforgiveness towards one or more individuals – or vice versa.

While forgiveness may be available as a coping resource for individuals who have been downsized, the idea may be problematic for those who have been outsourced as well as those who survive downsizing. In fact, it could even be maladaptive. Govier and Verwoerd (2002) write that individuals who forgive should stop short of reconciling with the perpetrator of the wrongdoing, especially if further risk is associated with the relationship. Outsourced and surviving employees still have a relationship with the organization that committed the transgression, so forgiveness might be inappropriate. Miley and Spinella (2006) state that forgiving individuals should not allow themselves to continue to be harmed; yet individuals who still depend on the organization for employment remain at risk of being downsized. Implications may also exist for future employment relations. Worthington and Scherer (2004) and others comment that those who have forgiven mobilize to protect themselves from further damage.

Positive Psychology

For those who remain susceptible to re-victimization, positive psychology (Seligman, 2002) may offer more adaptive value than forgiveness because it addresses making the best of one's signature strengths regardless of physical circumstances. For an easy-to-understand and inspiring introduction to this emerging field, the reader is referred to the book *Authentic Happiness* (Seligman, 2002). Rather than an organizational intervention, positive psychology might best be conceptualized as a pursuit that individuals could undertake on their own behalf. Though the field continues to attract proponents, evidence for interventions is not yet clear.

An Organizational Perspective

How organizations can best offset the costs of employee stress, what role personality variables might play, and whether a particular approach might mitigate negative organizational outcomes related to downsizing are important questions.

Grant and Langan-Fox (2007) suggest that the NEO Five factors, particularly neuroticism, could be used to identify individuals who may be creating higher levels of perceived stress due to their own thinking and behaviour. They note that the vulnerability of this group might be reduced through cognitive-behavioural therapy specific to the workplace. They also suggest that personality criteria could be utilized even earlier to identify people best suited for particular high-stress jobs. While this view is logical, it also raises issues of employee privacy and ethical use of potentially damaging information. Knowledge that can be used to identify and segregate can also be used to manipulate and discriminate, so safeguards against Machiavellian use of personal information would need to be in place if, indeed, they are possible at all.

Le Fevre, Kolt, and Matheny (2006) claim that although a growing body of theoretical work exists for organization-based stress management, it is thus far not backed by much evidence. Instead, they favour secondary approaches, which focus on the individual as a first-line intervention. Niven and Johnson (1989) emphasize the need for an evidence-based approach when offering stress-management interventions in the workplace. They say that a number of interventions, including relaxation training and day-away seminars, are too brief to work. Instead, they argue for employee choice in identifying particular behaviours to be modified and a long-term approach punctuated with opportunities to return and discuss what is working versus what is not. They advocate a theoretical approach that encompasses three variables: emotions, behaviours and cognitions.

Finally, an emerging organizational parallel to positive psychology offers a cultural approach suggested to buffer against organizational strains such as downsizing. It's called 'positive organizational scholarship', and it advocates for the creation of 'virtuous' organizations (Cameron 2006). Cameron and his colleagues at the University of Michigan in the US propose that like individuals, organizations are at their best when they aspire to 'virtuousness', which embraces ideas such as 'honor, goodness, benevolence and ennoblement' as well as 'human impact, moral goodness, and unconditional societal betterment' (Bright, Cameron, & Caza, 2006, p. 249). Being virtuous extends beyond merely being ethical. It layers on a concept called 'positive deviance' which encompasses virtuous aspirations that serve as 'fixed points to guide individual and organizational behaviour in times of ambiguity, turbulence, and high-velocity change (Cameron, 2006, p. 320). Virtuousness is said to have an amplifying effect, which eventually embeds itself as part of an organization's culture, and a buffering effect, which is protective during times of change. Virtuousness is also not constrained by cultural differences (Cameron 2006a), so it is appropriate in a global context.

Cameron, and others (2003; in Cameron 2006) found that virtuous firms recovered from the predictably negative effects of downsizing and retained their customers and employees to a greater extent than organizations that did not display virtuousness. In subsequent work (Bright et al., 2006), these researchers studied two virtuous organizations that had turned around financially after downsizing and found that employees clearly viewed their employers as being less affected than usual by the long-term negative effects associated with downsizing.

Cameron and Lavine have developed a management programme that teaches virtuousness to executives. In addition, their account of how a virtuous engineering firm transformed a radiation-contaminated Cold War-era nuclear weapons production facility into a wildlife refuge can be found in *Making the Impossible Possible* (2006). As with its sister field of positive psychology, positive organizational psychology is so new that evidence to support desired outcomes is still needed.

Conclusion

If downsizing has a human side, we hope that a glimpse of it has been presented here. We have examined associated health risks to individuals, why some people may fare better than others, and where resources might be utilized to help both individuals and organizations achieve mutually beneficial outcomes in association with outsourcing and downsizing.

As technology and globalization continue to drive organizational change, the need intensifies to find better ways of achieving short-term goals without sacrificing long-range survival. A more compelling question is whether, in some imaginable future, individual and organizational health might be viewed as means to an optimal common end.

Time will tell.

Acknowledgement

Luis Acosta, J.D., M.S.L.S. of the US Law Library of Congress for his review of the section on US employment law.

References

Ahmadjian, C. (2001). Safety in numbers: Downsizing and the deinstitutionalization of permanent employment in Japan. *Administrative Science Quarterly*, *46*, 622–654.

Amundson, N., Borgen, W., Jordan, S., & Erlebach, A. (2004). Survivors of downsizing: Helpful and hindering experiences. *The Career Development Quarterly*, *52*, 256–271.

Anderson, C. (1977). Locus of control, coping behaviors, and performance in a stress setting: A longitudinal study. *Journal of Applied Psychology*, *62*, 446–451.

Armstrong-Stassen, M. (2001). Reactions of older employees to organizational downsizing: The role of gender, job level, and time. *Journals of Gerontology: Series B: Psychological Sciences and Social Sciences*, *56B*, 234–243.

Arroba, T. (1979). The social and psychological aspects of redundancy. *Personnel Review*, *8*, 26–29.

Bandura, A. (1977). Self-efficacy: Toward a unifying theory of behavioral change. *Psychological Review*, *84*, 191–215.

Bandura, A. (2001). The changing face of psychology at the dawning of a globalization era. *Canadian Psychology*, *42*, 12–24.

Bandura, A. (2002). Social cognitive theory in cultural context. *Applied Psychology: An International Review, 51*, 269–290.

Baron, R., & Kenny, D. (1986). The moderator–mediator variable distinction in social psychological research: Conceptual, strategic, and statistical considerations. *Journal of Personality and Social Psychology, 51*, 1173–1182.

Basgall, J., & Snyder, C. (1988). Excuses in waiting: External locus of control and reactions to success–failure feedback. *Journal of Personality and Social Psychology, 54*, 656–662.

Battle, E., & Rotter, J. (1963). Children's feelings of personal control as related to social class and ethnic group. *Journal of Personality, 31*, 482–490.

Bright, D., Cameron, K., & Caza, A. (2006). The amplifying and buffering effects of virtuousness in downsized organizations. *Journal of Business Ethics, 64*, 249–269.

Briscoe, J., Hall, D., & De Muth, R. (2006). Protean and boundaryless careers: An empirical exploration. *Journal of Vocational Behavior, 69*, 30–47.

Bühler, K., & Land, T. (2003). Burnout and personality in intensive care: An empirical study. *Hospital Topics: Research and Perspectives on Healthcare, 81*, 5–12.

Cameron, K. (2006). Good or not bad: Standards and ethics in managing change. *Academy of Management Learning & Education, 5*, 317–323.

Cameron, K. S., & Lavine, M. (2006). *Making the impossible possible*. San Francisco: Berrett Koehler.

Campbell-Jamison, F., Worrall, L., & Cooper, C. (2001). Downsizing in Britain and its effect on survivors and their organizations. *Anxiety, Stress, and Coping, 14*, 35–58.

Cascio, W. (1993). Downsizing: What do we know? What have we learned? *Academy of Management Executive, 7*, 95–104.

Cascio, W. (2004). Managing a downsizing process. *Human Resource Management, 43*, 425–436.

Cavanaugh, M., Boswell, W., Roehling, M., & Boudreau, J. W. (2000). An empirical examination of self-reported work stress among US managers. *Journal of Applied Psychology, 85*, 165–174.

Chen, J., & Goligorsky, M. (2006). Premature senescence of endothelial cells: Methusaleh's dilemma. *American Journal of Physiology: Heart & Circulatory Physiology, 59*, 1729–1739.

Conraads, V., Denollet, J., De Clerck, L., Stevens, W., Bridts, C., & Vrints, C. (2006). Type D personality is associated with increased levels of tumour necrosis factor (TNF)-α and TNF-α receptors in chronic heart failure. *International Journal of Cardiology, 113*, 34–58.

Costa, P., & McCrae, P. (1980). Influence of extraversion and neuroticism on subjective well-being: Happy and unhappy people. *Journal of Personality and Social Psychology, 38*, 668–678.

Creed, P., & Watson, T. (2003). Age, gender, psychological wellbeing and the impact of losing the latent and manifest benefits of employment in unemployed people. *Australian Journal of Psychology, 55*, 95–103.

Cropanzano, R., Byrne, Z., Bobocel, R., & Rupp, D. (2001). Moral virtues, fairness heuristics, social entities, and other denizens of organizational justice. *Journal of Vocational Behavior, 58*, 164–209.

Davis, W., & Davis, D. (1972). Internal and external control and attribution of responsibility for success and failure. *Journal of Personality, 40*, 123–126.

de Fruyt, F., & Denollet, J. (2002). Type D personality: A five-factor model perspective. *Psychology and Health, 17*, 671–683.

De Meuse, K., Bergmann, T., Vanderheiden, P., & Roraff, C. (2004). New evidence regarding organizational downsizing and a firm's financial performance: A long-term analysis. *Journal of Managerial Issues, 16*, 155–177.

Deneve, K., & Cooper, H. (1998). The happy personality: A meta-analysis of 137 personality traits and subjective well-being. *Psychological Bulletin, 124*, 197–220.

Denollet, J. (1991). Negative affectivity and repressive coping: Pervasive influence on self-reported mood, health, and coronary-prone behavior. *Psychosomatic Medicine, 53*, 538–556.

Denollet, J. (2005). DS14: Standard assessment of negative affectivity, social inhibition, and Type D personality. *Psychosomatic Medicine, 67*, 89–97.

Denollet, J., Conraads, V., Brutsaert, D., De Clerck, L., Stevens, W., & Vrints, C. (2003). Cytokines immune activation in systolic heart failure: The role of Type D personality. *Brain, Behavior & Immunity, 17*, 304–310.

Denollet, J., Sys, S., Stroobant, N., Rombouts, H., Gillebert, T., & Brutseaert, D. (1996). Personality as independent predictor of long-term mortality in patients with coronary heart disease. *Lancet, 17*, S0140–6736.

Denollet, J., Vrints, C., & Conraads, V. (2007). Comparing Type D personality and older age as correlates of tumor necrosis factor-dysregulation in chronic heart failure. *Brain, Behavior, & Immunity, 17*, 736–343.

Doherty, W. (1983). Impact of divorce on locus of control orientation in adult women: A longitudinal study. *Journal of Personality, 44*, 834–840.

Doherty, W., & Baldwin, C. (1985). Shifts and stability in locus of control during the 1970s: Divergence of the sexes. *Journal of Personality and Social Psychology, 48*, 1048–1053.

Epel, E., Blackburn, E., Lin, J., Dhabhar, F., Adler, N., Morrow, J., & Cawthon, R. (2004). Accelerated telomere shortening in response to life stress. *PNAS, 101*, 17312–17315.

Farrell, J. (2003). The effect of downsizing on market orientation: The mediating roles of trust and commitment. *Journal of Strategic Marketing, 11*, 55–74.

Fisher, S., & White, M. (2000). Downsizing in a learning organization: Are there hidden costs? *Academy of Management Review, 25*, 244–251.

Folkman, S., & Moskowitz, J. (2000). Positive affect and the other side of coping. *American Psychologist, 55*, 647–654.

Fornell, C., Johnson, M., Anderson, E., Cha, J., & Everitt, B. (1996). The American customer satisfaction index: Nature, purpose and findings. *Journal of Marketing, 60*, 7–18.

Freeman, S., & Cameron, K. (1993). Organizational downsizing: A convergence and reorientation framework. *Organization Science, 4*, 10–29.

Ganster, D., Schaubroeck, J., Sime, W., & Mayes, B. (1991). The nomological validity of the Type A personality. *Journal of Applied Psychology Monograph, 76*, 1143–168.

Govier, T., & Verwoerd, W. (2002). Forgiveness: The victim's prerogative. *South African Journal of Philosophy, 21*, 97–111.

Grande, G., Jordan, J., Kümmel, M., Struwe, C., Schubmann, R., Schulze, F., et al. (2003). Evaluation of the German type D Scale (DS14) and prevalence of the Type D personality pattern in cardiological and psychosomatic patients and healthy subjects. *Psychotherapie, Psychosomatik, Medizinische Psychologie, 54*, 413–422.

Grant, S., & Langan-Fox, S. (2007). Personality and the occupational stressor–strain relationship: The role of the big five. *Journal of Occupational Health Psychology, 12*, 20–33.

Greenglass, E., Burke, R., & Moore, K. (2003). Reactions to increased workload: Effects on professional efficacy of nurses. *Applied Psychology: An International Review, 52*, 580–597.

Gruen, R., Folkman, S., & Lazarus, R. (1988). Centrality and individual differences in the meaning of daily hassles. *Journal of Personality, 56*, 743–762.

Hayflick, L. (1996). *How and why we age.* New York: Ballantine Books.

Hayflick, L., & Moorhead, P. (1961). The serial cultivation of human diploid cell strains. *Experimental Cell Research, 25*, 585–621.

Herriot, P., & Pemberton, C. (1996). Contracting careers. *Human Relations, 49*, 757–790.

Hertzog, R. (2006). Ancestral telomere shortening: A countdown that will increase mean life span? *Medical Hypotheses, 67*, 157–60.

Holmes, R., & Masuda, M. (1974). Life change and illness susceptibility. In B. Dohrenwend & B. Dohrenwend (Eds.), *Stressful life events: Their nature and effects* (pp. 45–72). New York: John Wiley & Sons.

Hopkins, S., & Weathington, B. (2006). The relationships between justice perceptions, trust and employee attitudes in a downsized organization. *Journal of Psychology, 140*, 477–498.

Internal Revenue Service, Department of the Treasury. (2008) Independent contractor (self-employed) or employee? Retrieved June 2008 from www.irs.gov/businesses/small/article/0,,id=99921,00.html

Kalimo, J., Taris, T., & Schaufeli, W. (2003). The effects of past and anticipated future downsizing on survivor well-being: An equity perspective. *Journal of Occupational Health Psychology, 8*, 91–109.

Kanter, R. (1989). Careers and the wealth of nations: A macroperspective on the structure and implications of career forms. In M. B. Arthur, D. T. Hall & B. S. Lawrence (Eds.), *Handbook of career theory* (pp. 506–521). Cambridge: Cambridge University Press.

Kets de Vries, M. (1997). The downside of downsizing. *Human Relations, 50*, 11–50.

Kickul, J., Neuman, G., Parker, C., & Finkl, J. (2001). Settling the score: The role of organizational justice in the relationship between psychological contract breach and anticitizenship behavior. *Employee Responsibilities & Rights Journal, 13*, 77–93.

Kobasa, S. (1979). Stressful life events, personality, and health: An inquiry into hardiness. *Journal of Personality and Social Psychology, 37*, 1–11.

Kraemer, T. (2001). Generating new metaphors; downsizing as cancer. *Advances in Developing Human Resources, 3*, 355–365.

Leana, C., & Ivancevich, J. (1987). Involuntary job loss: Institutional interventions and a research agenda. *Academy of Management Review, 2*, 201–312.

Le Fevre, M., Kolt, G., & Matheny, J. (2006). Eustress, distress and their interpretation in primary and secondary occupational stress management interventions: Which way first? *Journal of Managerial Psychology, 21*, 547–565.

Lepine, J., Podsakoff, N., & Lepine, M. (2005). A meta-analytic test of the challenge stressor–hindrance stressor framework: An explanation for inconsistent relationships among stressors and performance. *Academy of Management Journal, 48*, 764–775.

Levenson, H. (1972). Distinctions within the concept of internal–external control: Development of a new scale. *Proceedings of the Annual Convention of the American Psychological Association, 7*, 261–262.

Marchiori, D., & Henkin, A. (2004). Organizational commitment of a health profession faculty: Dimensions, correlates and conditions. *Medical Teacher, 26*, 353–358.

Mathieu, J., & Zajac, D. (1990). A review and meta-analysis of the antecedents, correlates, and consequences of organizational commitment. *Psychological Bulletin, 108*, 171–194.

McCrae, R., & Costa, P. (1986). Personality, coping, and coping effectiveness in an adult sample. *Journal of Personality, 54*, 385–405.

McCrae, R., & Costa, P. (2007). Brief versions of the NEO-PI-3. *Journal of Individual Differences, 28,* 116–128.

McCrae, R., Costa, P., Ostendorf, F., Angleitner, A., Hřebíčková, M., Avia, M., et al. (2000). Nature over nurture: Temperament, personality, and life span development. *Journal of Personality and Social Psychology, 78,* 173–186.

McCullough, M., Sandage, S., Brown, S., Rachal, K., Worthington, E., & Hight, T. (1998). Interpersonal forgiving in close relationships: II. Theoretical elaboration and measurement. *Journal of Personality and Social Psychology, 75,* 1586–1603.

McKinley, W., Zhao, J., & Rust, K. (2000). A sociocognitive interpretation of organizational downsizing. *Academy of Management Review, 25,* 227–24.

Miley, W., & Spinella, M. (2006). Correlations among measures of executive function and positive psychological attributes in college students. *Journal of General Psychology, 133,* 175–182.

Miller, D. (2003). Homeodynamics in consciousness. *Advances, 19,* 35–46.

Miller, M. (2005). What is Type D personality? *Harvard Mental Health Letter, 22,* 8.

Moore, S., Grunberg, L., & Greenberg, E. (2004). Repeated downsizing contact: The effects of similar and dissimilar layoff experiences on work and well-being outcomes. *Journal of Occupational Health Psychology, 9,* 247–257.

Morgan, G. (1997). *Images of organization.* Thousand Oaks, CA: Sage.

Muhl, C. (2001). The employment-at-will doctrine: Three major exceptions. *Monthly Labor Review, 124,* 3–12.

Niven, N., & Johnson, D. (1989). Taking the lid off stress management. *Industrial and Commercial Training, 21,* 8–11.

Ogińiska-Bulik, N. (2006). Occupational stress and its consequences in healthcare professionals: The role of Type D personality. *International Journal of Occupational Medicine and Environmental Health, 19,* 113–122.

Ogińiska-Bulik, N., & Langer I. (2007). Type D personality, coping with stress and intensity of PTSD symptoms in firefighters. *Medycyna Pracy, 58,* 307–316.

One Hundred Seventh Congress of the United States of America (2002). *An Act to Protect Investors by Improving the Accuracy of Corporate Disclosures Made Pursuant to the Securities Laws, and for Other Purposes.* Retrieved June 2008 from frwebgate.access.gpo.gov/cgibin/getdoc.cgi?dbname=107_cong_bills&docid=f:h3763enr.txt.pdf

Orlando, J. (1999). The fourth wave: The ethics of corporate downsizing. *Business Ethics Quarterly, 9,* 295–314.

Pacak, K., Palkovits, M., Yadid, G., Kvetnansky, R., Kopin, I., & Goldstein, D. (1998). Heterogeneous neurochemical responses to different stressors: A test of Selye's doctrine of nonspecificity. *American Journal of Physiology, 275,* 247–55.

Pedersen, S., & Denollet, J. (2003). Type D personality, cardiac events, and impaired quality of life: A review. *European Journal of Cardiovascular Prevention and Rehabilitation, 10,* 241–248.

Rosenman, R., Friedman, M., Jenkins, D., Straus, R., Moses, W., & Kositchek, R. (1967). Clinically unrecognized myocardial infarction in the Western Collaborative Group Study. *American Journal of Cardiology, 19,* 776–782.

Rotter, J., & Mulry, R. (1965). Internal versus external control of reinforcement and decision time. *Journal of Personality and Social Psychology, 2,* 598–604.

Rousseau, D. (1990). New hire perceptions of their own and their employers' obligations: A study of psychological contracts. *Journal of Organizational Behavior, 11,* 389–400.

Russell, A. (2007). Stress milestones. *Stress, 10*, 1–2.

Scott, M. (2007). *Scott on outsourcing law and practice.* Austin, TX: Aspen.

Scully, J., Tosi, H., & Banning, K. (2000). Revisiting the social readjustment rating scale after 30 years. *Educational and Psychological Measurement, 60*, 864–876.

Seligman, M. (2002). *Authentic happiness.* New York: Free Press.

Seligman, M., & Maier, S. (1967). Failure to escape traumatic shock. *Journal of Experimental Psychology, 74*, 1–9.

Selye, H. (1976). *The stress of life.* New York: McGraw-Hill.

Song, E., & Son, Y. (2008). The analysis of type D personality research as a psychosocial risk factor in cardiovascular disease for elders with a chronic disease. *Taehan Kanho Hakhoe Chi, 38*, 19–28.

Strelan, P., & Covic, T. (2006). A review of forgiveness process models and a coping framework to guide future research. *Journal of Social and Clinical Psychology, 25*, 1059–1085.

Sverke, M., Hellgren, J., & Näswall, K. (2002). No security: A meta-analysis and review of job insecurity and its consequences. *Journal of Health Psychology, 7*, 242–264.

Thompson, L., Snyder, C., Hoffman, L., Michael, S., Rasmussen, H., Billings, L., et al. (2005). Dispositional forgiveness of self, others, and situations. *Journal of Personality, 73*, 313–359.

Toussaint, O., Remacle, J., Dierick, J., Pascal, T., Frippiat, C., Zdanov, S., et al. (2002). From the Hayflick mosaic to the mosaics of ageing: Role of stress-induced premature senescence in human aging. *International Journal of Biochemistry & Cell Biology, 34*, 1415–1430.

Twenge, J. M., Zhang, L., & Im, C. (2004). It's beyond my control: A cross-temporal meta-analysis of increasing externality in locus of control – 1960–2002. *Personality and Social Psychology Review, 8*, 308–319.

US Equal Employment Opportunity Commission (1964). *Title VII of the Civil Rights Act of 1964.* Retrieved June 2008 from www.eeoc.gov/policy/vii.html

US Equal Employment Opportunity Commission (1967). *The Age Discrimination Employment Act of 1967.* Retrieved June 2008 from www.eeoc.gov/policy/adea.html

Vahtera, J., Kivimaki, M., Pentti, J., Linna, A., Virtanen, M., Virtanen, P., et al. (2004). Organizational downsizing, sickness, absence, and mortality: 10-town prospective cohort study. *British Medical Journal, 328*, 555–559.

Viner, R. (1999). Putting stress in lie: Hans Selye and the making of stress theory. *Social Studies of Science, 29*, 391–410.

Wade, N., & Worthington, E. (2003). Overcoming interpersonal offences: Is forgiveness the only way to deal with unforgiveness? *Journal of Counseling & Development, 81*, 343–353.

Watson, D., Clark, L., & Tellegen, A. (1988). Development and validation of brief measures of positive and negative affect: The PANAS Scales. *Journal of Personality and Social Psychology, 54*, 1063–1070.

Wendland, C. (1973). Internal–external control expectancies of institutionalized physically disabled. *Rehabilitation Psychology, 20*, 180–186.

Whitehead, D., Perkins-Porras, L., Strike, P., & Magid, K. (2007). Cortisol awakening response is elevated in acute coronary syndrome patients with type-D personality. *Journal of Psychosomatic Research, 62*, 419–425.

Wiedenfeld, S., O'Leary, A., Bandura, A., Brown, S., Levine, S., & Raska, K. (1990). Impact of perceived self-efficacy in coping with stressors on components of the immune system. *Journal of Personality and Social Psychology, 59*, 1082–1094.

Williams, L., O'Connor, R., Howard, S., Hughes, B., Johnston, D., Hay, J., et al. (2008). Neurobiology of the metabolic syndrome: An allostatic perspective. *Journal of Psychosomatic Research, 64,* 63–60.

Witvliet, C., Ludwig, T., & Vander Laan, K. (2001). Granting forgiveness or harboring grudges: Implications for emotion, physiology and health. *Psychological Science, 12,* 117–123.

Worthington, E., & Scherer, M. (2004). Forgiveness is an emotion-focused coping strategy that can reduce health risks and promote health resilience: Theory, review, and hypothesis, *Psychology and Health, 19,* 385–405.

Yegorov, Y., & Zelenin, A. (2003). Duration of senescent cell survival in vitro as a character-istic of organism longevity, an additional to the proliferative potential of fibroblasts. *Febs Letters, 541,* 5–11.

Zyglidopoulos, S. (2003). The impact of downsizing on the corporate reputation for social performance. *Journal of Public Affairs, 4,* 11–25.

Secondary References

Allen, N., & Meyer, J. (1996). Affective, continuance, and normative commitment to the organization: An examination of construct validity. *Journal of Vocational Behavior, 49,* 252–276.

Brockner, J., Wiesenfeld, B., & Martin, C. (1995). Decision frame, procedural justice, and survivors' reactions to job layoffs. *Organizational Behavior and Human Decision Process, 63,* 59–68.

Cameron, K. (2003). Organizational virtuousness and performance. In K. S. Cameron, J. E. Dutton, & R. E. Quinn (Eds), *Positive organizational scholarship: Foundations of a new discipline.* San Francisco: Berrett-Koehler.

Cobb, S., & Kasl, S. (1977). *Termination: The consequences of job loss.* (Report No 76-1261). Cincinnati, OH: National Institute for Occupational Safety and Health Research.

Cook, D., Cummings, R., Bartley, M., & Shaper, A. (1982). Health of unemployed middle-aged men in Great Britain. *Lancet, 5,* 1290–1294.

Dembroski, T., & Czajkowski, S. (1989). Historical and current developments in coronary-prone behavior. In A. W. Siegman & T. M. Dembroski (Eds.), *In search of coronary-prone behavior: Beyond Type A.* Hillsdale, NJ: Erlbaum.

Enright, R., & Zell, R. (1989). Problems encountered when we forgive another. *Journal of Psychology and Christianity, 8,* 52–60.

Fombrun, C. (1996). *Reputation.* Boston: Harvard Business School Press.

Graves, T. (1961). *Time perspective and the deferred gratification pattern in a tri-ethnic com-munity.* Research report No. 5. Tri-Ethnic Research Project. University of Colorado, Institute of Behavioral Science.

Kübler-Ross, E. (1969). *On death and dying.* New York: Macmillan.

Love, S., Ollendick, T., Johnson, C., & Schlezinger, S. (1985). A preliminary report of the prediction of bulimic behavior: A social learning analysis. *Bulletin of the Society of Psychologists in Addictive Behavior, 4,* 93–101.

Luthans, B., & Sommer, S. (1999). The impact of downsizing on workplace attitudes. *Group and Organizational Management, 24,* 46–71.

Noer, D. (1993). *Healing the wounds: Overcoming the trauma of layoffs and revitalizing down-sized organizations.* San Francisco: Jossey-Bass.

Rousseau, D. M. (1995). *Psychological contracts in organizations: Understanding written and unwritten agreements.* Thousand Oaks, CA: Sage.

Tellegen, A. (1985). Structures of mood and personality and their relevance to assessing anxiety, with an emphasis on self-report. In A. H. Tuma & J. D. Maser (Eds.), *Anxiety and the anxiety disorders.* Hillsdale, NJ: Erlbaum.

Sartorius, N., & Ban, T. (Eds). (1986). *Assessment of depression.* New York: Springer Verlag.

Worthington, E. (1998). Empirical research in forgiveness: Looking backward, looking forward. In E. L. Worthington, Jr. (Ed.), *Dimensions of forgiveness.* Philadelphia: Templeton Foundation Press.

Chapter 13

Transitioning and the Psychological Contract

Stephanie J. Morgan

In a number of the chapters we have raised the concept of the psychological contract and, linked to that, issues of justice. As previously explained, the psychological contract is an invisible or implicit psychological contract that supplements the formal written employment contract (see Chapters 6 and 12). However, although the concept has a range of implications for the behaviour of people in organizations, there are some remaining issues about its practical use and the discussions still continue regarding the nature of the contract and with whom (or what) the contract is (see Conway & Briner, 2005). Disputes remain regarding whether the contract is developed through promises or obligations, and whether it is with the organization or individuals in it. Wellin (2007) emphasizes that it helps to focus on a 'personal deal' and the individual relationships that enable the psychological contract to develop and influence perceptions of breach or violation. In this chapter we will discuss findings from research which explicitly questioned the expectations of staff when they were being outsourced, and the extent to which these expectations were met. Implications for outsourcing contracts, particularly where transitions have occurred, are discussed. The interview data is primarily from staff transferred through IT outsourcing contracts (a number of different contracts were investigated), but to retain anonymity as much as possible, the words NewCo and OldCo are used throughout to refer to either their new employer or their original company. The analysis was completed using the philosophy of Heidegger to aid understanding (Heidegger, 1962). This is a hermeneutic approach (see Smith, 2007), which enables focus on the meaning of an experience as well as shifts of time – particularly useful, we found, to this study.

The Human Side of Outsourcing: Psychological Theory and Management Practice
Edited by Stephanie J. Morgan

The Psychological Contract and Expectations

Expectations and promises are likely to influence the nature of the attachments to both companies, and are linked to form a psychological contract that participants may build with their new employer. In terms of hermeneutics, expectations for the future are closely linked to how one understands the present. Indeed Heidegger (1962) argues that the future possibilities are more important than perceived current consequences in developing an understanding of both present and past, therefore an awareness of what participants felt they were expecting when they were transferred may be important in our understanding.

Our research has given us strong evidence to suggest that most participants felt their psychological contract with their previous employer had been violated. The feelings of anger expressed by many indicate that this was a serious violation, not a simple breach (Robinson & Wolfe Morrison, 2000). Many participants suggested that they had no relationship worth speaking of with the previous organization, and that they would prefer not to have any further dealings. Ending the relationship may have helped them towards closure. The nature of outsourcing means that this is not possible, although the earlier analysis suggests that people find ways of dealing with this. When asked about expectations for the future, all the participants discussed their potential relationship with NewCo. The focus of this section therefore is on this aspect, and the potential building of a new psychological contract with the new employer.

Expectations of NewCo

Many of the participants suggested in the first interview that they had few expectations of NewCo initially. No one seemed to have a clear concept of 'obligations', another term used in the literature. Perhaps this is because of the nature of the transfer. As outlined earlier, many were not sure whether they were even wanted by the new company. In many cases there was a sense in which they gave the new company the benefit of the doubt, at least initially. In some cases this was explicitly linked to the idea that there would be no real change involved in the transfer:

> I'm not sure what I expected, apart from not expecting much because I was doing the same job and I didn't think it could be changed very much, but I know, erm, people were saying things could be procured quicker, and in fact I think ordering, erm, office equipment is a bit easier. (Participant 20-21, public/staff/male)

As most of the participants were from the public sector or from large private organizations, it is perhaps not surprising that some of them suggested that the reduced bureaucracy was viewed positively. However, this experience did seem to vary, with some being surprised at how similar the organizations were, and suggestions of bureaucracy in the new company:

> I don't think we could have foreseen how things were going to progress. I don't, if, it's, it's been a difficult nine months, let's put it that way. Erm, we did not know what to expect, erm, I don't think my managers knew what to expect. Erm, it has been a fire-fighting period. We were not, we are not able at the moment to feel proactive at all. Erm, partly because of NewCo red tape, partly because of the awkwardness of the customer. Erm, so it's been, if you can call it that, an interesting nine months. (Participant 07-2, public/mgr/male)

This excerpt also demonstrates a form of understanding shown by a number of participants, particularly those that had been interviewed early on in the transfer, that of making excuses on behalf of the new company. In the above excerpt it is partly the awkwardness of the customer, for others it was 'too early', or because 'the transfer was too rushed'. Despite having been transferred in a forced situation, then, many participants seemed to want to be 'fair' to their new employer.

Some participants focused on their expectations of training and development opportunities; this is indeed an aspect that many systems houses propose as a potential benefit. Not surprisingly, there was disappointment when this did not happen, especially by the time of the second interviews. However, some participants were still hopeful that it was only a matter of time:

Interviewer: are there any other things that you felt, perhaps at these general presentations, that met or didn't meet your expectations?
Participant: erm [pause] I think probably the, er, there are certain, certain things not quite there yet,
Interviewer: hmm
Participant: I mean they made a big thing about the career development side, but if you actually look at our ability to get at that, I'm sure it's there, but it's not straightforward. (Participant 13-2, public/mgr/male)

This participant, and many others, highlighted the problems of being expected to find out about jobs for themselves on the company intranet, an aspect many found difficult. For now this focus on self-development is potentially an element of the unexpected for many people working in large corporations or the public sector. Similarly, he discussed a change of manager, and how in OldCo his conversations with one manager regarding expectations would have been documented. There was no element of surprise in his discussion, more an indication of the difficulty of a change of culture. The emphasis was on how vague ideas of what might be found when working in a systems house may influence relationships, rather than on 'expectations' in any clearly formulated manner.

In contrast, some suggested that their developing expectations of a large systems house may be one of the problems. In particular, they spoke of how the early presentations had set certain expectations, of professionalism, of having real expertise in managing transfers. This led to disappointment, as one participant stated, 'instead they re-invent the wheel every time' (Participant 25-1, private/mgr). Another pointed out the long-term implications of raising people's expectations during these presentations, having experienced redundancies despite being reassured that this would not happen:

Interviewer: You must have had some expectations then of NewCo?
Participant: Yes, I would have thought they would have been better at doing it, than they were, I mean, one could excuse it if this was the first time they'd ever done it, yeah, I don't think we can excuse it, theoretically after so many attempts, and it's just, ah, I suppose, what really hurts is when people lie to you, yeah, you can take it, ok if they say we are going through a troubled period, we are having trouble, y'know we are having to look at numbers, we are thinking about these, but we want to make sure we do the best for you, but, y'know it's not the biggest rosy picture in the world, you should be aware that we are going through a redundancy programme, or at least through a re-organization or something, and people can read what they like into that, but when people stand up and say, like they did with NewCo, we are looking for hundreds and hundreds of people, y'know, nobody leaves when we do these things, and, they, it would have been better if they hadn't said it at all, y'know, just left that, blank. (Participant 16-1, private/mgr/male)

Again the importance of these initial presentations is highlighted, and it is suggested that the pain of downsizing was increased due to the perception that they had been purposely misled.

In most instances, where participants were clearly able to articulate unmet expectations, as in the above example, it was to do with very explicit contractual aspects. This participant highlights her dissatisfaction with the new company and the terms and conditions they have been offered, but also includes the less concrete aspect of not being listened to:

Interviewer: But erm, what, well you obviously expected them to be a bit better organized and to have ready this is what you do, but did erm, did you have any other expectations, that they have either met or not met or,
Participant: yeah, I mean all this business about not being financially disadvantaged and all that, yes we have been
Interviewer: oh right
Participant: We definitely have been. Erm, they are not as nice to us, as they were.
Interviewer: In what ways
Participant: erm, whereas before it would be y'know, 'oh well we will listen to you' they are not anymore, the attitude is take it or leave it.
Interviewer: hmm
Participant: erm, they have now offered us the NewCo grades, well they did say that we would have our NewCo grade offers within six months
Interviewer: yes they should have

Participant: It's taken them a year. We have only just had them. Erm, and there is definitely a difference, so they want us to work 42 hours instead of 35, but for no extra money. And er, y'know there's all these sort of issues really. (Participant 33-1, private/staff/female)

It is possible that the more explicit aspects of the contract, and a number of perceived breaches, build up to generate stronger feelings about other relational aspects. By the time of the second interview, although she was more positive about certain aspects of her relationship with the company, it was clear that the term 'expectations' generated ill-feeling, as she felt that, in their case, the hard work was not rewarded:

Interviewer: Have the last 18 months met up to your expectations?
Participant: No,
Interviewer: right
Participant: Not at all.
Interviewer: In what ways?
Participant: Because we thought that we were going to something, better. The way it was sort of sold, y'know, you work hard, but there's lots of other rewards [pause]
Interviewer: yes, and you don't feel that they've appeared,
Participant: No, no no not at all. [pause] You get the working hard bit, but [pause]
Interviewer: right
Participant: I think people feel that they have been, very cheated
Interviewer: Okay, do you feel cheated?
Participant: [pause] It, hasn't made a lot of difference to me, sort of, financially and things, because I am part time I just get my, same hours and everything, y'know the only thing I have lost out on is flexitime but then I have gained a company car, so, erm, no. I do feel, erm, that, things could have been done a lot better, I feel a lot of personal pain has been caused. (Participant 33-2, private/staff/female)

Others highlighted the pain of the process, which may well have influenced their expectations. The feeling that they were not doing well enough and needed to be managed by a more efficient organization may have also made the change more significant, and sense-making possibly more difficult. As with this participant, a number suggested that they had expected to work harder; indeed, for most this seemed to be the case. However, it was felt to be acceptable, if the extra work was acknowledged:

Participant: erm, expectations, I think, one, we knew we would have to work harder, I think, that you were prepared to accept that, if, erm, they were acknowledging the fact that you were working harder. As I said earlier, good work was applauded, whatever, then, yes. Erm, [pause] I can't really erm, think off the top of my head on that.
Interviewer: It is hard, it is because of some theory I have read about the impact peoples expectations may have on their work, but people I talk to have trouble thinking of expectations, and I wonder if the theory is wrong, because people

don't seem to have such a clear idea about what they want or expect, so don't be surprised if you can't think of an expectation, it's not, you help me even then because it's clear you are not sure what you expected.

Participant: no, no, I hadn't really erm, I can't say I had really thought about it, I didn't know what to expect. (Participant 19-1, public/staff/male)

Note the emphasis again on not knowing what else to expect other than harder work. However, the interview context should also be highlighted. First, he suggests that he cannot think 'off the top of his head', indicating that this perhaps needed more thought, and then I suggest that it may indeed be difficult to form expectations. This may have given him the cue that it was acceptable to say he did not know. In the second interview, this participant said again that he needed to think hard to work out what his expectations were, or whether he had any. However, it is interesting that many others said they did not know what to expect, indicating, as in the above excerpt, that they perhaps had not thought it through explicitly. Whether this is because of the involuntary nature of the transfer process is uncertain; perhaps expectations are less likely to be built if one feels there is no choice in the matter? Alternatively, perhaps expectations are difficult to assess in retrospect, or possibly, one does not think about expectations until they are breached. A further factor may be that these are mature staff. Perhaps newly employed graduates, the focus of much psychological contract research, have clearer expectations.

Evidence for the influence of the transfer process on expectations is clear in this example:

Interviewer: So, do you feel the experience has changed you, erm, you said that you feel differently about work now.

Participant: Yes. Yes, but also that you don't have any expectations really, erm, other than, well one of the expectations is you say this is what I am giving you, what do I get back in return. (Participant 09-2, public/staff/female)

This supports the view that individuals develop more transactional contracts after major violation. However, only a few participants were this clear-cut about their future relationships, suggesting that there is a problem with trying to generalize.

Another individual pointed out the differences between members of her team who felt that they were technical, and therefore hoped for career development, and her own experience, as she questioned her own ability to succeed in such an organization:

Interviewer: Your expectations were probably low to start with.

Participant: yes, yes, but I haven't gone even further down, I don't think its an even crappier organization, it's probably what I expected from them, y'know the communication's fairly bad, they haven't changed anything, but only because they don't really know what we are doing and until things start happening. (Participant 08-1, public/staff/female)

This suggests that expectations may tend to be low for some people in this type of transfer, and that, in principle, the company has an opportunity to exceed expectations. Conversely, perhaps more effort is needed to help involuntary transfers develop 'realistic' expectations.

Still there is an element here of waiting; many participants who were interviewed early in the process suggested that it was too early to know what to expect:

Interviewer: and do you feel that they have lived up to your expectations?
Participant: Well, it's early days yet, but I mean, erm, well yes, not for everybody, erm, well, the basic underlying feeling is I think is that, we are not integrated with what's happening totally yet. Yeah, erm, there are all these streams going on and we've had these, we've had these presentations from them and we've gone to other areas to talk with people and that sort of thing. (Participant 11-1, public/staff/male)

This participant is a useful example of the importance of assessing the impact of individual experience. In his case, by the time of the second interview, a promotion made him feel that his own expectations had been met, but he was very aware that his team still felt let-down, and suggests that he is privileged:

Interviewer: It sounds as if the last few months have met up to your expectations.
Participant: yeah, yeah I think because I am in a privileged position, having been moved to team leader and being able to integrate and all that sort of thing. I feel, I feel more part of, I have got a way forward now. (Participant 11-2, public/staff/male)

The other members of his team that were interviewed certainly showed no feeling of being integrated, and focused on either unmet expectations, or no expectations at all, as part of their problem.

Of those who were initially positive about the transfer, one was able to articulate his expectations quite clearly. This suggests that a reduced perception of violation can facilitate development of expectations. Even so, expectations were not always met, yet in the first interview he assumes that it is a question of time:

I hope that actually going to work for a company that is primarily involved in IT erm, that it will be treated a bit more seriously. Erm, I haven't been disappointed in that respect, what I have been a bit disappointed in is that, the organization and things would be done a bit more professionally than what they had been in the civil service. I have to say, I appreciate the fact that it's very much early days, we are two months into the contract, erm, and things are still a bit chaotic, but that isn't necessarily reflected on NewCo, I think it's the situation. (?) I think it would have happened regardless of what company had actually been successful. (Participant 12-1, public/staff/male)

Again it is noticeable that the time element is considered important, and that care is taken to reduce the blame on the organization. This can help to make sense of the disappointment – it is the situation, not the company, that is to blame.

Promises

Similarly, many participants suggested that no promises had really been made, yet during the interviews a few did discuss promises:

> They did promise us one-to-one interviews which they never kept to, that never happened. And I think, a lot of the chaps here, would have really welcomed that. They are all individuals they all say their circumstances are different to anybody else's, and I think that would have, in hindsight it was the one bit, not very good to promise it and then not come up with the goods. I mean it has been forgotten now, it's been forgotten but you do remember those things. They seemed to forget it very soon after the promise. (Participant 9-1, public/staff/female)

It is interesting that the participant suggests that things are forgotten by the company, yet are remembered by the staff. This indicates they feel that the promise was more important to them than to the company, or its representatives, the managers concerned.

For others, quite specific and seemingly minor promises seemed to gather in importance as time passed and they had not (yet) been met:

> Erm, yes the director has promised me that he will get me an interview with the new director, in the area I want to work in, there was something about doing some work for him, although when I spoke to him again about it he was a bit erm, not reticent, but I just felt he was concerned about putting me above (manager). So there is that, and now there's supposed to be two meetings on Wednesday I've got that, so I'm going to go (?) erm, but I do feel I've been promised that. Apart from that no, I don't think they have promised us anything just that there will be change etc. (Participant 32-1, private/staff/female)

There was indeed variation between transfers where change had been guaranteed and where the emphasis was on no change. Whether these were seen as promises by all involved is a moot point. Certainly this manager felt that discussions of no change did not amount to a promise:

> I, I think I am pretty safe in saying that no promises were made, to me personally, well to anybody for that matter. Well, no promises were made full stop. We were told we had been brought in to do a job and we would do it, y'know in the way we did before. And if things have changed that's not breaking a promise that's a business decision that has been made that we have to, change the way that you work that benefits the business. Which is fair enough, I can understand that. I think, although a number of colleagues that came across with me, weren't able to accept it so easily, so I wouldn't say that promises were made and broken, because I don't think promises were made to start with. Nobody is going to, y'know, it's like a lot of people were expecting, at the presentation about standard terms, that they were going to get huge pay rises, we

tried to dampen that, and we were told quite clearly that that wasn't the case. (Participant 07-2, public/mgr/male)

Note how this manager is able to make sense of changes as part of a business benefit scenario. This particular manager appears to be more closely identifying with NewCo by the second interview, which may make it easier for him to take this stance. Similarly, his discussion here regarding people having too high an expectation shows him taking the position of NewCo. Other participants found this a lot more difficult, indicating the links between perceptions of promises and attachment:

Interviewer: yes, were there any promises that were made that have not been met, when you came across?

Participant: There was a lot about, being made to feel a part of the organization, and keep you informed about, y'know what's going on, there would be a lot of communication, and in fact there's been none of that. (Participant 12-2, public/staff/male)

Again it is the transfer presentations that are highlighted here, and the disappointment that little seemed to be done to socialize the staff after these. The perception that promises were made of a future belonging may be an important one, and indicates that participants were hoping to feel a part of the organization. In the first interview, the participant cited above had been disappointed, but was holding on to the hope that communication would improve. However, his focus then had been on taking technology seriously; the lack of communication clearly became more important over time. This could be viewed as a developing expectation, perhaps becoming more pertinent because of its absence.

Participants who had been interviewed later in the transfer process were still able to remember this feeling of holding expectations in abeyance. This stability over time indicates that this might be an important way of helping to make sense of the situation. In hermeneutics the temporal element is important, and when one goes back to the past one retrieves possibilities, or 'forgets' due to the concerns of the present. The similarity of 'remembering' over these timescales suggests that participants have not created expectations to fit their current situation. This participant was interviewed two years after the transfer, and still remembers the feeling of holding expectations in abeyance:

Interviewer: Once you heard it was NewCo, did you have any particular expectations about what was going to happen?

Participant: No, not really, no, we were just like, going to wait and see what happens. We were, we felt, this time two years ago, between sort of October and Christmas, we felt it was all happening very quickly, once the contract had been awarded, we felt a bit like we were caught up in a sort of whirlwind, and things were flying at us from all directions, to fill in, and check this and check that, and we were just keeping our fingers crossed that everything was going through and all our pay and pension would be okay. (Participant 15-1, public/staff/female)

Similarly, most of those first interviewed two years after transfer had difficulty articulating expectations, although one was clear that some things had been promised:

> Pretty much, I didn't know what to expect, really I mean, having, having accepted I was coming across, I mean, I didn't know what to expect, I had no knowledge of the company, no knowledge of what business life would have on me, but erm, they'd promised me, I mean they offered me a job which was a better job than I had, I had a, prior to the, I had the whole organization here under my belt, so I had a better job out of it, I got a company car, which, of course I didn't get as a civil servant, I had cost centres to manage and some flexibility, so, that I knew I was getting before, just before takeover, and all of that was delivered, the expectations then were probably that, I had a job and er, the things that went with it, so, after that I don't know really, I'm still not sure what my expectations are. (Participant 05-1, public/mgr/male)

In a similar way to those interviewed early on in the process, some of the 'later' interviewees remembered clearly their concern regarding how much harder they might need to work. At the same time, perhaps they were better able to appreciate some of the positive aspects; in psychological contract terms their expectations had been exceeded:

> And erm, well I knew that it was a profit-making organization and therefore, well, actually everything that has happened since, I did sort of think would come, because as I say, with my husband's work, well anyone actually, if you listen to anything on the news you know how different private organizations work. So erm, I just think that I am going to make sure that I am one of those people that is always indispensable, or has always got a job or that they want to retain, erm, so I, I look after myself and I, I give, try to keep my career going in the right way so that I am, a worthwhile asset to the organization, erm, but I, I expected there to be job, redundancies, I expected to have to work harder. [pause] erm, y'know the nice bits, the social stuff, I didn't expect, it didn't really, didn't really expect, so some of the positive things that have come out of it. Although I think they mentioned it. (Participant 21-1, public/staff/female)

The positive aspects generally seemed to come as a pleasant surprise to participants, even though most transfer presentations highlight these. It is possible that they are not clearly remembered because they were not initially believed, or perceived as empty rhetoric.

In terms of promises, reports were very similar. It was again clear that the perceived promises only became important if they were broken. However, one aspect was noticeable from participants interviewed early on in the process. By the time of the second interview they showed more signs of disillusionment. Where expectations of training and communication had been generated, and originally held in abeyance, by about eight or nine months, the lack of these processes was causing concern. Although not always clearly expressed by the participants, these could be viewed as unmet expectations. It is possible that those first interviewed at two years had adapted more to the distance and lack of communication.

Conclusion

This research supports the view that a forced transfer is viewed as a serious violation of the psychological contract and is likely to lead to feelings of anger and resentment. Withdrawal of citizenship behaviours and loss of both identification with and commitment to the original organization seemed prevalent. However, the focus of blame seemed to vary somewhat, and in some cases was very specific. These findings suggest that there may indeed be problems with generalizing the organizational 'agent', and that multiple agents and multiple levels of analysis may be necessary in psychological contract research (Hallier & James, 1997). Managers who had also been transferred, while expressing a need to care for their staff, were less likely to be viewed, or see themselves, as agents of the new organization. They did not seem to be blamed for weaknesses in the new organization, nor did they suggest any felt responsibility for creating expectations, indicating that they were as much 'in the dark' as the staff. This suggests that the organizational 'agent' will also vary depending on the circumstances. Outsourcing might further complicate perceptions of contract development; it is possible that over a long timescale some transferred managers may eventually be viewed as agents of the organization, although this would require further research.

The analysis also suggests that employees in an outsourcing transfer may be uncertain of what to expect from their new employer. Perceptions of promises or obligations are even more unclear, indicating that expectations may be the better term to use in these circumstances. As suggested by Conway (1999), researchers in this area need to consider in more depth the fundamental question of which 'belief' should be measured. This thesis suggests that there may be variation in the usefulness of terms such as promise, obligation or expectation depending on the broader context.

In outsourcing, the few expectations that are formed appear to be held in abeyance, giving the new organization the 'benefit of the doubt' for some time. On the other hand, there was talk of exchange mechanisms, or reciprocity, for example commitment only being maintained while being treated well. This supports the view of Coyle-Shapiro and Kessler (2002) that employees do consider reciprocity important and balance future hoped-for benefits with current contributions, having some level of trust in their employer. However, this thesis offers insight into the timescales that may be involved in obligation fulfilment, with signs of disillusionment setting in between the first and second interviews for those interviewed shortly after the transfer. This suggests that the first six to nine months of a transfer may be particularly important in both developing and fulfilling expectations.

Although there were some signs of reverting to a more 'transactional' contract after the transfer, this varied somewhat, with other participants showing a desire for a relational form of attachment. Again this suggests that assumptions must not be made regarding the impact of violations on future contract development (Millward & Brewerton, 1999; Rousseau, 1995). The findings offer limited insight to the contract development process, possibly due to the difficulty participants had in expressing expectations or obligations. However, this in itself is useful as it could indicate that new contracts take longer to develop in such circumstances. Elements of trust, fairness, and good communication were highlighted by participants as important to their understanding (or lack of understanding) of the new organization, supporting the findings of Hubbard and Purcell (2001). It is also possible that the limited and individually focused socialization received by this sample is a contributory factor to the slow contract development, which supports the view that socialization and contract development are linked (Thomas & Anderson, 1998). Outsourcing appears to further complicate conceptions of the organizational 'agent', as transferred managers are less likely to be regarded as agents of the new organization. Theoretical development of the psychological contract construct needs to include more explicit assessment of the organizational agent. Further links between experience of violation, organizational socialization, and the development of new psychological contracts need to be developed. Such development may enable the psychological contract to be used as a more practical framework to help organizations manage transitions more effectively, as argued by Wellin (2007).

References

Conway, N. (1999). *Using the psychological contract to explain attitudinal and behavioural differences between full-time and part-time employees.* London: Birkbeck College.

Conway, N., & Briner, R. (2005). *Understanding psychological contracts at work: A critical evaluation of theory and research.* Oxford: Oxford University Press.

Coyle-Shapiro, J. A. M., & Kessler, I. (2002). Exploring reciprocity through the lens of the psychological contract: Employee and employer perspectives. *European Journal of Work and Organizational Psychology, 11*(1), 69–86.

Hallier, J., & James, P. (1997). Middle managers and the employee psychological contract: Agency, protection and advancement. *Journal of Management Studies, 34*(5), 703–728.

Heidegger, M. (1962). *Being and time* (trans. John Macquarrie & Edward Robinson). Oxford: Blackwell.

Hubbard, N., & Purcell, J. (2001). Managing employee expectations during acquisitions. *Human Resource Management Journal, 11*(2), 17–33.

Millward, L. J., & Brewerton, P. M. (1999). Contractors and their psychological contracts. *British Journal of Management, 10*, 253–274.

Robinson, S. L., & Wolfe Morrison, E. (2000). The development of psychological contract breach and violation: A longitudinal study. *Journal of Organizational Behavior, 21*, 525–546.

Rousseau, D. M. (1995). *Psychological contracts in organizations: Understanding written and unwritten agreements.* Thousand Oaks, CA: Sage.

Smith, J. A. (2007). Hermeneutics, human sciences and health: Linking theory and practice. *International Journal of Qualitative Studies on Health and Well-Being, 2,* 3–11.

Thomas, H. D. C., & Anderson, N. (1998). Changes in newcomers' psychological contracts during organizational socialization: A study of recruits entering the British Army. *Journal of Organizational Behavior, 19,* 745–767.

Wellin, M. (2007). *Managing the psychological contract: Using the personal deal to increase performance.* Aldershot: Gower.

Chapter 14

Conclusion: Towards a Model of Responses to Outsourcing

Stephanie J. Morgan

Introduction

Although this book has demonstrated a broad range of practical issues and theoretical approaches that can inform our understanding of the human side of outsourcing, there are some aspects, particularly of the requirement to work for two masters, that could benefit from a deeper understanding. In particular, Coyle-Shapiro, Morrow, and Kessler (2006) indicate the need for a better understanding of identification across two organizations. In this chapter I outline some events that may influence organizational attachment, particularly commitment and identification, and develop a process model that can result in real practical advice for those managing outsourcing transfers. In the final conclusion, I will return to other aspects of outsourcing that have been discussed, but here I feel that the transfer situation requires further consideration.

Events Influencing Attachment

At all these 'stages' highlighted in transition literature and the previous chapters events are rarely clear-cut, with different types of events in both OldCo and NewCo likely to impact upon the identification(s) of the individuals with the organization. (In rare cases where a 'deep'-level identification has been reached, there are likely to be fewer fluctuations; these more complex influences are discussed in a later

The Human Side of Outsourcing: Psychological Theory and Management Practice
Edited by Stephanie J. Morgan
Copyright © 2009 John Wiley & Sons Ltd.

section.) The analysis shows that identification with OldCo is lost quite quickly. For simplicity the focus of the following section is on the impact on potential identification with NewCo (the company to which employees are being transferred) only.

Events in OldCo

The type of events related to OldCo and their likely impact upon identification with NewCo includes:

- commercial decisions made against OldCo – potentially increase identification with NewCo;
- OldCo colleagues in meetings are derogatory about NewCo – potential decrease in identification with NewCo, or even explicit dis-identification, unless the employee is already deeply identified;
- continual monitoring of OldCo for e.g. salary changes – potential decrease in identification with NewCo likely as ties to OldCo remain;
- OldCo found to be 'refilling' staff in similar roles – likely to lead to an increase in identification with NewCo as all routes of return to OldCo are reduced, but only if NewCo is seen to be taking steps to integrate.

As indicated in the literature, there may be obstacles to identification, such as remoteness and isolation, that mean that even when events occur that could increase identification with NewCo (such as OldCo refilling roles), the identification does not occur, the transferees remain disconnected from both companies.

Events in NewCo

The following indicates some events specifically related to NewCo that can also help to increase or decrease identification:

- discussion of move to standard personal contract – potential increase or decrease in identification, depending on whether viewed positively or negatively;
- meetings about OldCo with NewCo colleagues – again a potentially positive or negative impact on identification depending on whether made to feel valued;
- presentations, social events and more general meetings with NewCo management and colleagues aimed at facilitating the transfer – if perceived as positive and sufficient in quantity may lead to increased identification.

Note that these events are mostly very specific to the outsourcing situation. Other aspects discussed by participants were more relevant to general socialization and identification in any organization. These included the nature of communications, motivational attempts and particularly good or weak line management.

Problems with Transition Models

Some events are likely to lead to either an increase or a decrease in identification depending on the individual and contextual circumstances. Some propositions can be made based on the analysis for our research, and these will be discussed later in the chapter. However, it is difficult to form individual predictions of changes in identification from any general stage model.

The extent and quality of communications and meetings with NewCo representatives are of vital importance and may have a cumulative effect, leading to a deeper, less situationally based level of identification. This cumulative effect is a particularly difficult aspect to conceptualize clearly in a pictorial form. The way in which these events build upon each other, and also the different ways in which similar events may be perceived, will depend upon where the employee is in the cycle when something occurs. This is not clear in Figure 14.1 as to allow for this would have made the model too complex.

Nicholson's (1990) model emphasizes socialization practices, individual and organizational 'tasks' at each stage, and possible outcomes for the individual, depending on how the transition progresses. According to Nicholson (1990), commitment is one potential outcome of the stabilization stage; however, there is no explicit link to organizational identification. This research suggests that our

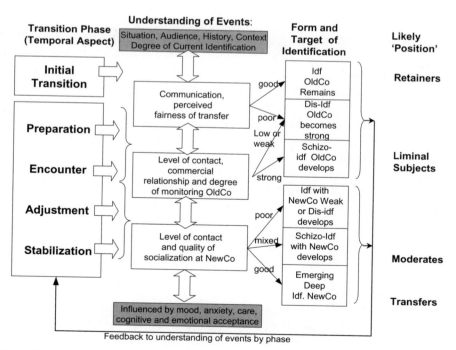

Figure 14.1 Process model of identification in outsourcing

understanding of identification may be increased by assessing the impact of social-ization processes throughout the transition cycle. To develop a process model of identification requires a mapping of current models of transition and identification, to gain a temporal element. To make this specific to outsourcing transitions requires integration of the findings from this research.

This first section has considered the findings from the analysis as related to transi-tion phases, and how these may impact upon identification. It is important now to consider current models of identification and integrate these with both the findings and the cycle.

Shaw and Jarvenpaa (1997) suggest that there is a tendency to focus on stages in models, such as with Nicholson (1990), whereas the real key is the transition between these and the underlying mechanisms. Linking identification and transition cycles may facilitate an understanding of this.

Current models of identification tend to be static. However, with the understand-ing of process gained from the analysis in this research and the use of the transition cycle, it should be possible to develop these to generate a process model. Two models were discussed in the literature review, as they are the most recent and more complex models of identification developed to date. These will be briefly summa-rized, and critiqued based on the earlier analysis, to aid development of a processual version.

Elsbach's Expanded Model

Elsbach's (1999) expanded model of organizational identification allows for a broader range of identifications than other models. The analysis in our research suggests that identification is indeed complex, suggesting that this may be an appro-priate base to build upon in developing a process model. Elsbach argues that dis-identification is not a simple mirror opposite of identification. It is suggested that identification is linked to the prestige of the organization's identity and self-enhancement motivations. Dis-identification is linked to identity threats and self-verification (the need to verify the absence of a negative identification). That is, a clear disconnection from a negative aspect of the organization reduces the risk that one's identity will be threatened by these negative connotations and increases the chance of enhancing the self. The analysis presented in this research does indeed have examples of participants distancing themselves from an aspect of the organiza-tion that they believe to be negative, for example 'mechanistic' and 'uncaring' cul-tures. Instead the participants were keen to identify themselves as 'caring' and 'people' types.

The model also allows for schizo-identification, where individuals simultaneously identify and dis-identify with particular aspects of an organization. Again there are good examples in the analysis of participants being very specific about certain aspects of an organization (or indeed a specific department within the organization) with which they identified or dis-identified, and other aspects of the organization with the opposite identification or dis-identification. However, these were at times extremely complex, and changed by situational context and over time; for example, complaining about uncaring emails (when one identifies oneself as caring) yet at the same time suggesting that these help to show that the organization is alive (and identifying oneself as needing to feel a part of something alive).

Elsbach's final addition to identification models is that of neutral identification, where a person balances cognitive connections and disconnections with an organization intentionally to maintain a stance of impartiality. While there were no indications of this occurring as a state in my own research, there were discussions of attempting to achieve this in specific meetings. Again this highlights a weakness of Elsbach's model that has become more apparent during analysis. Although changes in identification are allowed for as a series of identification steps, identifications and dis-identifications themselves are presented as state-like. The model does not fully explicate fluctuations over time and in different contexts. This may be partly due to the cognitive emphasis, and partly because of the static nature of the model itself. For these reasons we need to look at a model that may allow for fluctuations during interactions.

Structuration Model of Identification

Scott, Corman, and Cheney (1998) use Giddens' (1984) structuration theory to highlight the ways in which identity structures both influence and are influenced by identification interactions. They argue against the stable and almost trait-like emphasis in much of the identification literature and show how identification can vary contextually and change over time. The duality of structure and agent is emphasized, which allows for individuals to be active in the process of identifying, and also for the influence of social structures on those individuals' identifications. Previous conceptualizations have tended to suggest that employees passively 'get committed' through organizational actions, or alternatively actively identify with an organization that appeals to them, suggesting a trait as the causal mechanism. This model allows for both active and passive forms of identification, and could allow for the outsourcing context to be explicitly taken into account.

For example, in outsourcing, participants may be more or less eager to identify with the new company because of their feelings of being let down by their previous employer, yet the level of 'identification potential' may be strongly influenced by their exposure to NewCo and the style of company. The two aspects feed into each other and are potentially recursive. The interview situation is likely to highlight the active aspects of identification, where participants feel they can identify, or wish to dis-identify, with the organization, but analysis of precise wording such as the use of 'we' indicates the extent of passive (dis)-identification that has occurred.

In Scott et al.'s model 'situated activities' mean that certain identities may be more or less salient, and will influence the strength and nature of identification with various targets, in different situations. They also highlight the communicative expression of identification, and the importance of interactions and language in the process of identification. There is certainly evidence in this analysis of participants expressing identification in one context, and actively using their identification or dis-identification within the interaction (e.g. a meeting, a social gathering) to position themselves as a member or not of the organization.

They suggest that multiple identities include rules and resources to help anchor the self, and that identities will be regionalized, or grouped, but at the same time may be overlapping. The front regions are associated with 'positive' identifications and the back regions are related to negative or dis-identifications. It is suggested that negative identifications include values and beliefs that are in opposition to positive 'front region' identifications. This is subtly different from Elsbach's (1999) notion of dis-identification, which is more strongly linked to the need for self-verification. The structuration version enables an identity target to be salient, yet for there to be active distancing from specific aspects (such as organizational changes that appear to lead to a mechanistic attitude towards workers, as in this outsourcing research).

In this model the very act of telling someone that one feels a member of the organization may further establish one's feelings of belonging, which is likely to feed back into expressions of identification. Similarly, they suggest that an expression of dis-identification (e.g. with the team) may at the same time increase the salience of another focus (e.g. the organization). This could help to explain why some participants immediately began to discuss the importance of a role after explicitly dis-identifying with the organization.

Structuration theory was originally developed as a sociological theory, but can be used at a number of levels of analysis (Orlikowski, 1992). A key weakness is that it can be difficult to apply; the ongoing interaction between agency and structure means that it can be difficult to determine outcomes or causal relationships. However, it is possible to suggest typical relationships within specific historical and contextual situations, which is perhaps all we should hope for. Scott et al. assert that their model can be used as a middle-range heuristic, and perhaps this generality is a weakness in their particular model. Certainly they suggest that more needs to be done to explore the activity–identification relationship.

Their broad model depicts recursive activity between identity and identification as an 'attachment modality' and between activity and activity foci as the 'activation modality'. However, because of the focus on the individual level it does not depict the influence of the organization on the modalities. Similarly, owing to the emphasis on symbolic interactionism inherent in structuration models (Giddens, 1976), little allowance is made for emotive influences such as wants and needs, and the depth of current identification is not explicitly allowed for in the pictorial model.

The aim of the above model is to demonstrate more explicitly how an individual's current social identities, and their individual history with the organization(s), will influence the extent to which they may want to identify (or dis-identify) with the target. It also allows for passive identification(s). These potential identifications are influenced by the extent that the organization's agents and the current organizational context are perceived to promote identification (e.g. actively socializing staff).

This perception is itself influenced by the more general organizational identity and culture. The individual appearing to want to identify, or appearing to be (not) identified, with the organization may also influence the extent to which organizational agents are perceived to promote any identification, hence the two-way arrows and feedback loop in Figure 14.1.

The specific situation and audience, along with the identity salience, will influence the extent of current 'situated' identification, which will in turn influence the individual's identification levels and potentially also the perception of organizational attempts to promote identification. This model suggests that in order to understand the likelihood of identification with a target, a variety of aspects of the individual, the organization and the situation will need to be taken into account.

Using this model allows us to consider important aspects of identification not covered by Elsbach (1999), or clearly shown in Scott et al. (1998). While this may be an improvement in pictorial terms on the Scott and Cheney model, the weaknesses inherent in structuration models remains. A more specific model can be produced, which will include context issues particular to outsourcing, and the different forms of identification posited by Elsbach. However, first there are some additional concepts that may need including.

Additional Concepts

Neither model fully allows for changes in the quality or depth of identification, although the structuration version implicitly accepts this in terms of identity 'size'. It is likely that the participants classified as 'moderates' have developed a more situational identification as suggested by Rousseau (1998). This enables more fluctuation in the nature of their identification depending on the situation. Conversely, the employee who had fully identified with the new company could be classed as having achieved a 'deep' level of identification, which would lead to more stable, less situationally driven form of identification.

A process model of identification within organizations would therefore need to include all of these elements. Furthermore, outcomes may not always be linear, and feedback mechanisms should be shown which enable changes in the nature and quality of identification. Therefore, although a sequence of events can be shown to lead to a range of outcomes, it should be acknowledged that these outcomes will be further influenced by events in the future. To aid simplicity the model proposed here outlines key events or phases and relevant forms of identification, specific to the outsourcing situation. It is not intended to include primary cognitive processes related to these (see Elsbach, 1999 for a discussion of these) or to develop the underlying cognitive processes (see George & Jones, 2001 for a suggested model of individual reactions to change at this level). However, the analysis does suggest that forms of understanding and related identifications could be linked to the emotional and cognitive acceptance processes proposed by Weiss (1990). It is suggested that this should be viewed more holistically, in a similar way to Heidegger's emphasis on emotions and understanding as fundamental to 'being in the world'.

Towards a Process Model of Identification in Outsourcing

The model in Figure 14.1 expands upon previous models by integrating their most useful concepts and by capturing some of the processes involved in identification during outsourcing situations. A more complex understanding can be developed, allowing for different forms of organizational identification (as highlighted in the Elsbach, 1999 model) to be shown as possible outcomes. By emphasizing how current identity and the situation can interact, as highlighted in Scott et al.'s (1998) model, the reciprocal influences between structure and agency can be included.

This new model also leads to propositions that these different forms of identification may lead to the types of attachment (retainers, liminal, moderates and transfers) found in this outsourcing research. By using language related to processes such as development, emerging and becoming, the dynamic nature of the potential outcomes is highlighted, reducing the static feel of most diagrams.

The underlying high-level processes are proposed as understanding of events including the meaning of levels of contact with each organization. The outcomes are proposed to be complex and dynamic forms of identification. This fulfils the criteria for a processual model highlighted earlier. The model also allows for recursive processes, as the form of current attachment impacts upon one's ability to understand events, the relevance of expectations etc., and therefore the meaning of future events. By showing possible forms of identification with both the OldCo and NewCo, this model improves our understanding of potential conflicting identifications with dual targets, as occurs in most outsourcing situations.

Form and Target of Identification Initial Transition Phase

The phases of the transition are highlighted in the first column, starting with the initial transition handling where perceptions of justice were perceived by the participants to be particularly important to their attachment to the original employer. This is considered to be such an important process, based on this outsourcing sample, that it is shown separately to the proposed transition phases. Indeed, it is proposed that the experience of this process and the resultant impact upon identification with OldCo is likely to influence all the remaining phases. Hence, reading across from the initial transition box, their understanding of levels of communication and perceived fairness will lead to differing forms of identification with OldCo, which in turn feed back into the experience of later stages. If the initial transition is fairly managed there is an increased likelihood that identification with OldCo will remain strong (leading to possible 'retainers' from the sample). However, this will be influenced over time as the relationship with OldCo post transition develops or reduces, and also as the relationship with NewCo develops during the encounter and adjustment stages.

Identification with NewCo at this stage is probably Neutral as so little is known; indeed, in many cases a specific 'NewCo' will not have been confirmed. However, it is again likely that this initial process may influence how receptive employees are to NewCo; if they feel that their 'psychological contract' has been broken in an extremely poor manner they may be less likely to identify with future employers, or be more resistant to early socialization.

It is also proposed that the nature of understanding and the meaning of events during these stages will influence processes of cognitive and emotional acceptance. Indeed, a full understanding of an event could be argued to occur when cognitive and emotional acceptance has taken place, but the term 'understanding' allows for social and situational processes to influence these, whereas cognitive and emotional acceptance suggests a focus on internal, individual factors. Aspects of care and anxiety are linked with understanding of past/present and future. For example, I propose that if fairness is understood as low and the change has high significance for the individual, this generates high levels of emotions, particularly anxiety. This in turn is likely to decrease the possibility of emotional acceptance (Weiss, 1990).

Understanding of events

The second column shows the influence of an employee's understanding of type and level of contact, particularly of aspects relevant to each phase. It is proposed that the phase an employee is in will impact upon the nature of the understanding, and that certain events may have more salience at specific times.

The first box in this column suggests certain historical and contextual factors that will influence or moderate how the employees understand events. This allows for the understanding of events and the development of identification (or dis-identification) to be influenced by the current activity and situation, as proposed in the Scott et al. model. The use of a two-way arrow allows this understanding, and an act of (dis)-identifying to influence the quality or depth of identification in turn. However, it is proposed that the influence of the situation will be less when the identification is deeply embedded (hence 'degree of current identification' is included).

As highlighted in the discussion on initial transition, the level of communication and perceived fairness or justice perceptions are linked to the most important specific events at that phase. However, other events will become more or less important as each phase develops. Specific events linked to each phase are indicated in the earlier transition model. These will be discussed shortly, but these can be generalized (as in the lower two boxes in this column) to: level of contact, commercial relationship and degree of monitoring of OldCo required; and the level of contact and quality of socialization at NewCo. The perceptions of these general events are likely to feed back to each other and be interrelated – hence the two-way arrows between the boxes. For example, a series of poor communications from NewCo and ongoing perception of lack of socialization will possibly influence the degree of monitoring of OldCo felt necessary, or change their understanding of OldCo relationships. At the same time the ongoing nature of these communications will influence the quality and target of identification, and feed back into their understanding of events at each stage.

Forms of identification

A key aspect of this model is the proposed outcome of specific forms of identification. However, these are viewed as dynamic and should be conceptualized as emergent, with the feedback arrow returning to the next phase in the cycle, allowing for a change in understanding and a further shift in identification. For example, someone strongly dis-identifying with NewCo may be less likely to view any socialization attempts in a positive way, particularly if they have moved beyond the encounter stage (where they may have been giving them the benefit of the doubt owing to 'early days'). Similarly, this apparent lack of socialization reduces the potential for them to understand the organization, minimizing the possibility of their identifying with any aspect of the company. This suggests that NewCo may have to do more to influence these employees than those already identifying with the new organization. However, it is also possible for someone developing a deep identification with NewCo (owing to early positive experiences) to experience a lower level of contact with NewCo during a later stage, and develop either schizo- or dis-identification with NewCo. Their understanding of the company will therefore reduce, increasing the likelihood that they will become disconnected.

The model also suggests that there will be an interaction between employees' understanding of relationships with OldCo and with NewCo. Although for simplicity only the key resulting outcomes (the quality of identification) are shown for main targets – hence a focus on OldCo based on perceptions of OldCo levels of contact, and a focus on NewCo for the NewCo-related contacts. Similarly, not all potential outcomes are shown (e.g. neutral identification could occur in outsourcing if employees decided to purposely take a neutral position and felt that this neutrality was self-defining – viewing themselves as a person that doesn't take sides). Although the sample studied for this research included little evidence of neutrality, it is possible that employees could develop this as a strategy, particularly if they had been through an outsourcing transfer before.

Further phases

Returning to the first column allows us to consider how the different phases of the transition cycle may influence the ongoing sense-making and possibly modify the form and strength of identification. The issues and events discussed in the earlier section, using Nicholson's (1990) life-cycle model, can be explicitly used to increase our understanding of shifting forms of understanding and what types of events may be particularly salient at each phase. Specific aspects of the earlier discussion are highlighted here to aid reading of the model.

Preparation – here the employees are likely to gather as much information as they can about the new company, and the quality of initial presentations will be important in developing their initial attachment to NewCo. Their justice concerns will be paramount, not only in terms of how fair OldCo processes are perceived to be, but also the fairness of proposals by NewCo. However, their actual level of contact with NewCo is still minimal, meaning that events in OldCo are likely to be focal. If the presentations are perceived in a positive manner, and contact with NewCo is high, employees may begin to identify with NewCo at this stage. For many the poor treatment during the initial process, or the lack of information or contact from NewCo, may lead to no or even dis-identification.

Encounter – Employees will be influenced by the degree of initial socialization they experience from NewCo; if this is perceived as poor they may remain weakly identified or even develop a dis-identification with NewCo. The level of contact with OldCo may also be a key influence at this stage, although in principle dual identification could develop. The model does allow for identification with OldCo and NewCo, although this is probably rare in any depth. Alternatively, some employees may remain so deeply identified with OldCo that they are not receptive to NewCo.

Adjustment – At this stage employees begin to take more note of met and unmet expectations; the time of giving NewCo the benefit of the doubt is over. They will also be likely to begin discussions of changing their personal contracts, and the need to make decisions about this, and the ensuing discussions, are likely to influence identification, either positively or negatively. The degree of ongoing socialization will be more important now (linked to expectations). This is where some employees may start to feel particularly remote, and if their level of contact with NewCo is poor or mixed, they may feel little or no identification with them. Liminality may become more of an issue, as employees begin to realize that this is not a temporary state.

Stabilization – The extent of continued contact with OldCo may actually become more salient here. As the situation appears to stabilize, employees may have expected less contact, or be irritated by the continued relationship, especially if it is perceived as problematic. Here dis-identification with either company may still occur, or some aspects of each company may be identified with, as more knowledge is gained, and schizo-identification may increase. Further triggers, such as major contract renegotiations or rumours of back-sourcing, may lead to changes in identification again, as staff are forced to consider which company they now identify with, if any.

Categories or 'positions' of attachment

The research conducted for this chapter suggests that employees could be loosely classified by the forms of attachment they developed for the two organizations involved. The model leads to the following propositions concerning these main types of attachment (retainers, liminals, moderates and transfers).

If justice is perceived as fair and the initial transition is well managed, the identification with OldCo will remain (where organizational context facilitates this and current identification levels are high, identification will be 'deep' level). If the level of contact with OldCo remains high, and perceptions of socialization at NewCo are poor, these employees are likely to remain strongly identified with OldCo. If both forms of identification remain stable, attachment type will remain 'retainers'.

If justice is perceived as poor during the initial transition, dis-identification with OldCo is likely to be strong. If contact with OldCo is weak and perceptions of socialization with NewCo poor, these employees are likely to be weakly identified or even dis-identified with both, leading to possible liminality. Indeed, based on this sample, it is possible that contact with OldCo could still be high, but owing to the strength of the dis-identification with the company, employees remain disengaged from both companies.

It is also proposed that moderates are more likely to occur when perceptions of the level of contact and quality of socialization at NewCo are mixed, i.e. some experiences are good and others are poor. This could be due to a form of schizo-identification with NewCo developing, as staff identify with some aspects of the organization and dis-identify with others (Elsbach, 1999).

If perceptions of contact and quality of socialization at NewCo are good, there is potential for an emerging deep identification with NewCo. This is likely to be strengthened if the level of contact at OldCo is reduced (this is not shown in the figure to reduce the complexity). This will likely lead to the 'transfers' found in the sample.

The proposal that different forms of identification lead to different categories of attachment is based on the earlier analysis. For example, those participants that had been assessed as liminal did show clear signs during the interviews of dis-identification from both companies. The moderates tended to appear identified with NewCo in some areas and dis-identified in other respects, indicating schizo-identification. A strength of the model, therefore, is that it has been derived from both the data from the sample and current models of identification, and can be linked to these categories of attachment.

Summary

The aim of this chapter was first to develop a general model of outsourcing and related attachment processes, which would increase understanding of the temporal context and nature of this form of change. Nicholson's (1990) stage model was used to indicate how the transition cycle might develop and what particular aspects of each phase would be important in an outsourcing situation. The specific events related to both OldCo and NewCo that would influence identification with the new organization were shown and discussed. A new model specific to identification processes in outsourcing situations, fulfilling the requirements of processual models, was then developed, achieving the second aim of this chapter.

The new model both integrates the existing models of identification and expands on them to accommodate the findings from this outsourcing analysis. This model proposes that different forms of identification are likely to lead to the general categories of attachment found in the outsourcing sample. It highlights the importance of (employees' understanding of) levels and quality of contact with OldCo and NewCo as key influences on the form and strength of identification. Furthermore, it highlights the dynamic and changing nature of identification, and the influence of the current 'identifying' situation as well as context and history. However, it is also suggested that depth of identification or dis-identification will lead to a reduction in the influence of the activity or situation. The 'categories' may become more stable over time.

The model explicitly includes the temporal aspects of the outsourcing process (using the concept of transition phases), and the influence of individual understanding of events. This understanding is influenced not only by events but the level of anxiety and other emotions that emerge during the process. Including these factors allows for a more holistic (albeit more complex) understanding of identification processes. In our view, the concept of identification (and identity) is fundamental to understanding how employees react to outsourcing transfers, and should be considered further by practitioners and academics.

Conclusion

This book has demonstrated a number of ways in which our understanding of the human side of outsourcing could be improved. The model of identification developed above gives an overview of just one of the processes involved in a transition. While I would argue that identification could be a core element in outsourcing relationships, and is likely to impact upon responses to clients and employers (and possibly have crucial links to other processes such as the development of the psychological contract, perceptions of justice, trust and so on), it is clear that the human side of outsourcing is complex and multifaceted, and that attention should be paid to many if not all of the concepts discussed in this book.

Our practitioners in Part I of this book emphasized the importance of understanding the whole outsourcing life cycle, the different skills needed at varying stages, and the importance of relationships throughout. The theories and evidence discussed in Part II suggest a number of ways in which employee and management behaviour may be affected in outsourcing contracts.

The chapters lead us to some practical advice that should be considered by all involved in outsourcing.

Firstly, if you are arranging or involved in an outsourcing transition of staff, remember the following:

- People are likely to feel insecure; a caring attitude will help them – don't avoid the issues as this will make things worse.
- Reduce the chances of anger by ensuring that procedures are fair – ensuring organizational justice perceptions can help to develop a new psychological contract without strong feelings of violation.
- Work is often linked to people's identity – that's why the feelings can run deep, so do not just assume that because they still have a job they will not be upset.
- Emotions can be useful – use them, not abuse them. You want these people to continue doing good work for your organization. Be pleased that they care and help them to develop their new identity so that they can successfully identify with both organizations involved.

In terms of the transition itself:

- Plan and implement an extensive communication activity – with feedback allowed.
- Ensure that managers are coached and trained to enable them to communicate the changes effectively. Do not assume that they know how to handle it.
- Concentrate on the positive aspects where you can, but remember that these may differ for certain individuals.
- Try to ensure that staff continue to feel they are being treated fairly.
- Give people plenty of opportunity to talk to managers and HR from both organizations – this can enable trust to develop.
- Do not avoid the emotional aspects; people have a right to feel anxious and often what appears to be negative resistance can throw up some useful important points.
- Do give people the time and opportunity to get to know your chosen outsourcing partner. This can be particularly problematic if transferring for a second or third time, but is worth the extra effort.
- Ensure that the remaining staff and departments understand their new roles and relationships. Clear roles and procedures will help to avoid confusion and develop (or redevelop) trust.
- Let go when the time comes – your staff have a right to develop a relationship with their new employer, and it can create confusion if they are being told what to do by two different masters.

In terms of developing new contracts where staff transfers are not required (including offshoring and nearshoring), remember:

- Don't underestimate the time and resource cost of managing the contract and ensure that you understand the different requirements during the life cycle.
- Ensure that you meet face to face on a regular basis to develop trust and understanding.
- Ensure that all involved are trained to understand the cultural differences involved when dealing with different nationalities, and be alert to differences in

organizational culture. It can be worth holding cultural audits across the organizations or at least discussing differences openly to gain some shared understanding.

- Consider carefully the different skills required at various stages of the life cycle, and ensure that you either acquire the right people or (preferably) develop your own.
- Remember the importance of knowledge – in our increasingly customer-centric world all staff can be crucial links in understanding your business and your clients. Develop processes to ensure that this knowledge is shared.
- In all dealings, remember the importance of trust, justice and identity in enabling (or ruining) a successful contract and set up processes to ensure that people are engaged.

We hope that this book has given you some ideas regarding how to manage the human side of outsourcing if you are a practitioner. If you are an academic or budding researcher, this book has surely given you some ideas regarding areas where more research is needed. In our opinion, there is a clear need for more in-depth qualitative research, and/or mixed method studies where surveys can inform on frequency but interviews and observations inform on processes. Our understanding of how to develop skills, how to ensure that knowledge is shared, and how staff experience transfers for the third or fourth time, or indeed being brought back in-house, needs more research.

References

Coyle-Shapiro, J., Morrow, P., & Kessler, I. (2006). Serving two organizations: Exploring the employment relationship of contracted employees. *Human Resource Management, 45*(4), 561–583.

Elsbach, K. D. (1999). An expanded model of organizational identification. *Research in Organizational Behavior, 21*, 163–200.

George, J. M., & Jones, G. R. (2001). Towards a process model of individual change in organizations. *Human Relations, 54*(4), 419–444.

Giddens, A. (1976). *New rules of sociological method: A positive critique of interpretative sociologies*. London: Hutchinson.

Giddens, A. (1984). *The constitution of society*. Berkeley: University of California Press.

Nicholson, N. (1990). The transition cycle: Causes, outcomes, processes and forms. In S. Fisher & G. L. Cooper (Eds.), *On the move: The psychology of change and transition* (pp. 241–246). Chichester: Wiley.

Orlikowski, W. (1992). The duality of technology: Rethinking the concept of technology in organizations. *Organization Science, 3*, 398–427.

Rousseau, D. M. (1998). Why workers still identify with organizations. *Journal of Organizational Behavior, 19*, 217–233.

Scott, C. R., Corman, S. R., & Cheney, G. (1998). Development of a structurational model of identification in the organization. *Communication Theory, 8*(3), 298–336.

Shaw, T., & Jarvenpaa, S. (1997). Process models in information systems. In A. S. Lee, J. Liebenau, & J. I. Degross (Eds.), *Proceedings of the IFIP International Conference on Information Systems and Qualitative Research*. Philadelphia: Chapman & Hall.

Weiss, R. S. (1990). Losses associated with mobility. In S. Fisher & G. L. Cooper (Eds.), *On the move: The psychology of change and transition* (pp. 3–12). Chichester: Wiley.

Index

The Human Side of Outsourcing: Psychological Theory and Management Practice
Edited by Stephanie J. Morgan
Copyright © 2009 John Wiley & Sons Ltd.

employee–consultant transition, 219–20
employee–employer relationships, 87, 219
  and dual organizational relationships, 74
  and trust, 184
employee–independent contractor
    transitions, 219
employment
  externalization, 4
  private vs. public sector, terms and
      conditions, 32–3
employment relationships, change
    management in, 32
English language, and outsourcing, 100
Enright, R. D., 237–8
entertainment, in China, 55–6
Epel, E., 228
Erlebach, A., 223
Ernst, H., 143
Europe, outsourcing opportunities, 45
European Commission (EC), Directives, 12
European Union (EU), 209
eustress–distress dichotomy, 229–30
evaluation apprehension, 183–4
  definition, 184
Evaristo, R. O., 123
Eveleth, D. M., 82
events, understanding of, 271–2
evidence
  and 'face', 66
  and theory, 73–94
exclusion, discourses of, 110–11
exit planning, 20–1
exiting, outsourcing, 42
exit–renewal processes, in outsourcing
    contracts, 20–3
expectations
  long-term implications, 252
  and psychological contracts, 250
  realistic, 255
  role of, 8
  staff transfers, 249, 250–5, 257–8
experience, vs. curricula vitae, 44

'face'
  concept of, 65–7
  and evidence, 66
face-to-face contacts, virtual teams, 154–9,
    172–3

fast-moving consumer goods (FMCGs),
    42
Feldman, D. C., 85
Finkl, J., 222
first impressions, trust and, 159–60
FMCGs (fast-moving consumer goods), 42
Folkman, S., 231
forgiveness, 237–8
free market policies, 100
Furst, S., 144

Gambetta, D., 147, 176
gaps, in transitions, 17
Gartner, 134
GAS (general adaptation syndrome), 226,
    227
GEC, 34
general adaptation syndrome (GAS), 226,
    227
George, B., 196
George, J. M., 147
Gezhou Dam (China), 60
Giddens, A., 267–9
Gilbert, N. L., 82
global communications, 99
global service provision, 18
goal-setting, 102
Good, D., 147
goodwill, and outsourcing contracts, 8
governance, and deal management, 17–18
Govier, T., 238
Grande, G., 235
Grangemouth dispute (Scotland) (2008),
    32, 33
Grant, S., 230, 238–9
grieving, and transitions, 76
Griffeth, R. W., 82
group socialization, 78
Gruen, R., 231
Gurung, A., 128

Haas, M. R., 144
Hackman, J. R., 182
Hall, E. T., 123, 128
Hamel, G., 108
handovers, issues, 14
Handy, C., 123
hardiness, 231–2